FRIGHTENING THE HORSES

FRIGHTENING THE HORSES

Eric Braun

Gay Icons of the Cinema

R·H

Reynolds & Hearn Ltd
London

During the Oscar Wilde trials, *grande dame* actress Mrs Patrick Campbell (1868-1940) remarked: 'I don't care what people do, as long as they don't do it in the street and frighten the horses!'

Front cover: Heath Ledger and Jake Gyllenhaal in *Brokeback Mountain* (2004).

Frontispiece: Danny Kaye and friends in *Up in Arms* (1944).

First published in 2002 by
Reynolds & Hearn Ltd
61a Priory Road
Kew Gardens
Richmond
Surrey TW9 3DH

© Eric Braun 2002

Second edition © Eric Braun 2007

A CIP catalogue record for this book is available from the British Library.

ISBN 978-1905287-37-6

Designed by Paul Chamberlain.
Cover by Peri Godbold.

Printed and bound by Biddles Ltd, King's Lynn, Norfolk.

ACKNOWLEDGMENTS

First and foremost, many thanks to my editor, Richard Reynolds, for his unfailing patience and support spiked with a welcome sense of humour. I owe him a debt of gratitude for understanding that the mysteries of computers and the Internet remain, to date, impenetrable to me. Which brings me to those friends and colleagues who can fathom how words get translated from typewriter to disc and from thence into book form. These miracle workers include David Peter Balhatchet and Pam Hughes, Jenny Branscombe, Kate Armstrong and the Silverstones, Jan and David.

When it comes to research, film lore of the most intricate and even obscure kind lies at the fingertips of, again, David Peter Balhatchet, whose help has been of inestimable value, ably supported by my long-standing friends Marjorie Cummins and Lyn Fairhurst, and by book reseacher Sarah Fordham, who has the gift of magicking up worldwide titles on any subject in the universe. My thanks also to Adrian Rigelsford, Jonathan Rigby, Josephine Botting at the British Film Institute, the Joel Finler Collection and the Tony Hillman Collection.

To writer Michael Thornton I am indebted for many helpful suggestions in the early stages of this book and last, but by no means least, thanks to my agent, Carolyn Whitaker, for her invaluable help and encouragement from start to finish.

ALSO BY ERIC BRAUN:

Deborah Kerr: A Biography
So Much Love: An Autobiography (with Beryl Reid)
The Cat's Whiskers (with Beryl Reid)
Beryl, Food and Friends (with Beryl Reid)
Doris Day: A Biography
The Elvis Film Encyclopedia: An Impartial Guide to the Films of Elvis Presley

CONTENTS

INTRODUCTION

My school holidays were almost entirely occupied by keeping up with film releases and a once-a-week trip to London for an early morning movie, usually at the Empire Leicester Square. My filmgoing was strictly censored by my mother, with musicals and Janet Gaynor heading the list. They came together in 1929's *Sunny-Side Up*, with her regular partner Charles Farrell and, as comic relief, El Brendel, who I always thought was Swedish, though he was born in Philadelphia. I found something odd about him, apart from the fact that he was not very funny. When he turned up again at the Empire in a futuristic musical called *Just Imagine* (1930), I asked mother if she thought the same, and why. 'Because he's a sissy.'

She explained that a 'sissy' meant someone who was not very masculine. Simpering and limp-wristed, I supposed. The same applied to Edward Everett Horton, with the exception that he was funny and likeable, in *The Hottentot* (1929) and in *The Gay Divorce* (1934), where he appeared in a song and dance sequence with Betty Grable called 'Knock Knees'. Both Brendel and Horton continued to play their camp characters through the decades ruled by the Production Code, perhaps because they were asexual and therefore posed no threat to anyone.

There were many like them; it was not discussed, but you *knew*. 'Little skimpy white men, with little moustaches and their hands folded – *so*,' says Whoopi Goldberg in the film of *The Celluloid Closet* (1995). They were all very prissy and were, in fact, Hollywood's first gay stock characters. Kenneth Williams and

Charles Hawtrey regressed to this level in the Carry On films in Britain. Thus, in an oblique way, the movies tacitly acknowledged a third sex – one with no sex at all and therefore to be tolerated, as they were in real life.

With my puberty – and boarding school – came the revelation that a very potent sexual force did exist and demanded to be exercised, a force that had little to do with holding hands in the cinema and ultimately walking down the aisle to be united in holy matrimony.

With tolerance, and the modification of the Production Code in the sixties, came an influx of movies dealing, as explicitly as discretion allowed, with gay and lesbian relationships. Many of these films were by no means financially or critically successful. There will always be antagonism in some quarters to public displays of homosexuality – or indeed, any overt sexuality – so the horses and any other beings liable to be frightened should be warned. However, as God made us all the way we are, including the horses, everyone is entitled to be catered for.

This book, then, aims to explore the highways and byways of the gradual realisation that the third sex, incorporating bisexual, lesbian and gay, not only exists but, after decades of being kept under wraps and forced to function underground, has emerged from the closet; often reviled, but undefeated. As comprehensive a list as possible of relevant movies is appended. □

Eric Braun
Strawberry Hill
April 2002

1 THE FORBIDDEN TOPIC

In the film version of Vito Russo's illuminating book *The Celluloid Closet*, a brief scene shows two men in shirt-sleeves and braces solemnly dancing together. This experimental movie of 1896 is remarkable in that it would be some 70 years before such occurrences would be accepted by cinema audiences in any other way than to get an easy laugh.

As such things as homosexuality and bisexuality were never discussed among the general public and only thought of, if at all, as a subject for ribaldry among straight men, censorship seemed superfluous in the early days of cinema. However, Britain went ahead as early as 1912 by founding the British Board of Film Censors, strictly regulating which films were suitable for adults and unsuitable for children. In America, it was not until scandals among the lives of some of the stars, culminating in the 'Fatty' Arbuckle trial in 1921 (when a call-girl died at one of his parties), brought about the formation of the Hays Office by the Motion Picture Producers and Distributors of America.

At the same time movies were becoming raunchier by the month: among the most popular were Cecil B DeMille's epic historical spectacles, presented as pseudo-religious tracts – spicy sexual themes with explicit scenes of sin redeemed by Christian ethics. The Bible formed an endless source of sexual misbehaviour, with orgies galore and titles like *Don't Change Your Husband* (1919) and *Why Change Your Wife?* (1920), along with *Forbidden Fruit* the following year. The first two featured the star of the moment, Gloria Swanson, who went on working intermittently until her last film, *Airport 1975* (1974).

The Production Code was at last drawn up in 1930 and put into strict effect in 1934, with Joseph I Breen installed as director of the Code of Administration. Outstanding in a rigid list of guides for 'good taste' was that homosexuality or bisexuality ('sex inversion') must never be depicted or even implied. The Catholic Legion of Decency was also founded in 1934 and added its own strictures, with classifications of films to be avoided, under pain of sin.

This created problems, particularly for Mae West's *She Done Him Wrong* (1933); the stage title *Diamond Lil* had such notorious connotations that it was thought politic to have a title change. The original title of her next movie was changed from *It Ain't No Sin* to *I'm No Angel* (1933). With its sexy innuendoes and Mae's outrageous performance, the film single-handedly saved Paramount from bankruptcy. From then on, the star's battles with the censors were unrelenting. In West's case the blue pencil was ineffective: she could suggest so much by an inflection of her voice or a lift of the eyebrow that the censors were frequently left with egg on their faces.

Although homosexuality played no overt part in her movies, West's flamboyant style inevitably placed her at the head of the list of Gay Icons, a fact which delighted her as a self-styled champion of 'The Boys'.

From the beginning, gay men were used in the movies, usually in brief scenes, for light relief, throughout the silent days and the early talkies. *The Celluloid Closet* gives a plenitude of examples about which at least one writer feels deeply resentful. Arthur Laurent says, 'They were a cliché. I don't care whether they were gay or what. I think they're disgusting and unfunny. I could never understand why people laughed: it's like Stepin Fetchit for blacks.'

A favourite ploy in silents was featured in the 1914 *A Florida Enchantment*. At a dance, when four friends are waiting to take the floor, they prepare to take their partners and the two girls waltz off together, leaving the men to do the same. The situation was still a favourite in the talkies. In *Wonder Bar* (1934), Al Jolson is conducting a dance band, with Dick Powell as the crooner. The music starts, dancers take the floor; a man goes up to a couple and says 'May I cut in?' The lady answers graciously 'Certainly' and opens her arms to take her partner. 'Thank you,' says the male of the species – and dances off with her man. 'Whoops!' says Jolson, with a limp hand gesture. 'Boys will be boys!'

Even the great stars were occasionally presented in a camp light. In *Behind the Screen* (1916), Chaplin's leading lady is dressed as a boy, for plot reasons, and he is caught kissing her passionately by big Eric Campbell, who features in so many Chaplin films. He flounces about, hand on hip, until Chaplin boots him on the backside and he hobbles off screen, thus establishing Charlie's masculinity. Laurel and Hardy were involved in more than one ambiguous scene, which added to the laughs. In *Their First Mistake* (1932), a film in which they raise a baby together, Stanley says to Ollie:

'She says that I think more of you than her.'
'Well, you do, don't you?'
'Well, we won't go into that!'

The 1933 short *Twice Two* pictures the pair in drag when they dress up as their own wives, and in the full-length *The Bohemian Girl* (1936) they are pictured cuddling on a sofa. Ollie bestows a kiss on Stan's cheek.

One aspect of inversion has never troubled the censor: that of cross-dressing. Pantomime dames have for decades delighted most sections of the public, although in the main directed at children in the Christmas holidays. Likewise, Principal Boys are traditionally played by handsome ladies with spectacular underpinnings. No problems and no questions asked, except initially by the little ones, until they are told: 'It has always been that way – it makes it more fun.'

The equivalent in the movies goes back to Mary Pickford as *Little Lord Fauntleroy* in 1921, a prissy little fellow in any case, and one for whom Mary's golden curls were deemed entirely suitable. In the panto dame tradition, Brandon Thomas' Victorian farce *Charley's Aunt* has been filmed many times: by Syd Chaplin (half-brother of Charlie) in 1925; as a talkie starring Charlie Ruggles in 1930, with Doris Lloyd as the real aunt (the very first film I remember at all clearly); by Arthur Askey in 1940 (*Charley's Big Hearted Aunt*, after the comedian's catchphrase) with Jeanne de Casalis; Jack Benny with Kay Francis in 1941 and Ray Bolger in the musical *Where's Charley* with Margaretta Scott as Donna Lucia in 1952.

The fact that all these actors were ludicrously old to play an Oxford undergraduate (and, in Benny's case at least, ten years older than the leading lady) has never bothered anyone a jot – except a few carping critics. Traditionally, the real aunt was elegant and feminine, while the pretend aunt was dressed as an old Victorian frump, in black bombazine and a lace mobcap. On English TV, in 1970, our top female impersonator, Danny La Rue, played the part for glamour, which rather missed the point, even with the eternally chic Coral Browne as the aunt from Brazil, 'where the nuts come from.'

When it came to cross-dressing, the implications were there but they can only be recognised with hindsight. In 1933, Britain's most effervescent and energetic stage and screen comedienne, Cicely Courtneidge, starred in a film called *Soldiers of the King* as Maisie, the leader of a music hall family, the Marvellos. Maisie is a male impersonator who parades in soldier's uniform, moustache a-twitch, marching up and down the stage singing the rousing title song. Even out of uniform she looks boyish, with an Eton crop, as she guides the beautiful ingenue, Dorothy Hyson, towards stardom and does her best to keep her away from the predatory clutches of stage-door-Johnnies. In top hat and tails, Maisie sings to her protégée: 'The moment I saw you I knew you were the one I was meant to adore.' The film was a major box-office success and Courtneidge's adoring fans saw nothing out of place in this kind of behaviour, quite alien to the star's off-screen persona.

In the USA, the film, directed by Maurice Elvey, was called *The Woman in Command*. Courtneidge, in a dual role, also played her own mother. Her leading man was America's Edward Everett Horton, as the adoring but downtrodden stage director who actually gets to plant a very tentative kiss on the star's lips. The romantically inclined Dorothy Hyson's absences from the stage in the arms of a stage-door-Johnny (Anthony Bushell) give Courtneidge an excuse to indulge in one of her famous set-pieces, an energetic adagio act, flying through the air with the greatest of ease.

In *Me and Marlborough* (1935), Courtneidge played a woman who dresses as a man, in order to get into the army – fact treated as farce. As squaddie Kit Carson she sings 'All for a Shilling a Day'. Victor Saville directed and Tom Walls was the eponymous Marlborough. A strange echo of this film occurred in 1941, during my wartime army service. My Sergeant Major took me to a later Courtneidge film, *Take My Tip* (1937), in which she co-starred, as so often, with her husband Jack Hulbert. As Cis was strutting her stuff, singing 'The Empire Depends on You', the Sergeant Major said admiringly, 'That's a real *soldierly* woman!'

Some 20 years later, in 1962, came an even more striking echo, this time in Courtneidge's career. She gave a tenderly understated performance as Mavis, a retired music hall star who is a lesbian, probably the first to be pictured on the British screen, in Bryan Forbes' *The L-Shaped Room*. The scene where she reminisces to Leslie Caron about the dead friend she loved, and the camera pans to a photograph to show that the dead friend was a woman, is typical of Forbes' subtlety as a director. The pan is so quick you could miss it. At the Christmas party Mavis sings 'Soldiers of the King'.

In *The Celluloid Closet*, Quentin Crisp says, 'When men dress as women, everybody laughs; in reverse, nobody laughs'. He is referring to Marlene Dietrich in a tuxedo in *Morocco* (1930), in which she presents a woman in a cabaret audience with a rose and kisses her full on the mouth. Crisp adds, 'They just thought she looked wonderful!' Referring to the same scene, gay scriptwriter Susie Wright says, 'I was stunned by Dietrich in her tuxedo, and when she kissed the

SYLVIA SCARLETT

1935 RKO 94 mins b/w
Producer: Pandro S Berman; Director: George
Cukor; Screenplay: Gladys Unger, John Collier,
Mortimer Offner (from the novel by Compton
Mackenzie); Cinematographer: Joseph August
Katharine Hepburn, Cary Grant, Edmund Gwenn,
Brian Aherne, Natalie Paley

Nobody could have laughed at Katharine Hepburn when she dressed as a boy in George Cukor's 1934 *Sylvia Scarlett*, her first teaming with Cary Grant, although she herself was not happy with the way the story turned out. Latterly, the film has become a cult classic and Hepburn said Cukor taught Grant how to play comedy. The director brought out the Archie Leach in Cary Grant, as it were. Grant plays a conman who gets involved with Sylvia and her father (Edmund Gwenn), on the run from the law, having pulled one scam too many. Brian Aherne and Gwenn gave staunch support in this quirky adaptation of Compton Mackenzie's bestselling book.

woman, her romance with Gary Cooper went right out of the window and I was thinking of quite another scenario!'

Dietrich went further later. In 1940's *Seven Sinners* she sang 'The Man's in the Navy' in an immaculate white naval officer's uniform. In the circumstances, the lyrics were a masterpiece of innuendo. In her international cabaret act, from the 1950s to the 1970s, Dietrich reprised the scene in a more lighthearted manner. Back in white tie and tails, she included 'One for My Baby and One More for the Road' and other songs in a bar room setting.

In the main, cross-dressing has been employed for comedy, especially (as Quentin Crisp observed) when men dress as women. But comediennes have also often resorted to drag. Another example, in British movies, was the most popular star of the pre-war years, Gracie Fields (1898-1979). In *Shipyard Sally* (1939), the final British film of her contract with Darryl Zanuck for Twentieth Century-Fox (directed by her husband-to-be, Monty Banks), Fields dresses as a man to gain access to the male-only Garrick Club. Unfortunately for her, the dress suit she hires belongs to a

conjuror, with foreseeable consequences. When silly-ass comedian Oliver Wakefield pulls at a tab attached to the suit, flowers bloom, doves fly out and the costume eventually disintegrates.

Much Shakespearean comedy is, of course, built around the complexities created by cross-dressing leads. In Elizabethan days, men played women playing men (as in *Twelfth Night* and *As You Like It*). One of the most notable cinematic examples pre-war is the 1936 version of *As You Like It*. It starred Britain's most distinguished Polish import, Elisabeth Bergner, as Rosalind, who, of course, is metamorphosed into Ganymede – much to the confusion of Laurence Olivier's Orlando, who finds the boy strongly attractive. Bergner's husband Paul Czinner directed, as he did many of her films.

Old Mother Riley (1937) starred music hall comedian Arthur Lucan (1887-1954) as a sentimental old Irish washerwoman, the first in a series of 15 low-budget farces which remained popular through the war years and right up to 1952. 'She' signed off with *Mother Riley Meets the Vampire*, where the old harridan met no less a co-star than Bela Lugosi, 22 years on from his first screen appearance as Dracula. Lucan's wife, Kitty McShane, in her late forties by the end of the series, always played his daughter Kitty. Their on-screen altercations played a poor second to their real-life fights as man and wife. The unfortunate director who dared to suggest a touch of maturity in Kitty's character was blasted with, 'What about Claudette Colbert?' *Mother Riley* was the most successful and, at the same time, the least attractive example of showbusiness cross-dressing in British movies.

The thirties in Britain were prolific in cross-dressing-themed films, such as the stagy farce *It's a Boy* with Leslie Henson and Albert Burdon in 1933. This was directed by Tim Whelan, an American director who turned out some of the brightest British movies of the period, such as Cicely Courtneidge's *Aunt Sally* (1933) and the notable drama *Farewell Again* (1937), starring Flora Robson. In *It's a Boy*, the two comedians, Henson and Burdon, dressed up as wives in a consulting room, make small talk. 'Are you married?' 'Oh, yes, I'm a divorcee, you know.' 'Oh, really – and what was the matter with your first husband?' 'The one I have now.' Hardly Oscar Wilde but good for a giggle in the school holidays.

Officially the first British movie in Technicolor, *Wings of the Morning* starred France's Annabella with Henry Fonda and Leslie Banks. Directed by Harold Shuster in 1937, it cast the French star as a girl who spends a major part of the film dressed as a boy, with considerable success; unsurprisingly, as her sexual inclinations veered toward the Sapphic. She later married Tyrone Power.

First a Girl, directed by Victor Saville in 1935, starred Britain's top musical star, Jessie Matthews, opposite her then husband, Sonnie Hale. Hale plays a drag artist whose starring role Matthews, dressed as a boy,

understudies. Leading man Griffith Jones and his girlfriend, Anna Lee, cannot understand why he is so drawn to the girl/boy. Some of the scenes between them were decidedly risqué for the time and the very feminine Matthews acquitted herself remarkably well as the transvestite star.

The film's history is interesting. First made as a German musical starring Renate Müller in 1933 under the title *Viktor und Viktoria*, it resurfaced as a vehicle for Julie Andrews called *Victor/Victoria* (1982). Andrews' transvestite act was more than matched by Robert Preston's outrageous drag queen. Julie Andrews' 'straight' man, James Garner, in those more enlightened days was able to show far more overt attraction to Andrews in her masculine role than had Griffith Jones in Victor Saville's daring early venture. *Victor/Victoria* was directed by Andrews' husband, Blake Edwards. Of all the 'experiments' he performed on behalf of his wife's career, this one was eminently suited to her square-jawed appeal.

Anna Neagle was one star who was almost exclusively directed by her husband, Herbert Wilcox. Before she ascended the cinematic throne in 1937's *Victoria the Great*, Neagle played such popular actresses and courtesans as *Nell Gwyn* in 1934 and *Peg* [Woffington] *of Old Drury* the following year. In the latter she dressed as a man to sing 'A Little Dash o' Dublin', about the pretty colleen she/he met and 'soon she was in me arms'. Trans-gender songs of the period were not unusual. Gracie Fields' debut in *Sally in Our Alley*, directed in 1931 by Maurice Elvey, introduced the song 'Sally', addressed to a girl, which became, despite her protests, Gracie's theme song for the rest of her long career. She was still singing it – as a Dame of the British Empire – at the London Palladium in the year of her death, 1979. □

2 OSCAR WILDE

Oscar Wilde's association with mainstream cinema dates back to 1923, when the most flamboyant of all Hollywood's silent female stars, Alla Nazimova, directed, under the name of her husband, Charles Bryant, an all-gay/lesbian version of *Salome*. It seems that not only were all the cast homosexual, but also the crew. It was the first production after Nazimova left Metro, the studio at which all her films since 1916 had been made.

But Nazimova's ambition outreached itself. Putting most of her fortune into the production of *Salome* proved to be an unwise move. Her lover Natasha Rambova, Rudolph Valentino's wife, designed the sets and costumes, based on the drawings by Aubrey Beardsley. Critical reaction was enthusiastic and the film is now considered a classic of avant-garde silent cinema. But it cost Nazimova dear; her subsequent return to the studio system was hardly an unqualified success. At 45 she was still playing ingenue roles in increasingly exaggerated style, and in 1925 she left Hollywood to return to the stage.

A pre-Salome-and-Hollywood attempt at a Wilde subject was made in Germany in 1917: *Des Bildnis des Dorian Gray*, reportedly with a

It was not until 1945 that talking pictures ventured to tackle perhaps the most famous Wilde plot to deal, albeit in a subtle and oblique way, with sinister forces and unspeakable vices. Ironically, it was Metro-Goldwyn-Mayer, the studio under the supposedly benevolent despotism of Louis B Mayer, which took on *The Picture of Dorian Gray*, although Mayer prided himself on turning out films for family audiences. Metro was Hollywood's leading production company, with the greatest stars, directors and production teams. Usually, Mayer and his associates allowed the filmmakers their heads, with the result that some memorable movies made vast profits and gained considerable prestige through the years.

Alexander Korda's opulent Technicolor version of *An Ideal Husband* in 1947 was the last film he directed. Korda brought over Paulette Goddard from Hollywood to star as the 'scarlet woman', Mrs Cheveley, presumably for box-office kudos. Despite her efficient performance, she was difficult to visualise as an English *grande dame*, especially when measured against the genuine article in the person of Diana Wynyard as Lady Gertrude Chiltern.

Lady Chiltern is one of the least rewarding

Opposite: Stephen Fry and Jude Law in *Wilde* (1997).

AND THE CINEMA

gay subplot. Ernst Lubitsch's 1925 *Lady Windermere's Fan*, updated for the twenties, starring Ronald Colman, May McAvoy and Irene Rich as Mrs Erlynne, was acclaimed as a triumph of style and elegance, even without Wilde's dialogue.

parts Wilde ever wrote for a woman: humourless, uptight and self-righteous, she is all too ready to believe her husband, Sir Robert (Hugh Williams), capable of deceiving her with the scandalous Mrs Cheveley, who, despite her colourful past, turns out to be the

THE PICTURE OF DORIAN GRAY

1945 MGM 110 mins b/w and Technicolor
Producer: Pandro S Berman; Director: Albert Lewin;
Screenplay Albert Lewin (based on the novel by
Oscar Wilde); Cinematographer: Harry Stradling
George Sanders, Hurd Hatfield, Donna Reed, Angela
Lansbury, Lowell Vilmore, Peter Lawford, Richard
Fraser, Reginald Owen, Lydia Bilbrook, Morton Lowry

Ideal casting for the title role was Hurd Hatfield, then 27. His only previous film, the year before, was *Dragon Seed* with Katharine Hepburn, in which they both played Chinese characters. Hatfield's inscrutable beauty in itself resembled a portrait. The story of a young aristocrat in 19th century society who falls heavily under the spell of the hedonistic and manipulative Lord Henry Wotton becomes intriguing as soon as George Sanders drawls his way onto the scene, ideally cast as the devil's advocate. Sanders was always at his best playing characters of ambiguous morals and sexuality, and Dorian's eager acceptance of the life to which Lord Henry introduces him is quite understandable. Unseen orgies and unthinkable vices are what lies beneath the elegant exterior of their social activities and Dorian, as much in love with himself as with his louche lifestyle, is delighted to have his portrait painted. The transaction involves trading his soul to the Devil in exchange for eternal youth. He also trades in whatever vestiges of conscience he originally had and callously breaks the heart of his fiancée, actress Sybil Vane.

For this role the young Angela Lansbury gained an Academy Award nomination, for Best Supporting Actress. Another nomination went to Cedric Gibbons and Hans Peters for Art Direction, while Harry Stradling won an Oscar for his deep focus cinematography. Hatfield had just the requisite, aloof features to portray the man whose sins and depravities leave him facially unblemished, while his portrait, banished to the attic, reflects faithfully the hideousness of the life he was leading.

This film had little difficulty with the censor, as none of the forbidden topics of the Code are presented, although undoubtedly all are broken – and then some – in Dorian's off-screen activities. Director Albert Lewin saves the big shock for the film's climax : a close-up of the portrait, in vivid Technicolor, painted in a frighteningly grotesque style by Ivan Albright.

Dorian Gray was resurrected in 1970, in an Italian-British co-production (*Il dio chiamato Dorian*) starring blond, blue-eyed Helmut Berger as an innocent young man who grows obsessed with his own portrait and sells his soul, in his quest for eternal youth and beauty, while the portrait grows increasingly old and repulsive as in the original story line. Dorian's homosexuality is referred to, along with a jet-setting international gay cabal, whose denizens ensure he goes the right way to Hell. The new explicitness adds little to the tale and the 1960s mod clothes are risible rather than seductive. Berger, 26 at the time, is undeniably attractive, but the shock of the portrait is less effective than the 1945 version. Director Massimo Dallamano occasionally allows his subject to veer into the tacky, but in the main keeps a reasonably tight rein on his cast. The alternative title is *The Secret of Dorian Gray*.

It would seem invidious to omit the 1983 *The Sins of Dorian Grey*, a ludicrous made-for-TV metamorphosis by US director Tony Maylam, whereby Dorian changes sex and becomes a beautiful actress (Belinda Bauer) who sells her soul to the Devil. Just to assure us we're in the electronic effects era, it's her voice which changes horribly, while she stays young and beautiful. One hopes this doesn't put ideas into the heads of any of our ageing beauties. Anthony Perkins and Joseph Bottoms also star, and again it's a case of just let the subject rest in peace.

Opposite: Joan Greenwood, Michael Redgrave and Michael Denison in *The Importance of Being Earnest* (1952).

noblest of them all. Miss Mabel Chiltern (Glynis Johns), far more go-ahead than her sister-in-law (she would need to be), decides that it's time she gained a husband of her own and is herself nearly involved in a scandal, from which it takes the worldly-wise Mrs C to extricate her, at the expense of her own reputation. The all-star cast included Michael Wilding, Christine Norden and C Aubrey Smith, who travelled from Hollywood aged 84, despite having declined to make the journey to appear in a British film ten years earlier, quoting 'anno domini' as the reason!

The 1999 remake of *An Ideal Husband* received mixed reviews. Adapted this time by Oliver Parker, the play has never been the most rewarding to translate to the screen. Filmmakers are up against the uninvolving characters of the senior Chilterns, played here by Jeremy Northam and Cate Blanchett. At least Minnie Driver holds her own as Mabel. The film is illuminated (indeed, virtually held together) by Rupert Everett as the Wildean prototype, Lord Goring, who gets the best lines and delivers them with superb panache. Julianne Moore's Mrs Cheveley, however, lacks the insolent glamour of some stage incumbents

THE IMPORTANCE OF BEING EARNEST

1952 Two Cities/Javelin British/Asquith 95 mins colour
Producer: Teddy Baird; Director: Anthony Asquith; Screenplay:
Anthony Asquith (based on the play by Oscar Wilde; Cinematographer:
Desmond Dickinson
Michael Redgrave, Edith Evans, Joan Greenwood, Dorothy Tutin, Margaret
Rutherford, Miles Malleson, Richard Wattis, Aubrey Mather, Walter Hudd

Wilde's most perfect comedy, *The Importance of Being Earnest*, directed by one of England's most talented gay artists of the cinema, Anthony Asquith, is a classic example of translating Wilde to the screen and in exquisite Technicolor. The cast is a combination of the cream of stage and screen actors of the period: Edith Evans as Lady Bracknell, Margaret Rutherford as Miss Prism, Miles Malleson as Canon Chasuble, Michael Redgrave as Jack Worthing, Michael Denison as Algy, Joan Greenwood as Gwendoline and Dorothy Tutin as Cecily.

The slender plot hinges on the subterfuges of best friends Jack and Algy to lead their own lives away from the strictures and constraints of polite society. Algy impersonates Jack's brother, the spendthrift Earnest, while Algy has a pretend friend called Bunbury, 'who lives in the country'. Into this world of make-believe come the larger-than-life characters, all representing extreme aspects of the society of the day: the overweening arrogance of Lady Bracknell, the twittering ineffectuality of Miss Prism and the upper-class snobbery of Gwendoline and Cecily, through all of whom the author mocks the hypocrisy abroad in the world. Talking to Cecily on the subject of men and marriage, Gwendoline says: 'The home seems to me to be the perfect sphere for a man, and certainly once a man begins to neglect his domestic duties he becomes painfully effeminate, does he not? And I don't like that.'

This mocking of marriage is the opposite of Wilde's own alliance to his devoted and long-suffering wife, whom he loved in spite of everything. Lady Bracknell's values of courtship are based solely upon class and wealth, the prevalent Victorian middle- and upper-class attitude which Wilde so despised. Jack and Algy represent lives elegantly groomed and correct on the surface, employing their alter-egos to conceal existences in which they can live out their secret fantasies. 'Wilde's genius is such that his players can exalt both normalcy and subterfuge,' said artist Victor Passmore in a letter to the *Listener*. Theories that 'Earnest' is a code word for gay and that Bunbury is something along the same lines may be far-fetched: the beauty of it is that one can put one's own interpretation on any of Wilde's words and witticisms.

JOAN GREENWOOD
MICHAEL REDGRAVE
MICHAEL DENISON
in a scene from
THE IMPORTANCE OF
BEING EARNEST U
Colour by TECHNICOLOR   GFD Release

Crain's honour that the Lady with a Past takes the blame for leaving her fan in the drawing room of the man with whom no decent girl would have anything to do. The lady with a tarnished reputation who is really on the side of virtue and honour is one of Wilde's stock characters and a rewarding part for actresses who combine maturity with glamour.

Preminger's picture was titled *The Fan* in America, and should not be confused with the violent 1981 movie, directed by Edward Bianchi, in which fan Michael Biehn's obsession for actress Lauren Bacall leads him to murder a gay stranger, then set him on fire.

Wilde's subtle ghost story *The Canterville Ghost* was updated by director Jules Dassin to England in 1944, with a spooky Charles Laughton carrying his head around, tucked underneath his arm, in a roguish manner. Among several remakes, a 1996 version for US TV was directed by Paul Bogart and starred John Gielgud. This is another updated version, which works because of the star's depiction of his high-spirited but ineffectual attempts to frighten an American family, who instead take him to their hearts.

The first film biography of Oscar Wilde was made in 1959 in Britain by Gregory Ratoff. Robert Morley was cast in the title role, which he had played on the stage with some success. Although he movingly portrayed the pathos of the playwright in the trial scenes, he looked too old on screen and the same may be said of John Neville, best known in the theatre for his distinction as an actor and his good looks, but out of place as Bosie. Phyllis Calvert's sympathetic performance as Mrs Wilde and Ralph Richardson as the Queen's Counsel are more successful. Ratoff died soon after the completion of the film, shot, to great effect, in black-and-white.

Almost simultaneously, Ken Hughes directed the Technicolor biography *The Trials*

of the role, such as Margaret Lockwood, Kate O'Mara and Anna Carteret. This is a play that has always worked better in the theatre.

The same may be true of *Lady Windermere's Fan*. This play was filmed in Hollywood by Twentieth Century-Fox in 1949, in a perfectly serviceable version directed by Otto Preminger. Mrs Erlynne was played by the translucently beautiful British export, Madeleine Carroll. After this film, Carroll retired from the screen at the early age of 43, rewarding parts having proved all too rare in her American career. She had become one of Britain's most popular stars in the thirties, playing Hitchcock's ideal blonde in 1935's *The Thirty-Nine Steps* with Robert Donat and in 1936's *Secret Agent* with John Gielgud. In 1942 Bob Hope named her *My Favourite Blonde*. Born in 1906, she died in Spain in 1987.

Preminger's *Lady Windermere's Fan* has latterly been neglected in favour of the 1925 version, despite a cast which included George Sanders as another Wildean prototype, Lord Darlington, Richard Greene and Fox's favourite ingenue, Jeanne Crain. It is to save

Above: Phyllis Calvert and Robert Morley in *Oscar Wilde* (1959).

Right: John Fraser and Peter Finch in *The Trials of Oscar Wilde* (1960).

of Oscar Wilde, a far more lively account which gained immeasurably from the deeply felt performance of Peter Finch, who captures the essence of Wilde's nature without in any way physically resembling him. John Fraser's Lord Alfred Douglas, moody, self-centred and essentially heartless, is an admirable reading of the unsympathetic Bosie. James Mason's QC, Sir Edward Carson, is formidably convincing. Ken Hughes concentrates on this section of the story and presents a courtroom drama compelling in its intensity. Lionel Jeffries as Bosie's father, the Marquis of Queensbury (whom Wilde ill-advisedly sued for calling him a sodomite), is a terrifying conception. Yvonne Mitchell as the gentle Constance Wilde and Sonia Dresdel as the playwright's understanding mother round out a superlative cast.

Forbidden Passion, produced for BBC TV in 1980, covered the now well-worn ground, presenting Wilde as a stubborn man who refused to live a lie and paid the price in an era when façade was everything. Director Henry Herbert drew an admirable performance from Michael Gambon, but it *is* a pity about the title, which suggests Nazimova in the early 1920s rather than England in the early 1980s.

The most perfect casting for Oscar Wilde to date has to be that of Stephen Fry in Brian Gilbert's admirably balanced 1997 film, *Wilde*. Fry, surprisingly, brings out the masculine side of the man, who, in the early scenes, can lecture to silver-miners in the Wild West on the subject of beauty and keep his audience respectful and attentive. The scenes with Wilde's wife, Constance, played tenderly by Jennifer Ehle, suggest that their marriage might have gone along comparatively calmly had the beautiful and narcissistic Bosie, as played so admirably by Jude Law, not taken over Wilde's life. The scenes in a male brothel are tastefully handled, as is the role of Lady Wilde (Vanessa Redgrave, with big billing but little screen time). Fry looks and acts the part magnificently. ☐

3 CIRCUMVENTING THE CENSOR

A few notable movies almost escaped the censor's frowns long before Gay Lib was even thought of as a possibility. All of them were, in their own way, classics.

In 1927 *Wings*, the first film ever to win an Academy Award for Best Picture, dealt with the comradeship between two men, Charles (Buddy) Rogers and Richard Arlen. At first, having enlisted in the Air Force at the beginning of World War I, they are sworn enemies because they both love the same girl, Mary (Clara Bow). At training camp, a boxing match gets out of control and Jack (Rogers) knocks David (Arlen) to the ground. Gazing up at his assailant with the look of a hurt puppy dog, blood oozing from the side of his mouth, animosity turns to affection as David is helped up by his new friend Jack, and they leave the scene arm-in-arm as the best of buddies.

When the war moves into the sky, director William Wellman has a great time photographing the air combats. I saw the film at the cinema as a child, during the summer holidays in Margate. The lady tinkled the ivories romantically in front of the screen with spirited Charleston music whenever Miss Bow appeared, then held her peace while sound effects of roaring engines took over, following the action in the skies. Actually, the screen was a large sheet suspended between poles at the front of the hall. When Mary enlisted as a nurse, the pianist (Florence De Jong, who had quite a following of her own) turned to romantic songs of the ilk of 'What'll I Do?'

When one of the boys is seriously wounded in combat, his friend visits him in hospital and bestows a gentle kiss on his cheek. Such was the innocence of those silent days in the cinema that the audience remained respectfully hushed during this episode. With Jack the kisser and David the kissee, the scene is touchingly played by Rogers and Arlen. Clara Bow looks on sympathetically.

As with wartime buddies, so with peacetime schoolgirls. The 1931 *Mädchen in Uniform*, made in Germany, tells of a young girl (Herthe Thiele) and her romantic feelings for her teacher, Fraulein von Bournburg (Dorothea Wieck). While the headmistress declares Manuela's affection to be a scandal, her classmates declare their support and understanding. Based on the play *Yesterday and Today* by lesbian poet Christa Winsloe, the film was a worldwide success, although when released in the US in 1932 the censors made cuts to remove lesbian references, diluting the passion between teacher and pupil to make it play as a simple schoolgirl crush.

Director Leontine Sagan left Germany soon after the general release, although the film was voted by the National Board of Review as one of the Ten Best Foreign Pictures of 1932. She was to become one of Ivor Novello's favourite directors of his Drury Lane spectacles. Sagan, who by her masculine suitings and hair *en brosse* resembled a European version of Hollywood's

Right: A portrait of Conrad Veidt, circa 1919, the year in which he starred in the first film to deal explicitly with homosexual issues.

Dorothy Arzner, planned to direct a London play for Lillian Gish. But the gentle Miss Gish shied off the project after the first week at the King's Theatre Glasgow in 1936; it was *The Old Maid*, in which she played Charlotte Lovell, Bette Davis' part in the movie.

Dorothea Wieck went to Hollywood on the strength of *Mädchen* but her debut in *Cradle Song* did not prove a lullaby to the American public and she returned to Germany. The 1958 remake of *Mädchen in Uniform* predictably contained more explicit lesbian input than the original but, despite sensitive performances by Romy Schneider and Lilli Palmer as student and teacher, the Technicolor film ran into censorship problems in the US again and was not released there until 1965.

Germany was in fact responsible for the first film ever to deal explicitly with homosexuality. Richard Oswald's controversial series of so-called Aufklärungsfilme ('enlightening films') yielded titles like *Es werde Licht* (Let There be Light), *Prostitution* and, in 1919, *Anders als die Andern* (Different from Others), in which the young Conrad Veidt plays a famous violinist targeted by a particularly odious blackmailer (Reinhold Schünzel). During his spell in Weimar Germany, Christopher Isherwood caught the picture and reported later that: 'Performances of it had often been broken up by the Nazis. In Vienna, one of them had fired a revolver into the audience, wounding several people … Three scenes remain in my memory. One is a ball at which the dancers, all male, are standing fully clothed in what seems about to become a daisy chain. It is here that the character played by Veidt meets the blackmailer who seduces and then ruins him. The next scene is a vision which Veidt has (while in prison?) of a long procession of kings, poets, scientists, philosophers and other famous victims of homophobia, moving slowly and sadly with heads bowed. Each of them cringes, in

turn, as he passes beneath a banner on which 'Paragraph 175' [of the German Penal Code] is inscribed. In the final scene, [sexologist] Dr Hirschfeld himself appears. I think the corpse of Veidt, who has committed suicide, is lying in the background. Hirschfeld delivers a speech – that is to say, a series of subtitles – appealing for justice for the Third Sex.'

Perpetuating the *Mädchen in Uniform* tradition, in 1950 the French film *Olivia* also dealt with love between mistresses and students. When it was released in Great Britain and the United States, the film had been heavily censored and was retitled in America *The Pit of Loneliness*, obviously hoping to appeal to those who remembered Radclyffe Hall's unfilmed lesbian novel, *The Well of Loneliness*. The stars were two of France's loveliest, Simone Simon, who made *Cat People* and a few musicals in Hollywood, and Edwige Feuillère, equally revered on stage and screen but not happy in her 1948 film debut in England opposite Stewart Granger in *Woman Hater*.

The stars played sisters, joint headmistresses, each with her coterie of girls. Feuillère develops a tender relationship with new girl Olivia (Claire Olivia) and their affair is affectionate, even sensual. In the States the film was released with the tagline 'The daring drama of an unnatural love!' The screenplay by Pierre Laroche, from Dorothy Bussy's novel, was directed by Jacqueline Audry, who made 18 films, including a 1955 adaptation of Jean-Paul Sartre's play *Huis Clos*, in which the author's concept of Hell was three human beings trapped for eternity in a single room with people they despise. ('L'enfer, c'est les autres.') In it, Frank Villard and Gaby Sylvia both desire Arletty, who finds them both anathema. Remade in 1962, the film was a sensation at the Berlin Film Festival, where Viveca Lindors and Rita Gam shared the Best Actress Award, this version being directed by Ted Danieliewski.

Right: A portrait of Greta Garbo.

Lindfors played Inez, the lesbian of the trio.

During the era of the Production Code, Hollywood's way of dealing with novels or plays which had achieved notable success through tackling 'forbidden' subjects was to buy the rights for vast sums of money, then simply remove the core of what had made them so popular in the first place. The next step, in many cases, was to alter the title for which so much money had been shelled out. Thus, Michael Arlen's twenties bestseller *The Green Hat* provided a vehicle for two of Hollywood's most prestigious stars. Greta Garbo, helmed by one of her favourite directors, Clarence Brown, starred in the silent *Woman of Affairs* in 1928 and, in 1934, 'the notorious Iris March' was played by Constance Bennett in *Outcast Lady* (*A Woman of the World* in Britain), directed by

Robert Z Leonard. Thus the studios were able to duck the censor.

Both films were written in the period before Joseph Breen had become heavy with his blue pencil. Even so, the title *The Green Hat* was too risqué to be permitted. Hence the daring reference to 'Iris March' in the advertising campaign, for the benefit of readers of the book. The main problem was a syphilitic character among the leading men, so he had his sexual problem painlessly removed. MGM boss Louis B Mayer had thought Iris' first husband 'Boy' was gay, but production head Irving Thalberg corrected him and his suicide was put down to an infamous but unspecified crime.

Another notable title with sexual connotations came about in 1936, when Sam Goldwyn bought the rights to Lillian Hellman's controversial play *The Children's Hour*, filmed as *These Three*. When told that the play was about lesbians, Goldwyn is reported to have uttered one of his most famous Goldwynisms: 'It doesn't matter; we'll make them Americans.' He cast two of his favourite leading ladies; Miriam Hopkins, whose contract allowed her single star billing above the title, as the lesbian schoolmistress Martha Dobie, with Merle Oberon as her friend and the unconscious object of her desire, Karen Wright. Furthermore, to ensure getting the subject off the ground, Joel McCrea shared their billing as Dr Joseph Cardin, the local doctor for whom Karen falls.

So subtle is the direction of William Wyler and the performance of Miriam Hopkins that the latterday interpretation of her being more interested in Oberon than McCrea is understandable, given hindsight, of course. The theme of a vicious schoolgirl (Bonita Granville, who was nominated for an Oscar) whispering to her grandmother that she had seen 'things' taking place between the doctor and Karen in a bedroom near the students' quarters had been substituted for 'carryings-on' between the two teachers.

Wyler's film, adapted by Hellman herself, was a magnificent achievement, considered by many critics to be superior to the director's remake in 1962, starring Shirley MacLaine and Audrey Hepburn, in which Martha's lesbianism is left in no doubt and she hangs herself at the end. This time Miriam Hopkins played the vicious Aunt Lily, who considers the relationship 'unnatural', though the word 'lesbian' is never mentioned. The British title was *The Loudest Whisper*.

Miriam Hopkins (1902-1972) was a leading glamour star from the thirties to the mid-forties, enjoying successive lucrative contracts with Paramount, Sam Goldwyn and Warner Bros. Her husky voice, blonde hair and sophisticated aura led critic David Quinlan to compare her with Cybill Shepherd. Plum roles, like those in *These Three* and, previously, Noël Coward's *Design for Living* (1933), came Hopkins' way. The original Coward play featured a ménage à trois between Bohemians in thirties Paris. The film starred Gary Cooper as an artist, Fredric March as a writer and Hopkins as the woman they both love. Ben Hecht's screenplay removed any implication that the men were more than just friends and Ernst Lubitsch's direction, with his uniquely sophisticated 'touch', ensured one of the most wittily entertaining films of its year. Edward Everett Horton played Miriam's dim-witted husband.

Caustic though Coward was about what Hollywood had done to his play, he had reason to be pleased with Ben Hecht and Charles MacArthur's script for his adult screen debut *The Scoundrel* (1935), which won an Oscar for Best Original Story in 1935. In 1918 he had appeared with Lillian and Dorothy Gish in D W Griffith's *Hearts of the World*; now grown up with a vengeance, he plays a cynical, callous breaker of hearts (female), who dies and is allowed to return to Earth to find just one person (Julie Haydon) who can truly love him.

One of the first lesbian vampires surfaced

Opposite: Glenn Ford and Rita Hayworth in *Gilda* (1946).

GILDA

1946 Columbia 110 mins b/w
Producer: Virginia Van Upp; Director:
Charles Vidor; Screenplay: Marion
Parsonnet (based on Jo Eisinger's adapta-
tion of E A Ellington's original story);
Cinematographer: Rudolph Maté
Rita Hayworth, Glenn Ford, George
Macready, Joseph Calleia, Steven Geray,
Joe Sawyer, Gerald Mohr, Robert Scott,
Ludwig Donath, Don Douglas

One of the most notable examples of
circumventing the censor 'by a mile'
(said the *Radio Times* in 1998) is the
Columbia film *Gilda*, which presented
Rita Hayworth at her most dazzlingly
erotic. Rudolph Maté's black-and-white
cinematography, Jean-Louis' gowns,
Jack Cole's choreography and Charles
Vidor's direction were all aimed at
deifying Rita as the woman straight
men would go crazy for. And not only
straight men: when we meet her with
her new husband, Ballin Munson
(George Macready), a Teutonic casino
owner, he has hired a handsome and
unsuccessful gambler, Johnny Farrell
(enter Glenn Ford), as bodyguard (one
of three) to himself and his new wife,
who once happened to be involved
with Johnny herself.

The animosity between the two is
immediate – desire mingled with jealousy. When the two men light each
other's cigarettes the look in their eyes
is reminiscent of Bette Davis and Paul
Henreid and the immortal line 'Why
ask for the moon when we have the
stars?' in *Now Voyager*. Macready
says to Ford, 'As you know, when I

buy something, I want it immediately!'
Both Ballin and Gilda tease Johnny
mercilessly: among her lines to him are
'You're looking very beautiful tonight'
and 'You look very pretty in your bed
gown.' The film was made in 1946,
when such jokey references left most of
the public unperturbed.

This spiky *ménage à trois*, played to
the hilt by the three protagonists, can
have only one ending. When Ballin
finds that his wife and lover have been
deceiving him, he is only stopped from
gunning them both down by a well-
aimed bullet from Uncle Pio, the cloak-
room attendant, who has a love-hate
relationship with all three of them. This
is a beautifully timed performance by
Steven Geray, a former member of the
Hungarian State Theatre who appeared
in over 100 character roles in the
movies. Joseph Calleia, as the gently
mannered, almost anonymous
Obregon, the cop who is keeping an

eye on all of them, is no less ambiguous in his attitudes to his quarry. After
Uncle Pio has killed Munson, he shrugs
and says 'Justifiable homicide' as he
strolls off. Blond Joseph Sawyer (usually
cast as army sergeants) is here the
heftiest of Ballin's bodyguards, clearly
jealous of Johnny's loyalty to their boss
and contrasting well with Glenn Ford,
who treats him with contempt as his
master's 'bit of rough on the side'.

The official plot about tungsten
smuggling is not too easy to follow with
all these tangled emotions going
on – but who cares? There's always
the lovely Rita, who ends up in
Glenn's arms. He is certainly in for a
bumpy ride but obviously that's something he can take in his stride. As one
critic said: 'Surely Ford's character is
the most ambiguous leading man
ever.' The actor himself once commented that he and Macready played the
parts as gay lovers.

REBECCA

1940 Selznick 130 mins b/w
Producer: David O Selznick: Director: Alfred Hitchcock;
Screenplay: Robert E Sherwood, Joan Harrison (based on the
novel by Daphne du Maurier, adapted by Philip MacDonald,
Michael Hogan); Cinematographer: George Barnes.
Laurence Olivier, Joan Fontaine, George Sanders, Judith
Anderson, Nigel Bruce, C Aubrey Smith, Reginald Denny,
Gladys Cooper, Philip Winter, Edward Fielding

The forties started with a movie which not only gained its producer a best picture Oscar, but was heavy with homo-erotic imagery. The author of the original novel, Daphne du Maurier, a happily married woman with three children, nevertheless referred to herself as 'not a lesbian, but a half-breed, someone internally male but externally female.' She was latterly thought to be emotionally involved with Gertrude Lawrence, for whom she wrote the play *September Tide*.

Rebecca is the unseen presence, dead before the story starts but dominating the plot from beginning to end. Joan Fontaine was nominated for an Oscar for her performance as the timid paid companion of a rich domineering dowager. While staying in Monte Carlo, the unassertive girl, permanently under the thumb of Mrs Van Hopper (Florence Bates), dares to fall in love with the rich and handsome Maxim de Winter (Laurence Olivier), whose proposal of marriage she is only too happy to accept. However, once in his mansion the new Mrs De Winter discovers not only that he is gloomily obsessed by the memory of his dead wife, but that she has exchanged one dominatrix for another, more sinister, in the shape of de Winter's ghostlike lesbian housekeeper, Mrs Danvers (Judith Anderson). Mrs Danvers seems still to be in love with the memory of the first Mrs de Winter, with whom she seems to have had a relationship and whose room she devotedly maintains as a shrine in which the interloper is totally unwelcome.

The scene where Mrs Danvers lovingly takes out and fingers her dead mistress' lingerie and insists on rubbing her furs against the shrinking girl's cheek is redolent with menace and Sapphic intensity. The film is a triumph for all concerned, including Academy nominations for Olivier, Anderson, Hitchcock, writers Robert E Sherwood and Joan Harrison, and five others. After all that it would seem churlish to omit praising the performances of a handful of the finest British actors in Hollywood in 1940: George Sanders, Nigel Bruce, C Aubrey Smith, Reginald Denny and Gladys Cooper.

(ever so subtly) in Lambert Hillyer's *Dracula's Daughter* (1936), played by the beautiful Gloria Holden (1908-1991), she of the mesmeric eyes. The lady enlists the help of a sympathetic doctor (Otto Kruger) to try to rid her of her father's bloodsucking propensities. These reassert themselves when she picks up a street girl (Nan Grey), whom she hypnotises. Holden murmurs words to the effect that she hopes the model will not object to taking her blouse off: cut to a big close-up of Holden's hypnotising stare, then Grey reacting first in trepidation and finally screaming horror as (we assume) Holden closes in… and the screen goes blank. This was 1936, when seduction was left to the imagination. The London-born actress played mostly dignified supporting roles for the remainder of her career, until the late fifties.

The unworldliness of the Hays Office allowed a real howler to slip by unnoticed in Howard Hawks' 1938 *Bringing Up Baby*, one of the funniest and most original screwball comedies, teaming Katharine Hepburn and Cary Grant at their most sparkling. She is a dizzy heiress involved with an unworldly zoologist and an escaped leopard, the 'baby' of the title. Undervalued at the time of its release, the film has since become acknowledged as a cult classic, while Hepburn not only survived being stigmatised, among several other leading stars, as 'Box-Office Poison' by a leading American distributor, but won four Best Actress Oscars, receiving eight nominations and soldiering on until 1994.

Robert Siodmak's 1944 *Christmas Holiday* has been described as 'black', despite starring Deanna Durbin and Gene Kelly. With these two sunnily disposed stars, who could suspect that, just beneath the film's surface, there could be wickedness and menace. Durbin's fans were outraged that their embodiment of lighthearted happiness should be cast in a film including murder, incest and the homosexuality implied in Kelly's effeminate portrayal. Britain's leading movie magazine, *Picturegoer* (amalgamated with the prestigious *Film Weekly* soon after the outbreak of World War II), had welcomed Deanna Durbin's debut at 15 in the 1936 Joe Pasternak musical *Three Smart Girls*. But the magazine seriously doubted whether Durbin should have been involved in such murky material as *Christmas Holiday*. Just eight years before *Three Smart Girls* had singlehandedly saved Universal Studios from bankruptcy. Had she and Mickey Rooney, in 1938, not been awarded a special Academy Award for 'bringing to the screen the spirit and personification of youth'? And now...

In fact, from her first appearance in *Christmas Holiday* – singing, in clinging black satin, the melancholy 'Spring Will Be a Little Late This Year' on the brink of her marriage to Gene Kelly's Robert – Durbin gives her finest dramatic performance, in a career which made her Hollywood's highest-paid female star in 1948. That year she suddenly retired to marry Charles David, a director with whom she has lived in wealthy seclusion in France ever since. All attempts to penetrate their sanctuary have proved unavailing.

Gene Kelly's charming Robert is gradually revealed as a murderer who hides a bookmaker's body with the help of his mother, with whom his relationship verges on the Oedipal. His homosexual tendencies, implied by his manner, provide another revelation for Durbin's Abigail. Kelly and Durbin give performances of considerable subtlety, while the ever-menacing Gale Sondergaard was never more so than as Robert's possessive mother. On my discharge from the army, I worked as assistant manager at the Capitol Cinema, Upminster. We played this film: it had a compelling quality, which sent me in to view it again and again.

Billy Wilder's *The Lost Weekend* (1945) swept the board at the Oscars, and deservedly so. The story of a writer who seeks to drown his writer's block with alcohol (Ray Milland as Don Birnam) was adapted for the screen by the director and producer Charles Brackett, from the best-selling novel by Charles R Jackson. It won Oscars for their adaptation, as well as for Wilder's superlative direction. Milland won in the Best Actor category, and the film also scooped the year's Best Picture Oscar.

The hero's homosexuality was painlessly removed, except for a scene when a bitchy male nurse in the sanatorium (a superb cameo by Frank Faylen) leers over the writer's bed, hissing 'I *know* you.' The implication was there for those in the know and lends probity to a character both weak and fatally lacking in self-confidence, all achingly implied by Milland's performance. Often underrated as an actor, Milland shared certain characteristics with Cary Grant, being British-born in 1905, a year after Grant. Both actors acquired distinctive American accents, tinged with Bristolian (Grant) and Welsh (Milland), and both had romantic good looks, with an apparent underlying sense of humour. Milland's career declined, latterly, through undistinguished roles in B-movies, until he returned, bald-pated, as a character actor. Grant retired while still at the top and fully thatched.

The compromise happy ending of *The Lost Weekend*, with Don reformed by the love of a

Left: Ray Milland and Philip Terry in *The Lost Weekend* (1945).

good woman (Jane Wyman, strongly supportive), was a Hollywood concession, forgivable at the time, and was outweighed by the film's other virtues. Academy Award nominations went to John F Seitz (cinematography), Doane Harrison (editing) and Miklos Rozsa (musical score). An interesting footnote to my cinema-managing days was that a moment cut from the released version in Britain turned up in the print supplied to the Towers Cinema, Hornchurch. A hallucinatory bat crawls down the wall at the height of Milland's alcoholic delirium. A note to Paramount brought forth profuse apologies and the promised excision of the 'offending' footage. In hindsight, I should have kept my mouth shut.

Alfred Hitchcock, like Billy Wilder, made a distinctive contribution to the forties *noir* cycle. After *Rebecca*, with its Sapphic undertones, 1941 produced *Suspicion*. Joan Fontaine, starring again, is suspicious that bridegroom Cary Grant intends to murder her. In 1943, *Shadow of a Doubt* disturbed audiences with its revelation that Teresa Wright's beloved uncle Joseph

Cotten had a pathological loathing of women. In 1944 came Tallulah Bankhead's finest work for the cinema in *Lifeboat*, with her throaty utterance, 'Some of my best friends are women', a little in-joke between Hitchcock and his star. The director's *Spellbound* (1945) presented Ingrid Bergman as a psychiatrist dealing with a lesbian patient, played by Rhonda Fleming. Bergman's love interest is Gregory Peck, who appears according to all the evidence to be a murderer.

In 1947, Peck, again for Hitchcock, starred in a murder story with a remarkable cast, *The Paradine Case*. Alida Valli, in a part suggested for Garbo, is a *femme fatale* accused of murder. She is contemptuous of her defence counsel (Gregory Peck), who has fallen in love with her. It is fascinating to speculate what Garbo would have made of the part, though Valli is impressive. Ann Todd, in her only film made in the USA, is Peck's wife and Charles Laughton plays the heartless and lascivious judge in the case who lusts after her. Ethel Barrymore was Oscar-nominated for her performance as his wife. ☐

ROPE

1948 Transatlantic 80 mins colour
Producer: Sidney Bernstein; Director: Alfred
Hitchcock; Screenplay: Arthur Laurents (based on
the play Rope's End *by Patrick Hamilton);*
Cinematography Joseph Valentine, William V Skall
James Stewart, John Dall, Farley Granger, Joan
Chandler, Cedric Hardwicke, Constance Collier, Edith
Evanson, Douglas Dick, Dick Hogan

In this movie, Hitchcock experimented with his ten-minute take method, filming the story like a play, except for the opening and a few other reverse-angle shots. The film is based on the true story of Leopold and Loeb, two wealthy homosexual Chicago students who in 1924 murdered another student for the fun of it – and to see whether they could get away with the motiveless crime. The boys here are played by John Dall and Farley Granger, both gay actors, whose performances are spot-on.

The script, by homosexual Arthur Laurents in collaboration with Hume Cronyn and Ben Hecht, is based on the play *Rope's End* by Patrick Hamilton, which hinges on the quirky killers throwing a dinner party on the antique chest in which they have hidden the corpse. The guests include the victim's father (Cedric Hardwicke), his fiancée (Joan Chandler), whose presence makes them ill-at-ease, and a philosophy professor (James Stewart) whose interpretation of Nietzsche's 'superman' theory had been the basis for the murder. He it is who unmasks the killers in a scene of mounting suspense. Some critics have poured cold water on the movie as a 'stunt', which Hitch himself admitted, but I think it works superbly. The implied homosexuality caused the film to be initially banned in Chicago and other towns, besides being morally con-demned. In Sioux City Iowa, it was only passed after the murder scene was deleted.

The Leopold-Loeb story was filmed again in 1959 as *Compulsion*, directed by Richard Fleischer. This film had a script by Richard

Murphy, based on the novel by Meyer Levin, sticking far more closely to the facts as set forth by Levin. It is quite as compelling as Hitchcock's take, with the homosexual aspect more obvious, though less imaginative. Orson Welles gives a towering performance as the defence lawyer Jonathan Wilk. His final summing-up on behalf of compassion is masterly, while Bradford Dillman and Dean Stockwell acquit themselves admirably as the amoral thrill-killers, in the best parts of their careers.

In *Swoon* (1992), the most recent version of the case, director Tom Kalin has gone for the new Queer Cinema angle on the relationship between the two lovers. The relationship is seen as perverted in that it leads them to kidnap and finally kill a boy as the culmination of their self-destructive passion for each other. The almost incidental killing prevents any involvement with the lovers and can be interpreted as a homopho-bic interpretation of gay love, which is probably the last thing Kalin intended. The couple are finally tracked down by the police and con-demned to life imprisonment. It is surely time to let the matter rest there, both for the victim and his killers, lest even the most liberal-minded of Mrs Pat's horses threaten to stampede.

Above: John Dall and Farley Granger in *Rope* (1948).

Although the Production Code officially stayed in force until 1966, during the fifties and early sixties its stranglehold was gradually being hacked away. As social restrictions were eroded by more broad-minded attitudes and television became a real threat to the cinema, ways were explored to

4 THE BARRIERS START TO

combat or outdo the newer form of entertainment. Themes and language which would have been unthinkable were tried and found acceptable.

One example of this was provided by the highly rated writer Patricia Highsmith, herself a lesbian. Usually in her stories Highsmith presented characters who either were, or veered towards, the homosexual and her works were (in consequence?) more popular in Europe than the USA. Alfred Hitchcock visualised her 1950 novel *Strangers on a Train* as a viable subject for a film, but eight writers turned down his offer to work on the script until crime writer Raymond Chandler agreed to have a go. Hitchcock and Highsmith never met but talked courteously to each other on the phone. She had never written specifically for the screen and was happy for filmmakers to adapt her stories as they saw fit, unlike many authors who regard their work as sacrosanct and keep trying to interfere during filming. Hitchcock, however, did disagree with Chandler over certain key scenes.

Hitchcock wanted William Holden to play the tennis pro, the more masculine of the two main characters who meet on a train. However, he was forced to cast Farley Granger, with whom he had already worked on *Rope*. Nor was Hitchcock keen to have Ruth Roman as leading lady, although both she and Granger acquitted themselves admirably.

The plot is thus: on a train, Granger runs into a neurotic playboy (Robert Walker) who is all too happy to discuss his hatred for his father. When Granger admits he has a wife he wants to get out of his life, but refuses him a divorce, his new acquaintance suggests, in all seriousness, that they swap murders. Walker will dispose of the troublesome wife, while Granger is to kill the hated father. The tennis pro refuses to take the proposition seriously and dismisses it as a bad joke, but Walker is in deadly earnest and disposes of the recalcitrant wife in a fairground, a scene which is unfor-

CRUMBLE

gettably and typically Hitchcock.

The Walker character demands that his friend fulfil his part of the bargain, and Granger desperately tries to warn Walker's father of the scheme that his son is trying to put into action. Robert Walker is first charming, then creepily sinister, as the psychotic playboy, who is clearly fascinated by his athletic friend. The whole film is gripping from start to finish. Stage actress Marion Lorne puts in an effective comedy cameo, in a very rare film performance.

A sad footnote to the film is that the emotionally fragile Walker, who had suffered a traumatic divorce from Jennifer Jones, died during the making of his next film *My Son John* in 1952, after taking a dose of sedatives which led to respiratory failure at 37. He had married Jones in 1939 but lost her to David O Selznick in 1945. A second marriage was a disaster: he had a spell in a psychiatric clinic and a conviction for drunken driving. One of his big successes was *The Clock* (1945) with Judy Garland (*Under the Clock* in the UK). Deborah Kerr, with whom he appeared in *Please Believe Me*, released in 1950, says in her autobiography, 'The main thing I remember about the film was the genuine charm and appeal of Robert Walker. He was *so* vulnerable and his tragic early death robbed the cinema of one of its most attractive light comedy actors.' It seems that Walker's brilliantly accurate portrayal of a psychopath in the Hitchcock movie, so soon after his hospitalisation for a nervous breakdown, was all too near to the truth, especially given the actor's disturbed childhood and the breakdown of his first marriage.

Another Highsmith novel, *The Talented Mr Ripley* (1955), as filmed by Anthony

SOME LIKE IT HOT

1959 UA/Mirisch 122mins b/w
Producer: Billy Wilder; Director:
Billy Wilder; Screenplay: Billy
Wilder, I A L Diamond;
Cinematographer: Charles Lang
Jack Lemmon, Tony Curtis,
Marilyn Monroe, Joe E Brown,
George Raft, Pat O'Brien,
Nehemiah Persoff, George E
Stone, Joan Shawlee

In *Some Like It Hot*, Tony
Curtis and Jack Lemmon
cruise through a cross-dressing act which caused no edi-
torial headaches at all, as
musicians who witness the St
Valentine's Day massacre in
1929 Chicago and flee for
their lives disguised as
Josephine and Daphne, members of an all-girl band. Director Billy
Wilder co-wrote the screenplay with I A L Diamond, producing one
of the comedy classics of all time and one of the biggest successes
Marilyn Monroe ever enjoyed.

For good measure, the cast included thirties actors associated
with gangster movies, George Raft, Pat O'Brien and George E
Stone, besides the big-mouthed comedian Joe E Brown, whose closing line is one of the best-remembered and most laughed-at in
movies. As millionaire Osgood E Fielding III, he falls heavily for Jack
Lemmon in his Daphne persona and takes 'her' out in a boat, where
he proposes marriage. Daphne coyly tries to dissuade him and in
desperation exclaims, 'Osgood, you don't understand… I'm a man',
as he whips off his wig. Osgood's unperturbed reply: 'Well,
nobody's perfect.' End of film.

Interestingly, in a May 2000 TV interview, when asked about
Marilyn, Curtis denied ever making the oft-repeated quote that kissing her was like 'kissing Hitler'. He had only kind words to say and
asserted that when they travelled somewhere together as small-part
actors, they looked at each other and saw in their eyes 'future great-
ness'… or words to that effect.

Minghella, became a blockbuster in the early
months of the 21st century. Minghella's 1999
film was in fact a remake of René Clément's
Plein Soleil (1960; *Purple Noon* in Britain),
with Alain Delon and Maurice Ronet. The
plot concerns a friendship which ends in
murder, when Tom Ripley (Delon) travels to
Europe to persuade his old friend, Philip
Greenleaf (Ronet), to return to his family in
America. On arrival he becomes so obsessed
by his friend's opulent lifestyle that he kills
him and assumes his identity, having meticu-
lously planned the whole thing in advance.
He even convinces Philip's girlfriend (Marie
Laforet) that her lover, with whom she has
quarreled, is still alive.

Delon, perversely, resembles Jude Law,
who plays the *victim* in the Minghella remake.
Probably due to the passage of time and the
relaxation of censorship, Minghella's Ripley is
far more overtly gay than in Clément's film.

Furthermore, Matt Damon plays him as far from glamorous, whereas the beautiful Delon could never have been anything but attractive. Conversely, Ronet's looks, although handsome, were more ordinary. Another Ripley story, *Ripley's Game*, was filmed in 1977 as a German/French co-production, directed by Wim Wenders, starring Dennis Hopper as Tom Ripley and Bruno Ganz as a character called Zimmerman. The film, made in Germany, was released as *The American Friend* and has been much acclaimed as a key film in Wenders' *auteur* career.

1960 saw the release of the first two Oscar Wilde biopics. Also released that year was the Bryan Forbes-scripted *The League of Gentlemen*. Directed by Basil Dearden, the film was produced by Michael Relph and co-produced by Richard Attenborough. Attenborough, along with Forbes and Relph, was a founder member of the Allied Film Makers Company, along with actor Jack Hawkins, who played the leading role in the film. Other members of the League were Nigel Patrick, Roger Livesey, Robert Coote, Terence Alexander and Kieron Moore, the Irish actor who made his film debut in *The Voice Within* (1945). As Stevens, Moore is drafted by his ex-commanding officer, Lieutenant Colonel Hyde (Jack Hawkins), into a force of army comrades, bored with the inactivity of civilian life, who plan an ambitious robbery, with military precision.

This far-from-magnificent seven are drawn from all walks of life and Stevens happens to be gay, which, in those days, was a bold addition. The brawny Moore was very far from the clichéd queers of earlier days. His orientation is made quite clear but not overemphasised, fitting naturally into this delightful, very British and, with Dearden at the helm, almost Ealing-type film, admirably scripted and acted. The heist, naturally, goes wrong: much

SPARTACUS

1960 Universal-International/Bryna 196 mins colour
Producer: Edward Lewis; Directors: Stanley Kubrick, Anthony Mann [uncredited]; Screenplay: Dalton Trumbo, based on the novel by Howard Fast; Cinematographers: Russell Metty, Clifford Stine
Kirk Douglas, Laurence Olivier, Tony Curtis, Jean Simmons, Charles Laughton, Peter Ustinov, John Gavin, Nina Foch, Herbert Lom, John Ireland

Spartacus is a story in which Hollywood dipped a tentative toe into forbidden waters, in what was, at that time, the most expensive film ever made in America. It was directed by Stanley Kubrick and an uncredited Anthony Mann. The story of the slaves' revolt, led by gladiator Spartacus, against the all-powerful Romans provided an ideal role for Kirk Douglas, who possessed the requisite muscle and suggestion of brain power to lend conviction to his heroic depiction of idealism versus Roman greed and cruelty.

Kubrick's resources as a director made this an epic movie with quality and a cast to die for. Not the least of Kubrick's problems was coping with starry egos such as Laurence Olivier and Charles Laughton, who had watched Rome burn so many years before in *The Sign of the Cross* and had lost none of his self-importance in the interim. Also on hand was Tony Curtis (whose ego seems to have increased with girth and maturity), Peter Ustinov, a wry spectator of the scene, and Jean Simmons, who, according to Kubrick 'was no trouble at all.'

The scene which put the cat among thecensorial pigeons was the one where all-powerful Senator Crassus (Olivier) is attended in his bath by his slave Antoninus (Curtis at his prettiest) and indicates that his desires go beyond a bath and a rubdown. The incident was excised from the original release, but has since been restored (with Anthony Hopkins providing Olivier's now-lost dialogue track) and seems more risible than sexually stimulating. It is tempting to speculate what the millennium take on the scene would be.

Opposite: Tony Curtis, Jack Lemmon and Marilyn Monroe in *Some Like It Hot* (1959).

of the fun stems from guessing how that will happen. Furthermore, Moore's effete boyfriend is none other than the young Oliver Reed, playing limp-wristed and sibilant.

1959 and 1960 were the peak years of the great historical epics. 1959 saw the remake of *Ben-Hur* (1925), one of the most successful silent films, which had starred Ramon Novarro and Francis X Bushman. There are

Left: May McAvoy and Ramon Novarro in *Ben-Hur* (1925).

still those who maintain that the silent version is superior, even as far as the chariot race is concerned, which I find hard to accept. Ramon Novarro gives a wonderful performance, which is also remarkable given his later far-from-masculine persona. The film was directed by Fred Niblo, who directed the silent versions of *The Mask of Zorro* (1920) and *Blood and Sand* (1922) and helped Garbo to an early triumph in *The Temptress* (1926). Niblo's main claim to fame, apart from *Ben-Hur*, was as the director of the two biggest male stars of the period, Douglas Fairbanks Sr and Rudolph Valentino.

The 1959 remake had Technicolor and widescreen, plus Charlton Heston and Stephen Boyd in the key roles, with Jack Hawkins leading the stellar supporting cast. The movie was directed by William Wyler. The story tells of boyhood friends Judah Ben-Hur (Heston) and Messala (Boyd), who

become enemies at the time of the Crucifixion, after Ben-Hur has spent years away, unjustly condemned to be a galley-slave.

Ben-Hur and Messala meet as representatives of Judaism and the might of Rome respectively. One stirring climax is the great chariot race, which can seem a long time a-coming. Debating the strong personal relationship between the two men, Gore Vidal, one of the uncredited scriptwriters, suggested to Wyler that they had been lovers in youth and Messala had returned from Rome, wanting to resume the relationship, but Ben-Hur did not. Wyler saw this as a way of pepping up a convoluted plot and agreed. He confided in Boyd but left Heston in the dark. Boyd later admitted he had played Messala as a lover. With hindsight, that is the way it comes across in the early scenes and in the ending when, as the loser in the race, Messala takes great pains not to let the victorious Ben-Hur see his broken body.

Jack Hawkins is impressive as the Roman Commander who frees Ben-Hur from his galley chains and is rewarded when the slave saves his life after a pirate attack. Later, the Roman raises him to a prominent social position. The film deserved its Oscars as a mighty spectacle, and both Heston, so butch that he suggests rigor mortis, and Boyd, strongly contrasted, could hardly have been bettered.

The late fifties were a prolific time for Gore Vidal as a screenwriter. *The Catered Affair*, in 1956, was adapted from a play by Paddy Chayevsky about a Bronx family – mother Bette Davis, father Ernest Borgnine – planning an elaborate wedding for their daughter Debbie Reynolds, and was directed by Richard Brooks. Far from being the kind of work usually associated with Vidal, and still less with Bette Davis (playing a Jewish mum), this was a creditable piece of work without being a box-office smash.

In 1958 Vidal scripted *I Accuse!*, based on the turn-of-the-century Captain Dreyfus affair, a *cause célèbre* which reverberated throughout the world with speculations that the captain was, in fact, being tried for homosexuality as well as for treason. José Ferrer played the leading role, as well as directing the film, with Emlyn Williams as activist/writer Emile Zola, who defended him. Dreyfus was found guilty, but tried again, due to the efforts of his wife and friends to secure his release from Devil's Island. He was again found guilty but pardoned in 1899 and in 1906 the verdict was reversed. Proof of Dreyfus' innocence was discovered when German military documents were uncovered in 1930. He was a victim of anti-Semitism as well as trumped-up charges of paedophilia. A key figure in the film scenario was Anton Walbrook as Major Esterhazy.

Also scripted by Vidal and released in 1958 was *The Left-Handed Gun*, a life of Billy the Kid, in which it is subtly implied that Billy, as played by Paul Newman at his most handsome, was a repressed homosexual. Arthur Penn, the director, has been accused by the writer of tampering with his original conception, a problem that Vidal sometimes had with his film scripts. He rewrote the story in 1989, as *Gore Vidal's Billy the Kid*, directed by William Graham for cable television. Val Kilmer was more heterosexual in his approach to the role and the net effect of the remake was less gripping and subtle than the original.

The Tennessee Williams-Gore Vidal script of Williams' play *Suddenly Last Summer* (1959) was a landmark in the cinema and has often been credited as being the first Hollywood film to deal openly with homosexuality, although the leading figure of Sebastian Venable is only seen in flashback in the narration by Elizabeth Taylor. There can be no doubt what the subject is, however, and, as directed by Joseph L Mankiewicz, it could hardly be more gripping even if it were more explicit. In fact, as so often, subtlety lends effectiveness to the over-all picture. An American friend of mine, who had seen Williams' original one-act play, was quite shaken by the subject and said, 'That's one story that will never make the cinema.'

Filmed in England, with closed sets, rumours leaked out about the tensions on set, mostly concerning Montgomery Clift's emotional problems. This was ironic, considering that Clift was playing the psychiatrist, Dr John Cukrowicz, in charge of solving Catherine Holly's mental breakdown (the Elizabeth Taylor part). The troubled gay actor had complete support from his two female co-stars, especially Katharine Hepburn, who upbraided the director at the end of filming for his insensitive handling of Clift, vowing she would never work for Mankiewicz again.

Left: Montgomery Clift and Elizabeth Taylor in *Suddenly Last Summer* (1959).

Neither did she. Her performance – in the part of Mrs Holly, Catherine's venomous aunt (played in New York by one of MGM's top stars of the thirties, Ann Harding) – was an unforgettable creation, elegant and as lethal as the man-eating plants she cultivates. She tries to persuade the psychiatrist to have her niece lobotomised to remove the memory of the day she witnessed Sebastian pursued and cannibalised by the hungry youths he had used as bait to lure her into his sexual web. Taylor gave one of her best characterizations, besides looking incredibly lovely in black-and-white. The fact that Sebastian had previously used his mother to entice the boys, and discarded her when he considered her too old, was an added reason for the mother to take revenge on her niece.

The previous year, 1958, had provided Elizabeth Taylor with another of her most rewarding roles, as Maggie the Cat in another Tennessee Williams play-into-movie, *Cat on a Hot Tin Roof*. This time she is the voluptuous, sexually frustrated wife of Brick (Paul

Right: Paul Newman and Elizabeth Taylor in *Cat on a Hot Tin Roof* (1958).

Newman). Brick is guilt-ridden over his inability to satisfy her, due to his anguish over the death of his best friend, Skipper, who committed suicide. MGM at that time could not address the fact of Brick's homosexuality, which is explored in depth in the play, so they gave him a pair of crutches to explain his disability, though the question of Skipper is referred to as an added irritant.

Williams hated what had been done to his play. He reportedly told people in a cinema queue, 'This film will set the industry back 50 years. Go home!' Director Richard Brooks' reaction has not been recorded. It has been said that Taylor's Oscar in 1960 for *Butterfield 8* was to make up for her not winning for *Cat*. Others believe it was because she had nearly died of pneumonia. She played a call-girl who refuses to believe she is a prostitute, co-star-

ring with the always handsome but decidedly suspect Laurence Harvey.

The Tennessee Williams play was filmed again for TV in 1984, directed by Jack Hofsiss, receiving exceptionally good reviews for the performances of Jessica Lange as Maggie, Rip Torn as Big Daddy (played in 1958 by Burl Ives) and Tommy Lee Jones as Brick. The strong cast included Kim Stanley, David Dukes and Penny Fuller as other members of the family and the film gained considerably from not having to employ the evasions of yesteryear.

1957 saw the third (and one of the best) of Elvis Presley's films, *Jailhouse Rock*, released by Metro-Goldwyn-Mayer. This was a strange film to emerge from the usually glossy Metro production line. Richard Thorpe's gritty, fast-moving prison musical was more the type of

JAILHOUSE ROCK

1957 MGM 96 mins b/w
Producer: Pandro S Berman; Director:
Richard Thorpe; Screenplay: Guy Trosper;
Cinematographer: Robert Bronner
Elvis Presley, Judy Tyler, Mickey
Shaughnessy, Vaughn Taylor, Dean Jones

The storyline establishes Elvis as truck driver Vince Everett, who gets into a bar-room fight over a girl and accidentally kills the man who started it. Sentenced to from one to ten years for manslaughter, his cell-mate is Hunk Haughton (Mickey Shaughnessy), a former Country and Western singer who rules the inmates by doing them favours in return for packs of cigarettes. Hunk has considerable clout with the prison officers as the 'fixer', who can pacify the unruly inmates by playing his guitar and singing to them. He lends Vince his guitar and senses his raw talent. He tells him: 'You play ball with me and I'll play ball with you. I can't have my cell-mate walking round and looking like a bum.'

And hereby hangs a subplot. In Ned Young's original story, from which Guy Trosper fashioned the screenplay, it is the often factual situation of the older, tougher convict falling for the good-looking young cell-mate and offering to look after him in return for certain favours – in the script, cigarettes. Vince holds out against the offer and finds himself on the coal-yard shift – extremely dirty work under a sadistic warder who keeps the men short of drinking water. Vince has a rethink (over cigarettes,

of course) and Hunk lends him his guitar, to which he sings 'You're So Young and Beautiful' with such effect that the other prisoners go mad with enthusiasm. Hunk sees a way back into showbusiness and, placed in charge of a live TV production from the prison, tells Vince he has fixed a spot for him. His impression on the viewers is immediate and the jail is flooded with fan mail for Vince, which Hunk jealously bribes the post officials to withhold.

Vince finds out that the contract Hunk had persuaded him to sign, giving him 50 per cent of all his earnings, is invalid. He tears it up, signing with a pretty girl who works for a major record company (Judy Tyler as Peggy Van Alden). She builds Vince into a star but falls out with him when he becomes too big for his boots. Vince forgivingly fixes Hunk a spot on his TV show and offers him a ten per cent fee to look after him again after his split from Peggy. The TV show, *Jailhouse Rock*, is a wild success. Elvis himself, in black-and-white, performs one of his most memorable song and dance spectacles, to his own choreography, under the seasoned guidance of producer Pandro S Berman, who had made magic out of the Astaire-Rogers musicals. Still resentful over Vince's rejection, coupled with his protégé's phenomenal success, Hunk lays into Vince with his fists. Vince refuses to hit back and a hard blow to the larynx nearly kills him and causes his throat to swell, cutting off his wind-

pipe. After a successful operation the doctor warns him he may not sing again, but Peggy and Hunk bring along a bunch of musicians and...

The Vince-Hunk subplot is as much in evidence as the Vince-Peggy success story and lends balance to the light musical side of the story. Presley was never better and O'Shaughnessy, alternately callous and bullying, ruthless, loyal and caring, invests the character of Hunk with a depth somewhat lacking in Trosper's screenplay. Judy Tyler, warm and sympathetic as Peggy, helps make the happy ending genuinely touching. Sadly, she died in a car crash soon after the film was completed.

as Smoke Willoughby, a pianist who traces the career of Rick Martin (ie, Beiderbecke) from his orphaned childhood, when he attracts the attention of the great jazzman Art Hazzard, who teaches him all there is to know about being a cornet player. Jo Jordan (Doris Day), a band singer, loves Rick in her own quiet way, until she introduces him to her friend, 'intellectual' playgirl Amy North (Bacall), who marries him as a casual experiment in man-catching, then is unable to come to terms with competing against his love for music. Eventually she sets him aside to go to Paris with a lady friend, an artist who 'understands' her. Rick tells Amy she is 'sick' and needs some help, the prevailing attitude of the day.

As pure Jo Jordan, Day, in an almost peripheral role, sings some wonderful old songs expressing her love for Rick ('I Only Have Eyes For You' etc), and Kirk Douglas acts with some passion. But it is the mesmeric Bacall who remains in the memory. Director Michael Curtiz was nothing if not sophisticated and gives her a highly suggestive scene which she plays to the hilt. A young lift-boy gazes at her with unabashed admiration, of which she is fully aware. She pauses in the hall, looks back and returns to the elevator as the doors close. In the next shot she has returned to Kirk Douglas' apartment on the top floor. Apparently a closet nympho, her motto is 'You don't know what anything's like until you've tried it.'

By 1956 the world had already moved on to the extent that Robert Anderson's daring play *Tea and Sympathy*, which had initially been banned and then created a furore on the New York stage, was bought by MGM, a mere three years after the wild acclaim accorded the play and its stars in the theatre. Deborah Kerr was awarded the *Variety* Drama Critics' Award for Best Actress in a straight play, the Donaldson Award went to her for Best Actress and the

film that Warner Bros turned out with such efficiency. It seemed set to steer the star into the mould of the bitter, sullen and ungracious tough guy whose fists and quick temper land him in serious trouble. But it was not to be: after *King Creole* (1958) and army service, Elvis was transformed into the likeable, easy-going nice guy – though still handy with his fists – and, as a bonus from the army, terrific with his karate kicks.

When Issur Danielovitch and Betty Jean Perske dated in New York, they could have hardly guessed that in 1950, re-christened Kirk Douglas and Lauren Bacall, they would co-star in a fictionalised screen biopic of their idol, jazz cornetist Bix Beiderbecke, in *Young Man with a Horn* (*Young Man of Music* in Britain).

The story is narrated by Hoagy Carmichael

Above: Elvis Presley in *Jailhouse Rock* (1957).

Left: Alec Guinness, Omar Sharif and Peter O'Toole in *Lawrence of Arabia* (1962).

1954/55 Sarah Siddons Award for Outstanding Performance was also hers. This was at a time when the press dubbed Kerr 'Broadway's favourite star, with four "Marquees"' (theatres in which she was billed). Apart from *Tea and Sympathy*, the films *Dream Wife*, *Julius Caesar* and *From Here to Eternity* (all 1953) were running simultaneously. After all that, how could Metro not star her in her original role, the first of her new three-picture deal with the studio, in March 1956. Also cast in the movie were the other stars of the play, John Kerr and Leif Erickson. The director was Vincente Minnelli and Robert Anderson adapted his play for the screen.

Anderson wrote to me about the film: 'The picture didn't come off as well as we had hoped... we had to make too many changes for censorship. We kept fooling ourselves that we were preserving the integrity of the theme, but we lost some of it.' The story concerns a schoolboy lacking interest in 'manly' pursuits, who is set on the (then) politically correct path of sexual orientation and straight love by his teacher's wife. No one really dared to face up to the twin problems of deviancy and adultery. The crucial point of the play, that the boy had been seen swimming with a master everyone assumed to be homosexual, had to be omitted from the film altogether. Anderson continued: 'I feel that the stage production was indeed beautiful and brought out the hardness and whatever bite the play possessed, but the film bordered on the pretty. However, it serves its purpose in preserving the performances of Deborah, Jack Kerr and Leif Erickson.'

Kerr commented in her autobiography, 'I suffered with Bob Anderson, who had to make these adjustments in his play. It seems impossible that so recently one couldn't say 'homosexual' or simply 'queer' or 'gay' even, and it took something out of the movie that the boy was persecuted simply because he wasn't good at sports and games and preferred sewing on buttons and associating with faculty wives – who did not figure in the original at all – and playing classical music... The scene with his room-mate, Darryl Hickman, is a marvellous one. Al says, "You walk funny: you ought to walk like this", and proceeds to demonstrate how to be a beefy all-American boy. Bob Anderson has always held that the play isn't about homosexuality at all: it's about persecution of people whose ideas are different from yours. Because someone is 'different' they're not necessarily a 'sissy'. 'Sister boy' was the quaint euphemism used for homosexual in the movie.'

Of the director, Vincente Minnelli, Kerr says, 'He was extremely sensitive to the subject, the only thing that might have diffused it a little was that his great talent for making pictures very beautiful pictorially might have softened it – lushed it up a little.' She explains how difficult it was to shoot the end, which Elia Kazan had handled so brilliantly in the 1953 stage production. In the play, Laura comes into the boy's bedroom, stands by his bed and says the classic lines: 'Years from now, when you talk about this – and you will – be kind.' She just undoes the top button of her blouse... and the lights fade. In the movie, the scene is set in the open. The boy follows her into a wood and the effect is far less explicit.

That the subject was tackled at all shows that the barriers were certainly crumbling. But there was a long way to go before they were swept away altogether. Five years later, William Wyler did his best with another 'difficult' subject in *The Children's Hour*. As we have seen, the word 'homosexual' or 'lesbian' could still not be mentioned.

In 1962, when David Lean completed his epic *Lawrence of Arabia*, the term did not need to be used. The restored version of the history of T E Lawrence's classic autobiography *Seven Pillars of Wisdom* contained graphic descriptions of his homosexual torture at the hands of a Turkish officer and of the Arab boys slaking their 'pure and almost sexless' love with each other. The book inspired Lean's great biopic, which had been waiting for some 30 years to be made, originally by Alexander Korda with Walter Hudd set for the title role. David Lean commented in an interview with the *Guardian* in 1991: 'The whole story, and certainly Lawrence, was very, if not entirely, gay. We thought we were being very daring.' Lean instanced the ambiguity of the relationships with the Arab boys, King Feisal (Alec Guinness), the Turkish officer (José Ferrer) and Sheriff Ali Ibn El Kharish (Omar Sharif), introduced to Lawrence and the world in Freddie Young's superb cinematography through an awesomely beautiful desert mirage.

Young's Oscar nomination was well deserved, as were those for Best Picture, Peter O'Toole's wonderfully complex portrayal of one of history's most enigmatic characters, David Lean for Best Director, Omar Sharif for Best Supporting Actor, Robert Bolt for Best Adapted Screenplay, and Maurice Jarre for Best Musical Score. The film swept the board, and won a total of seven awards. Other actors included Jack Hawkins, Anthony Quayle, Claude Rains, Arthur

Kennedy and Donald Wolfit. Noël Coward's summing-up to Peter O'Toole was: 'If you'd been any prettier the film would have been called *Florence of Arabia!*'

The 1963 British-made *The Leather Boys*, directed by Sidney J Furie, was something of a *cause célèbre* in its day and regarded as an unacceptably frank insight into the gay lifestyle. The implied homo-erotic tensions between friends Reggie (Colin Campbell) and Pete (Dudley Sutton) come to the surface when Reggie marries Dot (Rita Tushingham) and shows a marked lack of sexual interest in her. She is, in fact, a screaming virago (a 'cure for lust', as a friend of mine used to say) and Pete, who really is gay, hopes to make the comfortable home life for Reggie that Dot is incapable of providing. The boys are as interested in motorbikes as they are in each other. When Dot screams at them that they're 'queer' (we were bolder in Britain than they were in the USA seven years before), the boys insist they're 'just good friends', but Reggie decides to sail off to America with Pete. *En route* for the docks they look in at a waterfront gay bar and Reggie realises that Pete really is 'queer' and rejects him, walking out of his life. Thus the director backs out of a happy gay ending.

The film gains immeasurably by Dudley Sutton's sensitive performance. This greatly underrated actor was the first to play the rentboy lodger providing the title role in the original stage version of Joe Orton's *Entertaining Mr Sloane*. In its day, *The Leather Boys* was an involving piece of cinema, with highlights in the wedding scene and the shots of Butlin's Holiday Camp. But avoiding the logical ending was something of a let-down.

No gay terms are used in 1964's *Goldfinger*, directed by Guy Hamilton and often considered the most effective of the blockbusting Ian Fleming adaptations, this

time by Richard Maibaum and Paul Dehn. This is the macho world of a powerful and womanising man, James Bond. As played by Sean Connery, Bond happens to be beautiful enough to make the swooning women who fall for him credible. But there is one who is unassailable, the delectable Pussy Galore, who manages a band of all-female pilots, called Pussy's Flying Circus.

Sean Connery is the perfect Bond for the cinema; Fleming's creation was hardly glamorous or inventive enough. Add Honor Blackman as Ms Galore and you have a perfect team. She appears to Bond out of a swoon-induced mist as he regains consciousness, and at once makes it clear that she is very much in charge, physically and mentally. As he prepares to cast his spell, she purrs, 'You can turn off the charm. I'm immune.' She doesn't have to say 'I go for the girls'; as Quentin Crisp once said, 'You just know.' So does Bond/Connery. Having been nurtured on a diet of Honor Blackman as Catherine Gale, control freak in TV's *The Avengers*, he recognises his match. However, besides working to foil Goldfinger's (Gert Fröbe) scheme to contaminate America's gold supply, he also concentrates on lowering Pussy's resistance. She works for Goldfinger, who orders her to 'entertain Mr Bond'. 'Business before pleasure,' she replies and comes back in something slinky. After a spirited judo session (she throws him and he throws her), the pair dive into a convenient load of hay. After this encounter, Pussy switches loyalties to Bond's side (at least for business purposes) and the world is saved for democracy.

Ted Moore's cinematography does Honor Blackman proud, Shirley Eaton makes a pretty impression (before she is gilded to death by her unspeakable boss) and Lois Maxwell contributes her charmingly low-key, longing but understanding secretary, Miss Moneypenny.

Right: Honor Blackman and Sean Connery between takes on *Goldfinger* (1964).

It was to be 14 years before Blackman, who in the meantime had been kept busy with star roles on film, stage and television, was to play another gay role in the cinema. Bizarrely, this was in the second sound remake of the creepy silent movie, *The Cat and the Canary*, which had starred Laura La Plante, Creighton Hale and Tully Marshall in 1927. The original was directed by Paul Leni, a German director, whose first Hollywood film this was, for Universal, and a forerunner of their later horror output, such as *Dracula* (1930), *Frankenstein* (1931) and *The Invisible Man* (1933). The first sound version, directed by Elliott Nugent in 1939, starred Paulette Goddard and Bob Hope, so inevitably the accent was on laughs, but there were still thrills galore in the classic story of family members gathered together in an old dark house to hear the reading of a will. Goddard is named beneficiary and spends the rest of the movie avoiding death from clutching hands and creepy cousins after her inherited wealth. The cast included the magnificently sinister Gale Sondergaard as the doomy housekeeper, who knows all the secrets of the house, plus John Beal and Douglass Montgomery, who turns out to be the murderous Charley.

The British version followed a mere 38 years later, in 1977, under the direction of Radley Metzger, with the basics of the plot unchanged but with a prologue featuring Wilfrid Hyde White as the eccentric old millionaire who activates the legend of the cat and the canary and loves only his little curly-haired descendant, Charley. The old man makes a film to be screened after his death, by his ancient and devoted housekeeper (Beatrix Lehmann), at a dinner party to which he posthumously invites his 'greedy bastard' relatives, with the housekeeper as butler-in-waiting. First visitor is the old man's lawyer (Dame Wendy Hiller, no less), only a mite less forbidding than Lehmann. She introduces the family guests: Michael Callan, Carol Lynley (as the menaced heiress), plus Daniel Massey and Peter McEnery as warring rivals, the latter as the fatal Charley, in league with creepy asylum-keeper Edward Fox, only you don't know that.

Then there's the odd couple, Honor Blackman as feted sportswoman Susan Silsby with her friend and constant companion, Olivia Hussey as Cecily Young. They are to share the same bedroom, as observed by the lawyer with the arched eyebrow at which Dame Wendy was such an adept and by Lehmann's Mrs Danvers type with pursed lips. 'Don't worry,' says sportswoman Susan gaily, 'we're not going to have children!' After some nasty happenings, including the lawyer's demise through a secret panel, several fights between the rival cousins and barbed hints from Susan to her heiress cousin, Susan and Cecily lock themselves in their room, where the sportswoman tenderly massages her terrified friend's back. But Susan foolishly ventures out into the darkened hall...

The Cat and the Canary is a splendid cast in a load of jolly rubbish, updated for the late seventies. American Carol Lynley manages a credible English accent. As for Honor Blackman, she still retains her glamour, playing mature high-livers with a keen eye for a sturdy limb (male) in TV soaps such as *The Upper Hand*. And she maintains an unerring skill at delivering trenchant one-liners on stage in her one-woman show *Dishonorable Ladies* – from Delilah to Dietrich; Cleopatra to Carmen; Medusa to Madonna. Who could ask for anything more?

Before quitting echoes and film companions of Bond, Lotte Lenya deserves a special mention as the representative of the gay pre-Nazi German era of the twenties and thirties,

and as the wife of Kurt Weill. The mere mention of his name evokes chilling memories of 'Mack the Knife' and *The Threepenny Opera*, which G W Pabst made into a 1931 film, *Die Dreigroschenoper*, starring Lenya. There was a 30-year gap before she was Academy Award-nominated for her role as the hatchet-faced but elegant procuress in the Vivien Leigh-Warren Beatty film *The Roman Spring of Mrs Stone* (1961), directed by Jose Quintero and based on the novel by Tennessee Williams. Mrs Stone, a widowed actress (and still a comely Rosalind in *As You Like It*), at 48 is provided with a dishy gigolo (Beatty) by pimp Lenya and finds no good comes of the association. Leigh, exquisite as ever in an unusual offbeat 'romance', indicates that Rome is not the ideal place to go for peace and solitude.

For 1963's Bond movie *From Russia With Love*, Lotte Lenya created a formidable lesbian killer with lethal dagger-wielding shoes. With her looks she was limited in her choice of film roles and Rosa Klebb suited her from top to, as it were, toe. The second of the James Bond movies, *From Russia With Love* was directed by Terence Young. Klebb remains surely the most formidable female Bond has had to cope with to date. Lenya was to make only two more films, including *Semi-Tough* (1977), playing a chiropractor and guru called Clara Pelf. She died in 1981, aged 82.

Shelagh Delaney's 1957 play *A Taste of Honey* was filmed in 1961 by Tony Richardson, one-time husband of Vanessa Redgrave and one of Britain's finest directors from the late fifties to the late eighties. Richardson died of AIDS in 1991. His bisex-

Left: Charles Laughton and Burgess Meredith (far right) in *Advise and Consent* (1962).

uality was known to his close friends, though he never acknowledged himself as such. *A Taste of Honey*, scripted by Delaney and Richardson, was a classic exploration of social rejects in the industrial North, with Rita Tushingham as Jo, a tough young woman who has a brief affair with a black sailor (Paul Danquah), poetic while it lasts but leaving her pregnant when he deserts her. The friend who looks after her, Geoff (Murray Melvin), is an effeminate homosexual who becomes like a mother to her and the baby. Together they present a united front against the world and, in particular, Jo's brassy, fun-loving mother (Dora Bryan) and her man friend (Robert Stephens). Dora Bryan was given a BFA (British Film Award) for her performance and waited five years before her next film part, in

The Great St. Trinian's Train Robbery, in 1966. Her stage career has continued, profitably, and the odd film role has come her way, but the skill and subtlety she showed as Tushingham's terrible mother – she meant well at heart! – could have been profitably employed in the cinema all these years.

The heart of the movie lies in the tender relationship between Jo and Geoff, beautifully portrayed by Rita Tushingham and Murray Melvin, whose subsequent film parts could never have been so rewarding. The cinematography of Walter Lassally and the score by John Addison perfectly complement the poetic tone of Richardson's triumphant transcription of Shelagh Delaney's memorable play.

Perhaps the first of the dramas concerning men of the cloth involved in blackmail charges of homosexual molestation of a minor was the 1959 British movie *Serious Charge*, based on the play by Philip King. Vicar Anthony Quayle is stalked by a neurotic parishioner played by Sarah Churchill. He gently tries to keep their relationship on a platonic level, while at the same time doing his best to counsel the town's delinquent (Andrew Ray), whom he defends on the death of the boy's girlfriend. The vicar's would-be girlfriend, Churchill, having seen the pastor with the boy, is all too ready to listen to his vengeful accusation of sexual impropriety, and the eponymous Serious Charge is brought against him.

Director Terence Young handled this forerunner of Basil Dearden's *Victim* (which created such a deep impression just two years later) with tact and a neat sense of the dramatic, in a story about jealousy and homophobia. The acting is flawless. Anthony Quayle gives one of his most interesting performances in British films as the vicar whose innate goodness lands him in trouble. Sarah Churchill's display of frustrated viciousness is all too convincing, and Andrew Ray makes the boy disturbingly real. An interesting piece of casting was Britain's most enduring rock 'n' roll star, Cliff Richard, as Ray's younger brother, exemplifying youthful brio and twanging a mean guitar. More than 40 years later, he rocks on, remaining at the top of his particular tree. *Serious Charge* is a minor trail-blazer to cherish.

Advise and Consent (1962), directed by Otto Preminger, was an early and outstanding example of homosexuality not mixing happily with politics (at least in those days). The cast is wonderful: Charles Laughton in his last film as a worldly wise Southern senator, Henry Fonda as a Secretary of State under investigation and Don Murray as the idealistic chairman on the sub-committee doing the investigating, with Gene Tierney representing the distaff side but not involved in the political arena. Other distinguished cast members include Walter Pidgeon and Peter Lawford. *Advise and Consent* was Hollywood's first film to venture inside a gay bar, apart from the rather curious portrayal of a drag act in what purports to be one in Clara Bow's penultimate film *Call Her Savage* (1932).

Advise and Consent's plot is complex. Pidgeon and his cohorts are trying to push through Fonda's appointment as Secretary of State, but Murray will not commit to him as his party leader. This leads to Murray being blackmailed over homosexual activities which took place years before, when he was in the services. Murray tracks down his former lover, John Granger, now a hustler in a gay bar, the 602. Appalled at the meat-market ambience of the place, he hurries out, despite his former lover's pleas for him to come and join him. After a brief altercation beside his car, Senator Brigham Anderson (Murray) pushes his former boyfriend, Ray (Granger), down into the rain-soaked road and makes his getaway. The tragic upshot is that the Senator commits suicide, unable to face his wife and three children, or his fellow senators.

Murray's performance was a courageous one for the time, and his co-stars, including Burgess Meredith – a key witness in unravelling Anderson's past – are all excellent. Laughton impresses as the laconic and ultimately homophobic Senator Seabright and Franchot Tone and Lew Ayres shine in the small but pivotal roles of President and Vice President. Preminger showed again what an adroit director he could be, given the right material – as in this screenplay, adapted by Wendell Mayes from the novel by Allen Drury. We are here still in an era when homosexuality carries a stigma, which almost inevitably leads to disgrace and, often, suicide.

Two years later there was more of a cutting

Above: Margaret Leighton, Henry Fonda and Ann Sothern in *The Best Man* (1964).

edge to Gore Vidal's adaptation of his own play *The Best Man* (1964). Directed by Franklin J Schaffner, this also has a political theme, centred on the two rivals campaigning for the position of President and trying to win the support of the dying incumbent – a fitting swan song from Lee Tracy in his last role before his own death. Tracy had been a big star in the thirties until his fast-talking act became dated and he made the unwise career move of upsetting Louis B Mayer.

The rivals for the nomination, neither of whom the President favours, are played by Henry Fonda and Cliff Robertson. Fonda is the idealistic William Russell, who has a history of emotional instability. His wife Alice (Margaret Leighton) is putting their divorce on hold, to avoid damaging his chances of the nomination. Robertson is the ruthless and hypocritical Joe Cantwell, who is using a dossier on Russell's emotional problems to sway the election results. However, it transpires that Cantwell had a relationship with a fellow sailor a few years previously. The climax hinges on whether Russell will use this evidence to retaliate.

Two romantic stars of the thirties, Ann Sothern and Gene Raymond, contribute valuable supporting performances, along with Kevin McCarthy, while gospel singer Mahalia Jackson appears as herself. Vidal is here in his element and his dialogue is razor-sharp. The decent Fonda wants no part of the 'dirty politics' game. His attitude is, 'Even if it's true, so what?' Like *Advise and Consent*, this outspoken movie had a limited release. Many local cinemas were unwilling to show such 'risky' subjects.

The climate of the fifties and sixties made possible the enormous success in Britain of the Carry On comedies and, worldwide, the series of Italian-made spectacles built around such legendary heroes as Hercules, twice played by former Mr Universe, Steve Reeves. The Carry Ons began in 1958 with *Carry On Sergeant*, adapted from R F Delderfield's play *The Bull Boys*, a serious drama dealing with conscription, by producer Peter Rogers and scriptwriter Norman Hudis. The director was Gerald Thomas and the distributors Nat Cohen and Stuart Levy, on their first venture into film production.

At first they did not think the rushes at all funny, but when Rogers sent the finished product they became ecstatic and recognised the birth of a new comedy genre, very British and with much of the crass effrontery of the long popular saucy seaside postcards. At least, if they did not make that prognosis immediately, they certainly did when the series grew to 29 entries between 1958 and 1978, the last being *Carry On Emmannuelle*, in which the spirit seemed to have gone out of the series. The 'comeback' movie, *Carry On Columbus* in 1992, when so many of the original cast had died, received a trouncing from

Right: Jim Dale and Julian Clary in *Carry On Columbus* (1992).

the press, most of whom had not warmed to the Carry Ons in the first place. Nor did they welcome Julian Clary, who was delightful (if you're a fan), but literally all at sea with the old-timers, as a kind of Major Domo on the voyage of discovery, with the ever-handsome Jim Dale in the title role.

A feature of the earlier films was the inevitably camp contributions of the two inescapably gay characters, Kenneth Williams and Charles Hawtrey. Between them they put the representation of homosexuals back to the era of the silent movies, representing the stereotypes of the pouf, pansy or faggot, with their limp hand gestures and sibilant tones. The laughs they got were the reinforcement of the 'real man's' attitude to effeminacy and struck a regressive note with every camp *double entendre*.

Charles Hawtrey was the weedy-looking one who used to play ageing schoolboys in the Will Hay comedies, while Williams, of the falsetto voice and campily flaring nostrils, enjoyed 30 years of top radio, TV and film fame, often with his friend Barbara Windsor, who represented perky glamour in ten of the Carry On movies. Williams and Hawtrey were the ones most likely to adopt female attire, though they often played 'manly'-ish as well. Kenneth Williams (1926-88) was in private life an unhappy character and never was able to get on with the overtly macho Sid James, as he revealed in his published diaries. Hawtrey (1914-88), always in demand for film and radio appearances, was a less complicated character and altogether gentler. Barbara Windsor, virtually never out of work on stage or screen, took on a new persona as an actress,

Left: Steve Reeves in *The Thief of Baghdad* (1960).

playing the feisty bar owner, Peggy Mitchell, in the hugely successful TV soap *EastEnders*.

Over on the continent a cheap and cheerful genre grew up in Italy's Cinecittà studios. In a period when men were becoming increasingly aware of their bodies, even the weediest could sometimes be deluded into believing that a strenuous course of weightlifting could transform them into something approaching the Charles Atlas photographs in the magazines. This paved the way to a transformation for gays. Bodybuilding became the rage and out of it came the muscle contests which were held yearly around the world, especially in the USA and Britain. I know; I took it up and fled from the scene before the time came for me to strut my stuff at the Mr South East London contest in Putney!

All of this had a massive gay following and produced a legion of giants, of whom perhaps the most handsome and certainly the most muscular was the American-born Steve Reeves, who hailed from Montana, the state

from which his hero Gary Cooper originally came. At first his ambitions were concentrated on becoming Mr America in 1947, when he was 21, then Mr World and, in 1948, Mr Universe, a title which he won again in 1950.

In 1954 Reeves photographed so well in the Jane Powell musical *Athena* that Italian director Pietro Francisci thought of casting him as Hercules when he was preparing the film *Le fatiche di Ercole* in 1957. DeMille had tested Reeves for his epic *Samson and Delilah* (1949) but had chosen Victor Mature instead. Mature's muscles were more than adequate, though hardly in the Reeves category: the choice may have had something to do with acting ability, of which Mature had more than he was ever credited with. Italian musclemen characters like Maciste had been popular since the First World War, but *Le fatiche di Ercole* (*The Labours of Hercules* in the USA) brought a resurgence of international popularity after American tycoon Joseph E Levine bought it, dubbed it into

English and spent a million dollars publicising it. He made a $4 million profit. Steve Reeves clubs sprang up like mushrooms, predominantly around the gay community (it has been said that girls go for brain rather than brawn), and contests were held for the best lookalikes. Queues outside the cinemas were touted by chaps selling Reeves photos.

The new craze for mythological heroes grew, and as Reeves could only film a certain number in a year and his salaries increased with the demand, bodybuilders were being signed up by the dozen. Britain's own Reg Park from Leeds went to Rome to take on Reeves' role in *Ercole al centro della terra*. Reeves' greatest rival, Gordon Scott (who had played Tarzan), was cast with him in *Romulo a Remo* (*Duel of the Titans*) in 1961, directed by Sergio Corbucci. Reeves claimed to have been offered the part of James Bond before Sean Connery, who, incidentally, had won several bodybuilding contests. With the best will in the world, one doubts that he could have carried off the Bond role. For all his glamour, beauty and presence, Steve's acting was strictly by numbers, though he cut a handsome dash in the 1960 remake of *The Thief of Baghdad*, nominally directed by Hollywood veteran Arthur Lubin.

Reeves retired from movies in 1968, after at last making a western, *Viva per la tuo morte!* (*A Long Ride from Hell*), married his secretary Aline and settled on a ranch to breed horses in California. He wrote a bestseller, *Building the Classic Physique the Natural Way*, and spent the rest of his life keeping fit and instructing others in weight training, which he believed could turn youngsters away from drugs.

In 1962 I set up an interview with Reeves in his apartment in Rome for *Films and Filming*, having planned a cycling holiday to Capri to stay with Gracie Fields in her home there, La Canzone del Mare. Gracie had been interested in pedal cycling since her youth and once wrote to me, 'I wish I'd known you earlier – I'd always wanted someone to cycle across Europe with – now, I guess I'll just stick to me knitting!' This time she said 'If I know you're coming, I'll put the kettle on for you!' Realising Rome to be handily *en route* for Naples and Capri, I negotiated the interview with Reeves and arranged to go via Paris, where Dietrich was appearing in concert at the Olympia Theatre.

An article I had written about Dietrich's role in *Judgement at Nuremburg* (1961) had pleased her sufficiently for me to receive a telegram, out of the blue: 'Come see me Olympia ticket on your name Box Office.' Dietrich's friend, actress Marti Stevens, was in the dressing room and the main topic of conversation was that Marlene did not think her concert had been sufficiently on form to impress Edith Piaf, who had the seat next to me in the stalls with her new young husband, Theo. They had seemed happy and gay and applauded Dietrich to the echo. She asked Marti Stevens, who had kept watch from the wings, if it were so. She agreed, but Marlene shook her head mournfully. I did get a throaty chuckle from her when she grabbed my book, a biography of Catherine the Great with a formidable cover portrait of a remarkably plain woman, and I said, 'So she didn't really look like you at all!'

The eventful journey ran into a hitch in Rome. Steve Reeves' large and friendly housekeeper, who spoke a little English, explained that he had had to leave suddenly that morning to film in Czechoslovakia and there had been no way to contact me. She made me welcome with wine and a large spaghetti bolognese and rattled on about the master, of whom she was evidently very fond. So I lost my chance of meeting Hercules in this world. He died on 1 May 2000, aged 74. □

5 GAY ICONS

A handful of stars have qualified for the title of Gay Icon, either because of the roles they played, their outrageous mode of dressing, or by virtue of something in their personalities which appealed instinctively to lesbians and gays.

MAE WEST (1892-1980)

Top of the list has to be Mae West, whose sympathy for homosexuals was declared in her plays. This trend started with *Sex* in 1926, a title never paraded on the billboards before and a subject that landed all of the cast in jail for ten days. Her next, the following year, *The Drag*, dealing with gays and transvestites in New York, was advertised as 'a homosexual comedy'. She wrote and directed this, in which, unlike *Sex*, she did not appear. Mae combed Greenwich Village for suitable actors. She was advised to open it out of town, but soon called it in for a

Opposite: A portrait of Mae West.

Above: Mae West and Margaret Hamilton in *My Little Chickadee* (1940).

rewrite. It became *Pleasure Man*, which opened at the Biltmore Theatre on 1 October 1928, only to be closed the next day. Mae, in her autobiography *Goodness Had Nothing To Do With It* (1959), hints at dark forces at work, but her position as Queen of the Gays was assured. She said that gay actors became her 'sisters'. 'They were all crazy about me and my costumes. They were the first ones to imitate me in my presence.'

Not only gay actors. Some 20 years later, when *Diamond Lil* was playing at the Prince of Wales in London, I was to witness an echo of her effect on gays. I joined the crowd at the stage door to witness what I was told was a daily ritual. First a little queen, having checked that the great star was not on her way down, imitated her walk along the line of fans and, when the star did appear, led a chorus of cheers and called out, 'Mae – you wicked girl; you're taking all the best men in town away from us!' She swayed up to him, prodded his chest with a be-ringed forefinger and drawled, 'You know – I think you're "one of those"'. She pecked his cheek and continued her stroll along the line. My moment had come.

Having read that it was difficult to get a good American chewing gum in Britain now that most of the GIs had left, I had saved a piece and stepped up to her with it in my hand. A muscular swain stepped forward but she waved him away. 'For you, Miss West,' I said proudly, handing her the stick of gum. She turned it over in a bemused kind of way, said 'Oooh, thank you, honey!' and stepped into her lighted limousine, driving off with regal waves of a white-gloved hand. Her little impersonator, not used to being upstaged, hissed 'Bitch!' and the performance ended with a laugh at my expense.

When Mae West's first two starring movies single-handedly saved Paramount Studios from bankruptcy, her comment was 'I was better known than Einstein, Shaw or Picasso. And yet I had done merely in front of the camera what I had done for years, as well, on stage.'

Above: Mae West and Timothy Dalton in *Sextette* (1978).

As the nonagenarian Evelyn Laye intoned on her stage comeback: 'They don't make them like that any more!'

Born in Brooklyn in 1892, Mae's father was a heavyweight boxer, known as Battling Jack, and her mother Matilda Delker Doelger, a German-born immigrant who had been a corset and fashion model before her marriage. 'She added the colour and style, Father made a living for us,' she wrote in her autobiography. Mae began lessons at a Brooklyn dancing school at the age of seven, and so impressed her instructor that he featured her in one of his Sunday-night programmes at Brooklyn's Fulton Street Royal Theatre, where she sang 'Movin' Day', performed a tap dance and won the gold medal first prize. Soon her parents were persuaded to allow her to join Hal Clarendon's stock company and to oversee her education while she toured with the troupe.

From 13 to 17, Mae played juvenile leads, performing an act in front of the footlights during the interval when there was no suitable role for her in a production. Her salary rose from $13 to $30 weekly and she developed a vaudeville act. This led to a meeting and short-lived marriage with jazz singer Frank Wallace, whom she joined in a song and dance act, also short-lived. She did not bother to divorce him and some 20 years later, when she had established herself in films, he sued for alimony, revealing their marriage in 1911, when she was 19. *Film Weekly* commented at the time that the revelation that Mae was over 40 years of age might come as a shock to her fans. Mae stayed in bed and made no comment. She had risen from vaudeville through revue to musical comedy on Broadway and written several controversial plays leading to *Diamond Lil* (1928), which settled her into the persona she continued to play, with variations, for the rest of her long life.

A resumé of her films shows her box-office appeal waning from *Go West, Young Man* with Randolph Scott in 1936 and *Everday's a Holiday* (1938), in which she did a riotous impersonation of a French cabaret star in a black wig. There was a resurgence in *My Little Chickadee*, co-starring with W C Fields in 1940. *The Heat's On* (1943) played as a second feature in Britain, retitled *Tropicana*. The film was a musical directed by Gregory Ratoff, in which Mae fell foul of the Watch Committee, represented by Victor Moore who, bowing graciously over her hand, was told, 'Don't look now, honey, your hair's skiddin'' – as his toupée slipped.

After signing a contract with Paramount, Mae waited a long time for her debut in *Night after Night* (1932), directed by Archie Mayo, starring George Raft and Constance Cummings. Mae plays an old flame of speakeasy owner Raft, and upstages everyone in the club scenes from the moment she responds to the hat-check girl's remark, 'Goodness, what beautiful diamonds!' Mae then says, 'Goodness had nothing to do with it.' George Raft said, 'Mae walked off with everything but the camera', while Cummings found her ruthless. This especially applied to Alison Skipworth, 67 and slow with her lines. In one scene there was awkwardness when, after a binge, Skippy and Mae wake up in bed together. The incredible reaction led, in 1933, to *She Done Him Wrong*, directed by Lowell Sherman from Mae's stage hit *Diamond Lil*.

Lady Lou runs her nightclub, where anything goes. The missionary next door, Cary Grant, tries to convert her. She wins him over after taking him in from top to toe: 'Why don't you come up sometime, see me?' Their teaming was repeated, the same year, in *I'm No Angel*, directed by Wesley Ruggles. In this, carnival owner Tira tames men and lions, among the former a businessman, Cary Grant: 'When I'm good, I'm very good; but when I'm bad I'm even better.' This scraped in, virtually uncut, pre-Production Code. However, substantial cuts were made in 1934's *Belle of the Nineties*. Leo McCarey directed this story written, as virtually all Mae's material was, by herself. She emerged as raunchy as ever, sang with Duke Ellington's band and dressed up as the Statue of Liberty.

In *Goin' to Town* (1935), directed by Alexander Hall, Mae weds an oil tycoon, inherits his millions, falls for a snobbish British Lord (Paul Cavanagh), and goes to Buenos Aries to get 'culture'. *En route* she sings Saint-Saens' Delilah, surprisingly effectively, in the opera *Samson and Delilah*. The same year Raoul Walsh directed *Klondyke Annie*, which Mae adapted from her stage play. As an entertainer singing 'I'm an Occidental Woman in an Oriental Mood for Love', she murders her Chinese lover and escapes on a boat bound for Alaska, sharing a cabin with missionary Helen Jerome Eddy, who dies on the journey. (When Eddy asked 'Do you snore?', Mae's reply was, 'Mmmmmm – I ain't had no complaints.') Captain Victor McLaglen becomes besotted with Annie, who takes on the missionary's uniform and poke bonnet and finds herself preaching at

revivalist meetings and singing hymns. This was my first sight of a West movie, in Zurich. I, along with so many others, became besotted. However, from then on, all mention of Mae West movies was barred from William Randolph Hearst's newspaper chain because he alleged she had insulted his mistress, Marion Davies.

Mae West's films, albeit toned down by the censor, continued to attract a preponderance of gays, as did her plays when she returned to the stage in *Catherine Was Great*. Her final film, *Sextette* (1978), was developed from her original play, *Sextet*. The play was mostly notable for the fact that one of West's leading men, Alan Marshall, dropped dead at her feet during the tour. Another lead, Jack La Rue, most adept at playing gangsters, survived.

Originally, *Sextette* had been mooted in 1970 for Warner Bros-Seven Arts, with Cary Grant, Rock Hudson and David Niven suggested as co-stars. In the event, the line-up was still impressive, including Ringo Starr, George Hamilton, Alice Cooper and Tony Curtis as ex-husbands who keep interrupting the consummation of Mae's marriage to Timothy Dalton. British director Ken Hughes had made the excellent Peter Finch version of *The Trials of Oscar Wilde* in 1960. The film also features an audio tape from Mae West's autobiography which is destined to save civilisation (I think). With songs galore, including one with Alice Cooper, the gay ex, and a regurgitation of many of her one-liners, it was no wonder Mae had a 'prompt' microphone in her wig, as she could not memorise the lines, which changed from day to day.

Veteran film critic Dilys Powell was impressed by the many times Margo Manners, 'reigning sex queen', had to stomp uncomplainingly up and down stairs in her stilt-like platform shoes. Hughes recalls that once, not hearing the command 'Cut!', she swayed on, hand on hip, through studio equipment and scenery. It obviously never crossed her mind that there was anything unusual in an 85-year-old sex symbol bedding a 33-year-old groom. Her last line as she opens her arms to welcome Dalton into the marital four-poster is 'The British are coming!' How's that for *savoir faire*?!

Mae West died at 88, after a fall from bed resulted in pneumonia. She was survived by her constant companion in later years, Paul Novak, a muscleman from her Broadway act in the 1950s.

TALLULAH BANKHEAD [1903-1968]

Tallulah Bankhead's outrageous quips were, in her day, as famous as Mae West's. The difference was that, in West's case, they were carefully adapted to situations in her plays or films, so they have been handed down through the media and the periodic airing of her movies on TV. West's one-liners are created and honed, just as her public image was gradually built up until it took her over completely. She was her own work of art, as far as her public was concerned. Sometimes she said things that were unconsciously funny, like, 'Ho-Chi-Minh? – Mmmm, I think I know him', but, in the main, every quip was assessed and placed just where it fitted.

Bankhead's sayings, many of which have entered into the language by reason of their downright bawdiness, just came naturally, as did her no-holds-barred personality. She said and did whatever came into her mind – and the devil take the consequences. Sometimes he did.

At my prep school, rumours percolated through that actress and film star Tallulah Bankhead had been forced to leave the country because of corrupting the boys of Eton. This was in the early thirties and, as is usual in such cases, it was an exaggeration. What happened was that the high-living Tallulah, the toast of the London stage, and particularly the Gallery Girls, who worshipped at her shrine, had invited five Eton boys to meet her at the Hotel de Paris in

Bray, near Maidenhead. What occurred between them is still shrouded in mystery, except that the boys were expelled and that a police report, released 70 years after the event, announced 'although it is rumoured in theatrical circles that Miss Bankhead is a sexual pervert, and immoral with men, it has not been possible to gather any information to confirm this.' One Whitehall official noted that 'according to an informant, she is a lesbian and has 'kept' a black girl in America and that she 'keeps' a girl in London now.'

Several officials were keen to see her deported. Sir John Anderson, the Permanent Under Secretary at the Home Office, had asked William Bridgman, the First Lord of the Admiralty, to make a direct approach to Eton, but the headmaster refused to cooperate. Nor were the parents of the boys, some of whom were friendly with Tallulah, prepared to do anything to stop their sons from associating with her. However, notices were put up at the school, saying 'From this date onwards, Miss Tallulah Bankhead is out of bounds.' A further edict announced, 'Henceforth, all students will be forbidden to witness a Tallulah Bankhead play, for fear of corruption.' One doubts if any other actress in the twentieth century has ever caused such a flutter in the public school dovecote.

Tallulah did, in fact, leave for the US shortly afterwards to take up a Hollywood contract, but she was certainly not deported. Her aristocratic friends in the establishment saw to that. But there had been so much about the case in the tabloids that at school we were convinced that this 'decadent lady' had been thrown out of the country. And what a frisson it gave us as ten-years-olds: it could have happened to us, although we were perhaps a little underdeveloped to meet this lady's needs. We, too, were forbidden to discuss her, but we let our imaginations run wild during after-dark whisperings in the dormitory.

A British peer once said, 'There are only

three people in England who are front page news, the Prince of Wales, George Bernard Shaw and Tallulah Bankhead.' She had made films before – two silents when she was only 15, having won a beauty contest whose first prize was a role in a motion picture. This was *When Men Betray*, in 1918. The other film, the same year, was *Thirty a Week*, but it was not until the talkies that her whisky baritone added extra piquancy to her considerable beauty. Tallulah's recording of 'Don't Tell Him What Happened to Me' was fairly dreadful, but something of the 'decadent lady' came through.

In her eight years in London Bankhead appeared in 16 plays; in her autobiography she quotes five as 'ridiculous messes, fated for quick disaster'. Another three were described as a little better and 'prospered in varying degrees'. That leaves eight good ones, which presumably made her the darling of the Gallery Girls, who were her staunch supporters come hell or high water. She knew them all by name and was happy to entertain them in her Farm Street home. She was undoubtedly their icon and, through her films, Broadway triumphs and reports of overseas peccadilloes, the gay community continued to regard her as someone special and a supporter.

One of her successes on stage was as Iris March in *The Green Hat*, of which the *Daily Express* wrote, 'Miss Bankhead is a genius. She does not act Iris March. She is Iris March.' This was 1925. In 1928 she made her first British film, a silent version of Pinero's *His House in Order*. Like quite a few stage stars of the period she looked upon the screen as 'an unworthy upstart', only to be entertained for the salary involved. 'Whatever my role, whatever my play, whatever my success, I was always shuttling to and from the pawnshop.'

It was in this mood that Tallulah went to America: 'When Paramount waved a fancy long-term contract at me I was in no position to

haggle.' It is this honesty that is apparent in her book, which makes it seem fortunate that she left Hollywood before her putative five-year contract was up. After the 1934 Production Code she might have found it difficult to circumvent their 'moral turpitude' clause; curbing her instincts never came very high on her agenda. She did say, 'My eight years in London were the happiest and most exciting in my life.' Whatever the critics wrote, no less an authority than James Agate said, of her Marguerite Gautier in *Camille*, 'her Marguerite is so chaste as to be positively painful.' Tallulah said, 'My fanatics in the gallery remained loyal. They sobbed deliriously as I went through my death convulsions at the final curtain.'

Her silent films, besides the two previously mentioned, included *A Woman's Love* (1928), produced the same year as the aforementioned

Above: A portrait of Tallulah Bankhead.

His House in Order. Tallulah's early American films failed to ring resounding bells, despite leading directors and co-stars. In 1931 George Cukor directed her in *Tarnished Lady*, from the work of Donald Ogden Stewart, filmed at the Paramount Studios in Astoria when the company was teetering on the verge of bankruptcy. Bankhead said, 'The picture was made by trial and error. What appeared on the screen showed it ... it was a fizzle.' She did not acknowledge Mae West's lifeline to the studio, but Tallulah had already shaken the dust of Hollywood from her shoes at this time. Her leading man was Clive Brook, a major if somewhat pompous star – again not credited in her book. Bankhead plays a socialite who marries for money and her performance has been called 'Distinguished in a sombre but involving melodrama.'

The same year, she made *My Sin*: George Abbott was the director. Tallulah plays a woman of ill-repute, at large in the canal zone, up to some erotic nonsense in a cabaret. The leading man, Fredric March, was to go on to a more prestigious co-starring partnership with her, in Thornton Wilder's *The Skin of Our Teeth* on Broadway. *My Sin* created a minor international incident when it was banned in Argentina, on the grounds that the movie 'sullied the dignity of the homeland.' Tallulah went on to say that it was not just the homeland that was besmirched.

In 1932 Richard Wallace directed *The Cheat*, a remake of the 1915 silent in which Sessue Hayakawa was the Japanese businessman from whom the heroine borrows money to pay off her gambling debts. She agrees to his terms, to forfeit her honour if she defaults. The scene where Hayakawa brands Fanny Ward was all too realistic and caused outrage – he, an oriental, with a caucasian flapper, was deemed to be unacceptable. It did wonders for Fanny Ward, who, in her sixties, claimed to be the eternal flapper and toured the vaudeville circuits on the strength of it. In the Bankhead version it may be that she

shoots the villain before he can brand her; besides which, director-actor Irving Pichel did not look very oriental. In fact, he was American, born and bred. Harvey Stephens plays the husband, who tries to take the blame; she then confesses. This sounds like good fun, but is not as exciting as the Fanny Ward version.

After these three 'mishaps', as she called them, Tallulah's option was picked up, so the films obviously didn't bomb financially. She moved to Hollywood to star in *Thunder Below*, directed again by Richard Wallace. As in most of her movies, Bankhead played a wicked woman 'inclined to be promiscuous, double dealing and dark of design'. Even before the Production Code she had to be repentant at the final fade-out. The men with whom she dallied this time were Charles Pickford and Paul Lukas, but she thought the director divine. She let him take her to a mortuary – he had been an undertakers' assistant and was fascinated by cadavers. Pointing out the departed on their cool slabs, he said, 'Tallulah, this should cheer you up. See how peaceful they are.' This was after a particularly trying day at the studio. Despite this refreshing episode, the director's 'divinity' and her vitality, Tallulah's verdict was: *'Thunder Below* was a double-jointed dud, maudlin and messy.'

The same year, 1932, she made *The Devil and the Deep*, which Marion Gering directed. This was Charles Laughton's first American film. He played a submarine commander, married to Tallulah, whom he suspects is having an affair with Cary Grant. He then ships him out. Then Gary Cooper enters the picture and the real romance begins, several fathoms deep. There were tensions in the studio's summer heat in those days before air-conditioning. Tallulah had taken exception to Grant's firm rejection of her tentative pass at him and countered with allusions to his lack of virility. Laughton took his side and behaved like a big

Right: Tallulah
Bankhead (centre)
aboard the *Lifeboat*
(1944).

brother to get him through his depression. Laughton actively disliked Tallulah and her drinking, nor did she get on with the director. Only Cooper was his usual imperturbable self – an attitude Laughton admired, besides being considerably attracted to him.

Finally, in this very busy year of 1932, Tallulah, on loan to Metro, starred with Robert Montgomery in *Faithless*, directed by Harry Beaumont. This was to be her last movie in Hollywood for 12 years, a story of the rich impoverished by the Wall Street crash. This time she was faithless to Montgomery and suffered accordingly in the end.

Tallulah had put away $200,000 during her year in Hollywood and lucrative offers were being waved at her, despite the Depression. She was summoned by Louis B Mayer and offered the part, opposite Clark Gable, which Jean Harlow was playing in *Red Dust* when her husband committed suicide. Tallulah replied that to replace the tragic Harlow at a time when she was at her lowest ebb after the death of Paul Bern would be the shabbiest act of all time. Harlow kept the part and Tallulah left Hollywood.

She did not reappear on screen until 1943, as one of dozens of top stars of stage and screen who volunteered their services to entertain the fighting men on leave in *Stagedoor Canteen*, directed by Frank Borzage. Tallulah washed dishes, served food and danced with the boys in a story built around a shy GI named California, played by Lon McAllister. The same year she made her best film ever, Alfred Hitchcock's *Lifeboat*, playing a socialite marooned at sea in World War II, with burly John Hodiak as the sailor she falls for and Walter Slezak as the Nazi who tries to wreck the boat and its motley crew of passengers.

In 1945 Tallulah played Catherine the Great in *A Royal Scandal* (*Czarina* in the UK), directed by Otto Preminger. The producer Ernst Lubitsch declared Bankhead's performance the finest he had ever seen on screen. However, despite first-rate support from Vincent Price and Anne Baxter, the film was seriously undervalued and the role suggested for Tallulah in *Leave Her to Heaven* went to Gene Tierney. A scandal which followed this film in the early fifties was neither Royal nor publicised:

Tallulah's co-star William Eythe and the gentle Lon McAllister, both Twentieth Century-Fox contract artists, were reported to the homophobic studio head, Darryl F Zanuck, as being discovered in a relationship and their contracts were cancelled at the earliest possible moment. McAllister's small stature at 5'6" was given as the reason he could not graduate to adult parts. William Eythe made his last film in 1950 and died at the age of 38 from acute hepatitis following a long battle with alcoholism.

After the disappointing reception of *Czarina*, Tallulah hotfooted it back to Broadway and made only two more big-screen appearances. In 1953 she was guest star in a musical called *Main Street to Broadway*, directed by Tay Garnett. She plays herself, desperately searching for a new play to 'show her as she really is'. This is not forthcoming and she rampages as only Tallulah could. The stars of the film were Tom Morton, Mary Murphy and Agnes Moorehead; other guest stars included Lionel and Ethel Barrymoore.

Twelve years elapsed before her final film in 1965, a Hammer shocker called *Fanatic* (*Die! Die! My Darling* in the US). The director was Silvio Narizzano. Inspired by the 1963 success of Davis and Crawford in Robert Aldrich's *Whatever Happened to Baby Jane?*, Tallulah came to England to play another 'psychotic old bag'. She plays Mrs Trefoile, a religious zealot who kidnaps her son's fiancée, Stefanie Powers, to 'reform her' and ultimately, as Mrs T has a killer instinct, to do away with her. The cast includes Donald Sutherland, Peter Vaughan, Yootha Joyce and Maurice Kaufmann. The star's performance was completely over the top, which, in the circumstances, was not to be wondered at.

Born in Alabama in 1903, Tallulah's mother died in childbirth and she was brought up by her progressive grandmother. Her father was Senator William Bankhead, Speaker of the House from 1936 to 1940. Tallulah, too, was famous for her political views and was one of the first to warn against the spread of Nazism. In 1950 she lobbied Congress on behalf of the Unemployment Compensation Act.

Her Broadway triumphs were legion, including *The Little Foxes*, played on screen by Bette Davis, and *The Skin of Our Teeth*. When Miriam Hopkins took over, Tallulah told her understudy, Elizabeth Scott, 'You be as good as she is.' Her quips were prolific, including 'I'm pure as the driven slush' (as opposed to Mae West's 'I used to be Snow White, but I drifted'). Everyone was called 'dahling' because she claimed not to be able to remember names. Meeting Joan Crawford for the first time, she said, 'Dahling, I've had an affair with your husband. You'll be next.' She referred to herself as 'ambidextrous'. One of her most oft-quoted sayings, handed down in gay folklore, came about she was acting in Baltimore in Tennessee Williams' *The Milktrain Doesn't Stop Here Anymore*. Asked 'Is Tab Hunter gay?', she replied, 'I don't know, dahling. He's never sucked my cock.'

She had resounding success in Lucille Ball's long-running TV show *I Love Lucy* as the Celebrity Next Door. Tallulah let it all, as far as permitted on a family show, hang out. Her last barnstorming TV appearance was in a 1966 *Batman* episode as The Black Widow. When she died, Beryl Reid remarked, 'At least she didn't die wondering.'

MARLENE DIETRICH (1901-1992)
[Maria Magdalene Dietrich]

Paramount Studios, who had Marlene Dietrich under contract in the early 1930s, committed an unforgivable gaffe, at least in the eyes of their newest protégée, Tallulah Bankhead [qv]. They advertised the latter's arrival in the following manner:

Coming! Coming!
Tallulah the Glamorous
Tallulah the Mysterious
Tallulah the Woman
We gave you Marlene Dietrich
Now we give you Tallulah Bankhead

Bankhead was shocked and displeased. She attacked Walter Wanger, producer of her film *My Sin* (1931), and ranted: 'This is an outrage. You can't do this to me! In London Marlene is called the second Tallulah Bankhead.' Wanger brought her down to earth. 'Don't worry Tallulah,' he said. 'The trailer will be changed. Henceforth it will read, "We give you back Tallulah Bankhead".'

For all this, the feud the press tried to set up never happened. At the first sight Dietrich had of her 'rival', she left the company of Paramount bigwigs she was entertaining, came over and welcomed her to the studio with warmth and charm. She readily consented to let Tallulah watch her at work, at a time when visitors to the Dietrich set were strictly forbidden. Threats had been made to kidnap her daughter, Maria, who was eight at the time.

Bankhead was also cordially greeted by the elusive Garbo, whom she had met at the home of Salka and Berthold Viertel, the German director who had edited one of Tallulah's films. Then Garbo and Salka, her close friend and scriptwriter, accepted an invitation to one of Tallulah's dinner parties. The guests were late, but charming when they did arrive. 'Forget the bilge about Garbo,' Tallulah wrote. 'She's excessively shy. When at ease with people ... she can be as much fun as the next gal.'

It was another matter between Dietrich and Garbo. They avoided meeting for years and years and when, by Machiavellian slight of hand, a mutual friend engineered a meeting, the event was a damp squib. Marlene positively gushed over Greta, who remained noncommittal

and monosyllabic. Between these two there was a definite rivalry, if not hostility. Garbo had been established at Metro since the silent days of 1926. When Dietrich came to Hollywood with her discoverer (and, some said, Svengali) Josef von Sternberg in 1930, both stars maintained an aloof and discreet distance. Garbo had a mystique all her own as the temptress over whom men fought. Dietrich, in her first American film, *Morocco* (1930), went all out for androgyny from the word 'go'. In her cabaret act, dressed in top hat and tails, she presented a flower to a woman guest, then kissed her full on the mouth. From then on she became established as a lesbian icon, without forfeiting her attractiveness to men. Her approach to sexuality on the screen was startlingly different.

Though she appeared in a dozen or so German films before Josef von Sternberg put her into *The Blue Angel*, she once said, 'He breathed life into nothingness.' They made six films together, all of which were poems to her image. She became set in this mould and always remembered what her mentor had taught her: how to make the most of herself. Every angle of lighting, every pose she knew instinctively; this knowledge was to sustain her throughout her film career and, later, in her years as an international cabaret star.

The illusion was complete, and persisted. She was dismissive of the pre-Sternberg era, saying flatly, 'There were no films.' In her introduction to her stage appearances she would state, 'I was a student at a theatre school when Mr von Sternberg asked to see me. I was asked to sing a naughty song. I had been so sure that I would not get the job that I had taken no song with me: I was told to sing "any song you like". So I sang 'You're the Cream in My Coffee' – and that's the song that got me into pictures." A charming story, indeed. No mention of those early films, or of a lesbian cabaret act with Margo Lion in the revue *Die zwei Cravatten*.

Marlene had, in fact, been a student at a theatre school – Max Reinhardt's Deutsche Theaterschule, no less – in 1922, but she omitted to mention the plays and films she appeared in during the intervening eight years, demonstrating her unique ability to adapt facts to fit what best suited her image and emotional needs. Von Sternberg wrote that he had never asked her to sing a 'naughty song', as she maintained, and that he would never have required her to do anything so vulgar. He was delighted with her film test and the way she responded to his instructions. The rest is history. She was given the part of Lola Lola in *Der blaue Engel* (*The Blue Angel*), a crude cabaret singer who wins the love of the middle-aged Professor Rath. She also fires the boyish lustings of his pupils, who delight in blowing up the feathers pasted onto a picture postcard of her so they can look up her legs. She accepts the professor's proposal of marriage, then treats him with callous indifference, taking a lover and finally driving her husband to madness. Professor Rath was played by Germany's biggest male star, Emil Jannings, and the lover, Mazeppa, by Hans Albers, with whom Dietrich had co-starred on stage in *Die zwei Cravatten*.

Shooting of *The Blue Angel* started in November 1929 and the film premiered in Berlin in April 1930. Dietrich's English was good enough for her to record the English version simultaneously with the German. Dietrich stole all the publicity, though Jannings received respectful notices for his acting, as always. He was less than ecstatic, having not wanted Marlene in the film in the first place. Paramount's production head, B P Schulberg, was so enraptured by Dietrich's performance that he accepted von Sternberg's insistence that he sign her up for Hollywood.

The studios were looking for a new sensation. Gloria Swanson had departed the studio where she had reigned for so long and the Polish import Pola Negri was hampered by her guttural accent. Negri's American debut in *A Woman Commands* (1932) was not a success, enlivened only by her singing of the song 'Paradise'. Much publicity was garnered through the years by Negri's well-covered feud with Gloria Swanson, but the public were tiring of both stars' tantrums. Although initially hesitant about sailing to America, the fantastic reactions to *Der blaue Engel* persuaded Dietrich to sign for Hollywood immediately. She sailed in April 1930 with von Sternberg, leaving her husband, Rudy Steber, and daughter behind.

Dietrich's first American film was *Morocco* (1930). Von Sternberg was presented with the book *Amy Jolly* by Dietrich when he left Germany for America. Jules Furthman adapted the screenplay from Benno Vigny's novel, casting Dietrich in the title role, as a cabaret singer with a past, who falls for legionnaire Tom Brown (Gary Cooper), an appreciative member of her audience. Rich man Adolphe Menjou had offered to make life comfortable for her on the tramp steamer coming over. She turned him down, but when the legionnaire rejects her, ungallantly, after they have become lovers, she agrees to marry Menjou. Tom Brown is missing, presumed dead, but Amy finds him alive and well. She turns down Menjou's offer of cosy domesticity, kicks off her high-heeled shoes and follows her lover into the desert, as a camp follower. A likely story, one might think, and one which created many a merry quip in the press – but a highly dramatic conclusion.

Dishonored followed in 1931, also directed by von Sternberg. Dietrich's officer's widow turned prostitute becomes Agent X-27 for the Austrian government during World War I. She falls for Russian spy Victor McLaglen and is sentenced to death as a traitor for helping him to escape. She puts on her streetwalker's garb before facing the firing squad, and, memorably, applies her lipstick before the guns are fired. The part allows Marlene to show her skills as an

actress, creating many moods, including a highly convincing masquerade as a peasant maid,
apparently *sans* make-up. Not least of her
achievements is a convincing depiction of feeling for the McLaglen character, one of the most
unsuitable leading men in her career. Britain's
foremost impressionist at the time, Florence
Desmond, put on record in her *Hollywood Party*
a hilarious impersonation of Dietrich as spy X-
27, intoning 'I must go to bed early: I have to be
up at dawn to be shot by Mr von Sternberg'.

1932's *Shanghai Express* is arguably the most
perfect combination of Dietrich, von Sternberg,
and Lee Garmes, who was cinematographer on
the first three Dietrich Paramount movies, for
the first of which he was nominated for an Oscar.
Forty years later, after von Sternberg had been
assumed to have been totally responsible for all
Dietrich's camera angles and lighting, Garmes
stated: 'Von Sternberg left the lighting to me at
all times … quite a lot of the picture was done
in natural sunlight, rare at the time … I did
some of the best close-ups of Marlene Dietrich
against a white wall, artificially lit to simulate
daylight … she had a great mechanical mind
and knew the camera. She would always stop in
the exact position that was right for her … the
Dietrich face was my creation.'

The action aboard the Peking-Shanghai
express is tightly knit among a small galaxy of
characters, including Clive Brook (still stiff-
necked and pompous) as the British officer
who has been Marlene's lover, Anna May Wong
as a Chinese girl with a doubtful past and
Warner Oland as a rebel leader. The supreme
moment of high camp is when Dietrich tells
Brook, 'It took more than one man to change
my name to Shanghai Lily!'

The crux of the plot is that Dietrich agrees
to become Oland's mistress if the rebel leader
will free Brook. She is saved from this eventuality when Oland is stabbed by Anna May
Wong. Playing for von Sternberg was a high-

Above: Marlene
Dietrich and Robert
Donat in *Knight
Without Armour*
(1937).

light of Wong's talking picture career in
Hollywood, although she had been an international star from the late twenties. A deeply private person, Wong lectured in England and
Europe, was never reported in the press to have
dated anyone other than the co-stars of her current movie, and chose women of intellectual
status as her companions. As Hollywood's
favourite – indeed, only – Chinese top-liner,
the restriction of her oriental persona led her
into starring in B-pictures with titles like
Daughter of Shanghai (*Daughter of the Orient*
in Britain, 1937), *King of Chinatown* (1939)
and *The Lady from Chungking* (1942). Wong
was actually born in Chinatown, Los Angeles,
never married and died in 1961. Her oriental
inscrutability as Hui Fey on the Shanghai
express was paralleled by the way Dietrich's
acting, to quote the contemporary review in the

London *Times*, found 'its strength and impulses in her careful elimination of all emphasis.'

As Helen Faraday in von Sternberg's *Blonde Venus* (1932), the director's own storyline required Dietrich to be all things to all people. A noble wife and mother to Herbert Marshall and their seven-year-old son Dickie Moore. An exciting cabaret star, emerging from a gorilla suit to don a frizzy blonde wig and sing 'Hot Voodoo', before later changing into the sexually ambivalent white tuxedo, tie and top hat. Other permutations included being an adulterous mistress to playboy Cary Grant, sinking to the dregs in sleazy flop joints while on the run from her husband's detectives, and finally returning to her now understanding husband and facing a bright future with him and son Johnny, having quickly re-established herself as the toast of Paris.

Marlene did all that was required of her, now photographed by Bert Glennon and looking wonderful in every situation. Her leading men were nicely contrasted and Dickie Moore as Johnny was one of the most endearing of child stars. This kind of story, despite von Sternberg's 'original' plotline, was an old warhorse, used by other top stars such as Ruth Chatterton, Kay Francis and Nancy Carroll. The mother-love theme echoed Marlene's own absorption with daughter Maria, but the degradation theme had been overworked as recently as the previous year, by Greta Garbo in *Susan Lenox, Her Fall and Rise*.

Song of Songs (1933) was directed by Rouben Mamoulian. This project was urged on Dietrich by von Sternberg while he was preparing *The Scarlet Empress*. This did not make for a better or more popular movie, despite the publicity coverage gleaned by the nude statue supposedly sculpted by Brian Aherne (in his American film debut). Aherne plays the sculptor for whom Dietrich poses part-time when not working in her aunt's (Alison Skipworth) bookshop. In the scene as filmed, Dietrich's Lily Czapenak is only shown naked to the shoulder. Lily marries into money, namely the lecherous Baron Von Merzbach (Lionel Atwill), whom she leaves to become a singer in a German nightclub. Sculptor Waldow tracks her down and she accepts his proposal of marriage. Pictorially the film is a feast. Dramatically it did not enchant the public, although it did better business than *Blonde Venus*.

Von Sternberg's *The Scarlet Empress* duly followed in 1934. Even more sumptuous than the previous film, this history of Catherine II recreated the glories of Imperial Russia and the breathless beauty of its young Empress so exquisitely, with Bert Glennon back as cinematographer, that one remembers the film as a series of glorious still photographs rather than a historic drama. Officially based on a diary of Catherine's, the story traces her introduction to the Russian court as a young German princess, to be betrothed to the Empress Elizabeth's (Louise Dresser) halfwit son Peter (Sam Jaffe). One of Catherine's lovers, Count Alexi (the dashing John Lodge), supports her leading of the army and peasants in revolt to overthrow mad Peter, who has been plotting to murder Catherine on succeeding his mother to the throne. In fact, the story had been realised more accurately in Korda's British *Catherine the Great* (1934), released just previously, starring Elisabeth Bergner.

My first view of Dietrich in the cinema was sneaked during a school outing to Cambridge to see *The Scarlet Empress*. Her previous films had been judged quite unsuitable by my mother, who saw and vetted them all. I found the movie exciting and the star too impossibly beautiful to be true, but some of the critics were scathing. Daughter Maria, as the very young princess, showed that she had her mother's cheekbones. She was to become a major TV star as Maria Riva.

The ultimate Sternberg-Dietrich confection

was 1935's *The Devil is a Woman*. It was a favourite of both of them. This time he supervised all the cinematography, assisted by the great Lucien Ballard. Dietrich, as cigarette girl Concha Perez, poses against a bewilderment of Spanish carnival settings as she breaks men's hearts, including ex-lover Lionel Atwill and his army comrade, political refugee Cesar Romero. In the end the two duel over her, Atwill is seriously wounded and she prepares to leave with Romero. At the last minute Concha changes her mind and returns to look after her old lover.

One critic said, 'Marlene shakes her head provocatively from side to side so frequently that one first fears, and then prays, it will fall off.' A financial disaster and a latterday camp classic, this film saw the effective end of the Svengali-Trilby relationship. Said von Sternberg, 'Fraulein Dietrich and I have progressed as far as possible together. My being with Dietrich any further would not help her or me.'

In 1936's *Desire*, Ernst Lubitsch decided to present Marlene as a warm human being. She plays a jewel thief who hides a stolen pearl necklace in Gary Cooper's jacket pocket as they cross the Spanish border. She has to stay with him to retrieve it. Love blooms; she renounces her confederates, awaiting her in the sumptuous chateau owned by her partner in crime (John Halliday), retains the necklace, marries Cooper and departs for Detroit with him. The transformation was complete. As glamorous as ever, costumed by Travis Banton and photographed by Charles Lang and Victor Milner, Dietrich 'came out of the trance she has been in for so long and acts once more like a flesh and blood heroine,' wrote Kate Cameron in the *New York Daily News*. Lubitsch provided the wit and director Frank Borzage, who had won an Oscar for *Seventh Heaven* (1927), brought out the heart and warmth.

Filmed in the Mohave desert, 1936's *The Garden of Allah* proved that Dietrich filmed

Above: A portrait of Marlene Dietrich from *Kismet* (1944).

wonderfully in Technicolor and that she could portray religious fervour with conviction (though she herself poked fun at the whole conception) as a disillusioned socialite seeking peace of mind in the Algerian desert. She falls in love with Charles Boyer, a renegade Trappist monk, who keeps his secret from her. When this is revealed she persuades him to return to the monastery to make his peace with God. The impressive cast included Basil Rathbone, C Aubrey Smith, Joseph Schildkraut, Allan Marshall and Tilly Losch as Irena the dancer. The latter's sensual dance awakened long-repressed passions in Boris the apostate. Off screen, Losch was the centre of a scandalous divorce case she brought against her husband the Earl of Carnarvon, in which she cited several beach boys as co-respondents.

Knight Without Armour (1937), directed by

Jacques Feyder in the UK for producer Alexander Korda, was adapted from James Hilton's novel by Francis Marion, with a screenplay by Lajos Biro and Arthur Wimperis. The film gave Dietrich the role of Alexandra, a Russian aristocrat rescued from the revolutionaries by Robert Donat as a British undercover agent. The path leads through picturesque forest settings, allowing her to emerge from a dip in a pool with assorted flora and fauna picturesquely arranged in her hair (courtesy of cinematographer Harry Stradling). Then it's back to statuesque posing again, though director Feyder claimed to bring out the warm human side of Marlene. She created a credible Russian countess and teamed romantically with the charismatic Donat.

1937 was a backtracking year for Dietrich. Ernst Lubitsch's *Angel* tells the risqué story of a British diplomat (Herbert Marshall) whose wife visits an upmarket bordello in Paris, run by her old friend Laura Hope Crews. A visiting American (Melvyn Douglas) mistakes Marlene for one of the girls and the inevitable occurs. She meets him again in London and has to choose between him and her now-ardent husband. Critical brickbats were many and the laughs unintentional. When Lady Maria Barker finds husband Sir Frederick has not been sleeping too well, she inquires solicitously, 'What is it, darling? Czechoslovakia?' The question raised gales of laughter in London's West End. When I caught it again in Zurich shortly before the start of World War II, with French subtitles over the English dialogue, there was no laughter; the crisis was too near, even in neutral Switzerland, to be funny. Edward Everett Horton contributes his usual camp double-take performance.

Dietrich had slid to number 126 on the list of box-office attractions and she was paid $200,000 to bow out of the film version of Terence Rattigan's stage hit *French Without Tears* (1939), about a French au pair who sets British boys' hearts aflutter. Ellen Drew eventually played the part, with Ray Milland, in 1940. William LeBaron, for Paramount, announced that 'Marlene Dietrich will be permitted to work elsewhere.'

But where? A remake of the 1932 Kay Francis-William Powell weepie *One Way Passage* did not materialise, neither did *L'Image* opposite Maurice Chevalier, for Julien Duvivier. A personal invitation from Adolf Hitler, delivered in London by von Ribbentrop, former German Ambassador to the Court of St James, for Marlene to return to her homeland was declined, for the second time. Then came a deal with Universal to return to Hollywood for the low salary of $75,000. (Korda had paid Marlene $450,000 for *Knight Without Armour*.) The film was to be a spoof western, a remake of the 1932 Tom Mix vehicle *Destry*.

The movie was called *Destry Rides Again* (1939) – the comeback of a lifetime. From an elegant statue Dietrich metamorphosed into an all-action saloon gal without sacrificing one iota of her glamour. Lighting cameraman Hal Mohr introduced her in close-up singing 'See What the Boys in the Backroom Will Have', establishing the no-holds-barred character of Frenchy. The music was by the same Friedrich Hollander (with Frank Loesser) who had scored *The Blue Angel*. Frenchy falls heavily for the seemingly mild deputy sheriff Tom Destry (James Stewart) and, having first mocked him, helps him clean up the town of Bottleneck at the cost of her own life. Her rough-and-tumble brawl with uptight townswoman Una Merkel was publicised as 'The Greatest Feminine Fist Fight Ever Filmed'. Brian Donlevy (he of the startlingly plucked eyebrows) was the owner of the Last Chance Saloon and Frenchy's protector – till Destry comes along. All in all, a great movie that put Dietrich back at the top of the movie pile; her teaming with Stewart irresistible and ultimately moving.

After the overwhelming success of *Destry*, Universal contracted the now more-marketable-than-ever Marlene for several more movies. The next, *Seven Sinners* (1940), directed by Tay Garnett, presented the new contract artist as Bijou Blanche, infamous cabaret singer, ejected from countless South Sea islands for creating too much unrest among the natives. Costumier Irene created eye-catching baubles, bangles and beads for the shady lady tramp, none more androgynously fascinating that her Navy ensign's uniform, already referred to, for 'The Man's in the Navy', a clip of which was shown in *Myra Breckinridge* (1970).

Naval officer John Wayne, one of Marlene's handsomest conquests through the years, was at his peak as a desirable stud and Britain's Anna Lee was the perfect respectable lady for Bijou to score points off. The male support was exemplary, including camp Helen Broderick's brawny son, Broderick Crawford, fey Mischa Auer, dour Albert Dekker and roly-poly Billy Gilbert. Apart from the imperishable Hollander-Loesser original 'I Can't Give You Anything But Love, Baby', 'I've Been In Love Before' completes a trio of her most effective songs for the movies.

France's top satirical director, René Clair, manoeuvred Marlene through the plot of *The Flame of New Orleans* (1941). The film first presents her as a *grande dame* gracing a box at the opera and catching the eye of wealthy banker Roland Young, then she settles in New Orleans, pursuing a *louche* lifestyle to amass more wealth as a waterfront harpy, with Laura Hope Crews again as a disreputable 'Auntie'. Andy Devine, Frank Jenks and Eddie Quillan are sailor buddies, but the one who wins her heart is tough Bruce Cabot, whom Dietrich did not care for as a leading man, even though he had once rescued Fay Wray from the arms of *King Kong*. Nevertheless, she sacrifices Roland Young and respectable security to run away with seaman Cabot on his boat, symbolically tossing her wedding dress through a porthole into the river. Mischa Auer provides his

own brand of comedy in a generally witty and sophisticated pastiche.

In *Manpower* (1941), directed by Raoul Walsh, Dietrich plays Fay Duval, newly released from prison. Fay becomes a clip-joint hostess who marries the doting Edward G Robinson, although she really desires his best friend, power linesman George Raft. When the affair comes to a head, the men slug it out among the electricity pylons until Robinson is killed in a fatal fall. Publicity coverage had Dietrich breaking an ankle when her co-stars came to blows on the set. She actually tripped on a cable, but it is a moot point whether she was trying to come between them. The cast all did well in a typical Warners actioner, as critic C A Lejeune remarked. Lejeune also pointed out that this was an unusual setting for Dietrich, 'like passing the lady on a moving staircase to the tube, or seeing her in Lyons Corner House, having a cup of tea.'

The Lady Is Willing (1942) provided another unusual role for Dietrich. She plays actress Elizabeth Madden, who marries pediatrician Fred MacMurray so she can adopt abandoned baby David James. This was Dietrich's first go at motherhood since *Blonde Venus*. The film is charming, lightweight and very sentimental, as the actress struggles to get through her production number, 'Strange Thing', clad in a shimmering Irene-designed gown with a foot-high headdress, while awaiting word of the baby's condition after an emergency operation. All-purpose co-star MacMurray (from Barbara Stanwyck to Greer Garson), is, as always, a reassuring shoulder to cry on.

The Spoilers (1942) was another western remake (the fourth) of Rex Beach's novel, with Marlene as a gin club owner in Alaska. She slinked around in low-cut Vera West gowns, while John Wayne and Randolph Scott squared up to slug it out in the climactic brawl for her favours. Richard Barthlemess, star of early talkies, played Bronco Kid and Margaret

Lindsay a sweet lady who is not what she seems. No songs and, all in all, a let-down. Lewis Seiler's *Pittsburgh* (1942) found Marlene playing a Pennsylvania coal miner's daughter, Josie Winters. Winters, ex-mistress of a crooked fight promoter, falls for Wayne and Scott again and marries the latter after he deserts the mines to become a steel executive, while Wayne, whom Josie really fancies, marries Louise Allbritton, daughter of a steel tycoon. Apart from the statutory fisticuffs between the boys and the spectacle of Marlene down a mine, this is even more of a let-down than the previous movie. At the climax the cast all link arms to appeal to the audience to support Allied unity and buy user bonds.

Between movies Marlene had joined the USO to entertain the armed forces and in April 1943 she sailed for North Africa to begin a three-year tour of liberated countries from Africa to the Aleutians. She managed to fit in a guest appearance in Eddie Sutherland's allstar musical *Follow the Boys* (1944), in which she did part of her act for the GIs, playing a musical saw and allowing herself to be sawn in half by Orson Welles in his Mercury Wonder Show sketch, fluting, 'Oh, Orson, it tickles.'

In her review of *Kismet* (1944), C A Lejeune noted: 'Marlene Dietrich was sawn in half by Orson Welles and the lower half came back, gilded, in *Kismet*.' Her first venture into Technicolor since *The Garden of Allah* eight years previously was in Metro's lavish remake of Edward Knoblock's musical play, in which, as Grand Vizier Edward Arnold's mistress Jamilla, 'Queen of the harem dancers', Marlene falls in love with Ronald Colman as 'the King of Beggars' and sometime Prince. The highlight was Jamilla's exotic interpretive dance, covered in gold from head to toe. This inspired gay boys around the world to do the same, usually without the gold paint. The handsome Caliph was James Craig, the 'poor man's Clark Gable', and the whole *Arabian Nights* fantasy was

happy escapist fare for war-weary patrons.

Martin Roumagnac (1946), directed by Georges Lacombe, was Dietrich's only French film and the only time she starred with Jean Gabin, her lover, who had been making movies in the USA. At that time Marlene's husband, Rudolf Sieber, to whom she had been married since 1923, was employed by Universal in their foreign films department. In a typical Gabin-type role, he played a builder who loves Blanche Ferrand (Dietrich) but kills her when he discovers she is secretly a prostitute and is murdered in his turn by one of her rejected suitors. Both stars gave sensitive performances and cameraman Roger Hubert did Marlene proud. Her old friend Margo Lion (from *Die zwei Cravatten*) played Gabin's sister.

For *Golden Earrings* (1947), directed by Mitchell Leisen, Marlene's old studio, Paramount, welcomed her back in the role of the wild and fabulous gypsy cocotte, Lydia. Dietrich dyed her body brown, wore a matted black wig, dangling bracelets and golden earrings. She also chewed garlic, to the discomfort of co-star Ray Milland, fresh from his Oscar triumph in *The Lost Weekend*. He played a British Intelligence Officer, whom the amorous gypsy helps to smuggle a poison gas formula out of Nazi Germany. Their tongue-in-cheek camp performances made the film a delight. Marlene announced: 'No more enigmatic glamour for me.'

Nevertheless, for Billy Wilder's *A Foreign Affair* (1948), glamour it was, courtesy of Oscar-winning cameraman Charles B Lang. Wilder's trenchant comedy about corruption in post-war Germany was a personal triumph for Marlene as Erika von Schlutoe, former mistress of a top-ranking Nazi officer, who does battle for US officer John Lund with Congresswoman Jean Arthur, investigating undercover activities in occupied Berlin. The Friedrich Hollander songs 'Illusions' and 'Black Market' are delivered with spot-on cynicism, top-billed Jean

Arthur ruthlessly out-bitched in every scene. *Life* magazine called it 'a triumphant return to the same sexy role that made her famous 18 years ago – the heartless siren who lures men to degradation and goes on singing.' And all this the year before Marlene became the world's most glamorous grandma.

Jigsaw (1949) involved a brief walk-on as a nightclub patron for director Fletcher Markle, as a personal favour in his made-in-New York low-budget feature starring Franchot Tone. Other guests included Henry Fonda, John Garfied and Burgess Meredith. Alfred Hitchcock's *Stage Fright* (1950) was Dietrich's first British film for 13 years. Marlene provided 'enigmatic glamour' as actress Charlotte Inwood, suspected of murdering her husband. 'He was an abominable man. Why does God allow such abominable men?' Her young lover was a newcomer to films, Richard Todd, boyfriend of top-billed Jane Wyman. Wyman played a RADA student masquerading as Inwood's dresser in order to pick up clues about the murder, while Michael Wilding was a laconic detective. Wilding had only a brief scene with Dietrich, but he was soon to join the distinguished band of her lovers. Alastair Sim and Dame Sybil Thorndike were Wyman's parents – strange casting indeed. Marlene languished in Christian Dior gowns and waved her legs while singing Cole Porter's 'The Laziest Girl in Town'. Vastly entertaining. Hitchcock remarked: 'Marlene is a professional – a professional actress, a professional dress designer, a professional cameraman.'

Back in Britain and again dressed by Dior, Dietrich resumed her partnership with James Stewart in Henry Koster's *No Highway* (1951; *No Highway in the Sky* in the USA). Stewart is the boffin who persuades film star Monica Teasdale that he's right about the imminent disintegration of their aircraft. Marlene's role is eminently sympathetic, the dialogue adroitly delivered and master cameraman Georges

Above: Marlene Dietrich in *Rancho Notorious* (1952).

Perinal's photography is up to the highest standards demanded by the star. Janette Scott is touchingly sincere as Stewart's daughter: Marlene was especially supportive of Thora Hird's young daughter.

For *Rancho Notorious* (1952), Dietrich was delighted to work with her old friend, German director Fritz Lang, but they feuded constantly on set. He accused her of scheming to turn her 'seasoned' owner of the Chuck-a-Luck saloon, Altar Keane, into a youngish siren, which she achieved with the backing of Hal Mohr, who had photographed her so brilliantly in *Destry Rides*

Above: Marlene Dietrich in *Judgment at Nuremberg* (1961).

The Monte Carlo Story (1957), filmed in Italy, is a gentle Technicolor comedy that has been called creakingly old-fashioned, but it has a certain world-weary charm befitting its stars. Marlene is Maria, Marquise de Crevacoeur, and Vittorio de Sica plays Count Dino della Fabba, gambling away assets they do not possess and making love in romantic settings. Dietrich's elegant con-woman has echoes of her Madeleine de Beaupre in *Desire*. Her songs are also evocative (eg, 'Home in Indiana') and, for good measure, there's Mischa Auer, whey-faced as ever.

Witness for the Prosecution (1957), is a late-flowering of the Dietrich magic which contains arguably her best screen performance, in Billy Wilder's adaptation of one of Agatha Christie's most effective plays. Apart from von Sternberg, Billy Wilder was perhaps the director with whom she was happiest. To perpetuate her legend, Wilder added a wartime flashback, showing how serviceman Leonard Vole (Tyrone Power) met his German wife Christine singing 'I May Never Go Home Anymore', flashing her gams when her trousers are ripped, accompanying herself on the accordion and, of course, causing a brawl. When Power is accused of murdering doting rich widow Norma Varden, Defence Attorney Sir Wilfred Roberts (Charles Laughton) is hired to get him off. But can he count on help from Christine Vole?

It would still not be fair to give away the secret twists and turns of the plot, but, suffice to say, Dietrich should have won an Academy Award for her many-layered characterisation of Christine. Laughton and his wife Elsa Lanchester were both nominated. It has been suggested that the desire not to reveal the storyline militated against Marlene being nominated.

Dietrich's guest spot in Orson Welles' cracking film *Touch of Evil* (1958), about corruption in a Mexican border town, has become a cult classic. This despite Marlene having only a handful of scenes as Tania, cigar-smoking Mexican

Again. Keane falls for gunman Arthur Kennedy, on the trail of his fiancée's murderer. Mel Ferrer plays her other admirer and Altar gets to voice a few philosophical observations about the passage of time. On the same subject, the publicists were quick to point out that her measurements (36.5-23-37) were the same as in 1939.

To induce Dietrich to be one of myriad guest stars in *Around the World in 80 Days* (1956), producer Mike Todd promised her a Cinemascope close-up of her legs, extended across the whole screen. In the San Francisco sequence she plays a dance hall queen whose main line of dialogue is to respond to David Niven's 'I'm looking for my man' with 'Isn't everybody?' The scene features Frank Sinatra as the piano player and George Raft as the bouncer.

madam and one-time mistress of crooked cop Hank Quinlan (Welles). As a fortune teller she tells him, 'Your time's all used up,' and when he is shot her terse obituary is 'He was some sort of man. What does it matter what you say about people?' She claimed to have made up Tania's outfit from her *Golden Earrings* Lydia drag. Which brings us to Mercedes McCambridge as a butch, leather-jacketed lesbian who helps rough up Janet Leigh in husband Charlton Heston's absence. Among the other guest stars, Joseph Cotten is presumably there as a favour to his old friend Orson, while Zsa Zsa Gabor really need not have bothered.

After a break of three years Dietrich returned to the screen in Stanley Kramer's blockbusting drama *Judgement at Nuremberg* (1961), about the German war crime trials. Spencer Tracy topped the bill as Judge Heywood, opposite whom, as Madame Bertholt, widow of a high-ranking German officer, Dietrich had most of her key scenes. She, arrogant and resentful, finds a sympathetic listener in the judge and a warm friendship ensues. This relationship is the heart of a fairly harrowing film and beautifully played by both actors. When Heywood gives his impartial judgment against the war criminals, his understanding with Madame Bertholt is over: she withdraws into herself and refuses to answer his calls. Her husband was a Nazi officer and her performance touches to perfection her veiled arrogance, tempered with sensitivity. Maximilian Schell as the defence counsel received an Oscar, while Judy Garland and Montgomery Clift were both nominated.

David Hemmings' *Just A Gigolo* (1978) became a touching swan-song for Dietrich, tempted out of retirement to play the madam of a brothel which supplies young men to escort ladies who require the services of youthful studs. Into her emporium comes David Bowie, nominal star of the film, as an ex-German army serviceman who finds it difficult to make a liv-

ing any other way. Athough the film was made in Germany, Dietrich's scenes were shot in a Paris studio, at her insistence. This made it impossible for her scenes with rock star Bowie to be filmed together, as he was touring at the time. Director Hemmings, who also appears in the movie, welded the scenes together successfully, however.

An impressive international cast included Kim Novak (on the look-out for studs), Curt Jürgens and Maria Schell, sister of Maximilian. Effectively the leading lady was Sydne Rome, who supplied a needed vivacity and most of the singing and dancing. Bowie does his usual thing of inhabiting, rather than acting, a role, though it is Marlene who interprets the theme song huskily and wearily in close-up, wearing the large veiled hat she maintains throughout. Thus she retains her glamour, though her voice breaks on the last two words of 'As life goes on, without me'. It has been said this was life overtaking art. Whatever, the film and her performance were crudely and cruelly reviewed and this very special film barely given a chance.

I first met Marlene at a press conference at the Café de Paris prior to her opening there in June 1954. Clad in a scarlet suit, she looked stunning and was graciousness itself, spending time at each table to talk to the assembled writers. There had been a touch of hostility prior to her appearance, questioning whether it was wise to face the public without gauzes, as it were. She won over almost everybody, with the exception of a journalist who had made a fairly vicious attack in advance. When his name was announced, she jumped up and moved to the next table. We fared well in our session, perhaps because I had seen and admired her favourite film, *The Devil is a Woman*. I was also keen to ask about a mooted film for Orson Welles. She laughed and said, 'Maybe – but you know Orson.' Well, I didn't, so that was a stalemate. The film was to emerge four years later as *Touch of Evil* and was a personal triumph for the director and herself.

The cabaret, introduced by Noël Coward as 'Our legendary, lovely Marlene', proved, for London audiences, that away from the familiar protection of the movies, she had nothing to fear. Dietrich's precise knowledge of lighting, costuming, make-up and projection afforded her complete control over her 'living legend' status as the eternal female. In an interview she said, 'The legend created by Mr von Sternberg served me well ... even those who set out to debunk the legend and probe for better things behind the triple gauze curtains of his magic. It has been said that I was Trilby to his Svengali. I would rather say I was Eliza to his Henry Higgins.'

After our meeting, 18 years later, at the Olympia Theatre Paris, I was to learn how completely she had everything under control. I was given a list of how many copies she would need of the article I had written which had taken her fancy. They included copies for her daughter Maria Riva, Stanley Kramer, Noël Coward, Billy Wilder, Major Neville-Willing of the Café de Paris, Burt Bacharach (then her accompanist), her husband Rudolf Sieber and others – a round dozen. The editor of the paper was so impressed and astonished, he had them all dispatched personally from the office. This pattern was repeated over reviews of *The Black Fox* and an article in *Sight and Sound* (nothing to do with me).

Eventually, I left the service to her press cuttings agency, who were presumably being paid. Sometimes the message would be relayed through her close friend, actress Marti Stevens, such as 'Will you deliver to Marlene at the Dorchester your cuttings book on her life?' There were some 14: I regretted I could not go back before 1932, and was told that would be in order. They were for daughter Maria's inspection, I was informed. Dietrich designed the cover of every one.

I became further embroiled while doing press for the small-wheeled Moulton Bicycles,

on which I was following Marlene's tours. Stops included Oxford, Eastbourne and the Edinburgh Festival. At the Bristol Hippodrome there was a heckler in the gallery. Marlene was berating the manager when I arrived in her dressing room. She greeted me as normal: 'How is your bi-cycle?' Then it began. 'Any more of this, and I go back to Vegas!' she stormed.

Moultons asked me to approach her as to whether she would agree to be photographed on a Moulton cycle (no doubt prompted by the posters of her reclining on a couch for British Airways). In a letter she said her contract forbade any other commercial advertising, but if the company would send one of their machines to her daughter in Rome, she would be happy for Maria or one of her family to be photographed cycling in exclusive areas of the Italian capital. The bike was dispatched to the address stated, but what happened later is shrouded in mystery. There was no acknowledgment and one can only hope that their press cuttings agency picked up happy pictures of the Riva family taking their constitutionals on the world's smallest bicycle.

Marlene sent a card from Paris saying that her book *Marlene's ABC* had received the best reviews from behind the Iron Curtain – 'Wouldn't you know?' She then phoned to say she was off to Taormina with Audrey Hepburn to be given a prize for *Judgment at Nuremburg*.

After her appearance with the Beatles in a Royal Show – her picture appeared on every front page the next day; she had refused to be photographed with anyone but the Liverpool Wonders – there came another note: why had I not been at the rehearsals? The simple answer was that I was not allowed in. We were out of touch while Marlene was touring abroad, but I managed to cycle to the Edinburgh Festival on the Moulton and to go backstage after her show. Maria, then married to William Riva, was among the people in the dressing room and became very vague when I asked about the Moulton in Rome. Her mother had a car waiting to take her and her guests to supper. As I went to make my farewell, Dietrich raised her arm as if I had been about to gatecrash the party. Later I heard she had asked who I was and how I had got there. I cycled back to London with heavy limbs. However, at a 1971 press conference at Heathrow Airport, I boldly introduced myself and she said, 'Of course I know you. How is your bi-cycle?' It's a puzzlement.

But then so was the lady herself. Maria Riva had given up her acting career after a tour with *Tea and Sympathy*, in order to become her mother's manager. In her biography, *My Mother Marlene*, she lists the lovers, male and female, who were always around: 'I never questioned their gender, or what they were there for.' There were governesses, one of whom made a pass at 'the Child', as Maria was always called in her growing-up days. Marlene's attitude seemed to be, 'Well, she'll have to learn sometime.' One of the ladies she found particularly 'creepy' was Hollywood scriptwriter Mercedes de Acosta, known as 'lover to the stars', who had affairs with most of the available female star names of stage and screen, including Maud Adams (the first Peter Pan), Eva le Gallienne, Catherine Cornell, Pola Negri, Garbo and, of course, Marlene, to whom she wrote adoring love poems.

Though Maria seemed to be comfortable with her mother falling in love again and again and again, she was unhappy with the way her father, Rudolf Sieber, was treated, always in the background and complaisant. When he retired to a chicken farm in the San Fernando Valley to live peacefully with his mistress (William Riva's mother, Tami), Marlene's rhetoric elevated the humble farm to 'my husband's ranch' and she claimed to go there for a short stay each year for the peace and quiet. This was her recipe for 'the perfect marriage'.

Above: A 1960s portrait of Joan Crawford.

JOAN CRAWFORD (1904–1977)
(Lucille Fay LeSueur)

One of the few self-made stars, Joan Crawford created her own genre after a stills photographer said her features were 'built'. She worked on this, having made her only stage appearance in the chorus of a revue starring the legendary French icon Mistinguett. Born in 1874, Mistinguett became part of the Parisian scene for so long that some wiseacre, paraphrasing the description of the ancient city of Petra as a 'rose-red City, half as old as Time', nicknamed her ' a rose-red Cutie, half as old as Time'. She made her British debut at the London Casino at the age of 73, forgetting the lyrics of 'Mon Homme', her most famous song, which she had been singing for nearly 60 years. She recovered

JOHNNY GUITAR

1954 Republic 110 mins colour
Producer: Herbert J Yates;
Director: Nicholas Ray;
Photographer: Harry Stradling;
Screenplay: Philip Yordan (from
a novel by Roy Chanslor)
Joan Crawford, Sterling
Hayden, Mercedes
McCambridge, Scott Brady,
Ward Bond, Ben Cooper,
Ernest Borgnine, John
Carradine, Royal Dano

This film was dismissed on its initial release as of little consequence until the likes of François Truffaut and Jean-Luc Goddard acclaimed it as a classic, 'profound, beautiful'. It has also been called a pro-feminist statement, a gay/camp exercise and several other things. In the film version of Vito Russo's book *The Celluloid Closet*, scriptwriter Suzie Wright says, 'It's incredible, if you're a gay audience, how you will watch an entire movie, just to see someone wear an outfit to make you think they're homosexual – you're just sitting there, waiting for Joan Crawford to put on her black cowboy shirt again.' As she advances downstairs to confront her arch enemy Emma Small (Mercedes McCambridge), Vienna the saloon-bar owner, in her skin-tight chaps with gun holstered at the ready, defiance blazing from her black eyes, scarlet lips set in a steel jaw, is a fitting adversary for the snarling butch lesbian wonderfully played by McCambridge.

Crawford wrote of Mercedes: 'A good actress, but a rabble-rouser.' This was apparent on set, where the actors sided with one or the other of the two rivals who fight it out on screen. No prizes for guessing who wins. A truly Horse-Frightening Moment: in the film Emma covets Vienna's land, besides envying her power over her two handsome lovers, Sterling Hayden in the title role and Scott Brady as gang leader Dancin' Kid. In an interview Brady told me that Hayden tended to side with McCambridge, while he himself, wise man, tried to remain uninvolved – no easy task with a star like Joan Crawford.

and went on to complete the engagement but some critics maintained that perhaps she had left her first London stage appearance too late.

Lucille LeSueur studied the imperious *grande dame* persona, which she emulated to the extent of maintaining her own image into her seventies. Her 'built' features helped secure Joan Crawford, as she was re-christened, a contract with Metro-Goldwyn-Mayer, which lasted from 1925 to 1943, during which time she graduated from ingenue to Bright Young Thing, Charlestoning furiously on table tops and dance floors in musicals both silent and, from *Hollywood Revue of 1929*, all-talking and all-dancing. She progressed from bitchy flappers who fought their way from the wrong side of the tracks to playing elegant and poised career women or glamorous wives and mistresses. The roles barely changed – with the exception of her inspired performance as the terribly scarred heroine of *A Woman's Face* (1941), directed by George Cukor, opposite Melvyn Douglas and Conrad Veidt. The scene where two lesbians dance in the half-shadows of a dingy café sailed past the censor with gay

JOAN CRAWFORD

July 12, 1971

Dear Eric,

Thank you so much for your letter and for the program of "Hollywood Revue of 1929" and the clippings on "Trog".

I can't wait to see your own review of "Trog" in "Films and Filming". They were all very kind to me but, unfortunately, not to the film. I hope it still makes a lot of money for my darling, Herman Cohen.

You were very kind to say such lovely things about me in "Hollywood Revue". When you see Dorothy Dickson, please give her my love.

I continue to travel thousands of miles a year for Pepsi. Unfortunately, all scripts today are just plain bad.

Bless you for being my friend. With affection and gratitude -

insouciance and Frightened The Horses.

With the encroachment of the roaring forties and Crawford's new Warner contract, a touch of maturity manifested itself. Crawford set a new style with her Oscar-winning performance as *Mildred Pierce* (1945), a role turned down by Bette Davis and Barbara Stanwyck. The director was Michael Curtiz, who, like Cukor, could bring out the best in Joan. This was her career woman role *par excellence,* again playing a character from lowly beginnings who gets involved in murder to protect her spoilt daughter (Ann Blyth) from the clutches of the unscrupulous Zachary Scott. Crawford was Academy Award-nominated for *Possessed* in 1947 and soldiered on with Warners until *The Damned Don't Cry* (1950). 'Prophetic,' she said, and made her last film under the contract the following year, *This Woman is Dangerous* (1952).

From 1952 she freelanced with *Sudden Fear,* opposite her new 'menace' Jack Palance, which gained Crawford her second Oscar nomination. In 1953 she returned to MGM for the colour musical *Torch Song,* of which her dance partner, director and part-time lover, Charles Walters,

Opposite: Joan Crawford in *Johnny Guitar* (1955).

Above: Joan Crawford made her final film appearance, alongside Joe Cornelius, in *Trog* (1970).

said 'Only God could get your legs up so high!' – no doubt with a little help from the 51-year-old star herself. There is one Horse-Frightening Moment at the end of her song-and-dance number 'Two-Faced Woman'. This is performed in black-face with a gaggle of supportive chorus boys, with Jenny (Crawford) tearing off her black wig in close-up and letting her marmalade-coloured hair fall around her ferocious black-face maquillage. Poor Michael Wilding, as her blind pianist leading man, imagines 'marmalade' hair as 'Gypsy Madonna'. The actor had his problems on set as well as in the scenario: from their first meeting, apart from a cursory hello, Crawford wasted no more words on him.

She returned to delight her gay fans in Nicholas Ray's *Johnny Guitar* (1955), even more than she had in *Torch Song*. In *Female on the Beach* she unveiled her remarkable figure for the last time, before scaling down her film appearances, having married her fourth husband, Alfred Steele, King of Pepsi Cola, in 1956. Crawford's three actor husbands were Douglas Fairbanks Jr (1929-33), Franchot Tone (1935-39) and Philip Terry (1943-1946).

She also enjoyed a passionate affair with Clark Gable, her co-star in several movies up to Frank Borzage's *Strange Cargo* in 1940. This despite a pious denial in her autobiography.

In her adopted daughter Christina's biography *Mommie Dearest* (1978) – a no-holds-barred exercise for Faye Dunaway in the 1981 film version – Crawford is portrayed as a monster, cruel to both Christina and her siblings, with a voracious appetite for sex (lesbian as well as straight) and 100 proof alcohol. In her 1962 autobiography, Crawford vehemently denied making stag movies in her early career and certainly doesn't mention any Sapphic encounters, although a recently published photo reveals her buxom and naked in the arms of a young lady of the same ilk. A critique of her *Portrait of Joan* pointed out that it 'leaves the lady where she would wish to be, elegantly framed above the drawing room mantelpiece.'

I found myself one night at the St James' Theatre seated next to Miss Crawford, who was clad all in white, her new husband Alfred Steele on the other side of her. When the curtain rose she reached over to him, took his hands and placed them in her lap where they remained for the duration of the first act. At the interval they rose to leave and I noticed that she had dropped her white gloves on the floor. On her return I seized the moment and timidly proffered them to her, saying, 'You've dropped your gloves, Miss Crawford.' She seized them and, fixing me with her imperious gaze, said, '*My*! Aren't you *sweet*!' I found it difficult to concentrate on the play after this fleeting encounter with La Divine.

As Mrs Alfred Steele she revelled in her role of ambassador and consort of the 'King of Pepsi Cola', and he accompanied her to England for the filming of *The Story of Esther Costello* in 1957. Crawford scaled down her film appearances and played only a guest role when replacing Margaret Leighton in *The Best of Everything* in 1959, before her legendary 1962 teaming

with Bette Davis in Robert Aldrich's *Whatever Happened to Baby Jane?* This was Crawford and Davis' first outing as the high priestesses of Grand Guignol. Aldrich planned a follow-up in the 1964 *Hush…Hush, Sweet Charlotte*, but during preproduction Crawford was hospitalised and Olivia De Havilland took over her role.

In an interview, Myrna Loy once told me that in the event of her being offered a role like Crawford's in *Baby Jane* there was no way she was going to play the part of a 'psychotic old bag'. Tallulah Bankhead was apparently happy to do so in the 1965 *Fanatic* (aka *Die! Die! My Darling*). However, *Straitjacket* in 1964 and the British-made *Berserk* (1967) and *Trog* (1970) are all examples of Crawford excelling in this genre. During the filming of *Berserk*, I had arranged an interview at Pinewood Studios, which was cancelled at the last moment due to the film being behind schedule. Crawford's leading man Ty Hardin was late back from a weekend trip to Paris and sparks flew between them on set. There were also words between the star and Diana Dors; the atmosphere between them had been tense from the start. I phoned Joan at the Dorchester Hotel and received fulsome apologies. During a long conversation she told me of her forthcoming trip to Italy to film *I bastardi!* aka *Sons of Satan* (1969) opposite Italy's leading young male star at the time, Guiliano Gemma. After a dispute over finance, the role was eventually played by Rita Hayworth.

Having made an instalment of the TV anthology *Night Gallery* in late 1969 for the young Steven Spielberg, thus helping him in his rise to prominence as one of the great directors of our time, Joan Crawford was diagnosed with cancer in the mid-1970s and confined to her New York apartment under the care of a nurse. She saw only her closest friends and died alone at home in 1977, after her nurse had briefly left her side to run an errand.

BETTE DAVIS [1908-1989]
[Ruth Elizabeth Davis]

It is difficult to pinpoint exactly when Bette Davis became a Gay Icon. It may be as far back as *Cabin in the Cotton* (1932), in which she uttered the Southern belle's line, 'Ah'd love to kiss ya but I just washed ma hay-uh.' Or was it years later, in 1949, when she puffed out a wreath of smoke and exclaimed 'What a dump!' in *Beyond the Forest* (impersonated by Elizabeth Taylor in *Who's Afraid of Virginia Woolf?* in 1966). Or even 'Fasten your seat belts – it's going to be a bumpy night' in *All About Eve* (1950). She may be the most quoted actress of the century, apart from Mae West, and certainly the most imitated.

There was no hint of this future eminence when Bette Davis got off the train to take up her first Hollywood contract with Universal Studios in 1930. A studio representative reported that 'No one faintly like an actress got off the train.' When studio boss Carl Laemmle first set eyes on her he said, 'She has as much sex appeal as Slim Summerville!' – a tall, gangly, bumbling comedian of the day.

Davis' first acting experience had been in the theatre. On her first professional engagement with a stock company in Rochester NY, she was fired by director George Cukor, no less, but she did make Broadway, in 1930, in a domestic comedy called *Broken Dishes*. Her film debut was in a forgettable movie called *Bad Sister* (1931). The same year, she appeared in *Seed* and the first talkie version of *Waterloo Bridge*. Universal persisted in thinking she was without sex appeal and did their best to make her resemble the very popular and beautiful Constance Bennett, whom, in fact, she did favour marginally.

However, Davis was not inclined to be presented as a second edition of anybody. She continued with her dreary parts in dreary films until the great George Arliss, one of the stage and screen's most eminent senior stars, insisted Davis be cast as his leading lady in the Warner production *The Man who Played God* (1932), against the studio's wishes. Arliss was kind and encouraging and fought the studio, his word always law. Warner Bros were sufficiently impressed to sign Davis to a long-term contract; she always gave Arliss credit for her proper start in the movies. The film was called *The Silent Voice* in Britain.

Another major Warner star, Ruth Chatterton, was also helpful when they acted together in *The Rich Are Always With Us* (1932), and the same year Davis played an artist in the Barbara Stanwyck vehicle *So Big*. The cast also included Ruth Chatterton's then-husband, George Brent, who would be Davis' leading man so many times in the future. In 1933, Davis had her only chance to act with Spencer Tracy, in *20,000 Years in Sing Sing*. He plays a convict, she his gun-toting moll. That she carried a torch for him was indicated years later, when she declined to accept Katharine Hepburn as Joan Crawford's replacement in *Hush… Hush, Sweet Charlotte* (1964).

Davis' career as an A-list Hollywood star gained momentum with the RKO production *Of Human Bondage* (1934), based on the novel by W Somerset Maugham. Davis co-starred opposite British leading man Leslie Howard under the assured direction of John Cromwell. She had to fight for the prize role of sluttish cockney waitress Mildred, who spells doom for club-footed artist Philip (Howard) when he becomes obsessed by her. She tells him she can never love a cripple; stricken, he carries on with his studies and meets the attractive Nora (Kay Johnson), a romantic novelist. Mildred reappears on the scene, abandoned by her loutish salesman lover after she became pregnant. Philip sets her up in an apartment, intending to marry her once the child has been born. Mildred, ever the slattern, flirts outrageously

drama cast her as alcoholic actress Joyce Heath, with whom architect Dan Bellows (Franchot Tone) falls in love, although he is engaged to socialite Gail Armitage (Margaret Lindsay). Davis said the award should have gone to Katharine Hepburn for *Alice Adams*, though her own notices were ecstatic.

Davis did rather better in *The Petrified Forest* (1936), directed by Archie Mayo. Reunited with Leslie Howard, her performance as Gabby, the waitress at a service station in the barren Arizona Desert, is beautifully restrained. This memorable film version of Robert E Sherwood's acclaimed play gave Humphrey Bogart one of his first notable movie roles as Duke Mantee, a ruthless gangster who holds up the service station and everyone in it. Bogart steals the acting honours, but the all-round performances of the three stars could not have been bettered.

For the next decade, Bette Davis' films were of superior quality, commercially successful and often acclaimed by the critics. In 1937's *It's Love I'm After*, again directed by Archie Mayo, Davis and Leslie Howard proved themselves as adept at crazy comedy as tragic drama, as a stage couple who portray themselves as the perfect romantic partnership but battle incessantly in private life. Olivia de Havilland comes between them as an adoring fan of Howard's. Davis disposes of her by pretending she has children by him. De Havilland, disenchanted, runs back to fiancé Patric Knowles. The stars interact brilliantly, while butler Eric Blore's 'I love you, sir' brings the house down.

For *Jezebel* (1938), Bette Davis won her second Oscar as Julie Marston, the Southern belle whose behaviour out-Scarletts O'Hara, leading her beaux, Henry Fonda and George Brent, as merry a dance as ever Scarlett did. This was the studio's reward for Bette missing the role that Vivien Leigh made her own. Superbly directed by William Wyler, the cast includes Margaret Lindsay as Amy, the

with medical student Griffiths (Reginald Denny) at her engagement party. They run off together and Philip turns his attention back to his work. Several plot twists later, after Philip has had corrective surgery on his deformed foot, he finds that Mildred is dying in a charity hospital. Before he can get to her she dies in a coma. Nora agrees to marry him, after Mildred's demise.

The notices for Davis' performance were highly favourable, including *Life*'s 'Probably the best performance ever recorded on the screen by a US actress'. Scandal erupted when she was not nominated for an Academy Award; the Oscar went to Claudette Colbert for *It Happened One Night*. Many felt that Davis' subsequent Academy Award for *Dangerous* (1935) was little more than a consolation prize. Directed by Alfred E Green, this minor melo-

Above: Bette Davis won her second Academy Award for her performance in *Jezebel* (1938).

Northern belle Fonda marries to spite Julie, and Richard Cromwell as Fonda's younger brother, who kills Brent in a duel.

For my money, *Dark Victory* (1939) provided the most emotionally satisfying role of Davis' long career. Directed by Edmund Goulding, the film plays as an updated *Camille*, with Davis cast as Judith Traherne, a hard-living lady dying of a brain tumour. Before it's too late she has the good sense to marry her handsome brain specialist, Dr Frederick Steele (George Brent), who, alas, is away when the fatal moment comes. Her secretary Ann (a lovely performance by Geraldine Fitzgerald) helps her to her room; realising she has made the most of a few months of happiness, she dies with a smile on her face.

Based on a story by W Somerset Maugham, William Wyler's *The Letter* (1940) proved a superior Bette Davis vehicle, easily outclassing *Of Human Bondage*. Plantation owner's wife Leslie Crosby (Davis) shoots her lover, claiming self-defence. Husband Herbert Marshall believes her story that the man attacked her, but attorney James Stephenson has doubts, confirmed when the murdered man's widow demands $10,000 for an incriminating letter from Leslie. Husband Robert spends his life's savings to buy the letter and Leslie confesses to him that the man was her lover. He forgives her, but the widow (Gale Sondergaard) stabs Leslie, whom the jury had acquitted. A triumph for Wyler and his star, who extracts every ounce of drama from her beleaguered situation.

Bette Davis and William Wyler reunited for Samuel Goldwyn's *The Little Foxes* (1941), adapted by Lillian Hellman from her acclaimed stage play. Fussin' and feudin' throughout filming, Wyler and Davis (reportedly an *amour fou*) came through with a great melodrama set during the post-American Civil War era. Davis stars as Regina Giddens, cold, bitingly callous, cunning and vicious in what has been called her greatest performance in her most testing role. With her

two grasping brothers (Charles Dingle and Carl Benton Reid) and vile nephew (Dan Duryea), she schemes to get funds for a sweatshop enterprise from her ailing husband, Horace (Herbert Marshall), whom she goads into a coronary and murders by withholding his medication. Overhearing her relatives' double-crossing arguments, daughter Alexandra (Teresa Wright) realises how vicious Regina really is, and leaves her corrupt family to rejoin her newspaper editor fiancé, David (Richard Carlson). Regina is left alone and hated. All the acting is superb, including Herbert Marshall as the definitive put-upon spouse.

Now Voyager (1942), directed by Irving Rapper, saw Davis in much softer mode. British critic C A Lejeune, in one of her rare bitchy moments, could not restrain herself from writing 'Now, now Voyager!' Albeit sentimental, Casey Robinson's adaptation of the Olive Higgins Prouty novel has been rated one of Davis' most sensitive performances. She stars as Charlotte Vale, the plain, repressed spinster daughter of a selfish mother (Gladys Cooper). On the verge of a nervous breakdown, Charlotte is referred by her sophisticated sister-in-law (Ilka Chase) to psychiatrist Dr Jaquith (Claude Rains), who insists she takes a long rest at his sanatorium.

After analysis and therapy – not to mention a complete makeover, including gowns by Orry-Kolly and pencil-slim eyebrows – she emerges chic and glamorous, ready to go on a South American cruise arranged by her sister-in-law. She meets the great love of her life, Jerry Durrance (Paul Henreid), married to an unloving wife, whose poor health makes it impossible for him to divorce her. Back in the rest home, guilt-ridden over her mother's fatal heart attack, Charlotte meets Jerry's depressed and unwanted daughter, Tina (Janis Wilson), with whom she empathises. Declining a marriage proposal from a wealthy socialite (John Loder), Charlotte persuades Jerry to let her adopt Tina, with whom she has become very close. As the lovers part, they do the famous cigarette-swapping scene and she utters the immortal words, 'Oh, Jerry, don't let's ask for the moon. We have the stars.'

Seven years on, King Vidor's *Beyond the Forest* (1949) proved the end of the line for Davis and Warner Bros and a pretty sorry affair. As Rosa Moline, Davis verges on the psychotic. Rosa deserts her husband, Dr Lewis (Joseph Cotten), after she has wrung his patients' past debts from them to finance her trip to Chicago, where she plans to seduce and marry rich industrialist Neil Latimer (David Brian). He turns her down to marry a socialite (Ruth Roman). Pregnant and alone, the half-crazed Rosa shoots Neil's lodge keeper, who knows her secret, and jumps off a highway embankment to kill the baby, contracting peritonitis in the process. In high fever delirium, she gets out of bed and staggers to catch the nine o'clock train to Chicago, dropping dead *en route*.

Said Dorothy Manners in the *Los Angeles Examiner*: 'No night club caricaturist has ever turned in such a cruel imitation of the Davis mannerisms as Bette turns in herself in this one.' But she does get to spit out 'What a dump!' In her autobiography, Davis wrote, 'Actually weary of the whole business, I made, as it turned out, my last trip to [Mr Warner's] office to beg him not to make me play Rosa Moline in *Beyond the Forest* ... I was, at this point, not young enough to play her ... "Bette Davis as a twelve o'clock girl in a nine o'clock town." This is how it was advertised. This set was the scene of my last battle with the studio. This "twelve o'clock girl" asked for her release during this film.'

Fortunately for the newly unemployed Davis, Twentieth Century-Fox soon came calling with the offer of a starring role in writer-director Joseph L Mankiewicz's *All About Eve* (1950). Davis' wisdom in leaving Warner Bros was more than justified by this 'wittiest, most devastating, most adult and most literate picture ever made

that had anything to do with the New York stage. *All About Eve* is also a movie in which Bette Davis gives the finest, most compelling and the most perceptive performance she has ever played out on screen.' So wrote Leo Mishkin in the New York *Morning Telegraph*.

Due to constant replays on television and the smash hit musical *Applause! Applause!* with Lauren Bacall, the story is too familiar to need more that the sketchiest outline. Temperamental and ageing actress Margo Channing (Davis) hires an adoring fan, stage-struck Eve Harrington (Anne Baxter), to be her secretary-companion. Margo's friends, playwright Lloyd Richards (Hugh Marlowe) and his wife Karen (Celeste Holm), approve and take Eve under their wing. At Margo's homecoming party, Eve begins to show her true colours, making up to Bill, Margo's putative husband (Gary Merrill), until Margo lets fly: 'Fasten your seatbelts – it's going to be a bumpy night!' Step by step, Eve double-crosses everyone and ends up in Lloyd's new play, Margo having announced her retirement to marry Bill. The cast is superlative, including George Sanders as critic DeWitt, who helps Eve then claims his pound of flesh; Thelma Ritter as Margo's maid, who sees through Eve from the start, and the young Marilyn Monroe as DeWitt's girlfriend. The film won four Academy Awards, including Best Picture, Best Director, Best Screenplay and Best Supporting Actor for Sanders.

Despite her success in *All About Eve*, Davis' film career took a severe downturn during the mid-1950s, culminating in several years away from films altogether. After a handful of negligible roles late in the decade, she made a comeback, of sorts, in the horror-tinged melodrama *Whatever Happened to Baby Jane?* (1962), directed and produced by Robert Aldrich. Another watershed in the Davis career; the film united her for the first and only time with old adversary Joan Crawford. From the word go it was rivalry all the way, on and off screen, but the movie made a fortune and re-established them both as box-office names. In Crawford's case, it was a matter of variations on the horror theme, while Davis played an assortment of the same diet, interspersed by character roles.

Baby Jane's story of two sisters in a decaying Hollywood mansion, ex-film star Blanche (Crawford), crippled in a car accident, and ex-child star Jane (Davis), ushered a new genre of camp-Gothic extravagance into the cinema. The increasingly mad Jane torments her helpless sister with dishes of baked rats, and plans a vaudeville comeback as Baby Jane, gruesomely reprising her old act to the accompaniment of gross pianist Edwin Flagg (Victor Buono). Blanche's attempt to escape is foiled by Jane, who binds and gags her, kills their cleaning woman and takes the dying Blanche to Malibu Beach, where she intends to bury her body. The films ends with Jane doing her old act for a crowd of curiosity seekers on the beach. Davis' frightening all-stops-out performance gained her another Oscar nomination, while Crawford, un-nominated for her comparatively restrained acting, more than got her own back at the Awards Ceremony by graciously accepting Anne Bancroft's Oscar for *The Miracle Worker* on behalf of the absent star.

Realising they were on to a good thing, Davis and Aldrich soon reunited for the arguably superior Deep South Gothic *Hush… Hush, Sweet Charlotte* (1964). Joan Crawford agreed to partner Davis once more, but dropped out early in production, suffering from viral pneumonia. Bette's friend Olivia de Havilland took over and filming proceeded smoothly. This time around, Davis' Charlotte is haunted by memories of her married lover (Bruce Dern), found beheaded and mutilated 37 years before. Charlotte believes that her father (Victor Buono) had done the deed and invites her cousin Miriam (Olivia de Havilland) to stay, to stop the state authori-

Above: Joan Crawford and Bette Davis in *Whatever Happened to Baby Jane?* (1962).

ties from demolishing her decaying home.

After Miriam's arrival, strange happenings begin – a lullaby played on Charlotte's harpsichord, apparently by a disembodied hand, a severed head rolling down a staircase. The shock sends Charlotte into a faint and the family physician, Drew (Joseph Cotten), gives her an injection. It transpires that he and Miriam are lovers, plotting to send Charlotte insane to gain control of her fortune. When loyal housekeeper Velma (Agnes Moorehead) finds out, Miriam kills her, then deludes Charlotte into thinking she has killed Drew. She encounters his bloody and muddy 'corpse' at the top of the stairs. Collapsing in a frenzy, she recovers to see Drew and Miriam embracing on the verandah below – a large cement urn, which she dislodges from its pedestal, squashes the guilty pair. Bloodier and more contrived than *Baby Jane*, this is the peak of Gothic horror – all the stops out for Davis and the top-quality cast, including Cecil Kellaway, George Kennedy and, in her last film role, Mary Astor as

Charlotte's lover's wife, Jewel, his actual killer.

As Hollywood gradually lost interest in Davis' *Baby Jane* renaissance, the star looked for employment in England, following Tallulah Bankhead's example and making two films for horror specialists Hammer. Seth Holt's *The Nanny* (1965) features Davis in unusually restrained mode, cast as a homicidal child-minder driven insane by the squalid death of her own, neglected daughter.

The Anniversary (1968), directed by Roy Ward Baker, settled for more familiar high-camp bitchiness. The film was based on Bill MacIlwraith's hit West End play, which had starred Mona Washbourne as Mrs Taggart, a monstrous mother, blind in one eye from an air-pistol shot by her oldest son, Terry. Never one to dress down, Davis wore a designer eye-patch in the role, further exercising her star power by firing original director Alvin Rakoff. Three members of the stage cast were retained: James Cossins as the older son, a transvestite; Jack Hedley, the middle one, and Sheila Hancock as his shrew of a wife. New recruits were Christian Roberts as young Tom and Elaine Taylor as his pregnant girlfriend, Shirley. She stands up to her prospective mother-in-law, but almost has a miscarriage when she finds Mrs Taggart's glass eye under the mattress while she and Tom are making love. Cue for one of Davis' witchlike cackling laughs.

Davis' last film appearance of note came in *The Whales of August* (1987), directed by Lindsay Anderson. The film co-starred silent film legend Lillian Gish and proved a fitting valedictory for two of the screen's greatest and most durable stars, cast as sisters living out their final years together – Davis, naturally, as the more forceful of the two. Probably only the highly sensitive Anderson could have guided them through this touching tribute to old age – Davis, fractious as ever, and Gish, though frail, having the slight edge in the performances. This was

Above: Bette Davis in *The Nanny* (1965).

also the last film appearance of Ann Sothern, as a neighbour of the sisters, for which she won an Oscar nomination – her one and only. Vincent Price completed this quartet of venerable stars, playing another old friend of the ladies.

In later years, Bette Davis suffered serious illnesses, including a stroke, a mastectomy and a broken hip, which did not inhibit her from being eager to face movie and TV cameras again. Her last interviews in Britain, publicising a book, were painful, in that she wore very short skirts and puffed cigarette smoke at the interviewers throughout. Davis' spirit, at least, was explosive to the end; for the rest, her gay fans viewed her through multi-filtered lenses, apparently not available during the filming of *Wicked Stepmother* (1989), her last and definitely worst movie.

CARMEN MIRANDA [1909-1955]
[Maria do Carmo Miranda da Cunha]

Defining 'camp' as anything frivolous or paradoxical within a conventional framework, 'Brazilian Bombshell' Carmen Miranda has to be the quintessence of camp. With her two-piece, multi-hued, sequined, feathered and jeweled gowns, six-inch wedge heels and baskets of fruit among her headpieces, she gyrated and coruscated, spouting heavily accented lyrics, almost always attended by her Banda da Lua musicians.

A natural for the more lurid shades of Technicolor, Miranda adorned a series of Hollywood movies from *Down Argentine Way* (1940) through to *Scared Stiff* (1953). The 'conventional' framework was provided by lighthearted musicals, variously starring Betty Grable, Don Ameche, Alice Faye, Cesar Romero and John Payne, through whose melodious romances Miranda exploded like a firecracker, causing paroxysms of jealousy among the strictly proper and correct blondes, or scratching the boys with two-inch carmined fingernails, to match her generous gash of a mouth. She was just the startling new personality audiences were seeking in a war-torn world. The plots were formulaic rehashes but nobody cared, knowing that she would burst onto the screen whenever things needed livening up.

Carmen Miranda was not, of course, everybody's dish of chilli con carne. Outraged straitlaced patrons wrote to the fan magazines in words like 'I've never seen anything quite so crude and, yes, repulsive, on the screen. All slinks and slides and mouth and false eyelashes...' One reader was caused 'acute embarrassment', and another wrote of 'an ordinary face, heavily lipsticked and rouged.' But to gay audiences she was almost everybody's party popper, the campest thing since Mae West, and a boon to impersonators, who could outdo each other with outrageous headgear, shoes and dresses. Personalities as diverse as Mickey Rooney,

Bob Hope and Tommy Trinder 'did' her, and her stock as a Forces' pin-up rose sharply when a snap of the devoutly Catholic star swirling in her dressing room with Cesar Romero revealed her as knickerless. Pirated copies of the photo were at a premium, sadly, but she assured her Bishop it was all due to flashbulbs.

At one time Miranda was the highest-paid woman in America. In the penetrating documentary *Bananas is My Business*, narrated by Miranda's sister Aurora, Alice Faye explained that Carmen made more money than anyone else for Twentieth Century-Fox. She was the only star who could get away with speaking her mind to studio boss Darryl F Zanuck, although in her scripts even she had to knuckle down to repeating the same old temperamental malapropisms to everyone who got in her way. Alice Faye was a good friend to her but Betty Grable disliked her cordially, a feeling warmly reciprocated.

There was a downside to all this lighthearted bandinage. As the chief exponent of hands across the ocean Latin-American rapport – essential as the Allies grew closer together during World War Two – she was obliged to represent the North American take on South America, which went down very well in European countries. In Brazil, however, she was accused of having become Americanised and even of betraying her country. When Carmen returned for personal appearances, she was coldly received and attacked in the press.

She returned to the USA to carry on her film career, vowing never to return to Brazil, where she had moved with her working class family from their native Portugal. Her father did well as a wholesale fruiterer and Carmen was convent-educated. Success came easily in Brazil; from being a successful milliner to rich ladies, she was invited to extend her instinctive and unique style of movement and song, performing for private parties. From there it was an easy step to make a test record, which quickly became top of the Brazilian Hit Parade (as it used to be called). A contract with RCA was soon forthcoming and, in a continent where there was little opposition, stage shows and films followed and she became the top musical star in Latin America. American impresario Lee Shubert was so impressed with Miranda, he invited her to star on Broadway in his 1939 revue *Streets of Paris*. Her part in Fox's *Down Argentine Way*, Betty Grable's first big starring vehicle, was filmed in New York, and from thence came the trip to Hollywood for Darryl F Zanuck.

I met Carmen Miranda at a reception at the Brazilian Embassy during her London Palladium stint in April 1948, with her Banda da Lua. When Shubert had signed her for Broadway, she went only on the condition that they accompanied her. She had married the year before, to David Sebastian, the co-producer of her movie *Copacabana* (1947). The marriage had soon run into trouble on account of his violent temper. Her family were against the match and sister Aurora said Sebastian used to attack Carmen physically. At the reception, however, he danced attendance on her constantly; for her part she was lacking in the expected sparkle and virtually monosyllabic. When I asked her was it true she was returning to Hollywood to make *A Date With Judy* (1948) with Elizabeth Taylor (for MGM), she replied with a flat 'Yes.' Aurora, who had made *Three Caballeros* (1944) for Disney, was seated beside her and supplied most of her answers: she was as lively as one had hoped Carmen might be. Carmen gave the impression that she would rather be anywhere else and there was an aura, almost, of sadness about her.

Aurora said, in a documentary, that her sister had changed during and after her marriage; she later had a nervous breakdown and was hospitalised home to Brazil, where she suffered acute depression. After her return to America, she got back into the swing of her career with some show of enthusiasm, in cabaret at Las Vegas and in her last two films, *Nancy Goes to Rio* (1950) and *Scared Stiff* (1953). She later reconciled with David Sebastian.

The end was swift and tragic. In 1955, while making a TV show with Jimmy Durante on 6 August, she fell to her knees after an energetic dance, gasped 'I'm all out of breath' while Durante stopped the music, and managed to dance off the stage with some grace. She died that night, alone in her room, after saying good-night and kissing her husband, who went to his room. She had apparently rallied after a late supper and sang at a party before retiring. Sebastian later found her lying dead on the floor in her pyjamas. He accompanied the coffin and her grieving relatives to her funeral in Rio. A period of national mourning was declared and crowds blocked the streets to show their affection. A little late, perhaps. She was just 46. Rumours of her cocaine addiction have never been substantiated, but if true, could have accounted for her early and sudden death.

JUDY GARLAND [1922-1969] [Frances Gumm]

Vulnerability may be one of the qualities that made Judy Garland, almost from the start of her film career, appeal to gay audiences, along with a certain boyish quality and the way she stood out from the norm. She was never a conventional film star, nor, really, a beauty, and her singing voice had its rough edges, especially in later years. Yet something about Garland made both sexes want to put their arms around her and protect her from the world.

She never had that protection in real life. From the beginning there was no way she could be prevented from going into showbusiness. Both her parents were vaudevillians, known as Jack and Virginia Lee, and Judy made her first stage appearance at the age of three. She took to the footlights so readily that her father, after she had taken three encores, had to yank her off the stage. Jack Lee was gay, so it was really in her genes, just as one of her husbands would be gay, and there was an instinctive sympathy with people set apart. That said, her good-looking father ('a gay Irish gentleman,' she called him) seemed to be too preoccupied to have much time for Judy, although they loved each other. It was her mother who pushed her into showbusiness – not that Judy needed much pushing.

They moved to Hollywood when she was 13, and Judy was soon propelled by mama into a musical short called *Every Sunday* (1936), with a young Deanna Durbin representing the operatic side of song while Judy was clearly a jazz baby. After that appearance together, the budding juvenile stars went their separate ways, Durbin to become Universal's top diva, Garland to a contract with MGM. She made her feature debut in the musical *Pigskin Parade* (1936), the start of a long and lucrative career as the studio's premier teenage musical comedy sensation.

Garland's teaming with Mickey Rooney made them the audiences' favourite young couple, their hit musicals including *Babes in Arms* (1939). Sadly, the pressures on Garland soon began to mount. In her early days as an entertainer, her mother had introduced her to pills to make her sleep and pills for waking up. MGM, in their infinite wisdom, increased the diet of uppers and downers to help Garland through relentless shooting schedules. Judy had become the studio's biggest star and they were determined to fully exploit their valuable property. Ironically, she only won the part of Dorothy in *The Wizard of Oz* (1939) after Twentieth Century-Fox demanded too much money for the loan of Shirley Temple, MGM's first choice for the role.

Throughout the 1940s, Garland sold more tickets that any other star in the world with the exceptions of Bob Hope and Bing Crosby. Her

Above: Billie Burke and Judy Garland in *The Wizard of Oz* (1939).

mood swings and erratic behaviour, with consequent escalation of pill-taking, drove her into a mental breakdown. In 1950 she was fired from the MGM musical *Annie Get Your Gun* and replaced by Betty Hutton; the same year she attempted suicide. It took Garland four years to make a film comeback, in possibly her definitive role for gay audiences: *A Star is Born* (1954). From then on, her life was a roller-coaster ride of marriages, movies, wildly successful live concerts, including Carnegie Hall and the London Palladium, TV series and affairs with both men and women. Celebrity lovers included Tyrone Power, who introduced her to love across the sexual divide, Orson Welles and Yul Brynner.

Her tragic life, apart from her own persona, surely added to her popularity with the third sex. MGM's 'fatherly' Louis B Mayer contributed, in equal measure with her pill-pushing mother Ethel Gumm, to the downward spiral of Garland's life. Both insisted, after her marriage to David Rose in 1941, that she abort her first baby. Not content with fondling Judy's breasts while he called her his 'little hunchback' during their 'conferences' in his office, Mayer also made it known among his executives that his child star was 'available' for pleasuring.

Further, Mayer gave his blessing to Judy's 1945 marriage to Vincente Minnelli, his brilliant contract director, knowing that he was not only homosexual but positively averse to having sex with women. They did manage to have a child, Liza Minnelli, in 1946, but Mayer's strategical 'Hollywood royal family' came apart at the seams when Judy found her husband in bed with the handyman. She dashed from their bedroom to the Italian marble bathroom Minnelli had designed for her, and slashed her wrists. And so it went on, through fairly disastrous marriages with three more husbands, one of whom, Mark Heron, was having an affair with Liza Minnelli's husband, Peter Alken, even after their marriage.

The last act of Judy's pain-wracked saga came in London, where she was appearing in a few sad concerts, during which she was often unable to drag herself on stage. She had married husband number five, Mickey Deans, whom she met when he was providing her with illegally obtained drugs, at a ceremony attended by none of her Hollywood friends and described by the *Evening Standard* correspondent as 'The saddest and most pathetic party I have ever attended.' In her London home she took six sleeping pills, and on awakening forgot she had taken them. She took four more as she sat on the toilet and there she died on 17 July 1969. Judy's songs, beginning with the innocence of a love lyric to Clark Gable, became increasingly full of angst, pain and self-doubt, striking a chord with the romantic longings of her invisible admirers.

MARLON BRANDO [1924-]

One of the few film actors to have earned the title 'a legend in his own lifetime', Marlon Brando offered a unique combination of magnetic acting ability, brooding good looks, sensuous masculinity and outstanding physique. He maintained a 'wild one' image from the beginning, being expelled from military academy, and left home at 19 to study acting at Stella Adler's school. Brando's passion for drama and his innate talent soon led to his Broadway debut in *I Remember Mama* in 1944. Three years later Tennessee Williams considered him ideal casting opposite Jessica Tandy in *A Streetcar Named Desire*, in which he was an overnight sensation.

In 1950 Brando made his first film appearance in *The Men*, directed by Fred Zinnemann; a sensitive and highly praised offering, detailing the lives of disabled World War II veterans learning to adjust to civilian life. Not only his acting skills but his torso were given a full workout in the scenes where he learns to exercise his arm muscles by pulley control.

Despite Brando's quick rise to stardom, he continued to live modestly, declining to dress up for social occasions, which he avoided as much as possible. He shared his New York lodgings with a lifelong friend, actor Wally Cox – born the same year and best known for the weedy, bespectacled character he played in the TV series *Mr Peepers* and *Hiram Holliday*. Brando never bothered to contradict rumours that they were lovers; although predominantly straight, he has admitted to gay affairs. 'Like many men I have had homosexual experiences and I'm not ashamed.' A journalist friend of mine, sent to interview Brando in the star's hotel room when he was in England filming *The Nightcomers* (1971) for director Michael Winner, claims that he had to fend off a pass. 'Quien sabe?' as Coward's Madame Arcati was apt to say.

Brando's private life, with no lack of rumours

of affairs with both sexes, has sometimes been more highly publicised that any actor would have wished. Highly publicised encounters which ended up in the courts – on one occasion involving a tragic death and one of his nearest and dearest – have led the actor to become increasingly reclusive, while at the same time contributing to a certain air of mystery. These events, combined with some of his classic screen portrayals, have given him the air of a legendary figure.

Although his beauty, and more particularly his classic physique, have long gone, his occasional film roles still create a certain magic, even if they frequently suggest caricatures of *The Godfather* (1972). Sadly, one feels he has long since lost interest in his film career, accepting parts solely to help support his lifestyle. A case in point is *Christopher Columbus: The Discovery* (1992), in which his portrayal of the notorious inquisitor, Torquemada, might have been interesting. An unkind critic compared him to 'a tethered barrage balloon'. He reportedly wanted his name removed from the credits – but it is still a name to conjure with. The last films in which Brando, although overweight, purveyed sexual magnetism were *Last Tango in Paris* (1972), Bernardo Bertolucci's landmark movie about a doomed sexual liaison, which won Brando a seventh Oscar nomination, and *Superman* (1978). At 54, newly platinum, Marlon was paid over the odds for his ten-minute role as Superman's father, Jor-El.

MARILYN MONROE (1926-1962)
(Norma Jean Mortenson)

Marilyn Monroe was the reigning sex goddess of the fifties. She also became a Gay Icon: her exuberance and sensual manner, allied to a fragile vulnerability and an innocence shielding her own sexuality, made her non-threatening to a gay audience and irresistible to her

Above: Marlon Brando in *The Wild One* (1954).

lesbian following. She proved a gift, too, to female impersonators by reason of her exaggerated sexual posturing and breathy vocal delivery, in speech and song.

She established herself as Twentieth Century-Fox's premier blonde, in succession to Betty Grable, the year they co-starred with Lauren Bacall in Jean Negulesco's *How to Marry a Millionaire* (1953). Grable finally abdicated in 1955 after *How to Be Very Very Popular*. Her down-to-earth song and dance girl persona had been ideal for the Armed Forces pin-up but of minimal appeal to gays in general, although she had many admirers among them. After the end of her film career, Grable's stage work included the short-lived musical *Belle Star* at the Cambridge Theatre in London. When she bounced out of her dressing room, the personification of Technicolor maquillage, to sign photos with a cheery 'Rightee', the friend I was with found her entrancing.

by the film with which she is most often associated, *Gentlemen Prefer Blondes* (1953). Monroe was cast as gold-digger Lorelei Lee in this musical version of Anita Loos' famous novel, directed by Howard Hawks. From then on she could do no wrong with the public, though she increasingly became a problem for directors, often late on set and suffering frequent bouts of illness as her drug dependency grew. Being the world's favourite sex symbol called for a more robust constitution than Marilyn possessed.

Among the highlights of her glittering career were Billy Wilder's *The Seven Year Itch* (1955), Joshua Logan's *Bus Stop* (1956) – one of her most touching performances, Wilder's *Some Like It Hot* (1959) and John Huston's *The Misfits* (1961), the final film for her and Clark Gable, written by her then-husband Arthur Miller. The final curtain, after she was fired for constant absences and unpunctuality on the set of *Something's Got to Give*, has been analysed ad infinitum, with no really satisfactory conclusions. Surely the time has now come to wish her RIP.

JAMES DEAN (1931-1955)
(James Byron Dean)

James Dean is undoubtedly one of the most extraordinary Gay Icons, by reason of his incredible impact on American youth culture in only three films, his screen charisma allied to potentially great talent, and his tragic sudden death in a car crash at the age of 24. A generation of young people, teens to early twenties, straight as well as gay, empathised with his rebellious persona from the moment they set eyes on him in *East of Eden* (1955). His death occurred on 30 September of that year, before either of his subsequent films, *Rebel Without a Cause* (1955) and *Giant* (1956), reached cinema screens.

Dean's family had moved to Los Angeles in 1936 when his father was offered work there. His

Marilyn Monroe was born into unhappiness, her supposed father killed in a motorbike crash when she was only three. Her mother and maternal grandmother were both committed to mental hospitals, and from then on she was passed from one foster home to another. She began her quest to be a movie star in the late forties, after a brief marriage to an aircraft factory worker in 1942 and an even briefer career as a model (including the famous nude shots). Contracts with Twentieth Century-Fox and Columbia led to bit parts in musicals. Her second signing with Fox began a slow build-up in dumb blonde roles, including appearances in *All About Eve* (1950) and *Clash By Night* (1952).

Monroe's first starring role came opposite Richard Widmark in *Don't Bother to Knock* (1952), where she was impressive as a psychotic baby sitter. Her real breakthrough role was in *Niagara* (1953), as a scheming wife, followed

Above: Marilyn Monroe and Tony Curtis in *Some Like It Hot* (1959).

Right: Sal Mineo, James Dean and Natalie Wood in *Rebel Without a Cause* (1955).

mother died four years later and he returned to Indiana to live with relatives. After graduating from high school, he returned to Los Angeles to be reconciled with his father and to try for an acting career, working from time to time in a local theatre group and obtaining bit parts in such movies as *Sailor Beware* (1951), *Fixed Bayonets* (1951) and *Has Anybody Seen My Gal?* (1952), starring Rock Hudson. Progress was not fast enough for Dean's liking and he moved to New York to perfect his craft, attending classes at the celebrated Actors Studio, under Lee Strasberg. His Broadway debut as a homosexual Arab in *The Immoralist* (1954) was a sensation, leading to a screen test and contract at Warner Bros.

Dean's first starring role in the John Steinbeck-based *East of Eden* was scripted by Paul Osborn, who suggested Dean to director Elia Kazan for the part of Cal, a wild adolescent – a role Kazan had intended for Marlon Brando. The moment the director met Dean, 'a heap of denim rags and twisted legs, looking resentful for no particular reason', the part was his: the quintessential misunderstood youth, the very picture of alienation was there before Kazan's

eyes. Cal's fight with his father (Raymond Massey) is of epic proportions, when he discovers that his mother, whom he had long believed dead, is alive and running a brothel. Jo Van Fleet gained an Oscar for her performance.

From Kazan to Nicholas Ray to George Stevens: no young actor had ever before started his career with such prestigious directors. In truth, Dean's third and last starring role – as Jett Rink, the arrogant young ranch hand who rises to become a wealthy, elderly tycoon in Stevens' *Giant* – showed his inexperience as an actor. Elizabeth Taylor, as was her wont with fragile young stars, took fondly to him, but Rock Hudson and James Dean were anathema to each other. To Hudson, nearly 30 years before AIDS forced him to come out, Dean's casual attitude to his sexual behaviour was a threat. Hudson also expressed jealousy that someone else had achieved screen immortality in such a short time.

The role of Jett Rink had been coveted by Alan Ladd and his agents. Ladd was a much better actor than he was usually credited and, at 42, with clever make-up and lighting, he could have managed both the youthful and elderly scenes, but director Stevens was set on Dean. The film was an enormous success, boosted by the combined star power of Taylor, Hudson and Dean, who gained his second Academy Award nomination. George Stevens won the Oscar for best film.

Ironically, at the time of Dean's death he had just completed a short film on road safety. Driving and speed were, perhaps, his premier obsessions, but it is impossible now to assess in which order his other *raisons d'être* belonged; acting and sex were high on the list and his passion for both was insatiable. On the surface, there was his love for his *Rebel Without a Cause* co-star Natalie Wood, although the night before his death, at a Malibu party, he had a heated argument with a man who accused him of dating women 'for publicity purposes'. It was not until the seventies that books were written speculating on Dean's bisexuality or homosexuality. Either way, his love life was very far from straightforward.

One biographer reports that Dean had his first gay sexual experience with a pastor from Indiana, his birthplace. During his later days he was excited by sadomasochism – the make-up department were at pains to disguise the cigarette burns inflicted by his loving tormentors. His one-time flatmate William Bast was reputedly the love of his life and in 1976 scripted a TV movie called *James Dean*, which dealt more explicitly with Dean's homosexuality than Bast had been able to in his 1958 book *The Myth Makers*.

While trying for film parts before his big breakthrough, Dean began cultivating influential gay men, including actor Clifton Webb, whose protégé he was to become. A later friend was actor Nick Adams, who was making *Mister Roberts* the year of *East of Eden*. They were introduced by Natalie Wood and Adams rapidly became close to Dean, making himself available for whatever services were required of him. The year after Dean's death, Adams introduced himself to Elvis Presley on the set of the latter's first movie, *Love Me Tender* (1956), possibly seeing Elvis as the

friend who might fill the gap left by Jimmy. Elvis was attracted by Adams' outgoing personality and the young actors caused quite a stir, cruising round Los Angeles with Natalie Wood, Russ Tamblyn and others on their Hondas.

Sadly, these young and talented actors were to follow Dean to early deaths. Nick Adams died of an overdose at 37 in 1968. Natalie Wood drowned in an accident at sea, which has never been satisfactorily explained, in 1981 at age 43. Presley's untimely end in 1977, at 42, came when his system had simply broken down from a surfeit of prescribed drugs and overwork.

DORIS DAY [1924-]
[Doris von Kappelhoff]

The honey-smooth singing voice, ready smile and simpatico disposition notwithstanding, Doris Day, in whatever role she played, represented the bachelor girl par excellence. Her tomboy persona appealed to lesbians and gays alike, while her non-explicit sex appeal attracted straight males without threatening their wives. In other words, she was all things to most people. In 1950s and 1960s 'sex' comedies, she was asserting her independence over men by clinging desperately to her virginity, although always getting together with her male co-star for the final clinch. She was expert in having her cake and, eventually, eating it.

In Day's early life there was much to prompt her strong sense of independence. Her father abandoned the family for another woman, obliging her mother Alma to bring up Doris and her two brothers (one of whom died aged two) on her own. Doris' first marriage at 17 to a 'psychopath', the father of her son Terry, and the battle to overcome the consequences of a car crash which nearly cost her the use of her legs were other tragedies. Doris retained her femininity while developing a steely inner strength.

Born Doris von Kappelhoff to German Catholic parents in Cincinnati Ohio, and trained as a dancer, Doris formed a partnership with a boy called Jerry Doherty when they were both 12 years old. They won a $500 first prize in a contest and agreed with their mothers to spend the money on a trip to Hollywood for a course in tap dancing at the famous dance school, Panchon and Marco, under the leading dancer of tap, Louis Da Pron. Alma Kappelhoff rented a small apartment for four weeks, consisting of one bedroom and a living room with a bed attached to the door. Louis Da Pron was so impressed with Doris and Jerry's progress in tap dancing that they were signed to tour with the Panchon and Marco stage show at venues in and around Hollywood.

In the week they were due to leave to take up residence in Hollywood for good, on a cold and rainy night, the 14-year-old Doris and her friends, *en route* to a party, were involved in a crash with a train at a crossing with no lights or signs. Doris suffered a double-compound fracture on her right leg. She was allowed to stay out of school while she recuperated and the family moved to a tavern bought by her Uncle Charley with the proceeds of the family bakery's sale: Alma did the cooking and they shared an apartment upstairs. Doris was the only victim of the near-fatal crash to suffer serious injury. Her ex-partner Jerry gave up his dreams of succeeding in showbusiness and went on to become a milkman.

During this period Doris had little to do but listen to the radio – those were the great days of the wireless. Ella Fitzgerald inspired her to sing along, as she said, 'to catch the subtle ways she shaded her voice, the casual yet clear way she sang the words.' This new interest prompted the ever-attentive Alma – the nicest kind of un-pushy stage mother – to hire a singing teacher, Grace Raine, who was so impressed with Doris' potential as a singer she volunteered to give her three lessons a week, although her mother could only afford one at five dollars. The other two

Above: A portrait of Doris Day.

were free. Raine's husband had contacts with radio station WLW, where Doris got her first chance to sing on the air in a local radio show called *Carlin's Carnival*, broadcast from a department store. She sang 'Day After Day'.

From this, she was engaged as a singer, for a fee of five dollars a week, at the Shanghai Inn in downtown Cincinnati, run by Charlie Yee, who accepted the 15-year-old's assurance that she was 18. To reach the cabaret in the restaurant on the second floor, Doris had to inch up the stairs on her backside before making her entrance on crutches to front a three-piece combo – a fairly original way to start a career in cabaret. When it seemed she might be able to swap her crutches for a cane, she impulsively tried a tiny tap dance to 'Tea for Two', supporting herself on her crutches, one of which slipped on the edge of a rug. She crashed down onto her injured leg, putting her back at least another year.

Doris was free of her crutches when Grace Raine was approached by a bandleader friend, Barney Rapp, who had heard her protégée singing on *Carlin's Carnival*, to enquire whether Doris would be interested in singing with his band in a club he was opening in Cincinnati, called The Sign of the Drum. She passed the audition with flying colours, though she had to sing a song she loathed: 'Jeepers, Creepers', surely the nadir of all crass jingles of the thirties. A new name had to be found – von Kappelhof did not sit easily on the marquee outside the club. She had made 'Day After Day' something of a signature tune, so Barney Rapp suggested Day as a surname. Doris was the first name of her mother's favourite film star, Doris Kenyon, sometime leading lady to Rudolph Valentino, so a new Day dawned.

She went on to sing with other bands, including Bob Crosby and His Bobcats. Crosby was the brother of Bing, but Day established no particular rapport with him and was happy to switch to the latest sensation in town, Les Brown and His Band of Renown. Brown signed Day after listening to her for five minutes at the Edison Hotel in New York. Brown's new band sound, different from all the others, was typified by his theme tune, 'Leap Frog' – staccato, like the unexpected leaps and bounds of that lively amphibian. The new association worked out very happily, until Doris presented Les Brown with a bombshell, announcing her marriage to Al Jorden, a trombonist with Barney Rapp's band, to whom she had become engaged when they were both still with Barney. She also announced her imminent retirement, and neither Les Brown nor Alma could make her change her mind.

Doris went ahead with the marriage, which was a disaster from the word go. For all his good looks, Al Jorden was insanely jealous, beating Doris up the day after their wedding because she accepted a wedding present from the man-

ager of the Jimmy Dorsey Band, with whom Al was then playing. This kind of behaviour continued after Doris became pregnant, interspersed with crying fits and begging her forgiveness. Twice during a car ride he threatened to kill her and the unborn baby, and eight months into the pregnancy he came home drunk and gave her the worst beating of all. Al was away on tour when baby Terry was born on 8 February 1942; Alma was with Doris at the hospital. After several unbearable months with the always unpredictable Al and her mother, constantly on the alert to protect her and the baby (with Uncle Charley, Doris's older brother Paul and a supportive Aunt Marie as neighbours), Doris locked Al out of the house and instructed her lawyers to initiate divorce proceedings.

Three times Les Brown begged Doris to rejoin him and the band; on the third occasion she agreed, with the persuasive influences of Alma and her Aunt Marie, who devoted themselves to looking after little Terry. There was a tearful reunion with Les and three happy years of touring, during which time she had a major hit record with 'Sentimental Journey', of which Les Brown was co-author with Bud Green, whose previous hit had been 'Flat Foot Floogie'. With World War Two in full swing, the song, predictably, became a kind of signature tune for Doris and she joined Betty Grable – a long-time favourite of hers – and Rita Hayworth as pin-ups for the Services. Doris was on her way to becoming an icon for the Armed Forces, if not yet for the gay community.

After a few months back with the Band of Renown, Doris fell in love again, this time with lead alto sax player George Weidler, brother of film actress Virginia Weidler. Again Les Brown tried to talk her out of it and again she decided this was the love of her life. After eight months, George, a very pleasant and fair-minded young man, wrote from his tour with Stan Kenton's band that he did not intend to be known as Mr

Doris Day – he saw great things ahead for her – and wanted to end the marriage.

An agent called Al Levy had it in mind to propel Doris into movies, and invited her to a party at the home of composer Jule Styne. Styne's partner Sammy Cahn practically forced Day over to the piano, where Jule Styne was tinkling the ivories. Much against her will, she sang a chorus of 'Embraceable You' perched on Styne's piano. Her agent Al, with Jule and Sammy, then took Doris aside and told her about their score for a new film musical, *Romance on the High Seas* (1948). Director Michael Curtiz, unable to get Judy Garland or Betty Hutton, was testing other singers and Doris was asked to do a test at Warner Bros. She was very unenthusiastic and said she was on the point of returning to New York to play her second month at the Little Club there. Al Levy persuaded her to be collected and taken to Curtiz's office bungalow. Two choruses of 'Embraceable You' and two floods of tears later, Curtiz said 'We make test.' They did and the result was a hit movie and a million-dollar seller for Doris in the song 'It's Magic', which was used as the film's title in Great Britain.

From 1951's *On Moonlight Bay*, where Doris played tomboy Marjorie, spending much of the film fighting off amorous co-star Gordon Macrae, her feisty roles were interspersed with more dramatic women-in-peril parts. Day struggled to preserve her sanity and her life from psychopathic husbands in *Julie* (1956), with Louis Jourdan, and *Midnight Lace* (1960), co-starring Rex Harrison. She was a shop steward babe in *The Pajama Game* (1957), a lecturer in journalism to reporter Clark Gable in *Teacher's Pet* (1958) and a fighter for women's rights in *The Ballad of Josie* (1968). As real-life torch singer Ruth Etting, she battled to maintain her independence from bullying gangster husband the Gimp (James Cagney) in *Love Me or Leave Me* (1955). In Alfred

Hitchcock's remake of *The Man Who Knew Too Much* (1956), she protected her son from murderous foreign agents. She still attracts a large lesbian following through the remarkable bipolarity of her movie roles, often repeated on TV.

Summing up, in the words of Kris Kirk in *Gay Times*, 'As well as appealing to musical queens, Doris Day was the big heart-throb of fifties dykes. Partly, one presumes, because of that husky voice and the boyish crop she wore so often and, no doubt, the tomboy energy she displayed so well as the pistol-packing, thigh-slapping, two-fisted Calamity Jane. But it wasn't just sex, it was image too. All great Icons have a dual personality and the other side of Doris' homely as apple pie/good sport, perfect wife image was the girl who always says no until the right man comes around, the foremost practitioner of prolonged avoidance of sex ... a potent brew for all those dykes who looked beyond the freckles and saw Sex on Legs.'

An added *frisson* for her admirers in the know during the fifties could be found in the comedies with Rock Hudson. More than once, his character pretended to be gay to avoid romantic advances until Doris was close enough for him to swoop, providing the spectacle of a gay man playing a straight man pretending to be gay. Whether this was an in-joke between scriptwriter Stanley Shapiro and Hudson in *Pillow Talk* (1959) and *Lover Come Back* (1962), or Cary Grant in *That Touch of Mink* (1962), is a thought to conjure with. Or was it all mere coincidence? And was Doris Day, who was no simpleton, in on the joke?

Doris' friendship with Hudson, warm but never intimate, continued up until he was the first guest on her cable TV series, *Doris Day and Friends*, in September 1985, when he was already terminally ill with AIDS. She knew nothing of Hudson's condition and was deeply shocked at his changed appearance. She later wrote, 'The filming had clearly been a major

Left: Nick Nolte and Barbra Streisand in *The Prince of Tides* (1991).

effort for him and I was all in favour of calling it off. I had no idea of his condition and he told me he'd had 'flu, which he was finding difficult to throw off. When we were walking around out there together, it crossed my mind it might be the last time. But I didn't really know. I hoped and prayed that it wouldn't be. I didn't know what was wrong with him, but I knew he was determined to do that show, if it took his last breath. It was his last thing and I really cherish that.' He died on 2 October 1985. The last shot of Rock in the show is as his white bus rattles away and Doris softly sings 'My Buddy'.

BARBRA STREISAND [1942-]
[Barbara Joan Streisand]

Since her arrival on the entertainment scene in the 1960s, Barbra Streisand has been a special favourite with gay audiences. Her initial gay fan-base has remained loyal through the years, and helped propel her to mainstream popularity in the first place. As an early supporter of gay and lesbian rights, she has been involved

in numerous AIDS charities.

She got an early career break when she entered a singing contest in Greenwich Village, with a prize of money, food and a job, all of which she was in dire need of, having had no luck at the numerous auditions she tried for. Streisand won the contest at The Lion Bar, which turned out to be a gay bar, and she was awarded a brief engagement singing there. She stunned the patrons, not only with her vocal expertise but also her bohemian outfits and sharp sense of comedy. From then on, her rise to superstardom was rapid and spectacular, via the trendy supper club Bon Soir and the famous nightclub The Blue Angel.

Writer Arthur Laurents saw her perform at the latter establishment and auditioned her for his new Broadway musical *I Can Get It for You Wholesale* (1962), which won Streisand a Tony award for her small role of the lovelorn secretary Miss Mapleshein. Working on the show, she met and married Elliott Gould in 1963, the year she released her first record, *The Barbra Streisand Album*, for which she was named *Cue*'s Entertainer of the Year.

All of this was a remarkable achievement, in

view of Streisand's poverty-stricken childhood, her father's death when she was only 15 months old, and her conviction that she was different from other children, besides being ugly. Barbra escaped into a fantasy world of being a rich, famous and beautiful actress. She persuaded her mother, against her inclinations, to send her to summer acting school for two years. Odd jobs as an usherette and switchboard operator kept her going until the break at the Lion Bar.

Streisand's second Broadway show, *Funny Girl* (1964), gave her the coveted role of Fanny Brice, the Jewish comedienne, who had her own gay following. The show proved the definitive turning point in her career. After *Funny Girl*'s smash success on Broadway, Streisand and her husband came to London, where she repeated her triumph at the Prince of Wales Theatre. She gave a lavish theatrical party, to which most of the stars of the London stage were invited. Beryl Reid, who was enjoying an enormous success in Frank Marcus' breakthrough black comedy about lesbian relationships, *The Killing of Sister George*, at the Duke of York's, went with her co-star Eileen Atkins. They were ignored by the hostess throughout the evening. 'I couldn't help wondering why she had asked us,' Beryl said later. The film of *Funny Girl* (1968), directed by William Wyler, won her an Oscar and she went on to become the most popular female star of the seventies.

Besides releasing more that 20 albums, Streisand starred in a succession of big movies, including *Hello Dolly!* (1969), *The Owl and the Pussycat* (1970), *What's Up Doc?* (1972) and *The Way We Were* (1973). *Funny Lady* (1975) saw her playing Fanny Brice one more time, opposite original co-star Omar Sharif as first husband Nick Arnstein, James Caan as second husband Billy Rose, and Roddy McDowell as her gay confidant Bobby Moore, whom Billy addresses as Pansy, Pet Poodle and Dear.

A Star is Born (1976), directed by Streisand

protégé Frank Pierson, was hated by many who loved the Janet Gaynor and Judy Garland versions, regarding this one as a travesty of the story of a fading star who helps an unknown actress to stardom while his own career ends in alcoholism and tragedy. The role originated by Fredric March and reprised by James Mason was played by Kris Kristofferson as a rock star, while Vicky Lester (Streisand) is now an aspiring singer. Personally I rated it as comparable to the first two.

Streisand has been called a control freak and other less polite things, which she counters by saying if she were a man nobody would remark on the matter. Her subsequent forays into directing as well as acting have been mostly widely praised.

BETTE MIDLER [1945-]

Like her near-contemporary Barbra Streisand, Bette Midler is Jewish. Born in Honolulu, her parents lived in a poor Samoan neighbourhood. Like Streisand, she got her initial start in show-business before New York's gay audiences. In Midler's case, after the usual round of clubs and auditions, she learned that Manhattan's Continental Baths were providing live entertainment at weekends. She presented herself, with her pianist and musical director Barry Manilow at her side, and was an immediate hit. Midler already had the requisite theatrical know-how, learned on stage in the Broadway production of *Fiddler on the Roof*, in which she graduated from the chorus to play the eldest daughter Tzeitel. The encouragement of the enthusiastic gay audience helped her to put aside her naturally shy and serious personality to become the boisterous, foul-mouthed 'Divine Miss M', the title of her best-selling 1973 album.

In a 1991 TV interview, Midler told Oprah Winfrey, 'They just loved me and they supported me and they bought my records and they carried on. When I stood in front of them – a couple of thousand men in towels ... I thought it was completely natural. You know, I must be a pretty odd person. They kicked me into the mainstream.' They were also pretty damn helpful to Barry Manilow in his ascent to the stars.

Midler made her starring film debut in *The Rose* (1979), a Twentieth Century-Fox release directed by Mark Rydell. Rose, a high-living rock singer exhausted from touring, wants a year off to rest, but her ambitious manager Rudge (Alan Bates) will not hear of it. Going into overdrive, Rose picks up a chauffeur, Dyer (Frederick Forrest), for casual sex which turns into the most fulfilling romance of her life. But he cannot take the pace and leaves her to her music. Her triumphant performance before a hometown audience turns out to be the last of her life. She succumbs to a combination of drink and drugs and dies, in a Horse Frightening scene. Midler's supercharged performance as the Janis Joplin-inspired singer won her an Oscar nomination for Best Actress, while Frederick Forrest was also nominated for Best Supporting Actor.

Apart from the filmed concert *Divine Madness* (1980), strictly for Midler fans only – her gags and jokes veer between the raunchy and the sick – her film career struck an impasse with *Jinxed!* (1982), a disastrous black comedy with Ken Wahl and Rip Torn. The production proved a nightmare for all concerned, Midler clashing with leading man Wahl and veteran director Don Siegel. The explosions on set were more talked about than the finished film and drove Midler into a nervous breakdown, from which it took her almost three years to recover.

The revival of Midler's film fortunes came via the unexpected agency of a Disney film, released through its 'adult' distribution arm, Touchstone. *Down and Out in Beverly Hills* (1986), produced, co-written and directed by Paul Mazursky, proved an extremely funny comedy, based on the old French classic *Boudu*

Above: Lily Tomlin and Bette Midler in *Big Business* (1988).

sauvé des eaux, about a tramp (Nick Nolte) who tries to drown himself in the swimming pool of a *nouveau riche* couple (Midler and Richard Dreyfuss). They 'adopt' him as an offbeat *deus ex machina*, who proceeds to turn their lives upside-down and awaken them to a new set of values they never knew existed. In character, Midler makes a tasteless AIDS joke which upset her public. Also in 1986, Midler played another *nouveau riche* wife, this time to Danny De Vito, in *Ruthless People*. De Vito plans to kill her, but she is kidnapped by a couple he has swindled, played by Judge Reinhold and Helen Slater. The ensuing black farce is well handled by directors Jim Abrahams, David Zucker and Jerry Zucker.

In 1987, with her movie career now heading into its stride, Midler co-starred alongside Shelley Long in *Outrageous Fortune*, as a couple searching for a missing boyfriend. One of the girls is outrageous and flamboyant (guess which), the other snidely bitchy, although prim and pretty. The plot goes to outrageous lengths for laughs, involving the main characters with chemical warfare, Russian agents and the CIA.

In *Big Business* (1988), Midler and Lily Tomlin star as two sets of identical twins, switched at birth, who come across each other as grown-ups in the Big Apple. One Midler-Tomlin pairing heads a ruthless New York City Corporation, the other organises an oppressed trade union, setting the scene for a major clash. The corporate Midler's lovers, played by Edward Herrmann and Daniel Gerroll, are seduced by the rustic charm of country boy Fred Ward – the Horse-Frightening moment.

After the comic turbulence of *Big Business*, the Divine Miss M plunged into tear-jerking territory, first with Barbara Hershey in *Beaches* (1989), which Midler also co-produced. Hershey plays an upper-class attorney, Midler a singer/actress determined to make the big time. The second weepie was *Stella* (1990), directed by John Erman, a remake of the Barbara Stanwyck hit *Stella Dallas* (1937). This was a sad mistake. Not only was Miss M miscast as the slovenly mother of teenage Trini Alvarado, but the storyline, already dated in the thirties, was bathetic in the nineties. One wonders what her bath-house admirers made of it. A teaming with Woody Allen for *Scenes From a Mall* (1991) – she a high-powered psychologist, he a major promoter – turned out flat, stale and unprofitable, despite the best efforts of director Paul Mazursky.

The sentimental showbiz drama *For the Boys* (1991), which reunited Midler with *Rose* director Mark Rydell, has its moments but never quite gels. Midler and an uncomfortable James Caan star as a bickering singer and comedian, whose professional and personal relationship stretches from the 1940s to the 1960s. While the World War Two scenes work well enough, the film overreaches itself when trying to deal with the Hollywood blacklist and the Korean and Vietnam wars.

In Disney's *Hocus Pocus* (1993), Midler starred as a 17th century witch, awakened from a 300-year siesta with sisters Kathy Najimy and Sarah Jessica Parker. The movie briefly comes alive when Bette sings 'I Put a Spell on You'; otherwise this is only for tolerant kiddies. Other nineties offerings include the made-for-TV *Gypsy* (1993), with Midler in the Mama Rose role previously played by Angela Lansbury and Rosalind Russell. *The First Wives Club* (1996), directed by Hugh Wilson, has a strong cast, including Goldie Hawn, Diane Keaton, Maggie Smith and Sarah Jessica Parker, yet Midler seems uncomfortable as a wistful single mother – her occasional catty lines are out of character.

For some, the Divine Miss M remains 'caviar to the general'.

CHER (1946-) (Cherilyn Sarkisian La Pierre)

Cher's outgoing image reminds one of a latter-day Tallulah Bankhead, although Cher is technically 'straight' – whatever that really means. Her outspokenness, penchant for costumes so skimpily cut as to show most of her credentials, multi-faceted career and a taste for younger men that only Joan Collins exceeds – all have appealed to gay audiences from the beginning.

Her recipe for living is an expansive one: 'a girl could wait for the right man to come along, but in the meantime that still doesn't mean she can't have a wonderful time with all the wrong ones!' Nevertheless, she was unhappy when her daughter Chastity came out as a lesbian. Cher claimed that it wasn't the fact of her sexuality that upset her, but that everyone else seemed to know but her mother. Chastity, the daughter of Sonny Bono, Cher's first partner and husband, may have felt like reminding her of her oft-repeated dictum, 'I answer to two people:

myself and my God.' In any case, mother and
daughter soon became best friends again.

Born in El Centro California, Cher's mother
was part Cherokee Indian, her father
Armenian. *En route* to fulfilling her ambition to
be accepted as a serious actress, Cher teamed
up with musician Sonny Bono, whom she married in 1969. Their act took off like greased
lightening and their top forty hits and TV series
in the sixties and seventies brought a sanitised
version of contemporary youth culture into the
mainstream. Their television shows combined
music and comedy, with Cher as either host or
co-host with Sonny, starting with *The Sonny
and Cher Nitty Gritty Hour* in 1970. *The Sonny
and Cher Comedy Hour* followed the next year
and *The Sonny and Cher Show* in 1976.

Sonny and Cher's joint film career was rather
less successful, although *Chastity* (1969) – the
inspiration for their daughter's name – now enjoys
a certain notoriety. Bono wrote and produced the
film (and composed the music) for Cher, who
stars in the title role. Her character chooses the
name Chastity for herself as it means purity and

abstinence. She speaks her lines in a detached,
unemotional way and much of it is in voiceover
soliloquies as she addresses herself at various
junctures, almost pushing herself to experience
everything she can. Chastity has run away from
home in search of a more meaningful life and
hitchhikes her way around Arizona. She shares a
room with a truck driver but he is so bewildered
by her philosophising that he doesn't attempt to
sleep with her. She then meets a young student
who takes her for food and coffee and lets her
sleep in his bed. Attracted by the idea of domesticity, she goes out to buy some groceries but,
stepping into a church on the way, gets freaked
out by the confessional box and hitches another
ride, ending up in a Mexican border town. There,
she persuades a pimp to take her to a bordello
where she humiliates a shy, gawky American student and takes $40 for the privilege. She meets
the madam, Diana Midnight (played by Barbara
London), a tough but attractive older woman, who
takes a fancy to her and there follows a long
sequence of the two going shopping and Diana
buying Chastity clothes. The two then go to a park

and Chastity plays on the slides while Diana looks on maternally. During one scene Diana takes Chastity into the room where all the prostitutes wait for punters and touches one of them suggestively. She kisses another one on the lips, an act received with pleasure by the prostitute, but then slaps her viciously on the cheek, to demonstrate to Chastity the power that she has over them. There is then a suggestion of lesbian sex, mainly consisting of close-ups of fingers on unidentifiable bits of flesh, with a voiceover by Chastity reflecting on why she likes being touched by this woman when she's never enjoyed it before, and on the nature of lesbianism ('maybe they want to be mothers'). Chastity then turns on Diana and runs away back to the student and they spend a night together. Once again she is enamoured of the idea of domesticity but, alone in the house, she is haunted by memories of being molested by her father, and she runs out onto the highway and collapses. Surprised at the film's R rating in the US, *Motion Picture Herald* opined that 'not even the bordello scenes carry any suggestion of pornographic intent.'

Sonny and Cher had appeared together in William Friedkin's *Goodtime*, but Cher's film career really took off in Robert Altman's *Come Back to the Five and Dime, Jimmy Dean, Jimmy Dean* in 1982. One year later, she was nominated for a best supporting actress Academy Award for her performance as Meryl Streep's hardheaded, unglamorous, lesbian roommate in *Silkwood*. Meanwhile, Cher did not sacrifice the camp flamboyance of her singing career, her fondness for tattoos and her exhibitionist fashion sense. Rumours circulated of plastic surgery, even of having ribs removed to enhance her figure, which she later denied. She owned up only to having had a nose job. She stoked the fires of her publicity while appearing to douse them.

Cher's clashes on set with Peter Bogdanovich were reported in full, although her performance in his film *Mask* earned her a Best Actress

Award at Cannes in 1985, along with Norma Alexandra. Emmys, Golden Globes and other awards proliferated, but it was the Oscar she coveted and won in 1987, playing the mother of an eccentric Brooklyn/Italian family in *Moonstruck*. The same year she joined Susan Sarandon and Michelle Pfeiffer in *The Witches of Eastwick* and then turned back to her lucrative singing career for a few years, before her next film *Mermaids* in 1990. This was chiefly notable for her having replaced the original director, Frank Oz, with ex-actor Richard Benjamin.

Hugely successful exercise videos, à la Jane Fonda, kept Cher busy until she filmed *Faceless* in 1995. She then concentrated furiously again on her recording career. Among her hits was a tribute to Elvis, 'Walking in Memphis', accompanied by a spot-on impression, in costume, of the King himself. In 1998 she beat Celine Dion's 'My Heart Will Go On' as the best-selling single of the year with 'Believe'. A highlight of 1999 was the Italian-made comedy *Tea with Mussolini*, in which she held her own with the cream of Britain's Damehood – Maggie Smith, Joan Plowright and Judi Dench. Reports are that they all behaved like perfect ladies.

Her raven, shoulder-length tresses have lately turned to platinum blonde. She's a knockout in any colour.

MADONNA [1958-]
[Madonna Louise Veronica Ciccone]

Throughout her career, Madonna has supported gay lifestyles and gay rights. The images in her music videos and picture book, *Sex* (1992), are frequently homo-erotic. She was one of the first showbusiness supporters of AIDS charities, and the honours she has received from the Gay and Lesbian Alliance Against Defamation speak for themselves. Her identification with the gay world came when her dance teacher

Above: Jonathan Pryce and Madonna in *Evita* (1996).

took her, at the age of 16, to a gay club, where she immediately felt at ease. Previously, at high school dances, she had felt an outsider. There was obviously something very different about her even then: girlfriends of mine have often felt acutely out of place in gay bars.

Born in Bay City Michigan, Madonna was brought up by her father after her mother's death when she was six. After a year at the University of Michigan, she left to become a dancer in New York. Fame did not come swiftly enough to satisfy her overwhelming ambition, so she recorded a demo, played drums and guitar, and made an impression on the disco scene. A recording contract with Sire Records set her on a meteoric musical career, much helped by her own powerful instinct for self-publicity.

Despite a film career that has rarely lived up to its hype, Madonna has become the most famous woman of her generation. She has a talent for constantly redefining her image, through her music videos, notably 'Like a Virgin' (a number one hit in 1984) and 'Justify My Love' (1990), the documentary *Truth or Dare* (1991; *In Bed with Madonna* in the UK) and, to a lesser extent, her movies. She has been sex goddess, whore (in 1990 the Vatican described her Blond Ambition tour as 'one of the most satanic shows in the history of humanity'), virgin and gender-bender,

alternately excoriated and lauded by the critics.

Her troubled marriage to Sean Penn (1985-89), which spawned their joint appearance in the disastrous comedy *Shanghai Surprise* (1986), made headlines on an almost daily basis for their spectacular fall-outs. The movie rapidly qualified as one of the Worst Films of All Time. Love affairs with Warren Beatty and a host of others have been covered by tabloid and mainstream press alike, while her relationship with comedienne Sandra Bernhard has been left with a large question mark. Sandra has said Madonna was the best lover she ever had, while Madonna stokes the fires of speculation by saying maybe she did and maybe she didn't, though she confesses she would rather people think she did, just so they can fantasise while buying her records that she 'was eating someone's pussy.' Has the Divine Miss M ever excelled this for a public utterance? Maybe with 'Every straight guy should have a man's tongue in his mouth at least once.'

Leaving aside the softcore 'art' movie *A Certain Sacrifice* (1979), Madonna's film breakthrough came in *Desperately Seeking Susan* (1985). She was ideally cast as the free spirit Susan, who helps bored New Jersey housewife Rosanna Arquette lose her inhibitions in the bohemian atmosphere of Greenwich Village. Directed by Susan Seidelman, the film proved a runaway success with audiences and critics alike. Madonna had to wait five years for another hit movie, Warren Beatty's *Dick Tracy* (1990). A successful spoof on the Chester Gould comic strip, the film featured a fine cast, including Dustin Hoffman as Mumbles and Al Pacino as Tracy's arch rival, Big Boy Caprice. Madonna appeared as chanteuse Breathless Mahoney, singing a couple of Stephen Sondheim songs, besides being at her kookiest and most alluring. Director-star Beatty again proved that he is more than just an enduringly pretty face and Madonna showed herself to be an effective team player.

She demonstrated this further in *A League of*

Their Own (1992), directed by Penny Marshall, based on a real-life all-girl baseball team of 1943, formed when most of the major league's players were away at war. Geena Davis, Lori Petty, Rosie O'Donnell and Madonna are the Rockford Peaches of Illinois, with Tom Hanks as their alcoholic over-the-hill manager in a wonderfully offbeat comedy performance. Madonna successfully plays against type, offering a hilariously rambunctious characterisation in an outstandingly funny movie.

From these delightful sorties into comedy, it's a swift and painful descent to *Body of Evidence* (1993), directed by Uli Edel. The body is the over-exposed but nubile one of Madonna herself, playing an S & M hellcat, manipulating handcuffs, candle wax and rock-hard thighs. Sleazy lawyer Willem Dafoe is out to prove her innocent of murdering her elderly lover with rough sex. The script defeats him, and his all-too-limp performance is not helped by the leading lady's gyrating, lip-licking, eyelash-batting displays, both in and out of bed. Frank Langella, soon off the screen, plays her bisexual husband. It's films like this that give Madonna a bad name.

That said, Abel Ferrara's *Dangerous Game* (1993) plumbed the lowest depths to which Ms Ciccone's movie career has so far descended. It's the story of a *ménage à trois* in a film-within-in-a-film, fictional director Harvey Keitel leading 'stars' Madonna and James Russo through a tale of violence, drug abuse and debauchery. The distinction between illusion and reality becomes blurred and the resultant threesome provides several Horse Frightening scenes. The film is well directed and acted but 'rotten to the core' (vide Coward lyric) and ultimately nihilistic. From here on, Madonna could only rise to the surface and beyond.

Madonna's film career finally got back on track with the lavish musical *Evita* (1996), based on the smash hit Andrew Lloyd Webber-Tim Rice stage show. Her performance as Eva Peron, from prostitute to actress to dictator's wife and, ultimately, to uncanonised saint, is, in my eyes, magnificent. It may come to be remembered as her supreme cinematic achievement, aided by co-producer, co-writer and director Alan Parker. Madonna strikes the right chord between the inherent humanity which made the people love Evita Peron and the ruthlessness that took her to the top and made her many enemies. Alan Parker handles the *mise en scéne* with superlative skill, and there are outstanding performances from Antonio Banderas, as Che Guevara, on-screen narrator and purveyor of the film's moral viewpoint, and Jonathan Pryce, who fleshes out the shadowy figure of General Peron as definitively as possible. An Academy Award went to Lloyd Webber and Rice for Best Original Song, 'You Must Love Me', though the nominations omitted the star, who amply deserved her Golden Globe Award for Best Everything.

The Millennium Madonna has moved into motherly mode, with two children of her own and marriage to British film director Guy Ritchie. In *The Next Best Thing* (2000), directed by John Schlesinger, she is again a mother, but with a slight difference. The father is her gay best friend on and, perhaps, off screen, Rupert Everett, the handsomest male star to come out for gay rights. In the story they fall into bed together, after much drink has been taken, and the result is baby Sammy. They are happy as a family for five years, until mother falls for a hunky investment banker (Benjamin Bratt). Everett, standing up for his parental rights, takes the matter to court. The ending is a compromise – Hollywood is still not prepared to come right out for gay rights. Peter Preston, in the *Guardian*, wrote, 'The best thing by far is Madonna, here cast as an identifiable human being, possessed of warmth and some feelings. This suits her well …who knows, she may even be playing herself at last.'

Madonna may be one of those rare mortals capable of having their cake and eating it. □

6 NOWT SO QUEER...

PRIVATE LIVES OF THE STARS, PART ONE

ALLA NAZIMOVA (1879-1945)

Born in the Crimea, Russia, Nazimova emigrated in 1905 and went to Hollywood in 1916. By that time she had established herself as a darling of the Russian, then the American, stage, distinguishing herself as a leading interpreter of Ibsen on Broadway. She was the first student of Stanislavsky to make an American reputation, indeed, under the single name of Nazimova, a towering one. Her bold, stylised acting was highly idiosyncratic, not to say downright bizarre, her personality distant and aloof.

Her film contract was an extraordinary one, bringing her not only an enormous salary but her own production unit and final approval on all stories, casts and directors. Contemporary female stars, such as Mary Pickford, Lillian and Dorothy Gish, and Mae Marsh, exemplified innocent American maidenhood. Among these women, Nazimova created scandal and dismay as the official hostess of Hollywood's lesbian community. Her outrageous parties at her famous home on Sunset Boulevard, the Garden of Allah, became the talk of the town.

She produced many of her own films and was

Opposite: Cary Grant in *I Was A Male War Bride* (1949).

often directed by her *soi-disant* husband, Charles Bryant, whom she had met on Broadway, and he co-starred in several of her films, including the first, *War Brides* (1916). In *Camille* (1921), she played the title role and, as producer, selected the already brightly shining luminary Rudolph Valentino to co-star as Armand. His next films were to establish him as the greatest male star of silent cinema. His wife, Natasha Rambova, was also Nazimova's lover.

After the financial debacle of her *Salome* (1923), Nazimova sought to reinstate herself in the privileged position she had enjoyed at Metro: inflated salary, control over almost everything. Instead, she found how unforgiving the studio system could be. She had persisted in playing young parts well into her forties – at 40, she was a ten-year-old in *The Brat* (1919), her teenage Salome was 43, and her 1924 *Madonna of the Streets* looked every day of her 45 years. With her popularity waning, Nazimova reluctantly agreed to play Jack Pickford's mother in *My Son* (1925). Her reviews mostly welcomed this overdue change of image, but no film offers followed and she returned to the stage.

It would be 15 years before Nazimova faced the movie cameras again. In 1940, with a helping hand from her old friend George Cukor, she played a once-famous German-Jewish actress in MGM's anti-Nazi melodrama *Escape*. Her character, Emmy Ritter, is rescued from a concentration camp by screen son Robert Taylor, who co-starred in this smoothly packaged propaganda with Norma Shearer, directed by Mervyn LeRoy. The following year, Nazimova had another famous bisexual son, Tyrone Power, in Rouben Mamoulian's lush Technicolor remake of *Blood and Sand* (1941). Power had specially asked for her in the part and again she received good notices. Nazimova's final movies, the year before her death at 66, were *Since You Went Away* and *The Bridge of San Luis Rey* (both 1944).

MONTY WOOLLEY [1888-1963]
[Edgar Montillion Woolley]

Monty Woolley was born in New York City, where his father owned the Grand Union Hotel, famous for the celebrities who stayed there. At Yale he met and became close friends with Cole Porter and they put on student shows together. Before World War One, Woolley had studied at Harvard as well as Yale, returning to the latter after the war as a teacher of Drama and English Literature. At 27 he went to Broadway to direct Cole Porter's musical *Fifty Million Frenchmen* (1918), which was a huge success, as was *Porter's Jubilee*. In 1919 Woolley made his acting debut at 30 in his friend's *On Your Toes*.

Twenty-seven years later, he played himself in Michael Curtiz's biopic *Night and Day* (1946), starring Cary Grant as Porter, with no hint of the composer's homosexuality; Alexis Smith played his wife. In the 1980 TV show *Song by Song by Porter*, Ned Sherrin referred to Cole's 'well-manicured public married life' as being glossy and brittle, and bullet-proof.

Monty Woolley, however, did not pretend about his sexual orientation. He saw no reason to get married, but 'coming out' was not the practice in those days. His preference for sex with black men, towards the end of his life, led to his estrangement from his long-time best friend, Cole Porter, after Woolley set up house with his black manservant, with whom he had fallen in love. Cole, two years Monty's junior, outlived him by one year. In *The Man Who Came to Dinner* (1941), based on the hit Broadway play, Woolley's character Sheridan Whiteside is asexual, in accordance with the mores of the time, although the critic Alexander Woollcott, the inspiration for the character, was famously gay.

Woolley, bypassed for an Academy Award for his classic first starring part, was awarded a Best Actor nomination for *The Pied Piper* (1942), directed by Irving Pichel. Woolley played a British father who lost his son in the war and escorts a group of children from Nazi-occupied France back to safety in England. Irving Pichel also directed the 1942 film version of Emlyn Williams' excellent play *The Light of Heart*, translated to the screen with only medium success. It is partially redeemed by the performances of Woolley as a once-famous actor whose career has been ruined by alcoholism (shades of John Barrymore) and Ida Lupino as the daughter who has devoted her life to looking after him. The American title was *Life Begins at Eight-Thirty* – then the usual time for curtain-up in the States. Woolley's drunken Santa Claus provides a comedy highlight amidst all the sentimentality. But, after three movies in rapid succession, he began to scale down his screen appearances.

The next year, Woolley made the most charming yet low-key comedy of his career: *Holy Matrimony* (1943), with Gracie Fields. After this comic gem, Woolley joined John Cromwell's all-star David O Selznick-scripted study of a family left at home when the menfolk go off to fight in

World War Two, *Since You Went Away* (1944). The film was a smash hit worldwide, Claudette Colbert giving one of her most richly satisfying performances as the army wife coping with her two daughters, Jennifer Jones and Shirley Temple, when her husband leaves for the war. Monty Woolley plays Colbert's irascible lodger, a retired army colonel, whose sarcastic remarks provide much of the film's humour. He, Colbert and Jones were all Oscar-nominated, among a cast which included Robert Walker, then married to Jennifer Jones, Joseph Cotten, Lionel Barrymore, Agnes Moorehead and Nazimova, in her penultimate film role.

Woolley was teamed again with Gracie Fields in *Molly and Me* (1945), directed by Lewis Seiler, with Fields as an ex-actress who takes a job as housekeeper to Lord of the Manor Woolley. Once again their teaming was incomparable but the film, although amusing when they are on the scene, came several years too late. The story had been devised as a vehicle for Red-Hot Momma Sophie Tucker when MGM had her under contract some five years previously. When her talking picture career did not materialise, the story was hastily dusted down for Gracie Fields and Roddy McDowall, then aged 12. By the time the movie came to be made, Roddy was 17 and the idea of Gracie willing him to sleep by singing 'Christopher Robin' was faintly ludicrous. Both actors protested but director Seiler was intractable. Fields had hoped for John Stahl again but he was busy on another project. Discussing her career in Capri, she told me that, at the end of filming, Seiler had the bright idea of adding a scene in a pub where she could sing some of her well-known songs. In *Holy Matrimony*, during the final scene (when Alice and her husband have decamped to a tropical island), she sings a few bars of 'Genevieve, Sweet Genevieve' while preparing lunch (kangaroo chops with crocodile sauce!).

An idea of Twentieth Century-Fox boss Daryll

THE MAN WHO CAME TO DINNER

1941 Warner Bros 112 mins b/w
Producers: Jerry Wald, Jack Saper; Director: William Keighley;
Screenplay: Julius J Epstein, Philip G Epstein (based on the play by
George S Kaufman and Moss Hart); Cinematographer: Tony Gaudio
Bette Davis, Ann Sheridan, Monty Woolley, Jimmy Durante, Richard Travis, Reginald Gardiner, Billie Burke, Grant Mitchell, Elisabeth Fraser, George Barbier

Monty Woolley was one of America's favourite character comedians, invariably cast as an irascible and bombastic senior citizen. His bushy white beard was already a trademark by the time he repeated his Broadway triumph in the film version of *The Man Who Came to Dinner*. He played the part of Sheridan Whiteside, a character based on theatre critic Alexander Woollcott, one of the witty celebrities who met regularly at New York's Algonquin Hotel over lunch. The others included Noël Coward, Harpo Marx, Dorothy Parker and John Barrymore. Barrymore had been earmarked for the Whiteside role, but by that time in his career he was no longer able to memorise lines.

Happily for Warner Bros, Bette Davis was so entranced with the witty script that she was happy to play the secondary part of the celebrity's secretary, Maggie Cutler, as a welcome change from her usual heavy histrionics. She took top billing and praise for her restrained and witty performance, but Woolley ran away with the honours. He became an 'overnight' star after 25 years of playing movie cameos which always stood out because of his appearance and resonant voice.

William Keighley directed the cast of stars, thinly disguised as the kind of alumni with whom Woollcott came into contact. They included Jimmy Durante as a Harpo Marx-like comedian and Ann Sheridan, delightful as the actress so eager to ingratiate herself with the venomous-tongued radio critic that she gets herself smuggled into the house in a mummy case, forcing Whiteside to offer hospitality. After the latter's fall on the ice outside the front door of the social-climbing Stanleys (Billie Burke and Grant Mitchell), they are happy to accept the cantankerous intruder and his acolytes in exchange for their moment of glory. The aforementioned acolytes include mimic Reginald Gardiner, in a very funny impression of Noël Coward.

F Zanuck's – for a Technicolor musical to co-star Woolley and Fields with Joan Bennett and Cornel Wilde, called *Waltz Me Around Again, Willie* and to be directed by Walter Lang – did not, alas, come to fruition. Woolley's last top starring role, in 1951, a lighthearted dig at big business called *As Young As You Feel*, was based on a Paddy Chayevsky story and directed by Harmon Jones. The movie saw him cast as an employee who is retired at 65. To get even, he impersonates the president of his firm's parent company, lording it over everyone as only Woolley could. His unlikely co-star was the abrasive Thelma Ritter as his daughter-in-law and the excellent supporting cast included Jean Peters, David Wayne, Marilyn Monroe, Albert Dekker as an executive and Constance Bennett as his bored and glamorous wife, whose elegant exhibition dance with Woolley is one of the film's highlights. Bennett said of Monroe as she wiggled by, 'there goes a broad with her future behind her', which eventually turned out to be sadly true.

Monty Woolley made only one more movie appearance, in the 1955 remake of the musical *Kismet* with Howard Keel, Dolores Gray and Ann Blyth. He died at 75 from a kidney infection.

CLIFTON WEBB [1891-1966]
[Parmallee Hollenbeck Webb]

Clifton Webb was trained as a dancer and actor as soon as he could walk and was a seasoned performer by the age of ten. From singing with the Boston Opera Company at 17, he turned to ballroom dancing in earnest at 19 and often partnered one of the top dancers of the period, Bonnie Glass. When he left her to play straight dramatic roles on the London stage, he introduced her to his protégé, Rudolph Valentino, as her new partner. Valentino's sensual grace had received ample workouts in his days as a taxi dancer (polite term for gigolo).

Webb's first film, in 1920, was *Polly With a Past* and he made a few silents up to 1925, including *The Heart of a Siren* (1925). He gave up the screen for some 20 years in favour of the theatre, specialising in the polished wit of roles like Sheridan Whiteside in *The Man Who Came to Dinner*, which he toured in the US in 1940-41. He also performed in Wilde's *The Importance of Being Earnest* and Coward's *Blithe Spirit*.

In the thirties Joan Crawford was keen to co-star with Webb in an MGM musical to be called *Glitter*. During rushes it became apparent that his talking voice, a compound of hauteur, prissiness and boredom, would not be suitable for a romantic leading man and the project was quietly dropped. It was not until 1944 that he made his talkie breakthrough in Otto Preminger's classic thriller, *Laura*. The movie starred Gene Tierney in her finest performance, as the heroine who has already been murdered – apparently – at the beginning of the film. The storyline traces who did it through the narration of Webb's Waldo Lydecker, an acerbic columnist. The detective investigating the case (Dana Andrews) falls in love with the image of the dead girl which begins to emerge, and becomes deeply and personally involved in unmasking her killer. The suspects are Webb himself, Vincent Price as Laura's fiancé and Judith Anderson as his socialite lover and Laura's aunt.

For Webb this was the perfect star role – cynical, snobbish, sexually ambivalent and surrounded by characters who are all the antithesis of conventional. These include Tierney herself, the sex symbol embodied in Laura's portrait, her actual face supposedly obliterated by an assailant's shotgun blast; Andrews, whose obsession with her suggests necrophilia; Price, whose androgynous persona lent an extra dimension to any character he played; and the soon-to-be Dame Judith, inescapably trailing an ambience of Mrs Danvers, the actress as complex in performance as any of her peers on screen or stage. (Closest to Anderson in terms of quirky undertones was Agnes Moorehead, so adept at playing witches and devious women of all kinds.) Preminger's subtle direction, allied to the brilliant screenplay by a clutch of writers, and the atmospheric black-and-white photography by Joseph LaShelle, who won an Oscar, all did credit to Vera Caspary's riveting novel.

From this kick-start to major cinema stardom, Webb's career went from strength to strength. Already fifty-ish and at no point handsome or hunky, the passage of time never altered his style, or, noticeably, his looks.

Webb's sexual preferences were no secret in Hollywood. Reputedly, among several husky young stars to whom he extended a helping hand was James Dean. Webb had no need of a pretty girl as 'beard' to public occasions; his mother, Maybelle, was invariably his escort. They were among the film capital's legendary couples and Webb was inconsolable when she died in 1960. Noël Coward named him 'the world's oldest surviving orphan' and he only survived her by six years.

Webb's run of film hits was virtually uninterrupted. His second was another *film noir*, *The Dark Corner* (1946), directed by Henry Hathaway, in which he was the acerbic, wealthy art dealer who frames Lucille Ball's private detective employer, Mark Stevens, for murder. Webb was again Oscar-nominated for Best Supporting Actor in Edmund Goulding's superior 1946 film version of W Somerset Maugham's novel *The Razor's Edge*, about a young man (Tyrone Power) trying to find spiritual fulfilment. The film co-stars Gene Tierney and Anne Baxter who, along with Webb, give the standout performances.

The same year, 1948, Webb struck his comedy vein, which sustained his career for the next four years, with *Sitting Pretty*, directed by Walter Lang. Webb plays the remarkable housekeeper/babysitter, Mr Belvedere, to Maureen O'Hara and Robert Young. Webb repeated his hilarious

Above: A portrait of Clifton Webb in character.

performance in 1948, directed by Elliott Nugent, in *Mr Belvedere Goes to College*. Shirley Temple co-starred. In a change of pace and image, Webb proved his versatility (and his screen virility) by playing husband to the movies' 'perfect wife', Myrna Loy, and father of their copious offspring, among them Jeanne Crain, in *Cheaper by the Dozen* (1950), directed by Walter Lang. In this charming and witty comedy Webb played an efficiency expert, bereft of his customary acerbity. Also in 1950, he and Edmund Gwenn were cast as angels in *For Heaven's Sake* (1950), caring for married couple Joan Bennett and Robert Cummings, who are expecting their first-born. George Seaton was the director.

A third reprise of his old friend, in *Mr Belvedere Rings the Bell*, directed by Henry Koster in 1951, led to a successful teaming with

Ginger Rogers in *Dreamboat* (1952), written and directed by Claude Binyon, in which they played silent screen stars whose popularity has been revived by television – an early satire on the then-new medium. She, now a cabaret artiste, is all for the publicity, while he, a college professor, tries to dodge it. Webb returned to drama in Jean Negulesco's 1953 *Titanic*, with Barbara Stanwyck, Thelma Ritter and Robert Wagner. In his sixties he played Dorothy McGuire's love interest in *Three Coins in the Fountain* (1954), also helmed by Negulesco, and again for Henry Levin in 1959's *The Remarkable Mr Pennypacker*.

In 1956 Webb came to England to make *The Man Who Never Was* for director Ronald Neame, playing a British Intelligence officer who fools the Nazis by strategically positioning a dead body carrying misinformation. The film was a big success. Webb then went to Greece to film *Boy on a Dolphin* (1957), directed by Jean Negulesco. Webb plays villain to Alan Ladd's heroic archaeologist on the trail of sunken treasure in the Aegean Sea. Peasant girl Sophia Loren was along for glamour and added box-office appeal.

Webb died of a heart attack in 1966, four years after his final film *Satan Never Sleeps* (1962), directed by Leo McCarey. It was also McCarey's last movie. Webb and William Holden played Catholic missionaries in post-World War Two China.

Back in 1956, during a break in filming *The Man Who Never Was*, Webb's friend from the twenties, actress Dorothy Dickson, arranged a party at her Eaton Square flat for him and his mother Maybelle. The guests included Emlyn Williams plus John Clements and his wife Kay Hammond (the original ghost wife Elvira in Noël Coward's *Blithe Spirit*). The hostess thought it might please the Webbs if I, as her PR at the time, tipped off the London *Evening Standard* about the occasion. It did *not* please him when a reporter and photographer appeared. Webb, seated beside Maybelle, thundered 'Who is responsible for this?'

I owned up and, in his most intimidating Mr Belvedere manner, he asked how I had the effrontery to allow the press into Dorothy's private soirée. I explained I had thought it would be a nice gesture towards Maybelle to have a photo of her with her son and the other stars. Maybelle was a charming, twittery lady of the ilk of actress Laura Hope Crews (1880-1942) the Aunt Pittypat of *Gone With the Wind* fame. Maybelle beamed and Mr Belvedere became Mr Gracious. A photo was set up, Clifton on the couch with his arm round his mother's shoulder on one side, Dorothy Dickson on the other, the star guests ranged around. He asked if I would like to sit in front, at their feet: I explained that it would not be fitting, but thanked him profusely. From then on we were friends and at the end of the evening he invited me to join him and Maybelle at the Savoy for champagne. How could I refuse?

IVOR NOVELLO [1893-1951]
[Ivor Novello Davies]

The ultimate matinée idol from the twenties to his death, Novello was Wales' answer to Hollywood's Valentino, Novarro and the other Italianate lovers of the twenties and thirties. His classical profile was exactly right for the movies.

He made his name as a composer at the beginning of World War I with 'Keep the Home Fires Burning', which was to become one of the war's great marching songs. With the Valentino boom about to burst into full force, the so-similar Novello made his first film in 1920, *L'Appel du sang* (*The Call of the Blood*), a French film made in Sicily, in which he played the romantic lead. He hated himself in it, but it proved so popular that he was inundated with offers from movie producers. He made *Carnival* in 1922 and the same year saw *The Bohemian Girl*, his first film with Gladys Cooper, who had been

Britain's pin-up girl in WWI and by the twenties was a shining light of London's West End theatre. *The Bohemian Girl* was followed by another with Cooper, *Bonnie Prince Charlie*(1923), by which time the press had dreamed up a romantic affair between the two of them.

They were, in fact, close friends and remained so until Ivor's death but the one true female love of his life was his mother, 'Mam'. Madame Clara Novello Davies was an eccentric and flamboyant Welsh singer and music teacher, who had formed the Welsh Ladies' Choir. The latter's fame caused Queen Victoria to summon them to perform before her at her summer residence of Osborne, where she bestowed upon Madame Clara a jewelled medal, which she removed only on retiring to bed. Her eccentricity grew as the years passed, as did her fondness for a glass of bubbly, always on hand for a sip during her singing lessons; she would return from her withdrawing room as the lesson progressed, increasingly unsteady, and tell her astonished pupil, 'Metropolitan Opera, you!'

Novello's film career flourished during the twenties and thirties: in 1923 D W Griffith invited him to make *The White Rose* for him in the USA. The Griffith publicity machine called him 'the second Valentino' and trumpeted his great love for Gladys Cooper, with headlines calling them 'the most famous and beautiful couple in the British theatre'. *The White Rose* was filmed in Florida and was in no way comparable to Griffith's *Birth of a Nation* (1915) or *Intolerance* (1916), but Novello received excellent notices.

He was eager to return to England to work on his new play, *The Rat*, which he co-wrote with his old friend, actress Constance Collier. The story concerns a handsome Apache dancer in Paris, wanted by the police and 'adopted' by a lady of substance, played by Isabel Jeans, who also co-starred in the film version in 1925. This was one of his earliest successes and there were to be two further 'Rat' movies, *The Triumph of*

Above: Ivor Novello and June Tripp in *The Lodger: A Story of the London Fog* (1926).

the Rat (1927), again with Isabel Jeans, in 1926 and *Return of the Rat* in 1929. However, *The Lodger: A Story of the London Fog* (1926), an Alfred Hitchcock thriller in which the hero is suspected of being Jack the Ripper, is probably the best known of Novello's silent movies.

He made the transition to talkies with ease and went to Hollywood to star with Ruth Chatterton, Warner's First Lady at the time, in *Once a Lady* in 1931. She later co-starred with Anton Walbrook in the British-made talkie version of *The Rat* in 1937. There was a 1932 sound remake of *The Lodger* and a romance, *Sleeping Car*, with Madeleine Carroll in 1933, in which he played the train conductor, followed by the film version of his play *I Lived with You* in 1934, with Ursula Jeans and the young Ida Lupino. He was to give his final acting performance for the cinema the same year in *Autumn Crocus*, playing a Tyrolean mountaineer opposite Fay Compton.

During his time in Hollywood he was asked to transcribe his play, *The Truth Game*, which had successfully transferred to New York for a long run, into an MGM film vehicle for Robert Montgomery. On Broadway, Ivor had co-starred with Billie Burke; the film version emerged as

But the Flesh is Weak (1932), with Britain's Heather Thatcher opposite Montgomery. Another script to which Ivor contributed, and for which he was paid a substantial sum, was the first MGM version of Edgar Rice Burroughs' *Tarzan the Ape Man* (1932); there had been several versions before Johnny Weismuller inherited the role. The key words which Novello made part of film history were, from Maureen O'Sullivan to Weismuller: 'Me Jane – you Tarzan.' There's nowt so queer as Hollywood.

During his stay in the film capital, Novello, with his charm and outstandingly friendly nature, along with his celebrity as actor, playwright and film star, became part of the social scene. He was on intimate terms with such luminaries as Garbo, Clifton Webb, Grace Moore and singer Libby Holman, attending regular Saturday night parties, often fuelled by bathtub gin, at the apartment of his friend and fellow theatrical producer, Richard Rose. Joan Crawford had met Ivor upon his arrival and then introduced him to everybody who was anybody at MGM.

Back in England, he became the most influential figure in British theatre in the late 1930s as lessee of the vast Drury Lane Theatre, where he presented a series of his own spectacular musicals. The first of these was *Glamorous Night*, starring ex-Metropolitan diva Mary Ellis, which was to enjoy phenomenal success and a long run. Indeed, it was to continue to tour England throughout the war years. Ivor went on to act in his next two box-office triumphs, *Careless Rapture* and *Crest of the Wave*, both of which co-starred Dorothy Dickson. His run of seemingly unstoppable successes only came to an end with his production of Shakespeare's *Henry V* in 1938, the patriotic and stirring historical epic with himself in the title role and Dorothy Dickson as Princess Katharine of France. The play, which had won them both glowing notices and attracted enormous crowds to the opening, was taken off in its third week, a casualty of the blanket closing of all London theatres during the Munich Crisis.

Around this time, Ivor had his own small personal problem: his mother, who had grown in eccentricity as the years passed. Her spell teaching singing in New York had come to an end with her so deeply in debt that her school had to be forcibly foreclosed; Ivor sent $15,000 through his lawyer and she was put on the boat for England. Unfortunately, the shock of all this induced a stroke and she was unconscious throughout the journey. When she recovered, her loving son promised never to mention the American debacle and bought her a small house near Marble Arch; she began to teach again. She also re-organised her Welsh Ladies' Choir into 'The Singing Grandmothers'.

Times had changed and their concerts were a resounding failure, despite the free tickets she distributed so lavishly. 'Mam' was in her late seventies, with most of her choir ten years younger. Undaunted, she formulated a plan and announced to Ivor that she was going to take 60 of 'her girls' to Berlin to sing for Hitler – their slogan was to be 'Singing for Peace'! She said, 'When we sing for Hitler at the stadium there we're going to change from our Welsh costumes into little white angel dresses for our Grand Finale and release hundreds of pigeons, each one carrying on its leg a little message of peace.' Ivor could not dissuade her. She told him that everything had been arranged, the expenses paid by a titled friend of hers, and off The Singing Grandmothers went, first to Holland.

She sent a telegram, 'Concert halls filled to capacity. Deafening applause. Greatest success of my career. Onto Berlin. Send four thousand pounds immediately.' In fact, audiences were so sparse the Amsterdam Opera House cancelled the night's concert. Ivor despatched his secretary to Holland with a cheque to pay off the accumulated debts and ship the 61 ladies back home. Madame Clara fought all the way up the gangplank and, back in London, locked herself in her house for a month admitting no one, not even her son. During the week of the Munich Crisis she sat at her window watching buildings being sandbagged and said bitterly, 'If they had let us go to Berlin all this would never have happened.'

During 1949 Novello wrote another musical for Mary Ellis, *The Dancing Years*, which was his greatest success ever. When the theatres, which had been closed after the declaration of war in September 1939, re-opened, he took *The Dancing Years* on an 18-month grand tour and then returned with it to the West End where it ran, intermittently, for the next ten years. Mary Ellis, who had starred in the film version of Novello's *Glamorous Night* in 1936, had given up her part in *The Dancing Years* to do war work, her role being taken by Muriel Barron. Dorothy Dickson starred with Edith Evans in the first production to re-open in London during World War Two (at first for afternoons only) – the hugely successful Herbert Farjeon revue, *Diversion*. I visited each and every time I was able to wangle an army pass.

The ladies who were constantly portrayed in the press as being the loves of Novello's life did, in fact, have romantic aspirations regarding him, especially Gladys Cooper, whose coldness towards Dorothy Dickson endured until Ivor's death from a sudden heart attack in March 1951. He was, however, a loving friend to all of them and to everyone he worked with on stage and screen, but his enduring love was for actor Robert (Bobbie) Andrews, who stayed with him for most of his adult life and for whom Ivor wrote parts in many of his plays. Andrews outlived him for many years, as did Richard Rose and so many of his friends from the early days.

His relationship with Noël Coward was guardedly cordial. Coward, although he had no reason to do so, envied Novello's success as a composer and could not resist the occasional barbed remark, as on the opening night of one of Novello's Mary Ellis musicals, *Arc de Triomphe*. He said, 'Darling, the music was

wonderful and Mary adorable', then quickly changed the subject.

Though Novello was usually kind, supportive and gentle to everyone, there was a limit to his tolerance. In Hollywood Tallulah Bankhead invited him and Richard Rose to a dinner party for which she had been preparing all day; drink had been taken in copious quantities and she had obviously decided to shock everyone. She received her guests from the top of the stairs in a scanty costume which reminded everyone that she was famous for wearing no underwear – Hitchcock had to admonish her during *Lifeboat* that she was putting the crew off their work. At the party she flung her arms round everyone and when she finally put her legs on the table during dinner, they slid off, nearly sending Ivor's soup crashing to the ground. She talked incessantly about herself all night and succeeded in ruining the party for everyone. Ivor suddenly got up to leave, saying he had a very early call at the studio next morning. The hostess said, 'Darling, I haven't shocked you, have I?' He replied 'You haven't shocked me at all, but you have bored me intensely.' And he left.

POLA NEGRI [1894-1987]
[Barbara Apolonia Chalupiec]

Pola Negri was born in Janowa, Poland, supposedly the daughter of a gypsy violinist who died in Siberian exile. She studied ballet in Russia, began appearing in Polish films in 1914, and in 1917 went to Berlin at the invitation of Max Reinhardt. She became one of Germany's top stars, especially in films for Ernst Lubitsch. In 1921, she played the title role of the poet *Sappho*, an icon for all lesbians. Inundated with lucrative Hollywood offers, Negri signed with Paramount in 1923, making her American debut in the melodrama *Bella Donna*. Among a number of less rewarding roles, she played Catherine the Great in *Forbidden Paradise* (1924), directed by Lubitsch.

Apart from acting in so many films – sometimes four a year – what made Pola Negri a reigning queen of Hollywood was her earthy, exotic personality. She had a knack of courting publicity with high-profile marriages (to a count, then to a prince), also indulging in a protracted celebrity feud with Gloria Swanson. Not least among her Hollywood conquests were Charles Chaplin, who quickly got cold feet after their engagement, and Rudolph Valentino, whose high-pressure 'love affair' with Negri received wide press coverage. Negri subsequently did her damnedest to upstage Valentino at his own funeral, throwing herself on his coffin with armfuls of flowers and emitting passionate wails. Eventually she had to be prised loose from the bier, when she swooned with a low but penetrating moan, to be carried off and comforted by her admirers. Tallulah Bankhead called Negri a 'lying, lesbo, Polish dyke.'

The American public eventually tired of such displays, as well as Negri's increasingly phoney, offbeat screen image. The coming of sound presented another problem. Pola was handicapped by a thick, guttural accent, though she sang 'Paradise' charmingly, the theme song for *A Woman Commands* (1932). She flitted around Europe's film capitals, making *The Woman He Scorned* (1930) in Britain and *Fanatisme* (1932) in France before re-establishing herself in Germany in the late thirties, having convinced the Nazi authorities that she was not of Jewish origin. Showing at least some scruples, Negri sued a French journal for starting rumours that she was romantically involved with Adolf Hitler. Her biggest hits of the thirties were *Mazurka* (1935) and *Madame Bovary* (1936).

In 1943, after her grief over Valentino had subsided a little and Chaplin was happily married to Oona O'Neill, Negri made the headlines once more when she threatened to sue her long-time lover, a Texan heiress, because the lady got married. The marriage was short-lived, and after her divorce the heiress moved back in with Poland's gift to the movies.

When Negri made a brief screen comeback in 1964, after an absence of 21 years, in Disney's *The Moonspinners*, she showed that she had lost none of her flair for self-publicity. As Madame Habib, a wealthy jewellery expert, she was supposed to have a pet Siamese cat. But, referring back to her glory days when, between affairs with Valentino and Chaplin, Pola used to parade down Sunset Boulevard with a tiger on a leash, she suggested a cheetah would be more in character. Accordingly, the day Marlene Dietrich arrived in London for a concert, the front pages of the evening papers featured a picture of Marlene in an unflattering mini skirt, which was quite overshadowed by one of Negri walking her cheetah down Park Lane. Dietrich was not impressed and was reported to have said, 'Where does she think she is? Old Hollywood?'

RUDOLPH VALENTINO (1895-1926)
(Rodolfo Alfonzo Raffaele Pierre Philibert Guglielmi di Valentina d'Antonguolla)

Rudolph Valentino was the greatest idol of the silent screen. There had been popular male stars before him, but Valentino transcended the matinée idol status of Ronald Colman, reigning supreme from the early twenties to 1926, the year of his death. Valentino was unique: the wildly passionate sheik from far-off lands, with bedroom eyes, sweeping his female conquests off their feet in an aggressively sensual fashion totally at variance with the macho approach of the all-American screen idols of the day, like Wallace Reid and Douglas Fairbanks Sr.

Born and raised in the small Italian town of Castellaneta, Valentino emigrated at 18 to the USA, hoping to become an agricultural engineer. The nearest he came to that goal was working as a part-time jobbing gardener. He was twice arrested for petty theft and blackmail and sent to the Tombs, a notorious detention centre, after which he was reportedly kept off the streets by a couple of rich gentlemen. Valentino subsequently found a niche as a taxi dancer, earning substantial small change as a gigolo to enraptured dowagers.

A friend suggested he try motion pictures and his looks soon gained him a walk-on role in *Alimony* (1918). Various small parts as thugs and villains followed, until Valentino became an established member of Nazimova's exotic coterie. It was she who had secured his release from the Tombs. After playing Armand to her *Camille* (1921), Valentino's tango and passionate derring-do with Alice Terry in *The Four Horsemen of the Apocalypse* (1921), closely followed by *The Sheik* (1921), set the seal on his fame.

Nazimova arranged two marriages for Valentino with her ex-lovers. Reputedly, the first, to Jean Acker, was never consummated. When Natasha Rambova, his second wife, took over the direction of Valentino's career, she feminised his persona to such a degree that eventually she was banned from his sets and all her control removed. In films like *The Young Rajah* (1922), in which he was attired in a minimum of satins and beads, and *Monsieur Beaucaire* (1924), in powdered wigs and a maximum of heavy make-up, Valentino earned the lasting derision of his straight male fans.

Further embarrassment followed. Valentino was arrested on a bigamy charge for having married Rambova before receiving his *decree nisi* from Jean Acker, who was not above using the name Mrs Rudolph Valentino on her billing. This matter settled, Valentino made two films which seemed to restore his dwindling popularity: United Artist's *The Eagle* (1925) and *The Son of the Sheik* (1926). Then came a blast from the *Chicago Tribune*, headlined 'Pink Powder Puff'. It continued: 'When will we be rid of these effeminate youths, pomaded, powdered,

Above: Rudolph Valentino in *The Son of the Sheik* (1926).

bejewelled and bedizened, in the image of Rudy – that painted pansy.' A few months after this, Valentino was taken to a New York hospital with a perforated ulcer and died suddenly on 23 August 1926. Mass hysteria took over the population – and not only the females. Suicides were rife. Rumours were spread that Valentino had been poisoned by a discarded male lover.

Fan clubs today still honour Valentino's memory. On the anniversary of his death, a mysterious woman in black used to lay a wreath of flowers on his grave. Her anonymity was always protected.

JACK PICKFORD (1896-1933)
(Jack Smith)

The younger brother of Mary Pickford, one of the most popular and powerful female stars of the silent era, whose business acumen also made her one of the richest. She was devoted to her blondly handsome sibling, who started as a stage actor and, as the leading star of Biograph, she got him in there at the age of 14 as a juvenile.

When she signed her unprecedented million-dollar deal with First National, one of her conditions was a lucrative contract for Jack, who became a star in his own right and later co-directed a couple of movies. One of these, *Little Lord Fauntleroy* (1921), had Mary as producer, besides playing a dual role as Fauntleroy and his mother, Dearest. Jack did not appear in this one, although he did co-star with his sister in *A Girl of Yesterday* (1915), among others.

Jack Pickford's private life was wild and chaotic, not to say ambidextrous, and of his three actress wives, musical comedy star Marilyn Miller was the most famous. He starred in a variety of romantic roles and was perhaps the first Tom Sawyer on the screen, in 1917. He left movies in 1928, after *Gang War*, and devoted himself to his own pursuit of happiness, through alcohol and gay amours. He fell to his death from a window, after a bitter quarrel with a young man whose name was never disclosed. The cause of death was given as suicide while the balance of his mind was disturbed.

TULLIO CARMINATI (1899-1971)
(Count Tullio Carminati de Brambilla)

This 1930s forerunner to 1950s star Rossano Brazzi as the US and British movies' resident aristocratic Italian charmer was on the stage from the age of 15, made his film debut in

Above: A portrait of Tullio Carminati.

1912 and soon became one of Italy's top screen stars. With the coming of sound he was much in demand for romantic leads, with his attractive Italian accent.

In the mid-1930s he starred with a selection of Hollywood divas. These included dancer Lillian Harvey (born in England) in *Let's Live Tonight* (1935), Constance Bennett in *Moulin Rouge* (1934), and opera star Grace Moore in *One Night of Love* (1934). He starred with Mary Ellis in *Paris in the Spring* in 1935, the year he travelled to England after a return to Italian films for *La marcia nuziali* (1935). English producer-director Herbert Wilcox chose him as a romantic lead for his wife Anna Neagle in a triangular love story on the high wires in the circus drama *The Three Maxims* (1937), with Robert Douglas, and in *London*

Melody/Girl in the Street (1937), again vying for her affections with Robert Douglas. In this busy year in the UK, providing continental charm for top British stars, Carminati starred with Gracie Fields in *The Show Goes On*, Margaret Lockwood in *The Street Singer* and our leading Viennese import, Lilli Palmer, in *Sunset in Vienna/Suicide Squad*, from which he made a record of the English title song.

Carminati also had a couple of near-brushes with the law during all this career activity, thanks to his predilection for guardsmen. He was not always discreet in his choices and, during public appearances in connection with promotions, a studio publicity man was delegated to accompany him to see he did not stray too far towards the barracks.

During World War Two, Carminati had a period of relative inactivity – as an Italian, England was no longer an option for filming, but he did appear later in a British film with an Italian theme, starring opposite Phyllis Calvert in *The Golden Madonna* (1949). It was while he was making this that I interviewed him at his villa in Rome, overlooking the Tiber. He could not have been more charming, but, understandably, seemed a little sad that stardom had passed him by, although he did play supporting roles in several Italian films in the fifties and sixties.

He was seen again in the Hollywood production *Roman Holiday* in 1953, with Audrey Hepburn, produced and directed by William Wyler, and *El Cid* (1961), directed by Anthony Mann. After the American-made *The Cardinal* in 1963, Tullio Carminati retired, to watch the Tiber and his dreams of past glories flow by. The interview for which I saw him in Rome did not, in the end, materialise; the magazine *Picturegoer* was in a state of flux, trying to cater for television and what was then called The Hit Parade, and stars no longer entirely current did not get a look in.

RAMON NOVARRO [1899-1968]
[Ramon Samaniegos]

Ramon Novarro was born in Durango, Mexico. He was a dark and handsome Latin lover of silents and early talkies, in which his light singing voice was much in demand. He started in Los Angeles as a vaudeville performer and singing waiter, then went into films as an extra in 1917. In 1922, with Rudolph Valentino's sudden rise to superstardom, Novarro was publicised as a rival 'Latin Lover', starring in such movies as *The Prisoner of Zenda* (1922), *Scaramouche* (1923) and *The Arab* (1924).

He never achieved Valentino's phenomenal popularity, but had a good following of his own and really made his mark in the title role of *Ben-Hur* (1926). Novarro and Valentino had become

Above: A portrait of Ramon Novarro.

Above: John Williams, Elsa Lanchester and Charles Laughton in *Witness for the Prosecution* (1957).

before returning to Hollywood, playing only five character parts between 1949 and 1960.

Novarro's tragic end is, sadly, the main reason he is remembered now. With the collapse of his stardom he had become an alcoholic, haunting the gay bars to alleviate his loneliness. He picked up two young men, brothers, and took them home for sex. Unable to find his money, they took it in turns to beat him to death, using (it is said) a bronze dildo given to him (and modelled) by Rudolph Valentino. An even more ghoulish aspect of the slaying is that one of the boys called his girlfriend on the phone and described to her what was going on. Which is how they were caught. Appalled, she called the police and the assailants were jailed for life, after a sensational trial.

CHARLES LAUGHTON (1899-1962) and ELSA LANCHESTER (1902-1986) (Elizabeth Sullivan)

With respect, I think it would be fair to label these two 'The Odd Couple'. Their companionable but often rocky marriage endured from the late twenties until Laughton's death.

Laughton was one of the movies' truly great actors, yet he only won a single Oscar, for his performance in *The Private Life of Henry VIII*, filmed by Alexander Korda in England in 1933. In life, Lanchester was a genuine eccentric. Her early stage appearances included quirky cabaret acts in London's Bohemian clubs, while her film performances, often with her husband, were almost always extraordinary. These ranged from *Bride of Frankenstein* (1935) to her manic song and dance called 'Yoga Is as Yoga Does' as Madame Nehrina in 1967's *Easy Come, Easy Go* with Elvis Presley.

Laughton was the most unlikely film star of the thirties. At 28 he was portly and said of him-

close friends but Novarro was something of a loner and never married. He remained a romantic lead until the end of the silent era, with notable hits in *The Pagan* (1929), *In Gay Madrid* (1930) and *Call of the Flesh* (1930). His speaking voice passed the crucial test of early talking pictures and led to extra kudos as Greta Garbo's co-star in *Mata Hari* (1931).

Novarro's singing voice was heard to good advantage in *The Barbarian/A Night in Cairo* (1933), with Myrna Loy, and in the musicals *The Cat and the Fiddle* (1934) with Jeanette MacDonald, and *The Night is Young* (1934) with Britain's Evelyn Laye – although the latter film was a flop and Laye's last in Hollywood. *The Sheik Steps Out* (1937), a lame Valentino spoof, and the aptly titled *A Desperate Adventure* (1938) were his last starring roles in the USA, and Novarro filmed in France and Mexico self, 'I have a face like the behind of an elephant.' He often overacted, as did Elsa, but his best performances were pure magic. The first of her biographies, *Charles Laughton and I* (1938), pictured their marriage as idyllic, indulging in teenage larks and flying high on a swing they built between trees in the garden. In her 1983 book, published 21 years after Laughton's death, reality had been allowed to intrude to the extent that Lanchester claimed that two years into their partnership Laughton admitted his homosexuality, because he faced possible prosecution and incarceration after he had picked up a youth in a park. Her reaction, after he showed her the couch on which they had consummated their passion, was, 'Fine, but let's get rid of the couch', which she subsequently burned.

A more objective view of Laughton's life was taken by Simon Callow in his 1987 biography *Charles Laughton: A Difficult Actor*. Callow, a great admirer, did much to restore the balance away from Elsa's biased view by interviewing Charles' last lover, Terry Jenkins, in a 1987 TV programme and concentrating on Laughton's compassionate and intuitive acting, rather than the self-denigrating and unhappy picture he had widely circulated about himself.

As a team, the Laughtons created some memorable characters. In 1933, Elsa was Anne of Cleves to Charles' Henry VIII in a hilarious scene depicting the King and his new wife spending their honeymoon night playing cards. Alexander Korda directed with a great sense of period. The same director elicited two more remarkable performances from the couple. Laughton played the title role of the Dutch painter *Rembrandt* (1936), whose religious fervour inspired him to persevere in his art, despite poverty and lack of sponsorship. Lanchester played Hendrikje Stoeffels, the maidservant who becomes first the painter's mistress, then his wife. Gertrude Lawrence co-stars as her predecessor, a coarse woman who deserts him as his

Above: A portrait of Elsa Lanchester.

fortunes fail. Hendrikje dies in childbirth in a deeply moving scene. Artistically brilliant, the film was a financial failure.

Their next film together was Erich Pommer's *Vessel of Wrath* (1938), with Laughton as a drunken beachcomber and Lanchester as the prim missionary who sets out to reform him. The US title was *The Beachcomber*. All three films were made in England, as were two earlier silent shorts *Daydreams* (1928) and *Bluebottles* (1928), the year after which Charles excelled as a silent diner at a table in *Piccadilly* (1929), starring Anna May Wong.

Back in the USA, where they had first settled in 1932, the Laughtons made two all-star blockbusters together. The first was *Tales of Manhattan*, directed by Julien Duvivier in 1942. Laughton plays a conductor whose fortunes plummet after his wife picks up, in a pawnshop,

THE SIGN OF THE CROSS

1932 Paramount 124mins, 118 mins [1944 reissue] b/w
Producer: Cecil B DeMille; Director: Cecil B DeMille; Screenplay: Sidney
Buchman, Waldemar Young (from the play by Wilson Barrett);
Cinematography: Karl Struss
Fredric March, Elissa Landi, Charles Laughton, Claudette Colbert

DeMille's epic is typical Cecil B lavish history, with Laughton as an effeminate Nero, who actually mouths 'delicious debauchery' and fiddles while Rome burns. He clearly relishes the role, while a scorching lesbian dance scene merits a Horse-Frightening_award: religious groups protested indignantly and also objected to Nero fondling a nearly naked slave boy. Claudette Colbert, in training for her later role as DeMille's *Cleopatra*, plays Nero's nymphomaniac wife Poppaea beautifully, but somewhat toned down for the censor. Fredric March is the handsome but pure centurion after whom she lusts and Elissa Landi the Christian girl Flavia, to whom his heart belongs.

the tailcoat around which the story revolves. The second was *Forever and a Day*, in which Laughton is a Victorian butler to married couple Ian Hunter and Jessie Matthews, in her only American film. Lanchester plays a below-stairs tweenie; their segment was directed by Victor Saville in 1943. In 1948 Laughton played a publishing mogul who murders his wife, Rita Johnson, in *The Big Clock*. Lanchester played a dotty artist who becomes involved in the plot. Ray Milland and Maureen O'Sullivan also star, with O'Sullivan's husband, John Farrow, directing. The Laughtons' final film together was the 1957 *Witness for the Prosecution*, perhaps their most rewarding teaming. Lanchester was Oscar-nominated for Best Supporting Actress as Laughton's bullying nurse, Miss Plimsoll, upstaging everyone at their best, including her husband, Marlene Dietrich and Tyrone Power.

Charles Laughton was born in Scarborough, England, where his father was a hotel owner. He served on the front line in World War One and was gassed shortly before the Armistice. At 25 he entered the Royal Academy of Dramatic Art, then became a star of the West End stage, where he met and married Elsa Lanchester in 1929. His performance in *Payment Deferred* as a bank clerk whose financial difficulties lead him to commit murder took him and his wife to New York in 1931, where he recreated his original role. Laughton also starred in the film version, released the following year (1932), with Ray Milland and Maureen O'Sullivan, directed by Lothar Mendes.

Also in 1932, Laughton made one of the classic horror movies of all time, directed by the master of the genre, James Whale: *The Old Dark House*. Laughton plays Sir William Porterhouse, one of a group of young people forced to seek shelter from a rainstorm in a sinister house, where the mute, psychotic butler is played by Boris Karloff, in his first starring role. Other *Benighted* (to quote the original J B Priestley title) travellers are Gloria Stuart, Raymond Massey, Melvyn Douglas and Lillian Bond as the chorus girl partner of Sir William. At the end of the year, he starred in another horror classic, the kinky and much-banned H G Wells adaptation, *Island of Lost Souls*.

Of the 37 or so other Laughton films not already dealt with, it is possible to itemise only those which were classics in their own right or are memorable because of Laughton's outstanding performances and unusual co-stars. There were two with Carole Lombard: *White Woman* (1933) and *They Knew What They Wanted* (1940). There were also two with Deanna Durbin: *It Started with Eve* (1941) and *Because of Him* (1946). *The Barretts of Wimpole Street* (1934), directed by Sidney Franklin, contains one of Laughton's greatest performances, as Edward Moulton Barrett. Barrett is the sadistic and clearly incestuous father of poet Elizabeth, one of Norma Shearer's most memorable characterisations. When told to avoid inferences of incest, the actor said, 'They can't censor the gleam in my eye.' An Oscar-winning role, if ever there was one, but Laughton was not even nominated, although Shearer was. Fredric March presents a highly romanticised Robert Browning.

Ruggles of Red Gap (1935) contains some of Laughton's best comedy acting as the correct English butler; the role was also played in 1923 by Edward Everett Horton. The butler is lost by his impoverished master in a poker game to a rough and ready American couple played by Charles Ruggles and Mary Boland. The film, directed by Leo McCarey, was nominated for a Best Picture award, which actually went to another Laughton film of the same year, Frank Lloyd's *Mutiny on The Bounty*. The role of the execrable Captain Bligh won Laughton an Academy Award nomination. Other Best Actor nominations went to Clark Gable and Franchot Tone, while Frank Lloyd was nominated for Best Director. This was the first time in motion picture history that three actors were nominated for the same film.

1935 was surely Laughton's year of achievement. The year also saw his magnificent portrayal of Javert, the merciless Chief of Police in the best version of Victor Hugo's *Les Misérables*, directed by Richard Boleslawski. Fredric March is equally fine as Javert's lifetime adversary, Jean Valjean, whom the Chief hunts down remorselessly for stealing a loaf of bread to survive. Cedric Hardwicke is impressive as the kindly Bishop who restores Valjean's faith in humanity. Rochelle Hudson is suitably fragile in her role as Cosette.

The Hunchback of Notre Dame (1939), directed by William Dieterle, is the most moving version to date of Victor Hugo's classic novel *Notre Dame de Paris*, with another superlative performance by Laughton as the lonely, pathetic, misshapen bellringer, who falls in love with the beautiful gypsy Esmeralda (Maureen O'Hara). *Salome* was also directed by Dieterle, in 1953, with Rita Hayworth's interpretation contrasting vividly with Nazimova's Sapphic temptress, while both Laughton and Judith Anderson are in scenery-chewing form as Herod and his evil queen Herodias. *Young Bess* (1953), with Jean Simmons in the title role (directed by George Sidney) allowed Laughton to reprise his Henry VIII to considerable, though brief, effect. Deborah Kerr plays Henry's last wife, Catherine Parr, who outlived him. *Spartacus* (1960), starred Laughton as Gracchus, a wily Roman senator, and his film career ended with *Advise and Consent* (1962).

Elsa Lanchester was born in the London borough of Lewisham, danced with Isadora Duncan's troupe as a child and at the age of 16 began acting with The Children's Theatre in Soho. Her first film, in 1928, was *The Constant Nymph* for Basil Dean. Perhaps her most famous Hollywood role is her portrayal of the *Bride of Frankenstein* (1935), directed, as was the original, by James Whale, with Karloff once again playing the monster. Her make-up is imaginatively grotesque and she portrays the bride with considerable pathos, matching the touch of genius Karloff imparts to his role as her consort. In addition, she plays a deceptively demure Mary Shelley in the prologue.

After her trip to America with Laughton, she appeared as Clickett the maid in *David Copperfield* (1935), directed by George Cukor. Other dotty ladies in her repertoire included the mad sister in *Ladies in Retirement* (1941), another eccentric in *The Spiral Staircase* (1946) and the flirtatious wife in Danny Kaye's *The Inspector General* (1949). In 1958 she played a genteel urban witch in *Bell, Book and Candle*. Her first nomination for Best Supporting Actress came in 1950 for playing a nun in *Come to the Stable* (1949) starring Loretta Young, who was nominated for Best Actress. Later film appearances included *Mary Poppins* (1964), *Willard* (1971) and *Murder by Death* (1976). Lanchester outlived her husband by 22 years.

WILLIAM HAINES [1900-1974]

The name of William Haines is unlikely to strike a chord with any but those whose film-going dates back to the twenties and early thirties, or film buffs and cinema historians. He was one of the jewels in MGM's crown, a well-loved romantic lead whose stock-in-trade was innocent boyishness, the kind that any girl would be happy to take home to mother.

Haines graduated with honours from military school, then worked on Wall Street as an office boy. In those days the traditional rise to stardom was via catching the eye of a talent scout – in Haines' case from Goldwyn – who offered the handsome youth a film test. He arrived in Hollywood in 1922 and one year later was already a leading man, making his debut in *Three Wise Fools* (1923). Among his most successful films were *Tower of Lies* (1924) and *Sally, Irene and Mary* (1925) with newcomers Joan Crawford and Constance Bennett. The following year *Brown of Harvard* was a big box-office hit. His best film, however, was *Show People* in 1928 with Marion Davies, a brilliant satire on Hollywood.

Haines had no problem making the transition from silents to sound and made a big success in *The Adventures of Get-Rich-Quick Wallingford* in 1931. Haines was a friend of director George Cukor and, like him, made no secret of his sexual orientation, to which the studio was prepared to turn a blind eye during the days of his success. By 1934 his time for playing young co-eds was drawing to a close. He made his last film during that year, *The Marines are Coming*. The same year Haines was caught in a local YMCA with a soldier. Louis B Mayer called him to his office and ended his tirade by threatening Haines that he had to give up his boyfriend, Jimmy Shields, or his contract would be cancelled. Without hesitation, Bill told him to tear it up.

Happily, Haines had more than one string to his bow. He had, at that time, already start-ed to dabble in interior design, encouraged by two of his best friends, Joan Crawford and Carole Lombard, who were his first clients. Claudette Colbert, Norma Shearer, Joan Bennett and Lucille Ball followed them.

Haines was a regular at George Cukor's parties, many of which were exclusively male. A story circulated that, on one occasion, after much drink had been taken, Billy, as his friends called him, seduced Clark Gable and thereby enraged the aggressively macho Gable, an incident which was to have repercussions some years later. During the filming of *Gone With the Wind*, there was a party at which someone gossiped, 'George is directing one of Billy's old tricks.'

In fact, it seems extremely unlikely that Haines, as a close friend of Gable's wife Carole Lombard, would have upset him, considering that they met so often socially. Cukor had worked for a year on pre-production before Vivien Leigh's Scarlett O'Hara had been chosen. The director got on extremely well with her and co-star Olivia De Havilland, but, so the story went, Gable thought Cukor was concentrating on the girls to his detriment. The star had stormed off the set, declaring 'I can't go on with this picture. I won't be directed by a fairy.' Three weeks into the filming, Cukor was replaced by Gable's choice, Victor Fleming.

Leigh and De Havilland continued to be coached by George Cukor, whom their co-star persisted in calling 'that fag'. This was a flagrant case of the pot calling the kettle black, considering the rumour that Clark Gable's all-male hunting parties were as carefully orchestrated by the studio as Tyrone Power's dates with Loretta Young, Janet Gaynor *et al*. The more likely reason for David O Selznick firing Cukor as director was the frequent clashing between the two dominant moguls.

Haines' second career in interior decorating benefited him far more financially than continuing as the oldest college boy in North America would have done. He had neither the staying power, nor the versatility, of Humphrey Bogart, Spencer Tracy, Fredric March or even Clark Gable, whose 'secret' was at least as well kept as Barbara Stanwyck's. Haines even designed the Mocambo Club and the London residence of the then American Ambassador. Ten years after he quit MGM, William Haines and Jimmy Shields sent Mayer an anniversary card, saying 'And you said it couldn't last!' Haines died at 73, in 1974.

ERIC PORTMAN [1903-1969]

'A scholar and a gentleman' is a fitting description for one of England's most distinguished stars of stage and screen for more than 30 years. Eric Portman made his name as a haughty, cynical aristocrat in the 1930s, culminating in the 1937 version of *The Prince and the Pauper*, one of his very rare movie appearances in Hollywood, starring Errol Flynn and the Mauch Twins, Billy and Bobby. In the forties he showed his versatility by making appearances in some of Britain's finest war movies, including, *49th Parallel* (1941), *One of Our Aircraft is Missing* (1942) and *We Dive at Dawn* (1943). Portman also played warm and sympathetic parts, including a bluff Yorkshire working man for Launder and Gilliat in *Millions Like Us* (1943) and *Great Day* (1945).

His most sensational role was in Michael Powell and Emeric Pressburger's *A Canterbury Tale* (1944), as a member of the gentry and pillar of the community, a secret woman-hater who pours glue on girls' heads in the black-out. The subject caused some ribaldry among the press but, like Powell's later *Peeping Tom* (1959), it was ahead of its time and eventually acclaimed as a classic. In 1946 he pursued Dulcie Gray with murderous intent through a wooded island in London's Serpentine Lake in *Wanted for Murder*; she was rescued by Derek Farr. Portman played a public hangman with Ann Todd in producer Sydney Box's *Daybreak* (1947).

Above: Eric Portman and Sheila Sim in *A Canterbury Tale* (1944).

Although Portman was far from being a hater of women – he made a fine impression as the betrayed husband of Vivien Leigh in the 1955 film version of Terence Rattigan's *The Deep Blue Sea* and, on stage, of Mary Ellis in the Rattigan play *The Browning Version* – his sexual orientation veered strongly towards the 'stronger' sex. He also had a predilection for the good life. Peg Pearson, the continuity girl on *Daybreak*, who adored him, used to marvel that he could get through his work so impeccably after his generous morning cocktails, a mixture of brandy and sherry. Portman continued to work consistently on film and stage throughout the sixties until the year before his death. In 1966 he was outstanding as Dame Edith Evans' estranged husband in *The Whisperers* and, in 1968, he played a bisexual man who was married to his own daughter in *Deadfall*. The same year he made a cameo appearance in his final American film, *Assignment to Kill*.

CLAUDETTE COLBERT (1903-1996)
(Lily Claudette Cauchoin)

If there was such a thing as the perfect Hollywood star of the Golden Era, it could well be Claudette Colbert. For sheer charm, grace and elegance, both on and off set, she had few peers. Her private life was as immaculately laundered as her screen and stage persona. Colbert's marriages, first to actor/director Norman Foster (1928-35) and then to Dr Joel Pressman, who had treated her for a sinus and was married to her from late 1935 till his death in 1968, were apparently happy and above reproach.

From the thirties to the fifties, when so many remarkable screen personalities flourished, stars were expected to live their lives by the standards embodied in the Production Code, based on how the millions who filled the cinemas were presumed to be living *their* lives. Same-sex relationships were covered by the 'moral turpitude' clause, which could be applied to even the greatest stars, and careers could be snuffed out if sexual or any other transgressions were made public. In Hollywood, women who were lesbian or bisexual were secretly known as the 'Sewing Circle' and would close ranks to protect the public reputations of their members.

An outstanding example of this was Claudette Colbert, so well-loved both in her professional and private life that, in the course of more than 60 years on stage and screen, everyone with whom she came in contact could only have wished her well. She told Lawrence J Quirk, one of America's foremost film historians, that she had never had any intention of writing her autobiography, but for his illustrated and extremely comprehensive biography she co-operated fully. The result is, in fact, virtually a hagiography; she insisted she had no deep dark miseries to reveal.

A rumour that she and the ubiquitous Marlene Dietrich had been lovers when they were both at Paramount may have been based on the fact that they had been photographed sharing a well-publicised helter-skelter ride at a charity function! (On the other hand, as screenwriter Gore Vidal said in *The Celluloid Closet*, gays were so starved of fantasy-fodder that they were able to conjure up whole new scenarios from the most slender evidence.) In her later years, after the death of her devoted husband, Dr Pressman, Colbert shared her Barbados home with the brilliant actress Claire Trevor, six years her junior.

Born in Paris, Claudette moved with her family to New York at the age of six and attended Washington Irving High School and the Arts Student League, with ambitions to become a fashion designer. A chance meeting at a party led to her stage debut in 1923 and to parts on Broadway from 1925. Her film debut, *For The Love of Mike* (1927), was a silent film directed on a shoestring by Frank Capra, with Ben Lyon. She hated making it and was always tired, as she had to travel from film locations back to Broadway to appear in her hit play *The Barker* each night. She vowed never to film again and tore up her contract with First National.

The play was an enormous success and she went to London with it in 1928. A few less successful plays followed *The Barker*. Despite her vows, she returned to films in 1929, with the advent of talkies, probably because she felt that, despite the primitive and cumbersome sound techniques, she would be able to use her voice, one of her greatest assets, to advantage. She signed with Paramount, with whom she was to stay for 14 years. She made *The Lady Lies* (1929) with Walter Huston and *The Hole in the Wall* (1929) with Edward G Robinson, another recruit from the stage. In 1930 she appeared with Maurice Chevalier in their first film together, *The Big Pond* (and also in the French version, *La grand mer*). She also appeared in *Young Man of Manhattan* (1930) with her husband, Norman Foster, whom she had met and married during the run of *The Barker*. Ginger

Rogers, then 18, also starred.

Colbert's seventh film, in 1930, was *Manslaughter* with Fredric March, her last at the Astoria Studios in Queens. She also co-starred with March the following year in *Honor Among Lovers* (1931) for Hollywood's only female director of the time, the extremely masculine Dorothy Arzner. March said of the latter: 'On a set she was tough-minded and no nonsense. I never felt that I was dealing with a woman – she was one of the guys. My guess is that she made Claudette a little nervous.' Quirk, in his biography of Colbert, says of Monroe Owsley's performance as her sadistic husband: 'Under Arzner's guidance he emerged as a monster male – the kind who would drive any woman to another woman. But even Arzner did not dare to go to that extreme in 1931.' However, Arzner did encourage cameraman George Folsey to light and photograph Claudette to better advantage than in any of her previous films, while Colbert's later insistence that she be photographed only from her left profile was shown to be a practical career move.

Her second film with Chevalier, *The Smiling Lieutenant* (1931), had the ineffable advantage of being produced and directed by the stylish and witty Ernst Lubitsch, who invariably brought out the best in his actors. Again, a French version was made with Colbert and Chevalier speaking their native language, with a different supporting cast. After an affair with a café entertainer (Colbert), Chevalier is duty-bound to marry an ugly-duckling princess, played by Miriam Hopkins in only her second movie. The good-natured cabaret girl helps turn the duckling into a swan; the two actresses had been friends on Broadway and got on well together. Miriam had not then developed into what her ex-husband Anatole Litvak called a 'Hollywood hellcat' and the person of whom Bette Davis later said 'God has been good – He has taken her from us!'

Of the six films Colbert made in 1932, the first, *The Wiser Sex*, teamed her with Melvyn

Above: Claudette Colbert in *Bluebeard's Eighth Wife* (1938).

Douglas, who played a crusading lawyer wrongly accused of murder. Colbert played the strong-minded and enterprising young woman who eventually gets him acquitted and uncovers the real murderer. My first ever view of her was in this film, waking up in bed with tousled hair. I asked my mother if all stars went to bed with their lipstick on. 'Of course,' she said. 'That's supposed to be natural, healthy colouring.' Melvyn Douglas was one of several leading men who talked of Colbert's 'walloping sex appeal'. Fredric March, another frequent co-star, was to encounter that side of her, later in the year, when she played Poppaea, 'the wickedest woman in the world', in *The Sign of the Cross*.

Also in *The Wiser Sex* was Lilyan Tashman (1899–1934), a sparkling, sophisticated ex-Ziegfeld Follies girl, famous for her diamonds and for being voted 'the best-dressed woman in Hollywood'. Witty ripostes and smart timing

IT HAPPENED ONE NIGHT

1934 Columbia 105 mins b/w
Executive Producer: Harry Cohn; Producer: Frank Capra, Director:
Frank Capra; Screenplay: Robert Riskin (from the story Night Bus by
Samuel Hopkins Adams); Cinematographer: Joseph Walker
Claudette Colbert, Clark Gable, Walter Connolly, Roscoe Karns, Alan
Hale, Jameson Thomas, Henry Wadsworth, Claire McDowell

The auspices for this all-time great romantic comedy were not favourable. The role of the madcap heiress who runs away from her irascible millionaire father (Walter Connolly) to avoid marriage had been turned down by Constance Bennett, Myrna Loy, Margaret Sullavan and Miriam Hopkins. Clark Gable considered the story foolish and had not wanted to do it, but the loan-out to Columbia was imposed on him by MGM as a disciplinary measure in response to their top male star's complaints about always being cast in 'brutish' roles. Claudette Colbert accepted her part as a chance to act with Gable. Frank Capra's imaginative direction of Robert Riskin's brilliant screenplay and the chemistry between the two leads worked a cinematic miracle, earning five Oscars for best picture, director, actor, actress and screen adaptation.

The movie sparked off the craze for screwball comedies. The scene in the motel where the heiress and the newspaper man travelling with her erect a blanket between their beds (which they call the 'Wall of Jericho') was a sly dig at the newly enforced Production Code, with delighted audiences filling in with their own imaginations. Walter Connolly, as the ranting father, created a role model he was to repeat profitably for the remainder of his career and Claudette's hitchhiking a lift by a gentle raising of her skirt to a passing motorist is another memorable screen gem.

film *The Misleading Lady* (1932), one of many routine pictures she illumined in the thirties.

This movie was followed by one of Cecil B De Mille's least inspired productions, *Four Frightened People*, in 1934. Set in the Malaysian jungle, Colbert is transformed from a mousy secretary into a Dorothy Lamour clone in a leopardskin bikini. The balance, however, was soon redressed by perhaps the finest film Colbert appeared in, *It Happened One Night*.

It is sad to reflect that the Gable-Colbert team, so profitably showcased in that film, was only to return once more, in MGM's disappointing *Boom Town* (1940), and that Colbert's reunion with Capra in the 1948 *State of the Union*, with Spencer Tracy, ended in tears. Colbert was to be paid $500,000, dress fittings with Irene were completed, then three days before shooting was due to start, she noticed that the director had not signed her usual proviso that she was not to work after 5.00 pm. This was a clause Garbo and others had insisted on and one that was well known in Colbert's case: at 44 she, her agent (who was her brother) and her doctor (who was her husband) felt that, after eight hours under the strong lights on the set, her energies would be flagging and she would not photograph as well as she had earlier in the day. Capra would not budge and insisted that this time she would have to waive the clause. Colbert said 'No contract, no picture.'

Katharine Hepburn, who had been helping her friend Tracy with his lines at home, happily leaped into the breach, turned up on the set, word-perfect after two days, and Irene's costumes were adapted to fit her angular frame. For Colbert's public, this was a disappointment after her great success in her previous Capra film, which made six million dollars. *The Egg and I*, however, proved more successful.

In 1950 Colbert changed pace with an intensely dramatic story, *Three Came Home*, based on Agnes Newton Keith's account of her

were her stock-in-trade and, from the silent days, she had often been typed as a 'vamp' or Other Woman. Attractive to both sexes, her rapport with Claudette Colbert was immediate and productive, both on screen and in private life. Colbert spoke of her as one of her more rewarding Hollywood encounters and mourned when she died of cancer in 1934 at the tragically early age of 35. Tashman was married to Edmund Lowe, Colbert's co-star in her next experiences as a prisoner of war under the Japanese, when they overran Borneo during World War Two. Director Jean Negulesco said, 'Colbert's performance was realistic and utterly convincing.' One of the most telling scenes was when she relates to another prisoner (Florence Desmond) the brutality she suffered at the hands of a Japanese officer after she reported an assault on her by a sentry the night before. There were glowing notices for Colbert and Desmond, in a role intended for Gracie Fields. Japan's greatest screen actor, Sessue Hayakawa, playing a colonel torn between his own humanity and the harshness of the regime under which he has to act, was much applauded.

Unfortunately, the back injuries Colbert sustained on this often brutal picture were what kept her out of the next role she was down to play, Margo Channing in *All About Eve* (1950) On a lighter note, Florence Desmond, known as England's best stage impressionist, who somehow contrived to resemble the subject of her impersonations besides getting the voice right, had done a virtually flawless take-off of Colbert in her 1940 film with Ray Milland, *Arise, My Love*. She reprised this on set for Claudette, to lighten the tensions in the scenes they had together.

In 1952 Colbert came to England to make *The Planter's Wife/Outpost in Malaya* for director Ken Annakin, with Jack Hawkins and Anthony Steel fighting terrorists in the Malayan jungle – a dispiriting experience for all concerned. In France she starred in *Love, Soldiers and Women/Daughters of Destiny* (1953) with Eleanora Rossi Drago, another misfire. She then returned to Hollywood for her first film there in three years, *Texas Lady* (1955), in Technicolor, directed by Tim Whelan, with Barry Sullivan. This was her penultimate American movie, into which she put all her former sparkle and vitality in the role of a gently reared Edwardian lady who takes over a Texas newspaper whose corrupt methods she blames for her father's suicide.

THE EGG AND I

1947 Universal-International 108 mins b/w
Producer: Chester Erskine; Director: Chester Erskine; Screenplay Chester Erskine, Fred Finklehoffe (based on the novel by Betty Macdonald); Cinematograper: Milton Krasner
Claudette Colbert, Fred MacMurray, Marjorie Main, Louise Allbritton, Percy Kilbride

As a team, Fred MacMurray and Claudette Colbert had been working together for 12 years, first co-starring in *The Gilded Lily* (1935). His 6'3" opposite her 5'4Ω", with the inference of her innate intellectual superiority acceding to his masculine stubbornness, worked extremely well. In all, they were together in seven movies and *The Egg and I* was the most financially successful.

As town dwellers experiencing life on a farm they had to undergo much slapstick physical indignity – she falling off a roof and into pig swill, he felling a tree which crashes down onto his henhouse and so on. They threw themselves into the situations so wholeheartedly that the laughs were continuous. In this they were aided by the contrasting teaming of Percy Kilbride and Marjorie Main as the un-handyman and his corncrake-voiced wife, who spawned no less than nine spin-offs with the Ma and Pa Kettle series. Main was Academy Award-nominated as Best Supporting Actress. The glamorous Louise Allbritton, Universal's resident other-woman player, tries to lure MacMurray with her sultry looks and mechanised farm across the way.

Despite the film's prodigious success it was not a favourite of either of the stars. MacMurray commented, 'Claudette and I worked damned hard. We were both at the turn of 40 then. I know she was a big asset and it wasn't easy for her, getting all dirtied up, sliding off roofs and whatnot ... but I never saw her hesitate to go after effects that would perk up the laughs.' She said, 'Fred was a big help with it – as always.'

It was not a world-beater, but Barry Sullivan was unstinting in his praise, having experienced the vagaries of working with Bette Davis in *Payment on Demand* (1951) and Joan Crawford in *Queen Bee* (1955). He told me, when in London for a TV commitment: 'She was one of my top favourites. She was 51 at the time and looked a good 15 years younger. She was always accessible in a scene, met you eye to eye, always played things back to you.'

Above: Claudette Colbert in the make-up chair for *Drums Along the Mohawk* (1939).

was the current male pin-up after *A Summer Place* (1959) with its chart-topping Max Steiner theme song. Donahue felt very insecure about his part as an aggressive young tobacco grower at odds with himself and the three girls in his life. Strong actors like Colbert and Malden were in for ballast, to help give Troy the self-confidence he lacked, while the lush Technicolor production values and the great cinematographer Harry Stradling saw that Colbert and the others were photographed to their best advantage. When I interviewed Claudette in the sixties at London's Connaught Hotel, I asked her to tell me frankly why she had made *Parrish*. 'Truthfully,' she said, 'the film paid for my home in Barbados.'

Her legendary charm and beauty were not changed and, more remarkably, when she starred with the famous curmudgeon Rex Harrison at the Haymarket Theatre in 1984 in a revival of Frederick Lonsdale's twenties comedy *Aren't We All?*, the Colbert looks were still amazingly youthful. She had appeared in the US run of *The Kingfisher* with Harrison, who presented her with the Sarah Siddons Award for Best Actress in 1979-80, and she had always managed to control his turbulent outbursts. I visited her backstage at the Haymarket with Dorothy Dickson, some five years her senior. They had been friends when Claudette was in London with *The Barker* in 1926. After enthusiastic compliments on both sides, Claudette said 'Well, I suppose I'll have to give up some day.' There was no sign of it then.

In 1987 she co-starred with Ann-Margret in the two-part TV drama, *The Two Mrs Grenvilles*, a Madame X-type story of an ambitious show-girl who marries the scion of a wealthy, influential and snobbish family (Stephen Collins), with Colbert as the matriarch, dispensing equal charm and venom, in probably the most malevolent character of her whole career. Based on a true story, the powerhouse performance of Ann-Margret – as the kitten whose claws are concealed until her mother-in-law, Colbert, reveals

In 1956, Colbert said she would get out of films 'before I'm pushed out' and returned to the stage for the first time in 27 years, taking over on Broadway from Margaret Sullivan in *Janus*. The same year she played with Noël Coward and Lauren Bacall in a TV version of Coward's *Blithe Spirit*, a success despite the tension between Coward and Colbert, after he told her at rehearsals that she was playing her part backward.

From then onwards until the end of her career, she was to concentrate her energies and talent on the theatre, apart from one final film in 1961, *Parrish*, as Troy Donahue's mother and Karl Malden's wife. Director Delmer Daves concentrated his energies on 24-year-old Donahue, who her real, destructive agenda – carries an old-fashioned plot reminiscent of Ruth Chatterton and Pauline Frederick in the 1930s. For added value, Sian Phillips delivers a spot-on characterisation of the Duchess of Windsor. After this fitting coda to a remarkable 66-year public life, Colbert's final appearance was to participate in the twelfth annual Kennedy Centre Honours, celebrating the best of the Performing Arts in 1989. She died in 1996 at her Barbados home.

Her friend Claire Trevor made her last TV movie, *Breaking Home Ties*, in 1998 and died in April 2000.

CARY GRANT (1904-1986)
(Archibald Alexander Leach)

Cary Grant was married five times, his wives including Virginia Cherrill, Chaplin's leading lady in *City Lights* (1931), Woolworth heiress Barbara Hutton, Betsy Drake and Dyan Cannon, with whom he had his only child. But Grant usually returned, between wives, to the house he had shared with his lifelong companion, Randolph Scott, since they met during a lunch break at their studio while Scott, one year Grant's senior, was making his first film, *Sky Bride* (1931).

Such an arrangement between two young, attractive, unmarried rising stars was highly unconventional and gossip rose to fever pitch when they used to attend premieres and public functions together without attendant females. Paramount, to whom they were both under contract, reacted to ambiguous remarks in gossip columns by insisting Cary and Randy (to his friends) find suitable young women as escorts. They chose two promising females, recently arrived in Hollywood: starlet Sari Maritza and her friend Vivian Gaye, a budding literary agent who had taken an apartment near to Grant and Scott. The girls created as much scandalous speculation as the boys, which amused everyone

and kept the studio happy. Carole Lombard, a friend of Cary's who appeared with him in 1932's *Sinners in the Sun*, summed up the situation with the classic remark: 'Their relationship is perfect. Randy pays the bills and Cary mails them!'

This allusion to Grant's well-known frugality with money probably had its origin in the deprivation of his childhood days. He was born Archie Leach in Bristol, a seaport town in the west of England. His father Elias was a handsome 32-year-old with a deep cleft in his chin which his son inherited; he worked as a suit-presser in a clothing factory on a minimal wage which barely paid the rent. His wife Elsie was a neurotic and bitter woman, whose only other son had died of meningitis before his first birthday. Her husband alleviated the monotony of working life with evening drinking sessions and numerous affairs with young women, including chorus girls from the Empire and Hippodrome Theatre, to which Elias took his little son for the only happy outing he enjoyed during his dreary upbringing.

Elsie resented him – he was perhaps the illegitimate son of a Jewish woman who disappeared from their lives – and frequently rapped his knuckles with a stick. Grant later confided in his friend, actress Mary Brian, with whom he made a film in England in 1936, *The Amazing Quest of Ernest Bliss*, that he was part-Jewish. To others, including playwright Clifford Odets, he denied the fact, but he nevertheless contributed lavishly to various Jewish causes.

Christmas pantomimes delighted the boy and his father, who, seeing him happy in the theatre, was pleased to hand him over to Robert Lomas, head of the Penders acrobatic act of tumblers and stilt-walkers. Elias signed a statement that Archie was ten, the minimum age for stage work then. Lomas later took him into the troupe, becoming more of a father to him than Elias ever was. As one of Bob Penders' 'Little Dandies', he travelled abroad with them to Germany and France, besides appearing at the Theatre Royal Drury

Lane in *Jack and the Beanstalk* in 1910, starring the great pantomime dame George Graves. The Penders, on stilts, were the giants. Archie often tumbled off onto the sloping stage; he was more secure as a stork, wearing a bird mask.

Archie was ten when he returned from a walk one day to be told that Elsie had suddenly died of a heart attack and had had to be buried immediately. He could never get an answer as to the location of her grave. Many years later he learned that his father had had Elsie committed to Fishponds Lunatic Asylum, where people were kept in appalling conditions for one pound a year. The reason for this criminal act was that Elias was about to install his mistress, Mabel Bass, in the home. Though disturbed and hysterical, Elsie was certainly not insane.

After the Penders travelled to New York, Archie decided to stay on and seek acting work. He became friendly with the female impersonator, Francis Renault, known as the 'Last of the Red Hot Papas', who specialised in impersonating Lillian Russell, although he was muscular and virile. He became Archie's patron and, it was popularly believed, lover. He also helped him financially through the years until he became established. Archie, then 17, also met and set up house with Australian Jack Kelly, who was 24 and soon to become famous as Orry-Kelly, costume designer for Warners and, later, Fox. They shared a large loft in Greenwich Village where they were joined by another gay Australian, Charlie Phelps, a steward who had jumped ship to join his friends and help share the $15-a-week rent. His stage name was Charlie Spangles and he appeared in a Greenwich Club doing an act called Josephine and Joseph, in which one half of his body was made up as female, the other male. Jack Kelly paid his way painting murals and drawing titles for silent films.

Archie was still with the Penders in the revue *Good Times* and remained regularly employed in vaudeville tours and, later, in musicals and other plays until he travelled west to Hollywood in Jack Kelly's car, after the latter moved to Warners with his new lover, Phil Charig. Charig was the composer of an unsuccessful musical called *Nikki*, a costume drama in which Archie appeared with Fay Wray, whose husband, John Monk Saunders, had written the original play. It was Fay who suggested the name Cary after the character he played; 'Grant' was an inspiration of Paramount Studios' publicists. The heads of the studio were B P Schulberg and Jesse L Lasky, who had brought young Leach to the States as a child and kept a friendly eye on his progress ever since. As a test they cast him in a short called *Singapore Sue*, the outcome of which was the move to Los Angeles with Phil Charig in 1932. Schulberg put the newly christened Cary Grant to work immediately in *This is the Night* (1932), co-starring with Lili Damita. Simultaneously, he was cast opposite Carole Lombard in *Sinners in the Sun*.

The studio had arranged an apartment in West Hollywood for Cary and Phil, who had planned to write scores for the movies. When Grant met Randolph Scott, Charig returned to New York without having written a single film score and Randy moved in. From 1932 to 1942 they maintained their joint accommodation, which was always available when needed. Grant was rushed from film to film, of varying importance, mainly in leading roles – seven in 1932 alone. His first in 1933 was the one that caused the biggest stir in his career to date: Mae West's *She Done Him Wrong*. Mae, whose sense of her own omnipotence was positively papal, claimed to have 'discovered' Grant and gave the impression that he had previously only done a few bit parts, more or less as an extra. When she 'spotted' him, she said 'If he can talk, I'll have 'im.' As she affected to be unaware of the presence of other female stars on the Paramount lot, the fact that Grant had played leads opposite Carole Lombard, Marlene Dietrich, Tallulah Bankhead and Sylvia Sidney in one year was neither here nor there.

Grant's first teaming with Katharine Hepburn in 1935, in *Sylvia Scarlett*, was a self-indulgent exercise by director George Cukor in seeing how far he could go, from a book by Compton Mackenzie, with Hepburn and Edmund Gwenn as father and daughter con artists and Grant as their new partner in crime. Hepburn spends much of the film disguised (attractively and convincingly) as a boy to avoid the law and the dialogue with Cary, caressing her in male attire, has such provocative lines as 'It's nippy tonight: you'll make a proper hotwater bottle' and 'There's something about you that gives me a queer feeling every time I look at you.' All this passed over the heads of the audiences – who stayed away in droves – and, presumably, the censors too.

During the filming, Howard Hughes paid two visits by plane to the location, ostensibly to see Hepburn, with whom he was supposed to be having an affair. The eccentric billionaire was not the full-blooded heterosexual his publicists paraded before the public. Brian Aherne, co-starring in the film, recalled, 'I think he was more interested in Cary.' On his second visit, Hughes took Cary for a joyride over Los Angeles – the only person to be so honoured. It was Randolph Scott who had introduced Howard Hughes to Grant: the filmmaker/aviator had taken Randy under his wing when he was a student at Northern Carolina University and brought him to Hollywood.

Cary made two movies on loan to MGM: *Suzy* (1936), a First World War thriller with Jean Harlow, directed by George Fitzmaurice, and, the following year, *Topper* (1937), from Thorne Smith's book *The Jovial Ghosts*, with Grant and Constance Bennett as two high-living ghosts, killed in a car crash and stranded on earth until they can perform something worthwhile. This involved Roland Young in the title role, Billie Burke as his wife and canine star Asta as Grant and Bennett's dog. Norman Z McLeod directed this delightful comedy with captivating performances from all concerned. The sequel in 1939

starred Bennett on her own, with Young and Burke and only a quick ghostly vision of Grant.

Bringing Up Baby (1938) provided a triumphant second team-up with Katharine Hepburn. *Holiday* (1938), directed by George Cukor, had been filmed in 1930 with Ann Harding, from the play by Philip Barry. It concerned romantic complications in high society, with Cary, engaged to Doris Nolan, discovering he prefers her free-spirited sister, Kate Hepburn. The stars were in sparkling form and Lew Ayres nearly stole the honours as Hepburn's alcoholic brother, played, as near the wind as possible, as being gay. Another outstanding performance, reprised from the first version, was Edward Everett Horton's, whose characterisations, while always amusing, were also inevitably camp.

The movie, despite favourable notices, did not help Hepburn out of the disfavour with which she was regarded at the time but Cary Grant could do no wrong. He had three big hits in 1939. These were George Stevens' classic adventure film, *Gunga Din*; another top-flight action movie, Howard Hawks' *Only Angels Have Wings*, co-starring Jean Arthur and the young Rita Hayworth; and *In Name Only*, directed by John Cromwell, with Carole Lombard. Lombard had helped her friend Kay Francis, whose career was at a low ebb, back into the big time by insisting she be cast as Cary's ruthless, social-climbing wife. During the shooting of *Gunga Din*, Cary received a startling telegram informing him that Elsie Leach, whom he had considered dead for so many years, had been released from Fishponds Asylum. When the filming was finished, he returned to England on the *Queen Mary* to visit his official mother in Bristol. What transpired between them was never divulged but, though he traveled to see her regularly through the years, their relationship was almost always strained. She had no interest in showbusiness or his career and was uneasy with his fame.

1940 was another eventful year, beginning

with a film reunion with Irene Dunne: their 1937 vehicle *The Awful Truth*, as a husband and wife on the verge of divorce, was a scintillating crazy comedy which earned director Leo McCarey a Best Picture Oscar. The follow-up, *My Favourite Wife*, three years later, was notable in that, apart from Irene Dunne, Grant's other co-star was Randolph Scott in a re-working of the old Enoch Arden story.

Another smash-hit comedy in 1940, *His Girl Friday*, teamed Grant with Rosalind Russell, one of the screen's most skilled farceurs, in Howard Hawks' remake of Lewis Milestone's *The Front Page* (1931). Chief reporter Hildy Johnson undergoes a sex-change from Pat O'Brien's original characterisation, now incarnated by Russell. Grant played her ex-husband editor, Walter Burns, previously played by Adolphe Menjou. The operation was eminently successful. The token heroine, Burns' one-time fiancée Mary Brian in the first take, has disappeared from the script altogether. Edward Everett Horton's 1931 role as the 'sensitive' reporter, played here by Cliff Edwards as poetry-reading and dandyish, metamorphosed in yet another remake, under the original title in 1974, into a downright swishy queen, played by David Wayne.

To top this 1940 set of sparkling comedy highlights in Grant's career, Katharine Hepburn herself jet-setted back into his life courtesy of their joint romantic partner, Howard Hughes. Hughes had secured the rights to Philip Barry's play *The Philadelphia Story* for her, in which she had scored an enormous success on Broadway in the central role of Tracy Lord, an eccentric heiress residing in a Main Line Philadelphia Estate. She sold the property to Louis B Mayer, retaining the right to choose the director (George Cukor) and cast. The latter included Cary Grant as her ex-husband, socialite C Dexter Haven, and James Stewart as reporter Macaulay. The intrigue and by-play as Grant and Stewart vie for Hepburn's affections are subtly handled, adding up to one of the wittiest and most sophisticated of all screen comedies, for which Stewart won Best Actor Oscar.

Grant was to gain his first Academy Award nomination for his next film, *Penny Serenade* (1941). This is a drama in which Grant and Irene Dunne play a married couple who attempt to adopt a child after the death of their own baby. The director was George Stevens. Grant's next Oscar nomination came in 1944 for another drama, *None But The Lonely Heart*, as a cockney (with an accent more Bristol than London) who returns home to look after his dying mother, played by Ethel Barrymore, who gained the Best Actress Oscar. This was the only film in which Grant was directed by his friend, Clifford Odets.

Grant's film career was to last for a further 22 years, always at the top, until he retired in 1966. His rewarding collaboration with Alfred Hitchcock began in 1941 with *Suspicion*, in which Joan Fontaine, reprising her *Rebecca* routine for Hitchcock, was to win a second Oscar opposite the charming but possibly murderous Cary. In 1946's *Notorious* his leading lady was Ingrid Bergman. They play fellow spies in postwar Brazil, where she marries Nazi Claude Rains in order to keep track of underground Fascist activities. In 1955 there was *To Catch a Thief* with Grace Kelly, who, wealthy and beautiful, falls for Grant on the French Riviera. He's a retired jewel thief – but are his intentions above board? The last – and best – of the classy Hitchcock romantic thrillers came in 1959: *North by Northwest*. Grant is an advertising executive mistaken for a spy, who tangles with James Mason and Martin Laundau and uses his 'feminine intuition' to unmask Eva Marie-Saint as the real spy. This movie abounds in memorable Hitchcock touches, such as the celebrated sequence in which a plane bears down on Cary in a cornfield.

There are few teamings as notable as Cary Grant's with Katharine Hepburn. But in his early

Right: Cary Grant, Eva Marie Saint, James Mason and Martin Landau in *North By North West* (1959).

movie days in 1935, Myrna Loy was Grant's co-star in *Wings in the Dark*, directed by James Flood. They are two pilots in love, until he gets blinded. In 1947, Loy was the judge who orders Grant to keep dating her teenage sister, Shirley Temple, to help her get over her crush on him – hence the title *The Bachelor and the Bobbysoxer* (UK: *Bachelor Knight*). Grant, of course, falls for Big Sister. Their third, most mature and most popular film together was *Mr Blandings Builds His Dream House* (1948). They are a married couple from the city who move to a ramshackle house in the country with traumatic and hilarious results, aided and abetted by Melvyn Douglas. The movie was directed by H C Potter.

Less felicitous were two films with Ginger Rogers. The first was *Once Upon a Honeymoon* (1942), a spy drama directed by Leo McCarey, not quite on top form, with Grant as a reporter trailing Nazi spy Walter Slezak and becoming involved with the agent's new wife, ex-burlesque queen Rogers. *Monkey Business* (1952), directed by Howard Hawks, has absent-minded professor

Grant finding a youth elixir, which sends him and wife Rogers into their second childhood with hilarious results. The film also features Marilyn Monroe, barely of out her first childhood.

A trial run with Deborah Kerr in *Dream Wife*, directed by Sidney Sheldon in 1953, saw her feminist attitudes as Grant's fiancée send him into the arms of foreign princess Betta St John, until Deborah is appointed to be their interpreter – with predictable results. Grant and Kerr were later cast in one of the most romantic films of all time, *An Affair to Remember* (1957). This time director Leo McCarey was at his considerable best. The stars were on top form in McCarey's remake of his classic 1939 *Love Story*, which had starred Irene Dunne and Charles Boyer. It's the one where the lovers promise to meet again at the top of the Empire State Building and an accident prevents her keeping the appointment. A genuine weepie which never loses its charm.

The relationship between Grant and Kerr was less happy in *The Grass Is Greener* (1960), directed by Stanley Donen from the West End comedy success by Hugh and Margaret Williams. Although Grant chose her for the part of Hilary Countess of Rhyall, opposite his Victor Earl of Rhyall, their old rapport had gone. Grant showed little concern for her and was often rude. Kerr told actor Moray Watson that Cary had changed and it was very sad. Also starring was Robert Mitchum as the American millionaire with whom the countess has a fling. Co-star Jean Simmons also found Grant different. He virtually ignored her, though they had been friends when she was married to Stewart Granger, of whom Cary became very fond, having been present at his marriage to Jean in Tucson Arizona. Cary obviously took Granger's part in the acrimonious divorce proceedings which were going on during the filming.

More personal upsets occurred on the two films Grant made with Sophia Loren. *The Pride and the Passion* (1957) was directed by Stanley Kramer, an ill-conceived and top-heavy epic set at the time of Napoleon, with Grant as a British naval officer and Frank Sinatra as a Spanish guerrilla fighter. Cary was not happy to be cast with newcomer Loren but soon decided he was in love with her, which was awkward as his relationship with Betsy Drake, whom he had married in 1949, was at an intensely difficult stage. As with his first wife, Virginia Cherrill, their fights would sometimes lead to him physically abusing her. Reading the gossip about Cary and Sophia, Betsy, who genuinely loved him, was distraught, though she did not know he had promised to divorce her and marry Loren, who, in fact, was dating Carlo Ponti, to whom she would soon be married.

In fact, despite all the moonlit dinners, Grant was using her more as a psychoanalyst than a lover, discussing his emotional problems and revealing the duality in his nature. He was passionately involved with a young Spanish male but, when Betsy Drake did eventually visit the Spanish location, Cary paid her little attention

and continued to take out Sophia, who said she loved him but seemed to take the matter lightly. Sinatra, at his lowest ebb temperamentally, insulted everyone and behaved appallingly. Grant ignored his co-star's outbursts and concentrated on Loren, who was cast as a passionate peasant girl. Sinatra refused to finish the film unless it was completed in Hollywood. Stanley Kramer was eternally grateful to Grant for his loyalty, doing everything he could to help ease the tensions.

Meanwhile, Cary had added to his own difficulties by offering Sophia the co-starring part in the forthcoming *Houseboat* (1958), which he had promised to wife Betsy Drake. The film he had made with her the year before their marriage, *Every Girl Should Be Married* (1948), had not been a success, nor was she rated very highly as an actress. But Grant did his best to secure her work, with *Houseboat* as a sort of consolation prize on which she had set her heart and for which she had written the storyline. The director, Melville Shavelson, after Cary had told him Sophia would be his co-star, negotiated with Paramount behind Cary's back. In the meantime, when Sophia rejected his offer of marriage, Grant had vengefully reverted to having his wife in the film.

Stanley Kramer doubted that the relationship with Sophia had become physical: she was devoted to Ponti, who often visited the set and did not appear to consider Cary as a rival. When he found he was forced to honour the contract to have Loren in the film, Grant had to humiliate Betsy again by breaking the news. She managed to put a brave face on things, though her husband's *soi-disant* lover was playing the part Drake had created for herself. After a brief rapprochement with Sophia, Cary reverted to his demands that she leave Ponti and marry him. He went completely out of control. Director Shavelson said, 'It was murder on the set. Cary made things very, very difficult for everybody.'

He now did all he could to humiliate Sophia as well as his wife. He tried to take over the

Right: Cary Grant and Audrey Hepburn in *Charade* (1963).

direction and screamed orders at second lead Martha Hyer. It was at this time that Betsy, ready to do anything to keep Cary, seemed happy to join him in experimenting with LSD, which he anticipated would help him draw together the tangled skeins of his life. This was the wonder drug of the time, advocated by writers such as Christopher Isherwood and Aldous Huxley, whom Grant met to discuss the magic qualities of mescalin, described so vividly in Huxley's book *The Doors of Perception*.

Also in 1958, Grant teamed again with Ingrid Bergman for *Indiscreet*, directed in England by one of the masters of comedy, Stanley Donen. Grant is an American who falls for European actress Bergman. This is a charming romantic comedy also featuring one of Britain's top stars, Phyllis Calvert. In 1962, Delbert Mann's *That Touch of Mink*, with Doris Day, earned Cary a fortune. Also lucrative was *Charade* (1963) with Audrey Hepburn, with the bonus that the film rights reverted to him after eight years. Cary worked well with Audrey,

though he had worried that at 58 to her 34 he might appear too old to be her romantic interest. However, with the expert playing of the stars, backed by Walter Matthau, George Kennedy and James Coburn, the skilled direction of Stanley Donen and the adroit photography of Charles Lang Jr, the film was another marked success at the box-office. Grant planned to team up with Audrey Hepburn again in *Father Goose*, directed by Ralph Nelson and released in 1964, but when she proved to be busy on another project, Leslie Caron stepped into the breach.

Betsy Drake had divorced Cary in 1959 and he began an intense affair with Dyan Cannon. In interviews he said that LSD had restored his composure and turned him into a tranquil and well-adjusted human being. That was not the side he showed Dyan Cannon, whom he would treat as harshly as he had Virginia Cherrill, beating her with his fists, locking her in her room and knocking her to the ground when she wore a mini-skirt. Yet she kept forgiving him and they were married in July 1965 at Howard Hughes'

Desert Inn. Their daughter Jennifer was born in February 1966. Grant became obsessive over the child, whom he idolised. His treatment of his wife became more cruel and irrational, driving her to the verge of a nervous breakdown, until she sued for divorce in August 1967.

The divorce dragged on. Cary tried to prevent it by encouraging Dyan to return to the stage and to appear in a film, *Bob and Carol and Ted and Alice* (1969), for which she won an Oscar nomination. The divorce was finally granted in 1968. Grant had already made his last film, *Walk, Don't Run* (1966), directed by Charles Walters. Cary played a businessman forced to share accommodation in Japan during the Olympics with Samantha Eggar and Jim Hutton.

In April 1970, Grant received his Honorary Oscar for Services to the Film Industry from Frank Sinatra, who delivered a brief but warm tribute. Four years earlier, Cary was established as a member of the board of Fabergé; as a travelling representative for the perfume, he threw himself into the promotions with complete dedication. He fell in love with their PR, the young and attractive Barbara Harris, who was English and whom he married in 1981. Ever since he had slapped a lawsuit on comedian Chevy Chase for alleging that Cary was homosexual (although the case petered out when Chase failed to respond), it seems Grant's interest in the male sex was no longer apparent and, of all his wives, Barbara had the most happy and peaceful time with him until his death in 1986 at the age of 82.

His friendship with Randolph Scott had continued through Randy's marriage to the fabulously wealthy Marion Dupont and his second marriage to another heiress, Patricia Stillman, in 1944. In the 1970s, Grant and Scott held a reunion at the Beverly Hillcrest Hotel and were observed by the maître d' holding hands in the darkened restaurant after the other guests had left. Randolph Scott died in March 1987, a year after Cary Grant.

GRETA GARBO [1905-1990]
[G Louisa Gustafson]

Garbo has been called the most famous film star of all time, and also the most enigmatic. The enigma is rooted in her sexuality – was she lesbian, was she bisexual? During her lifetime many men had been mooted to be her lovers, ranging from co-stars John Gilbert and George Brent, gay photographer Cecil Beaton, conductor Leopold Stokowski and the famous *ménage à trois* with George Schlee and his wife, designer Valentina. Garbo's famous catchphrase 'I want to be alone' – probably a studio invention – and her early retirement from filmmaking at 36 have been variously attributed to disillusionment over the comparative failure of her final film *Two-Faced Woman* (1941), her fear of growing old before the cameras and her intense shyness. All of which perhaps contributed to her years of nomadic wandering, up to her death at age 84.

Certainly, when I was staying in Rome with friends soon after the end of World War II, she was in town, negotiating one of many comebacks which never transpired. I passed her in the street, still instantly recognisable and beautiful, unmade-up and with hair awry, in slacks and a floppy hat, which she pulled down over her eyes, saying in the most intimate deep-throated accent, 'Please don't recognise me!'

After her death the floodgates opened to innumerable testimonials to her lesbianism, which is now the popular explanation of her early withdrawal from public scrutiny. Mercedes de Acosta, avowedly Hollywood's most active and wealthy lesbian, who had worked her way through half of the showbusiness world's available Sapphic stars, revealed in print her off-and-on passionate affair with Garbo and published a topless snapshot of her taken during one of their idylls. Everyone from Pola Negri to Marlene Dietrich appeared to find de Acosta irresistible. Among her other talents, she was a scriptwriter

Opposite: Charles Bickford and Greta Garbo in *Anna Christie* (1930).

ANNA CHRISTIE

1930 MGM 86 mins b/w
Director: Clarence Brown; Screenplay: Frances Marion (based on a play by Eugene O'Neill); Cinematographer: William H Daniels
Greta Garbo, Charles Bickford, Marie Dressler, George F Marion Sr, James T Mack, Lee Phelps

The subject chosen for Greta Garbo's talkie debut was just right, along with the famous first line of dialogue – 'Gimme a visky, ginger ale on the side and don't be stingy, baby' – which has gone down in screen history. She plays a prostitute who returns home after 15 years away, and received an Oscar nomination, as did Clarence Brown for Best Director and William H Daniels for Best Cinematographer. Marie Dressler, however, almost stole the film as Marthe, the aging prostitute who is Anna's confidante throughout the movie. She also became Garbo's lover in real life as the Swedish star took refuge from Hollywood and the world in Dressler's comforting and ample bosom. The part of Marthe in the German remake, directed by Jacques Feyder, was played by Salka Viertel.

Dressler had made her film debut with Charlie Chaplin in *Tillie's Punctured Romance* (1914) and a couple of sequels, but major stardom came only after *Anna Christie*. The same year she co-starred with Wallace Beery in *Min and Bill*, for which she won the Best Actress Academy Award. Also in 1930 she appeared with her butch sparring partner, Polly Moran, in one of their popular ladies-together farces, *Caught Short*. Their final and funniest team effort was *Reducing* (1931), partly set in a women's Turkish Bath.

In the following years, Dressler joined the ranks of Metro's top female stars, including the ravishing Jean Harlow, with whom she shared a gloriously camp scene in George Cukor's all-star *Dinner at Eight* (1933). Walking into dinner with Dressler, Harlow, as the gold-digging wife of magnate Wallace Beery, says, 'I was reading a book the other day.' Dressler, as *grande dame* actress Carlotta Vance (based on the Horses' champion, Mrs Patrick Campbell), does an exaggerated double-take and booms 'Reading a book?' Harlow: 'A nutty kind of a book: do you know, the guy says that machinery is going to take the place of every profession?' Dressler, looking her up and down, replies, 'Oh, my dear, that's something you need never worry about!' By the time of her death at 65 from cancer, in 1934, Dressler had, for four years, been the biggest box-office attraction in the USA. By 1938, Shirley Temple held the title, at ten years of age.

and playwright. Fear of discovery as to her driving sexual orientation, which at the time Garbo was filming could have destroyed her career along with her enigmatic legend, probably played a part in her obsessive reclusiveness.

Garbo was born in Stockholm, Sweden, of a peasant family. Her father was an unskilled labourer who died when she was 14 and she had to go to work in a department store to support her family. She was chosen for her looks to appear in a short film the store was producing for promotional purposes, which led directly to her first professional feature, *Peter the Tramp* (1922). Garbo's performance gained her a two-year course at Stockholm's Theatre Royal Dramatic Academy, where she met Mauritz Stiller, Sweden's top film director of the time. He was gay but saw great potential in Greta Gustafsson, re-christened her Garbo and cast her in her second film, *Gosta Berlings Saga* (1924).

This film prompted Louis B Mayer to offer a Hollywood contract to Stiller, who agreed to sign on condition that Garbo went with him. Garbo's plumpness caused Mayer to temper his enthusiasm; it was his opinion that 'Americans don't like fat women.' When she arrived in Hollywood with

Stiller in 1926, her weight was taken care of, her teeth straightened and in her first American film, *The Torrent* (1926), the reconstituted Garbo was an overnight sensation as a Spanish peasant girl who is the object of nobleman Ricardo Cortez's affection. Cortez was billed above her. The director was Monta Bell, with Mauritz Stiller, who spoke little English, as assistant and interpreter.

Stiller and Mayer detested each other but Garbo's stock had risen so high after her first picture that she was able to insist her mentor direct her next film, *The Temptress* (1926). However, after a series of clashes with studio personnel, Stiller was replaced by Fred Niblo, the director of the silent version of *Ben-Hur* (1925). Stiller moved to Paramount and directed two films with Pola Negri, *Hotel Imperial* (1926) and *The Woman On Trial* (1927), with considerable success. Stiller then started *The Street of Sin* (1928), starring the temperamental German star Emil Jannings, a gross and unattractive bisexual publicised as the greatest film actor in the world. He once said, 'I believe in men – in varying circumstances,' and revelled in the pre-

Hitler ambisexual Berlin clubs such as Le Silhouette and El Dorado. When Hitler came to power he turned a blind eye to Jannings' sexual orientation because of his great popularity, his marriage to Gussi Holl and the films he made under the Nazi regime, for which he was awarded a medal by Goebbels and was made the head of his own film company, Tobis, in 1932.

Clashes on the set led to Stiller being replaced as director of *The Street of Sin* by Josef von Sternberg, although when the film was released in 1928 Stiller received sole credit – his last. He died the next year after directing a musical, *Broadway*, back in Sweden. He was just 45 and had been suffering from a respiratory illness. Sentimentalists ascribed it to a broken heart over the Garbo debacle and he was said to have died clutching a photograph of her. The studio had not allowed her time off from filming to go to his funeral – one of the grudges she held against Mayer for the rest of her time there. Her third film, *Flesh and the Devil* (1927), directed by Clarence Brown, saw Garbo's first teaming with John Gilbert. Their torrid love scenes created such a sensation that two more Gilbert-Garbo romances followed in quick succession.

Love (1927), directed by Edmond Goulding, was a version of Tolstoy's *Anna Karenina.* The same story would be one of Garbo's biggest successes as a talkie opposite Fredric March in 1935, directed by her favourite director, Clarence Brown. Brown also directed Garbo and Gilbert in *A Woman of Affairs* (1928). The death of Valentino in 1926 had cleared the way for Gilbert, a swarthy Italian type, to be one of his most popular successors. As a box-office team, he and Garbo were incomparable and the studio were not slow to fan the flames of their scorching celluloid passion, which threatened to ignite her dressing room when he rushed there during each break on the set. Certainly, Gilbert was deeply enamoured but Garbo stated later that they never had an affair.

The coming of sound ruined the careers of many stars of the silent screen and MGM were anxious about how Garbo's deep voice and Swedish accent would record. They had kept her in silent films for two years after the arrival of sound in 1927. In 1930, Louis B Mayer – and the film world – held their breath after the slogan GARBO TALKS! was launched world-wide. The film in question was *Anna Christie.*

Following *Anna Christie,* Garbo was again Oscar-nominated in 1930 for her second talkie, Clarence Brown's *Romance,* in which she plays an opera star in love with a young clergyman. During the 1930s she was cast opposite three of Metro's most prestigious male stars: with Robert Montgomery in *Inspiration* (1931), Clark Gable in *Susan Lennox: Her Fall and Rise* (1931) and Ramon Novarro in *Mata Hari* (1931). In 1932 *Grand Hotel,* Edmund Goulding's all-star screen version of Vicki Baum's bestselling novel, won Best Picture Award. Besides Garbo as Grusinskaya, the fading ballerina, there was John Barrymore as her lover, the titled thief; brother Lionel as the dying man on a last fling;

Above: Greta Garbo and Melvyn Douglas in *Ninotchka* (1939).

Wallace Beery as the ruthless industrialist and Joan Crawford, out-acting them all as the ambitious stenographer, Flaemmchen.

Crawford and Garbo had no scenes together. Crawford recalled their meeting in an elevator in her autobiography, when Garbo said she regretted this and, caressing Joan's face, said how beautiful she was. Crawford then wrote, 'If ever I had been tempted to be lesbian, this would have been the time.' In 1933, Garbo followed up with *Queen Christina,* perhaps her most iconic film of all.

Garbo received two more Oscar nominations, the first for *Camille* (1937), directed by George Cukor, playing Dumas' dying courtesan opposite Robert Taylor's Armand – for my money, the greatest female screen performance I have ever seen. Perhaps the fact that I absconded from boarding school for its London premiere at the Empire Leicester Square heightened my enchantment. Then in 1939 she made *Ninotchka* for Ernst Lubitsch with Melvyn Douglas, her first comedy. GARBO LAUGHS! screamed the posters. Garbo gained her fourth Oscar nomination for this brilliantly funny classic co-written by Billy Wilder and Charles Brackett, in which she plays a Russian envoy won over to capitalist ways by Paris and by playboy Melvyn Douglas.

Douglas appeared again in Cukor's *Two-*

Faced Woman, torn between two Garbos, one a ski instructor who marries him, then masquerades as her raunchy twin sister to test his fidelity. Constance Bennett excels as Garbo's rival, a sophisticated playwright. Decried by the critics and not very popular with the public, this was Garbo's last film. I personally found it delightful, especially the dance 'la chica-chaca', originated by Garbo in her raunchy persona, leading to a conga round the nightclub floor and an exchange of barbed remarks with her love rival, Bennett, in which Garbo has the last laugh. Bennett retires to the powder room, lets out a high-pitched scream at her reflection in the mirror, smoothes her hair and swans back to the table, composure fully restored.

During her world travels the papers were ever-ready to announce new comebacks for Greta Garbo. These included *Woman of the Sea*, as the captain of a Swedish trawler; Daudet's biography of Sappho; the title role in *The Picture of Dorian Gray*; a biography of George Sand, eventually played by Merle Oberon in *A Song to Remember* (1945), and *The Paradine Case*, directed by Hitchcock in 1947 with Alida Valli as the mystery woman on trial for murder, the part for which Garbo was sought. In 1950 she seemed all set to face the cameras aged 45 in *The Duchess of Langais*, a romantic period drama of the kind in which she could have excelled. James Mason, her co-star, had already been paid part of his salary. Max Ophuls had been signed as director but, at the last moment, the financing was withdrawn.

This was a hurtful blow to Garbo's pride, especially as Dietrich, her nearest 'rival' and her senior by five years, went on working in films until 1978 and enjoyed a renaissance as a world-famed cabaret star from the fifties to the mid-seventies, returning to Germany in 1960 for the first time in 30 years. She and Garbo met once at Marlene's insistence at a party arranged by George Cukor in the sixties. Dietrich, it is said,

anxious to know how her rival was wearing after so many years away from the screen, was fulsome in her flattery. Garbo answered only monosyllabically. The occasion did not go down as the meeting of twin souls or the artistic liaison of the century. Marlene expended herself uncharacteristically, Greta kept her cool. A 1991 video called *Meetings of Two Queens* presumed to make art improve on real life. It so moulded the celluloid that it appears Garbo loves and is loved by Dietrich – in the video-maker's dreams.

JANET GAYNOR [1906-1984]
[Laura Gainor]
and
CHARLES FARRELL [1901-1990]
The World's Sweethearts

Born in Philadelphia, Janet Gaynor was one of the few Hollywood idols to have graduated from lowly work as an extra to top stardom. Her sweetly naïve quality quickly made her a family favourite. She was the only star whom I, as a child, was allowed to see in all her films without question, because she was so 'wholesome'. Under all that sweetness was a steely ambition and total professionalism in all that she did. She was the first actress to win an Academy Award, at the original 1928 ceremony, for *Seventh Heaven*, *Sunrise* and *Street Angel*; in those days the award could be for cumulative performances.

In the first of those films, her co-star was Charles Farrell, who shared her straightforward, innocent appeal. They were to inherit from Mary Pickford and Douglas Fairbanks the title of the World's Sweethearts, thanks to the many films in which they played young lovers, including the early musical *Sunny Side Up* (1929). In the latter film, Janet, in her nasal, plaintive voice, sang a number of contemporary hits, including the title song, 'I'm a Dreamer' and 'If I Had a Talking Picture of You'. Farrell, whose voice matched hers, joined her in duets. Gaynor was the highest-paid star of Fox Films from 1924, a position she maintained after they became Twentieth Century-Fox until she terminated her contract in 1936. In 1934 she was Hollywood's top box-office star. Other hits with Farrell included *Merely Mary Ann* (1931), *Delicious* (1931) and *Change of Heart* (1934).

Fans were keen for Farrell to divorce his wife, Virginia Valli, and marry Gaynor, who was first married to attorney Lydell Peck in 1932. Farrell remained married to Valli from 1932 until her death in 1968. Although Palm Springs had no Sapphic reputation when the Farrells moved there in 1941, their status as a 'twilight tandem' (term for a husband and wife who are both gay) soon brought a weekend and holiday exodus of industry lesbians to the resort, where Dinah Shore's golf tournaments drew 10,000 visitors every year as an established annual lesbian event. Charles Farrell left films in 1941 to go into the sports club industry full time, and before you could say 'Velvet Mafia', they were millionaires.

Off screen, Janet Gaynor was more butch than her fellow World's Sweetheart, although her little-girl looks in such movies as *Adorable* (1933) made her every red-blooded male's 'girl next door'. What fans could not know was that Janet's heart belonged to lovely Margaret Lindsay, star of many films, including *Cavalcade* (1933) and several Ellery Queen mysteries. She was four years younger than Gaynor and theirs was an on-going romance. After leaving Fox, Janet joined Selznick International and gave a sensational performance as the waitress turned film star in *A Star is Born* (1937). This was her only starring film in colour, for which she won an Oscar nomination, as did co-star Fredric March. Gaynor retired after another success with Selznick, *The Young in Heart* (1938), and then created a sensation in 1939 by marrying MGM's brilliant costume designer, Gilbert Adrian. Adrian had designed for the most glamorous stars at Metro,

Above: Charles Farrell and Janet Gaynor in *A Change of Heart* (1934).

including Garbo, Joan Crawford, Norma Shearer, Jean Harlow and Constance Bennett.

Adrian's persona was undeniably gay, and Janet – her mop of curly brown hair styled by Metro's Sydney Guilaroff into a short, severe bob – looked almost butch. Theirs was a highly successful partnership. From 1942, Adrian opened his own salon and most of his star clients followed him there. Margaret Lindsay remained a close friend – she never married, but her name was often coupled with Hollywood's most 'eligible' bachelors. She went on filming until 1963, six years after Gaynor made a brief screen comeback, playing a mother in the Pat Boone vehicle *Bernadine* (1957).

Gaynor was widowed two years later, and in 1964 married producer Paul Gregory, for whom she did some stage work. She died in 1984, outliving her friend Margaret Lindsay by three

years. Gaynor had never recovered from a near-fatal car crash in 1982, in which her friends and fellow sewing circle ladies, Mary Martin and Helen Hayes, were involved. Though neither of the other women were seriously injured in the crash, Hayes was to die of congestive lung disease in 1993 and Martin, mother of Larry Hagman, died in 1990 from cancer.

LOUISE BROOKS [1906-1985]

An outstanding example of what could happen to an actress who utterly refused to come to terms with Hollywood values, Louise Brooks became a superstar – before the term was invented – through her European films. G W Pabst's German-made *Pandora's Box* (1929) heads most

Above: Janet Gaynor in *A Star is Born* (1937).

Brooks fans' list, finding new devotees over 70 years after its original release. Brooks returned to the USA in 1930, determined to reclaim the stardom that had been hers after her appearance in Howard Hawks's *A Girl in Every Port* (1928).

Her outspoken opinions on the film industry ('The pestiferous disease that was Hollywood'), coupled with her 'desertion' to film in Europe, were two black marks against her. By refusing to sign a contract with RKO, turning down the lead in a talkie version of *The Cat and the Canary* – the 1927 version headlined Laura La Plante and the 1939 remake made a star of Paulette Goddard – plus scorning the female lead opposite James Cagney in *Public Enemy* (1931), which went to Jean Harlow, Brooks found herself spurned by Hollywood. The best she could get was a two-reel short, *Windy Reilly Goes to Hollywood/Gas Bags* (1931), directed by Fatty Arbuckle and, after two meaningless films, *God's Gift to Women* and *It Pays to Advertise*, both in 1931, she became a nightclub dancer.

In 1936 her attempt at a comeback yielded only bit parts or leads in such B-westerns as *Empty Saddles* (1936) and a John Wayne vehicle, *Overland Stage Raiders* (1938). These were the straws that finally broke the star's back. She left Hollywood forever at 32 and eventually settled in Rochester New York, making a few radio appearances in the forties and taking a brief spell as a saleslady at Saks.

In the mid-1950s Brooks enjoyed a literary renaissance when some of her old films were rediscovered in both Europe and the US. She became sought after for her perceptive and intelligent film criticism and was regarded as something of a film guru for her assessment of life in the film industry. She did not mince words and, although some of her contemporaries mentioned 'sour grapes', she evaluated in her own direct way regardless.

She published her autobiography *Lulu in Hollywood* in 1982. Her sexual attractiveness had actually become more potent over the years. In her classic films she projects a screen image which is a reflection of her own private life. Whereas Lillian Gish personified virginal purity and Clara Bow and the early Crawford the uninhibited flapper, Brooks projected a fiercely independent, sensual, sexually ambiguous woman who would go her own way no matter what the consequences. Garbo and Dietrich, about to come into her own in *The Blue Angel*, represented the European personification of these qualities, though Brooks spoke dismissively of Marlene as 'too old' for the part of Lulu. Brooks was not out to win friends or influence people.

Hence she was so perfectly right for Frank Wedekind's Lulu in *Pandora's Box/Die Büchse der Pandora*, as the nymphomaniac whose insatiable desires lead to her death at the hands of Jack the Ripper. Director G W Pabst chose her for the role after her performance in Hawks' *A Girl in Every Port* as the vamp who destroys the seemingly indestructible friendship of two carousing sailors by her indiscriminate passions. Among Lulu's lovers is the lesbian Countess Geschwitz, played by Alice Roberts, who thus became the first fully developed lesbian character to appear in the movies. Seemingly, Roberts so hated playing the role that her passionate declarations of love to Lulu were actually directed off-camera to Pabst himself, or any other suitable male presence. One of Brooks' other co-stars was the Prague-born matinée idol, Francis Lederer, who started a new career in Hollywood in 1934 in *Man of Two Worlds* and died, aged 94, in 2000.

Louise Brooks' second film for GW Pabst, *Diary of a Lost Girl/Das Tagebuch einer Verlorenen* (1929), was the director's final silent film and another notable *succès d'estime*, with Brooks as an innocent raped by her father's business partner and having a baby as a result. She is sent to a sexually charged but hellish 'school for wayward girls' and escapes to take refuge in a brothel. This time the lesbian element is represented by actress-dancer Valeska Gert, herself a practising Sapphist.

Brooks' last European film and final starring role was in *Prix de beauté* (1930), a melodrama in which she is a contestant in a Miss Europa Beauty Contest. Though this was no classic, Brooks' luminous performance was highly praised. Directed by Augusto Genina, who also co-scripted with René Clair, the film offered the novelty of Edith Piaf dubbing Brooks' singing voice. Following her belated return to film fame, Brooks' career was recaptured in the 1985 documentary *Lulu in Berlin*, directed by Richard Leacock and Susan Woll, which contains her only filmed interview.

Born in Cherryvale Kansas, Brooks moved to New York at 15 to study ballet and was soon asked by Florenz Ziegfeld to dance in his Follies. She signed a contract with Paramount to make films in their New York studio, starting with *The Street of Forgotten Men* (1925). Four films released in 1926 included *The American Venus* and *The Show-Off*. When the Astoria Studios closed, Brooks moved to Los Angeles and played bigger parts in *Evening Clothes* (1927) and *The City Gone Wild* (1927). Her films in 1928 were *The Canary Murder Case* and *Beggars of Life*, the latter directed by William Wellman, with Richard Arlen and Wallace Beery. After shooting her stepfather when he tries to rape her, Brooks' character disguises herself as a boy and hits the road with a personable tramp (Arlen).

Brooks claimed not to be a lesbian but admitted to several lesbian affairs, including one with Greta Garbo, besides frequenting gay and lesbian clubs in Berlin. She believed that being thought of as gay influenced Pabst in choosing her for *Pandora's Box*. She was briefly married to director/producer Edward Sutherland from 1926-28 and her captivating screen persona, combined with a fascinating personal life, made her a gay icon to discriminating lesbians for generations. She died of a heart attack aged 79. □

7 ... AS THESPIANS

PRIVATE LIVES OF THE STARS, PART TWO

BARBARA STANWYCK [1907-1990]
[Ruby Stevens]

Like her friend Joan Crawford, Barbara Stanwyck was the epitome of independence and determination. Her streak of nonconformity, toughness and resilience – though she could charm the birds off the trees when she wanted to – was probably what made her so popular with lesbian audiences. She could match, and sometimes outdo, any man (or woman) who came her way and, although she never came out of the closet, she lived through marriages to two homosexuals without a breath of any gay scandal.

Born Ruby Stevens in Brooklyn, her mother died when she was only four years old and she had to rely on relatives and foster parents for her upbringing. At the age of 15 she followed her sister Mildred into the Ziegfeld Follies and henceforth into burlesque, where she shared the stage with Mary Tomlinson, a clergyman's daughter who had run away from home to save her family from possible embarrassment over her lesbianism. Mary changed her name to Marjorie Main, later the raucous-voiced mother in the Ma and Pa Kettle series (1949-1957).

At the age of 19 Ruby Stevens became Barbara Stanwyck, during the Broadway run of *The Noose*, in which she had the female lead. At 21 she married the twice-divorced comedian Frank Fay, ten years her senior and then at the peak of his career in vaudeville. In 1929

Opposite: Barbara Stanwyck in *Sorry Wrong Number* (1948).

they moved to Los Angeles, where he became the founder of the modern gay movement. Besides being a closet homosexual, however, he was also an alcoholic and a wife-beater. At this time his wife was starting her meteoric rise to fame and stardom and, with her money, they bought a mansion in Brentwood. This made them the back-fence neighbours of Joan Crawford and her second husband, Franchot Tone. After starring in a number of B-movies, Stanwyck really made her mark between 1930 and 1931 in *Ladies of Leisure*, *Illicit*, *Night Nurse* and *Miracle Woman*. For two decades thereafter she was a top box-office attraction.

Stanwyck's first Academy Award nomination was for the downtrodden mother she played in the weepie *Stella Dallas* (1937), in which her old friend Marjorie Main played her mother-in-law. Three more nominations were to follow for *Ball of Fire* (1942), with Gary Cooper, *Double Indemnity* (1944) and *Sorry, Wrong Number* (1948) with Burt Lancaster. Stanwyck's second marriage to the beautiful Robert Taylor, in 1939, was studio-arranged, seemingly under pressure from the fan magazines complaining about the inapposite 'closeness' of certain star couples without benefit of clergy. Among those named were Clark Gable and Carole Lombard, who were as *bona fide* as anyone in Hollywood. Never mind that Stanwyck spent the honeymoon night at her ranch and Taylor went home to mother. At least the studios, the fans and Hedda Hopper

DOUBLE INDEMNITY

1944 Paramount 106 mins b/w
Producer: Joseph Sistrom; Director: Billy Wilder;
Screenplay: Raymond Chandler, Billy Wilder (from
story Three of a Kind by James M Cain);
Cinematographer: John Seitz
Barbara Stanwyck, Fred MacMurray, Edward G
Robinson, Tom Powers, Porter Hall, Jean Heather,
Tom Powers, Byron Barr, Richard Gaines

This classic *film noir* redefined Stanwyck's already highly successful movie career. Her stylised performance portrays an icy woman whose boredom and sexual drive lead her to involve her shifty lover (MacMurray) in murder with malice aforethought and without compunction. She, Phyllis Dietrichson, persuades Walter Neff to help her take out a life insurance policy on her husband, played by Tom Powers, without his knowledge and also to murder him in order to collect it. They have to contend with the claims adjuster, Barton Keyes (Edward G Robinson), who suspects that all is not as it should be. The lovers find their trust in each other sorely tested and a game of cat and mouse ensues with Robinson.

MacMurray gives the performance of his career and Robinson once again proves himself to be a consummate master of his craft. This sinister story gives Wilder the opportunity to hone his technique as a skilful and subtle exponent of the genre as well as highlighting how Chandler is able to treat this type of narrative with such cynical adroitness. Among a clutch of other Oscar nominations, Stanwyck was given her third: had there been any justice in Hollywood she would have won.

In the climax, Phyllis shoots her daughter Lola's boyfriend, with whom she has been having an affair. She hopes to pin the murder on Walter Neff, but he shoots her instead. Walter, wounded himself, manages to crawl to his office to narrate the story into a dictaphone. As he dies, Keys calls the police – bringing the story full circle to complete Walter's narrative, with which the film began.

were satisfied. When the two stars did move in together they had separate bedrooms. Stanwyck had a lifelong relationship with her publicist, Helen Ferguson, which could not be questioned and, to keep it all in the family, Ferguson went on to become Taylor's manager.

An early triumph for Stanwyck, George Stevens' 1935 *Annie Oakley*, was notable for the fact that her popular performance as the flamboyant and masculine markswoman was played as a feminine lass who gets all sentimental at the sight of rugged Preston Foster as a rival gunslinger. During the next four years Stanwyck had some great successes opposite charismatic co-stars. There were two team-ups in screwball comedies with Henry Fonda in *The Mad Miss Manton* (1938) and *The Lady Eve* (1941), which was directed by Preston Sturges. *Remember the Night* (1940), a charming sentimental romance, was Stanwyck's first film opposite Fred MacMurray. It was also her first with the great costumier Edith Head and ace photographer Ted Tetzlaff. The critic C A Lejeune, no fan of Barbara's, grudgingly referred to her as 'the now quite beautiful Miss Stanwyck'.

Aside from *Double Indemnity*, other highlights in Stanwyck's career included *The Two Mrs Carrolls* with Humphrey Bogart (1947), *Sorry, Wrong Number* (her fourth Oscar nomination, 1948) and *Titanic* (1953) with Clifton Webb, which prompted him to dub 'Missy' his 'Favourite Hollywood Lesbian'. Although her last two films for the cinema, Elvis Presley's *Roustabout* (1964) and *The Night Walker* (1964), with her ex-husband Robert Taylor, were hardly jewels in her crown, 1962's *Walk on*

Right: Capucine, Laurence Harvey and Barbara Stanwyck in *Walk on the Wild Side* (1962).

WALK ON THE WILD SIDE

1962 Columbia/Famous Artists 114 mins b/w
Producer: Charles K Feldman; Director: Edward Dmytryk; Screenplay: Joe Fante and Edmund Morris (from a novel by Nelson Algren); Cinematography: Joe Macdonald
Barbara Stanwyck, Laurence Harvey, Capucine, Jane Fonda, Anne Baxter, Richard Rust, Karl Swenson, Donald Barry, Juanita Moore

This was Stanwyck's return to the big screen after five years. She had made three films in 1957, including two Westerns (a genre she loved): *Trooper Hook* and *Forty Guns*, directed by Samuel Fuller. She received an Emmy for TV's *The Barbara Stanwyck Show* in 1961 and was happy to accept a good part in a film when it was offered – that of Jo Courtney, the lesbian Madame of a bordello in New Orleans who lusts after her new girl, Capucine. She bitterly resents the intrusion of the smooth Laurence Harvey, who falls heavily for Capucine. Among Jo's other trials is a legless husband who propels himself around on a trolley. Her vicious fight with Capucine is a Horse-Frightening Moment.

The film was not the huge success it was expected to be, despite the adult theme and the excellent cast, including Jane Fonda and Anne Baxter, probably because of the screenplay, which watered down Nelson Algren's novel. Harvey stated this in an interview, while the *New York Herald Tribune* wrote: 'The compassion, the sense of personal waste that could make the film unusual and penetrating is crowded out by constant underlining and melodramatic clichés.' Stanwyck herself said she 'always thought it could have been a damm good movie, but it just didn't work out.'

Again, her fellow workers admired and liked her. Baxter said: 'I unburdened to Barbara. She's that kind of person. You feel that you can trust her.' Harvey, whose sense of self importance was second to none, received a blistering tongue-lashing for reporting late on set on the last day's shooting. Nevertheless, he delivered a remarkable testimonial: 'Miss Stanwyck is one of the most startling and professional women I have ever worked with. She had a great air of honesty and directness about her and her relationship with cast and crew was totally unpretentious. In fact, I could never quite decide which side of the camera she was working on!'

Capucine, a great beauty, had been a model in Paris and was herself a lesbian. Rumours that she was transsexual were never substantiated and she went on to act opposite Peter Sellers in *The Pink Panther* (1964) and appear in two *Pink Panther* sequels in 1982 and 1983. However, her film career petered out after *My First 40 Years* (1989). Increasingly isolated in later years, she ended her life by jumping from the balcony of her eighth floor apartment in Switzerland, at the age of 57, in 1990.

the Wild Side was significant in that Stanwyck played her one and only screen lesbian.

For four years, from 1965, Barbara Stanwyck created a new image for herself as the 'blood and guts matriarch' Victoria Barkley in the western TV series *The Big Valley*. She loved the character, the work and most of her co-stars. One concession to the now-colour TV cameras was that she agreed Victoria should be portrayed as blonde, acknowledging that as 'an old broad who combines elegance with guts', her younger audiences would hesitate to accept the heroine of a TV soap with white hair. Throughout her film career, most of the movies were in black-and-white; as her hair became increasingly flecked with grey she declined to dye it, but if the screenplay called for a wig she would wear one.

In her later years she suffered from some severe illnesses, some of them near-fatal, but she continued to work. At 76 she made a strong impression as a woman of great wealth, deeply religious, who nevertheless falls in love with a young priest, played by Richard Chamberlain, in the TV series *The Thorn Birds* (1983). This series was based on the novel by Colleen McCullough, published in 1977. From 1985 to 1986 Stanwyck starred in *The Colbys*, an offshoot of *Dynasty* in which her 'daughter' Linda Evans had co-starred with Joan Collins and John Forsythe. Stanwyck's co-stars were Stephanie Beacham and, as Barbara's romantic interest, Charlton Heston. This was, perhaps, a trifle bizarre in the circumstances since he was in his early sixties and she was approaching 80. Her caustic wit had not deserted her: she said of her co-star, 'He still thinks he's parting the Red Sea!' After a long fight with illness, she finally succumbed to emphysema and died in 1990 at the age of 83. Her sexual orientation has been called the 'best kept secret in the movies', according to Axel Madsen in *The Sewing Circle*.

RICHARD CROMWELL [1910-1960]
[Roy M Radabough]

There has been a tendency to downgrade Richard Cromwell's career, due perhaps to his brief marriage to British-born star Angela Lansbury (1945-46) at a time when his own Hollywood fortunes were in decline. This was mainly due to his career being interrupted by World War II service in the Coast Guards from 1942.

Lansbury's overnight rise to stardom – being Oscar-nominated in her first film *Gaslight* (1944) at 19 and again in her third, *The Picture of Dorian Gray* (1945) – was the start of a career which has kept her constantly employed in films, TV and theatre for an incredible six decades. Mostly, she played parts much older than her years; as Laurence Harvey's mother in *The Manchurian Candidate* (1962), she was only three years his senior. In her seventies, she became the most powerful and richest woman on television after the triumph of her supersleuth character Jessica Spencer in the series *Murder, She Wrote*. When Cromwell walked out on her after 11 months, she married her second husband and agent, Peter Shaw.

Angela, as an adolescent, had admired photos of Cromwell in fan magazines and was thrilled to meet him in the flesh when she was evacuated during World War II to Hollywood. It seems to have been love at first sight on her side: her favourite pin-up was suddenly available. On his side, the vision that was Sybil Vane, the music hall singer besotted by the decadent Dorian Gray in the film, was responsive to his declaration of love. He told her that she was the prettiest thing on two feet and invited her and her mother, actress Moyna MacGill, to supper in his home on a hillside in Los Angeles, overlooking Sunset Boulevard. They were married three weeks before her 20th birthday in September 1945.

LIVES OF A BENGAL LANCER

1934 Paramount 109 mins b/w
Producer: Louis B Lighton; Director: Henry Hathaway;
Screenplay: Waldemar Young, John L Balderston,
Achmed Abdullah, Grover Jones, William Slavens
McNutt (from the novel by Major Francis Yeats-
Brown); Cinematographer: Charles Lang
Gary Cooper, Franchot Tone, Richard Cromwell, Sir
Guy Standing, C Aubrey Smith, Monte Blue,
Kathleen Burke, Douglas Dumbrille, Akim Tamiroff

This was hailed as the greatest war film ever made, despite the glorification of British imperialism, which was the accepted thing at the time. Richard Cromwell plays Lieutenant David Stone, son of the Commanding Officer of the 41st Bengal Lancers, an intractable military veteran and a rigid disciplinarian. The young lieutenant welcomes as allies Lieutenant Alan McGregor (Gary Cooper), a seasoned frontier fighter who speaks his mind but can be flexible when the need arises, and Lieutenant John Forsythe (Franchot Tone), who is relaxed and easy-going. The Colonel is trying to prevent an Indian uprising by blocking a local chieftan's attempt to steal two million rounds of ammunition from the friendly Emir of Gopal (Akim Tamiroff). David's situation with his father is tense and he gets support and understanding from Alan and John. There is torture and action galore. Such a film would be unthinkable today but was a massive box-office success in the mid-thirties.

Cromwell had become her first lover, probably in an attempt to change his sexuality and conform to the all-American male image the studio had created for him. He was financially beset, work was petering out after his absence in the Coast Guards, and he was becoming an alcoholic. Lansbury had met his friends, such as Joan Crawford, Gary Cooper and Cary Grant, as well as several homosexual companions, but she was busy with her work and believed in his love, even though their sex life was not great. She just thought that was the way things were and had no inkling anything was wrong until she returned home one day to find a note on the Steinway Grand piano he had given her for a wedding present. It said, 'I'm sorry, darling. I just can't go on.' He, his car and his clothes were gone.

None of their friends seemed surprised; it appeared that everyone but she had known — even, apparently, her mother. Such situations were not uncommon in the Hollywood of which she had so little experience. Since that time it has become commonplace to imply that Cromwell's career had consisted of just a string of bit parts, which is untrue. Equally insubstantial is the common gossip that Angela had found Richard in bed with another man. 'It was pure invention,' she says. He had done his best to be a good husband and had cracked under the strain.

Born in Los Angeles, Cromwell started his career as an artist-decorator and became interested in acting through painting masks of Hollywood stars. With his looks he soon gained work as a film extra and after just two days' employment on *King of Jazz* (1930), starring Paul Whiteman & His Orchestra, he was spotted by a talent scout and re-christened through a fan magazine competition, in which readers, judging by his photograph, suggested a name they considered most appropriate to his 'boy next door looks'. Out of 500 entries the studio chose 'Richard Cromwell' and the lucky winner was awarded a night on the town with the new star, accompanied by a photographer and a press agent. This dignitary announced that Cromwell was to play the lead in *Tol'able David* for director John G Blystone, a story that had been filmed in silent days. Despite having no experience of acting, Cromwell gave a good enough showing in this 1930 whimsy to continue playing the personification of innocent youth for the next 12 years.

Like William Haines, Cromwell was playing glowing youths into his thirties, appearing in juvenile leads from the start, his films including Marie Dressler's *Emma* (1932), directed by Clarence Brown. The same year he was best friend to Tom Brown, both army cadets in *Tom Brown of Culver*, in which Brown had the unusual distinction of having the film script written around his own name. In 1933 Cromwell co-starred with Clara Bow in her last film, *Hoopla*, but his most rewarding opportunity came two years later in *Lives of a Bengal Lancer*.

In 1936 Cromwell travelled to England to make his only British film, a change of armed forces to *Our Fighting Navy/Torpedoed!* (1937). The film's publicity agent, Bob Grahame, remembered Cromwell's charm and co-operation when it came to promoting the flag-waving epic, which was directed by Norman Walker for producer Herbert Wilcox. In 1938 Cromwell played Henry Fonda's young brother in *Jezebel* for director William Wyler. The next year he was again teamed with Fonda under another outstanding director, John Ford, in *The Young Mr Lincoln* (1939). This film offered a dramatic part for Cromwell as one of two brothers facing lynching when accused of murder. Lincoln (Fonda) takes on the boys' defence and traps the real killer into a confession.

At this vital point in Cromwell's career, after his success as *Baby Face Morgan*, directed by Arthur Dreifuss in 1942, his call-up was a bitter blow to his growing star status. On demobilisation he made only one more film, *Bungalow 13* (1948). Before his death from cancer at 50, he had become friends again with Angela Lansbury and her husband, Peter Shaw.

JEAN MARAIS [1913-1998]
[Jean Alfred Villain-Marais]

The film career of France's most glamorous leading man really took off when he met the poet, playwright and film director Jean Cocteau in the late thirties. Cocteau had started creating films of great pictorial beauty, usually based on classical themes, full of memorable, haunting images, which drew almost ethereal performances from his small company of actors. The group was soon to be headed by Marais, with whom he had fallen in love on sight.

Cocteau concentrated on guiding the career of his protégé and lover on stage and later in films. He knew just how to bring out the full capabilities and the blond, Nordic good looks of the young and athletic actor, who had entered movies in 1933 in *L'Epervier*, of which he was also assistant director. Cocteau began to write plays and film scripts for Marais, who became France's leading romantic actor during the forties and fifties. The relationship may be compared to the association between Josef von Sternberg and Marlene Dietrich in the early thirties, except that the Cocteau-Marais association endured considerably longer.

There was no secret about their relationship – France was always open about sexual matters – and Marais was genuinely loved by the public. Building workers, recognising him when he passed by, were wont to call out, 'C'est la belle Jeanne. Comment va tu, cherie?' He always answered with the cheerful bonhomie which was the key to his personality.

The most celebrated of the Cocteau-Marais collaborations was *La Belle et la bête/Beauty and the Beast* (1946), acclaimed as a poetic masterpiece. Marais played a triple role, including the Prince and the Beast. Their 1948 triumph *L'Aigle a deux têtes/The Eagle With Two Heads* was an intricate Ruritanian romance in which Marais co-starred with one of the greatest French film actresses, Edwige Feuillère. This was followed the same year by *Les Parents terribles/The Storm Within*, adapted by Cocteau from his novel. Two films in which Marais starred, for which Cocteau wrote the screenplays but did not direct, were in *L'Eterne retour/The Eternal Return/Love Eternal* and *Ruy Blas* (both 1943). In the latter Marais played the title role as well as the villain, Cesari.

Another of the team's most highly praised collaborations, *Orphée* (1949), featured Marais in the title role of Orpheus. This has been called one of the most remarkable films ever made, with natural settings distorted by light and shade to suggest the mystical regions of Orpheus' underworld. A reprise in 1960, *Le Testament d'Orphée*, was the last film they made together. Marais continued as a sought-after leading actor in films after his mentor's death in 1963, appearing in a French film based on the Leslie Charteris character The Saint, *Le Saint prend l'affut* (1965), which did not travel abroad. In 1964 he played master criminal *Fantômas*, with a sequel in 1967, *Fantômas contre Scotland Yard*. Without the guiding hand of Cocteau it is doubtful whether he would have reached as far as he did, the highest echelon of French film stardom. Whilst Marais was his most personally cherished creation, Cocteau's influence on such other great exponents of cinematic art as directors Luis Buñuel, André Delvaux and Georges Franju was both unmistakeable and understandable.

Born in Cherbourg, the son of a physician, Marais determined upon a career in acting while still at high school. Turned down as an actor by the Paris Conservatoire, he secured small parts in the theatre, then marked time in movies until his momentous meeting with Cocteau, who was the darling of the intellectual world, besides being a great poet, painter, novelist and playwright. Among the notable roles Marais played without his most influential director were *Le Secret de Mayerling/The Secret of Mayerling* (1949), as Crown Prince Rudolph, *Si Versailles*

m'était conté/Royal Affairs in Versailles (1954), as Louis XV, *Le Comte de Monte-Cristo* (1955), as Edmond Dantes, and *Ponzio Pilato* (1961), as Pontius Pilate, filmed in Italy.

Marais' last film, in 1996, was Bernardo Bertolucci's *Stealing Beauty/Lo ballo da sola*, an Italian/British/French co-production in which, at 83, he played a French art dealer who had become part of the adoptive family of Diana and Ian Grayson (Sinead Cusack and Donal McCann). Living in Tuscany, they are visited by Lucy (Liv Tyler), the daughter of their friend, Lucy's high-living mother, who had committed suicide. Another houseguest of the Graysons is the terminally ill Alex Parrish, played by Jeremy Irons, who becomes mentor to the young girl. Marais, white-haired and bearded, is still recognisable although the camera seldom lingers long on him – just long enough for him to utter a few philosophical remarks about love and destiny. A gentle swan song for one of French cinema's great romantics.

DANNY KAYE [1913-1987]
[David D Kaminski]

One of the most original American comedians, Danny Kaye was essentially a star for Technicolor, radiating with his red-gold hair and puckish features a glamour whose appeal was indefinably gay without ever becoming camp.

His marriage to Sylvia Fine in 1940 was a great professional relationship. She wrote the bulk of his unique tongue-twisting patter songs, used to such great effect in his movies and on records. His sexual orientation was accepted quite naturally; people who could not define the word homosexual accepted that he was 'different' and were content to leave it at that. His personality, originally defined in his stage work, radiated down from cinema screens with as much warmth as it did in the theatre. His seasons at the London Palladium played to standing room only from 1948 and he also entertained at Buckingham Palace. Rumours that circulated about Kaye's friendship with the Oliviers confused a public already concerned about Vivien Leigh's involvement with Peter Finch, leading to her nervous breakdown and subsequent withdrawal from the film *Elephant Walk* (1954), in which they were to co-star.

Kaye's real rise to fame came on Broadway in the 1941 hit *Lady in the Dark*, in which, as the gay secretary, Russell, he achieved the impossible by upstaging the star, Gertrude Lawrence, when he sang the patter song 'Tchaikovsky', rattling off the names of 50 Russian composers in 39 seconds flat. This brought him to the attention of Hollywood and he signed a film contract for Samuel Goldwyn. Following a high-powered publicity build-up by the Goldwyn Studios, he was introduced to cinemagoers in Elliott Nugent's 1944 musical extravaganza, *Up In Arms*. Two girls, Constance Dowling and Dinah Shore, are trapped on the Pacific-bound ship taking Kaye and his friend Dana Andrews to the war zone. The captain (Louis Calhern) discovers them and Danny is jailed after the ship docks. During an attack by the Japanese, he is captured but manages to escape in some hilariously funny scenes and even takes some of the enemy prisoner. The sets are spectacular. Some humorously tuneful songs, for which Harold Arlen and Ted Koehler received an Academy Award nomination, are shared by Kaye and American Forces Pin-Up Dinah Shore.

Kaye's movies through the forties and fifties brought an innovative gay presence to the screen. For example, Kaye and Andrews (proving himself as adept at comedy as he was in drama) are seated next to each other on a bus, while Dowling and Shore are seated opposite. Both sides are declaring their love for each other but to the other passengers it appears that they are hearing love talk from two gay partnerships. Cue: pursed lips

and shocked glances. Simplistic, but funny, in a manner to suit the attitudes of the day.

Kaye's follow-up movie proved just as popular. In *Wonder Man* (1945), he plays twin brothers, an outgoing and brash entertainer and an introverted intellectual librarian. The former is murdered and his ghost persuades the living sibling to impersonate him to discover the identity of the killer. Confusion sets in when the spirit of the dead twin enters the living one, providing a field day for Kaye's manic characterisations, backed by the usual superior production values and musical interludes, with Virginia Mayo as the dead man's fiancée and a bewildered Vera-Ellen as the stoic librarian's girlfriend. Samuel Goldwyn produced the film personally and Bruce Humberstone directed.

Goldwyn was again in charge of *The Secret Life of Walter Mitty* (1947), with Norman Z McLeod in the director's chair for this adaptation of James Thurber's classic short story about the timid daydreaming hero whose fantasies take him into all kinds of adventures. The producer invested over $8 million in the venture, with the glamorous Goldwyn Girls featured in some of Kaye's spectacular numbers and Virginia Mayo co-starring once again, one of his favourite and most beautiful leading ladies. Boris Karloff parodies himself as a sinister psychiatrist and Fay Bainter excels as Danny's mother from hell. This has been rated as Kaye's best film.

Howard Hawks remade his own *Ball of Fire* (1942) as the musical *A Song is Born* (1948), with Kaye in the Gary Cooper role of the stodgy professor researching slang for a new encyclopedia and Virginia Mayo in Barbara Stanwyck's role as the stripper, Sugarpuss O'Shea. There is an excellent jazz score with Benny Goodman, Louis Armstrong, Tommy Dorsey and Lionel Hampton, all in the same movie. Cool.

The fifties began with Kaye being given a Golden Globe Award for his delightful performance in *On the Riviera* (1951), a very funny updat-

Right: Jeanne Lafayette and Danny Kaye in *Hans Christian Andersen* (1952).

ing of *The Man from the Folies Bergère* (1935) and *That Night in Rio* (1941). Kaye took the dual role of a cabaret entertainer and a famous financier, played in the earlier films by, respectively, Maurice Chevalier and Don Ameche. Gene Tierney as the financier's wife inherited the part of the Baroness from Merle Oberon and Alice Faye. Musical specialist Walter Lang was the director.

In 1952 Charles Vidor helmed another brilliant musical, particularly for children: *Hans Christian Andersen*, a biopic of Hans Christian Andersen, the gay (but not in this version) author and teller of the world's most famous fairy stories, in which Kaye gets to sing Frank Loesser's 'The Ugly Duckling', 'Inchworm', 'The King's New Clothes' and 'Wonderful, Wonderful Copenhagen'. The British-made *Stories of a Flying Trunk* (1979) offers a more realistic oortrayal of Andersen, as played by Murray Melvin, but Samuel Goldwyn's earlier version proved far more popular. Andersen, who played with dolls as a child, aspired to be

a ballet dancer and was kept by a male lover, was definitely not a fit subject for the kiddies.

Knock on Wood (1954), with all the hilarity and none of the sentimentality of the previous film, cast Kaye as a ventriloquist opposite Mai Zetterling in her only American film, directed by Norman Panama and Melvin Frank. Also in 1954, Michael Curtiz directed the all-time perennial Yuletide favourite *White Christmas*, with Bing Crosby and Danny Kaye as wartime buddies who become an entertainment team and come to the rescue of the ski resort inn run by their old army commander, Dean Jagger. The Irving Berlin score, fashioned around the surefire title song, is interpreted to maximum effect by singer Rosemary Clooney and dancer Vera-Ellen, along with Crosby and Kaye, who perform a drag number with gusto and enthusiasm. Of the remainder of Kaye's fifties films – all extremely popular – the most brilliant is *The Court Jester*.

Kaye saw the fifties out with a semi-dramatic role in a biopic of jazz trumpeter Red Nichols,

THE COURT JESTER

1955 Paramount/Dena 101 mins Technicolor
Producers: Melvin Frank, Norman Panama; Directors: Norman Panama,
Melvin Frank; Screenplay: Norman Panama, Melvin Frank;
Cinematographer: Ray June
Danny Kaye, Glynis Johns, Basil Rathbone, Angela Lansbury, Cecil Parker,
Mildred Natwick, Robert Middleton, Michael Pate

With this picture, the Norman Panama/Melvin Frank team crafted a vehicle for Danny Kaye rated, along with *The Secret Life of Walter Mitty* (1948), as one of his two best and most inventive films. Kaye plays Hawkins, a lowly valet who rises to become the leader of a peasant revolt to restore the rightful King Roderick (Cecil Parker) to the throne of England. Hawkins transforms himself into a court jester to gain access to the wicked Sir Ravenhurst (Basil Rathbone), usurper of the royal prerogative, and to overthrow his oppressive rule. Naturally, the jester turns the palace protocol upside down.

On his side is Glynis Johns as Maid Jean, in her first American film, while Angela Lansbury as Princess Gwendolyn is his ally at the palace. Hawkins' plan to use poison inevitably goes haywire when the code words 'the vessel with the poison is the vessel with the pestle' gets changed in the translation, and another tongue-twister, 'the flagon with the dragon', not unnaturally gets distorted in being related from mouth to mouth. Despite these confusions, Sir Ravenhurst is vanquished and King Roderick is restored as ruler of the realm. Apart from Danny Kaye on his most sparkling form, the ladies enter happily into the spirit of this swashbuckling spoof, while Rathbone proves that his comedy timing makes him, with his urban villainy, the ideal foil for Danny Kaye.

The Five Pennies (1959), with Barbara Bel Geddes playing his wife and Louis Armstrong as himself. The film was voted an Academy nomination for Best Musical Score – Nichols played his own trumpet to Kaye's miming. Under Melville Shavelson's direction Kaye turns in a strong dramatic performance – the supreme farceur held well in check. The serious side of Kaye's nature became apparent when he began to devote more and more of his time to worldwide tours on behalf of UNICEF, entertaining children in developing countries. In 1954 he was awarded a special Oscar for his 'unique talent, his service to the Academy, the motion picture industry and the American people.'

Kaye's film appearances in the sixties were only sporadic. From 1963 to 1967 he starred in his own *Danny Kaye* TV Show, for which he won both an Emmy and a Peabody Award. He returned to comedy roles on the big screen in *On the Double* (1961), directed by Melville Shavelson, with a 'Special Guest Appearance of Miss Diana Dors', whose management had appropriated the 'Miss' title formerly reserved for such luminaries as 'Miss Ethel Barrymore' and opera singer 'Miss Grace Moore'. Danny had a special penchant for English leading ladies, including Mai Zetterling (Swedish-born but a star of British films), Glynis Johns, Elsa Lanchester (*The Inspector General*, 1949), Patricia Cutts (*Merry Andrew*, 1958), not to mention his long-standing friendship with Princess Margaret.

His last leading role was in Frank Tashlin's *The Man From the Diner's Club* (1963). In 1969, Kaye was the brightest spark among the many guest stars supporting Katharine Hepburn as the eccentric Countess in Bryan Forbes' *The Madwoman of Chaillot*. He plays the ragpicker who helps her outwit a gang of avaricious oil company bigwigs. Among Kaye's 60 TV appearances were *Peter Pan* (1975) and *Skokie* (1981), as a Jew trying to prevent a neo-Nazi march in a small American town. At the time of his death at 74, following an operation for cancer, Danny Kaye, who often claimed to be a 'wife-made man', had worked for the United Nations for 35 years. His wife, Sylvia Fine, outlived him.

DENNIS PRICE [1915-1973]
[Dennistoun Franklyn John Rose-Price]

Of all the male Rank stars, Dennis Price was the most elegant and cultivated. Educated at Oxford University, he began work as an actor in a stock company in 1937, from which he joined John Gielgud's company in the West End the same year. Invalided out of the army in 1944, he made his film debut the same year in *A Canterbury Tale*. From then on Price was in regular employment in leading roles, often as the romantic lead opposite the Rank Organisation's top female stars, such as Phyllis Calvert in *The Magic Bow*, *Caravan* with Jean Kent and *Hungry Hill* with Margaret Lockwood (all 1946). In 1947 Price was a murder victim in *Dear Murderer*, co-starring Eric Portman, Greta Gynt and Hugh Williams, and then switched to the murderer role in *Holiday Camp* (1947) as the homicidal Squadron Leader, Hardwick.

This was around the time I was working at Shepherd's Bush Studios as an assistant director and Dennis Price was always there on one set or another, polite, professional, urbane and slightly reserved. At one time, he was working on two films at once: *Easy Money*, a portmanteau film starring Greta Gynt and Jack Warner, and in the costumes of two centuries before in *The Bad Lord Byron* (both 1949).

Also in 1949, Price gave his subtle and deadly interpretation of Louis Mazzini, serial killer, in *Kind Hearts and Coronets*. He more than holds his own against eight Alec Guinnesses, playing members of the same family whom Mazzini must dispatch before he can inherit a dukedom. Robert Hamer was both writer and director. In 1950 Price was again a killer in *Murder Without Crime*, giving a performance which the *New York Times* wrote was 'exquisitely sadistic … A deadly dandy'. In the backstage story *Charley Moon* (1956), Price, long before it was 'safe' to do so, played Harold Armytage, a gay ham actor specialising in pantomime dames, in a cast which included Max Bygraves and Florence Desmond.

Price's marriage to Joan Schofield remained a closed book when she declined to co-operate with an aspiring biographer of Price after his death; the project was subsequently abandoned.

THE BAD LORD BYRON

1949 Triton 85 mins b/w
Producer: Aubrey Baring; Director: David MacDonald; Screenplay: Terence Young, Anthony Thorne, Peter Quennell, Laurence Kitchin, Paul Holt; Cinematographer: Stephen Dade
Dennis Price, Joan Greenwood, Mai Zetterling, Linden Travers, Sonia Holm, Irene Browne, Ernest Thesiger

Here we have the story of England's most romantic poet sanitised for Lord Rank's followers and played beautifully, if blandly, by Dennis Price. Price would have been more than qualified to interpret the real concept of the 'Byronic hero', who flourished from 1788 to 1824. Byron died in his mid-thirties of malaria contracted at Missolonghi, having joined the Greek insurgents in their uprising against the Turks. This was after his meeting with Shelley and the two years they spent in Switzerland and Italy, to which the story does not extend. There is no hint of bisexuality in the script and the affair with his half-sister Lady Augusta Leigh (Linden Travers), which caused Byron to be ostracised from polite society, is also glossed over.

Several of Rank's top leading ladies figure in the movie, notably Mai Zetterling as Teresa Guiccioli and Sonia Holm as Annabella Millbank, whom Byron married. Irene Browne excels as her formidable, gossip-mongering mother and Joan Greenwood surpasses herself as Caroline Lamb, uttering the most-often quoted line in the film in her inimitable gurgling basso profundo: 'Lord Byron, are you really mad, bad and dangerous to know?' This occasioned director David MacDonald several retakes due to unquenchable giggles among crew, cast and, not least, Miss Greenwood herself. No performance of hers was without interest, which goes for most of the leads and the venerably camp Ernest Thesiger. The latter, whose wildly gay Dr Praetorius in *Bride of Frankenstein* (1935) has become a classic, often joined Queen Mary in crocheting petit-point at Buckingham Palace.

Years later, actress Hermione Baddeley, in her 1984 autobiography *The Unsinkable Hermione Baddeley*, 'outed him' in her account of the period when she was having affairs simultaneously with Price and Laurence Harvey. She wrote that, when he observed her bruises, Dennis remarked, 'Some of my boyfriends knock me about, too.' Then he winked and said 'I quite enjoy it.' Baddeley, who was the opposite of

Victim, and almost certainly explains his descent into trashy British and European horror films towards the end of his career.

Born in Twyford near Reading, the son of a general, it was, perhaps, inevitable that the dandies, bachelors and aesthetes Price often played were mostly from an upper-class background. The exception was, notably, in the theatre when he toured with Noël Coward in 1942 as Sam Leadbetter, a friend of the working-class family in *This Happy Breed*. Despite his alcoholism, increasing as the years passed, Price was seldom out of work on stage, screen and TV. In *The Passing Show, Charles Cochran Presents*, he impersonated Noel Coward and in 1965 he became a major TV personality in the series *The World of Wooster*, playing the archetypal English valet, Jeeves, opposite Ian Carmichael's Bertie Wooster.

In the year of his death from cirrhosis of the liver, he played critic Hector Snipe in the comedy-thriller *Theatre of Blood* (1973), rapidly killed off by crazy Shakespearean actor Edward Lionheart (Vincent Price), who sets out to demolish the critics who denied him the Best Actor award. Jolly Grand Guignol and a fitting end to one of England's most accomplished actors.

MARY MORRIS [1915-1988]

Had this actress been more adaptable to the requirements of the cinema, she might well have become a world star. She was comparable to other great screen ladies of androgynous appeal, but remained a well-respected stage actress whose film career was spasmodic and confined exclusively to England. In the end, television afforded her more rewarding roles for the unconventional self-expression in which she excelled.

After running her own repertory company, the Stranger Players, in Oxted, Surrey at the age of 21 – the company name is, perhaps, significant –

straitlaced, stated, 'I did not wink back.' In a later TV interview, *By Myself* in 1992, Dirk Bogarde said that he thought all the actors in his film *Victim* (1961) were straight except Dennis Price, who was homosexual but didn't mind a bit – 'Nobody else had the courage to do it.'

Price was blackmailed throughout much of the fifties and sixties, with emotionally and financially crippling results. This may explain why he was cast as a blackmailed actor in

Above: Dennis Price and Joan Greenwood in *Kind Hearts and Coronets* (1949) and *(below)* Anthony Nicholls, Dennis Price and Dirk Bogarde in *Victim* (1961).

Right: Mary Morris, Raymond Huntley and Francis L Sullivan in *Pimpernel Smith* (1941).

Morris was awarded a contract with MGM and went to Hollywood. It is not difficult to imagine the effect she had on Louis B Mayer. He had, after all, been ready to dismiss Greta Garbo as a mere adjunct to Swedish director Mauritz Stiller until she capitulated, albeit unenthusiastically, to being 'made-over' and groomed for the movies. Morris, however, was a totally different kettle of fish, in no way ready to abandon her own clearly defined lesbian persona to suit the whims of any mere mogul, no matter how powerful. She refused to alter her name to avoid confusion with an already well-established actress of the same name, nor would she relinquish her favourite bicycle in favour of a studio limousine. Katharine Hepburn, the closest analogy in respect of unconventional behaviour and even looks, kept her bicycle in the shed until she was well-established enough to travel any way she wanted.

No parts were offered in Hollywood and the contract was terminated, by mutual consent, after six months. Back in England, having gathered a certain amount of publicity as the girl who 'turned down' Louis B Mayer, she made her film debut as a tough and potentially lesbian young offender in an all-girl penitentiary. The film was *Prison Without Bars* (1938), in which she was singled out as a promising hope for the future. Her high cheekbones, large luminous eyes, savage grace and throaty, clipped tones rendered her both photogenic and sexy in an ambiguous way.

For Michael Powell and Emeric Pressburger, she played an uncompromising chauffeuse who joins in enthusiastically with the abduction of a young woman in *The Spy in Black* (1939). In producer Alexander Korda's Technicolor fantasy *The Thief of Bagdad* (1940), she played a murderous mechanical doll. The part was, however, so radically cut that the strong impression Morris created was muted. Her biggest opportunity in movies came in 1941 when the astute Leslie Howard, fresh from his success in *Gone With the Wind* (1939), chose her for his leading lady in *Pimpernel Smith*.

1941 was also the year Mary Morris played Peter Pan to Alastair Sim's Captain Hook in probably the most effective rendering of J M Barrie's renowned fairy story. Stationed in Edinburgh at the time, I was lucky to catch the play at the Lyceum Theatre there. Soon after, having tea at Machie's restaurant in Princes Street, I was intrigued to see Morris a few tables away, to such an extent that I shovelled mustard into my tea (mistaking it for granulated sugar) while gazing at the first actress I had ever seen in person. This ludicrous incident made us both laugh when I related it to her in the sixties at E J Barnes' cycle shop in Notting Hill Gate, where we used to have our machines serviced before repairing to the Earl of Lonsdale pub across the road.

By this time, in her fifties, Mary Morris, being one of those rare actresses who did little or nothing to care for her complexion and wore no make-up, looked much older than her years. But her looks and throaty laugh were unmistakable; she was without any affectation and extremely friendly to everybody. She had moved in as companion to Mary Ellis in her Eaton Square flat after the death of Ellis' third husband, Jock Roberts. In Ellis' autobiography, the actress records how the entrance of 'the other Mary' into her world completely changed her way of life, Morris bringing a totally unconventional outlook and happy-go-lucky personality. Peter Pan had come home to roost.

The two had become friends during the run of the 1950 play *If This Be Error*, in which Morris played Ellis' stepdaughter. The younger actress' Notting Hill studio was on the point of demolition and she was looking for somewhere to live. In *The Dancing Years – The Autobiography of Mary Ellis*, the older woman writes of their 'stimulating few years together … she was an amazing, talented and chronically compassionate young actress … who could be startling in Pirandello, Eugene O'Neill or Shakespeare.' This side of Morris had little or no opportunity to be exploited in the movies.

Mary Ellis turned 101 in June 2001, still serene in Eaton Square. There must be something about Ivor Novello's leading ladies –

maybe a blessing from above combined with the rarefied air of London SW1. Mary's friend, Dorothy Dickson, who lived just a few doors away, also attained the age of 101.

Mary Morris was born in Suva in the Fiji Islands and studied for the stage at the Royal Academy of Dramatic Art. She was constantly employed in the theatre, one of her most noted successes being in 1945 opposite John Mills in *Duet for Two Hands*, written by his wife Mary Hayley Bell. After *Train of Events* (1949), in which she played Peter Finch's unsympathetic wife, whom he murders, her film career petered out. She continued in radio and made the last of many TV appearances in *Sometime in August* (1990), broadcast two years after her death. The last time I saw her she was waiting at a Sloane Square bus stop, less than a week before her sudden death from a heart attack in 1988.

TYRONE POWER [1915-1958]
[Tyrone Edmund Power Jr]

Born of a multi-generational theatrical family, Tyrone's destiny was to be an actor. His great-grandfather, Tyrone Power, was a famous Irish actor (1797-1841) and his father, Tyrone Power Sr (1869-1931) was a matinée idol on Broadway and a star of silent films. Power Jr (as he was billed in early screen appearances) was a natural for film stardom, as one of the most photogenic young men ever to make the transition from stage to motion pictures.

Having attended a Shakespearean drama school, his Broadway debut in 1936 led immediately to his being spotted by a talent scout for Darryl F Zanuck and signed to a long-term Twentieth Century-Fox contract. During his years in New York, Power had a love affair with Robin Thomas, stepson of John Barrymore, which lasted for several years until he moved to Hollywood. From an early age he found himself

Right: Jack Haley, Alice Faye, Don Ameche and Tyrone Power in *Alexander's Ragtime Band* (1938).

attracted to both men and women, and both sexes found *him* irresistible. This became manifest when he made an early film appearance at 19 in *Tom Brown of Culver* (1932), directed by William Wyler. The film was a breeding ground for handsome young male talent, with its story of a training school for cadets. Apart from the eponymous star of the movie, there were Richard Cromwell and Alan Ladd. Power's romance with another male contract artist at Fox, probably William Eythe, had unfortunate consequences for the actor in question.

The studio built up romantic affairs with Loretta Young, his co-star in several movies, and with ice-skating queen Sonja Henie, with whom he co-starred twice – this liaison may well have been for real. In 1939 Tyrone married French star Annabella, a union which lasted nine years. Their friendship endured after their divorce, when he was able to confide in the sexually versatile some of his tangled affairs of the heart.

Born in Cincinnati, Power's family moved to California when he was seven due to his ill-health: for all his shining good looks, he was never really robust. His first leading role, in 1936, was as a wealthy nobleman called Karl in *Ladies in Love* – his first teaming with Loretta Young, in an all-star cast including Constance Bennett, Janet Gaynor, Paul Lukas and Don Ameche, as well as Zanuck's new French discovery, Simone Simon. The same year he went straight into co-starring with Madeleine Carroll in Henry King's ambitious *Lloyds of London* (1936), which brought him instant stardom. Top-billed was Freddie Bartholomew as the young version of Power's character, the founder of the great banking corporation.

After the cool, aristocratic Carroll, British-born and one of the screen's most beautiful women, Power's film union with the vivacious all-American Loretta Young in lightweight, glossy romantic comedies proved surefire box-office gold. Their three films together in 1937 were *Love is News*, directed by Tay Garnett, *Café Metropole*, directed by Edward H Griffith, and *Second Honeymoon*, directed by Walter Lang. Henry King's *In Old Chicago* (1938), centred around the great Chicago fire of 1871, proved one of the most important and spectacular films of the thirties. Power played the feckless son of Oscar-winning Alice Brady, cast as Mrs O'Leary, whose cow supposedly kicked over the lamp which started the fire. Her other son, the city's mayor, is Don Ameche and the girl the brothers fight over is Alice Faye in a part intended for Jean Harlow, who died the year before.

In 1938 the three stars went into one of the best pre-war black-and-white musicals. This was *Alexander's Ragtime Band,* directed by Henry King, with Power and Ameche as musicians caught up in the birth of the jazz age, again competing for the favours of Faye. King brought out a humanity between the characters, whose saga takes them through World War I and a veritable cornucopia of Irving Berlin songs, some belted out by Ethel Merman. Alice Faye, like many of her peers, fell for Power and the relationship evidently left a scar. Many years later, she declined to co-operate in a much sought-after autobiography because she wanted to be honest and did not feel like going into the subject of Power's bisexuality.

For his third film of 1938 there could hardly have been a greater contrast between leading ladies: from the warm-hearted, melodious Alice Faye to the regal First Lady of MGM, Norma Shearer. Power was on loan to MGM, for extra box-office ballast, to co-star in *Marie Antionette* (1938) as the Queen's young lover, Count Axel von Fersen, who tries to help her escape the guillotine. W S Van Dyke's lavish re-telling of French Revolutionary history was a successful showcase for Shearer, with strong support from the Oscar-nominated Robert Morley as the ineffectual Louis XVI, John Barrymore as Louis XV and Gladys George as Madame Du Barry. (After Du Barry thanks the Queen for inviting her to a palace reception, she replies, 'Ah, Madame, even royalty enjoys an occasional roll in the gutter!') Power then starred as Ferdinand de Lesseps, the engineer of the Suez Canal, reunit-

ed with Loretta Young, as the Empress Eugenie, in Allan Dwan's *Suez* (1938). This was the only time Power played opposite Annabella, whom he was to marry the following year.

In 1939 it was back to musicals and Alice Faye in *Rose of Washington Square* (1939), directed by Gregory Ratoff, a story based on the career of singer Fanny Brice, with Power as her lover Nicky Arnstein and Al Jolson basically playing himself. Henry King, one of Power's favourite and best directors, elicited a strong performance from him in the title role of *Jesse James* (1939), which co-starred Henry Fonda as his brother Frank. This was a romanticised account but gripping entertainment. In the same year there was another musical with Sonja Henie, *Second Fiddle*, with Power as her skating instructor. It was directed by Sidney Lanfield, who made their first film together, *Thin Ice*, in 1937.

Another superior director, Clarence Brown, and a powerful first screen version of Louis Bromfield's bestseller, *The Rains Came* (1939), had Power handsomely brown-skinned but strangely cast as an idealistic Indian doctor, playing opposite Myrna Loy. She is the promiscuous Lady Eskith who, under his influence, gives up her wanton ways and, ultimately, her life to nurse the sick in plague-ridden Ranchipur. George Brent co-stars and the movie is virtually stolen by the great Russian actress Maria Ouspenskaya, who made her film debut at 60 three years earlier. As the Rhanee, a tiny wizened figure in a sari, she dispenses worldly wisdom in a voice midway between the croak of a bullfrog and the rustle of parchment, which she resembles. Power's last film in 1939, *Daytime Wife*, cast him as the executive husband of Linda Darnell, who suspects him of infidelity. Gregory Ratoff was again in the director's chair.

In 1940 Power made two films in quick succession for Henry Hathaway. In *Johnny Apollo* he plays the son of convicted criminal Edward Arnold, to help whom he turns to crime, falling for gangster's moll Dorothy Lamour. In *Brigham Young* he plays a follower of the eponymous 19th century Mormon leader (Dean Jagger), the latter guiding his people across the land, seeking freedom from religious persecution. The same year Tyrone, who had proved himself equally adept at historical drama, light comedy and musical romance, found his ideal metier as a swashbuckling adventurer. The film in question was *The Mark of Zorro*.

After this spectacularly successful film, Power and Rouben Mamoulian reunited with Linda Darnell in another swashbuckling remake, *Blood and Sand* (1941). The original 1922 film had consolidated Rudolph Valentino's standing as the world's most acclaimed star, playing the naïve bullfighter Juan Gallardo, a part which brought out both the magnetism and danger inherent in Valentino's best characterisations before anyone had reason to pin the 'pink powder puff' label on him. In the opinion of the critics of the day, Power could not match Valentino's example, yet it brought out his own unique blend of personal charm and romanticism. He also looked magnificent in his matador outfits. Mamoulian's lush Technicolor compositions recalled the great Spanish masters and brought an Oscar to cinematographers Ernest Palmer and Ray Rennahan. Gallardo's ladies match the overall beauty of the film. Linda Darnell is the virtuous Carmen Espinosa, approved by Gallardo's deeply religious mother, Senora Augustias (Nazimova). The matador's temptress and nemesis, Dona Sol, is played by Rita Hayworth, on her way to becoming the screen's most seductive star. There is fine support from some of Fox's best contract players, including Anthony Quinn, Laird Cregar, J Carrol Naish and Lynn Bari.

After this winner there was a quick change into modern uniform as *A Yank in the RAF* (1941). This cast Power opposite Betty Grable, just coming into her own as Fox's number one

musical star. The film, directed by Henry King, turned out, on account of their combined box-office appeal and the timeliness of the subject, to be Fox's second highest financial winner of the year, second only to *How Green Was My Valley* (1941), which won the Best Picture Oscar.

Power's next foray into uniform was as a British army deserter and conscientious objector in *This Above All* (1942). He is persuaded to do his patriotic duty after all by Joan Fontaine, playing the upper-class daughter of a doctor. She had won that year's Best Actress Oscar for *Suspicion* and did not wholly approve of Tyrone's androgynous wife, Annabella, who, she was at pains to point out, was 'several years older than he.' Anatole Litvak directed. Like George Cukor, it was felt Litvak favoured the females in his films and the fact that he did not insist Power try an English accent lessened the star's conviction in the role.

Henry King directed Power again in *The Black Swan* (1942), this time in one of his most effective swashbuckling roles. Power plays a pirate out to win the love of the governor's daughter, Maureen O'Hara. George Sanders played the villain, as he had three times before in *Lloyds of London*, *Love is News* and Power's other 1942 picture, *Son of Fury*, directed by John Cromwell. After playing a naval officer in *Crash Dive* (1943), directed by Archie Mayo, Tyrone Power, at 28, encountered the real armed forces when he enlisted in the United States Marine Corps in August 1942.

Power was discharged from the Marines in November 1945, having logged 1100 hours' flying time, much of it under enemy fire. He was reunited with Annabella and their social circle, which included Tyrone's long-time best friend and lover, Cesar Romero, David Niven and Keenan Wynn. Wynn was married to Evie Abbott, who had once been the female love of young Tyrone's life. Yet, when he had proposed marriage, she declined, sensing that

Left: Herbert Marshall, Tyrone Power and Clifton Webb in *The Razor's Edge* (1946).

something did not quite gell when it came to lifetime commitment.

Power's first movie in four years was an ambitious adaptation of Somerset Maugham's *The Razor's Edge* (1946). His war service had matured his looks and in *Nightmare Alley* (1947) he took on the most unpleasant character he every played – Stan Carlisle, a worker in a sleazy carnival. Carlisle steals the affections of the phoney mind-reading act, Joan Blondell, who persuades him to oust her drunken husband and partner. Together they become a successful nightclub act until Carlisle gets his comeuppance and sinks to being the 'geek' in a carnival sideshow – a performer who eats live chickens. A very nasty film, directed by Edmund Goulding, it earned Power the most enthusiastic notices of his career. Unsurprisingly, it did not please the public, who considered Blondell, at 38, too old for him.

This was a bleak period for Power. His marriage to Annabella was about to end in divorce and affairs with Judy Garland and Lana Turner had faded, the latter because the sexually vora-cious Turner could not resist Frank Sinatra's advances while Tyrone was away from her. Another lady had set her cap at Tyrone, the ambitious Linda Christian, who had marriage on her mind. She had her way in 1949, and years later she and her husband offered a home to Linda's school friend, Tita, and her husband, Edmund Purdom, who was in New York to play in *Caesar and Cleopatra*. The couples went everywhere together and the inevitable happened: both the Powers were attracted to the handsome Purdom and it was rumoured that Linda, wearying of commitment to just one man, used letters that had passed between Tyrone and Edmund, 11 years his junior, as a lever to get a divorce from Power in 1955. She and Purdom subsequently married. Tyrone and Linda's daughter Romina inherited her parents' looks and was to become a starlet in European films, along with her young sister, Taryn – egged on by their mother Linda.

The quality of Power's films after his return to civilian life was variable. His eagerness to appear opposite Orson Welles, a friend from his days in the theatre whom he admired inordinately, led him into two historical dramas. The first was a superior swashbuckling epic, *The Prince of Foxes* (1949), directed by Power's favourite, Henry King. Tyrone subtly underplays as Andrea Corsini, a soldier chosen to act as aide to Cesare Borgia, running rings round the full-blown histrionics of Welles as the notorious warlord. The second film opposite Welles, *The Black Rose* (1950), has Power playing a 13th century English noble journeying in the East. This is a more routine adventure story, directed by Henry Hathaway.

Power's revised contract with Fox to do only two films per year allowed him to return to his first love, the theatre. His most successful appearance in the theatre was his bare-stage reading of Stephen Vincent Benét's narrative poem *John Brown's Body*. This was an epic yet deeply human story set during the American Civil War, directed by Charles Laughton, who headed a company including Raymond Massey as Abraham Lincoln and Judith Anderson playing all the female roles. Laughton was exceptionally helpful in aiding Power to create an imposing theatrical presence. They were very close and Elsa Lanchester said, 'I know Charles adored Tyrone Power as a beauty ... Charles believed Ty would become a very fine actor.'

The 'travelling poem' had its first reading in Santa Barbara in November 1952. In Pasadena, Van and Evie Johnson brought a busload of friends to the performance and in Beverly Hills the young Rock Hudson sneaked in backstage with a friend. Noticing them, Tyrone brought them chairs to watch from the side. Hudson, who admitted to being a 'terrific fan', became a firm friend for the rest of Power's life. After a gruelling tour, *John Brown's Body* reached New York, having played 68 cities in ten weeks. The opening was on 14 February 1953, to a standing ovation. Power's notices were ecstatic – at last the critics recognised him as a stage actor of distinction.

In 1955 Power was directed for the first time by John Ford, in *The Long Gray Line* – too long by half, and overly sentimental to boot, although Power gives a fine performance as West Point athletics trainer Marty Maher. The character's ageing process, from 18 to 80, was less of a challenge than the teenage make-up. At 42 the actor's social life had accelerated out of control after his divorce from Linda. New female and male lovers proliferated, including Swedish actress Anita Ekberg. In 1956, when he traveled to England to film *Seven Waves Away/Abandon Ship*, directed by Richard Sale, Power began an affair with co-star Mai Zetterling, also Swedish, whom he found as strong as Annabella and as sensual as Linda. To complicate matters, he was still seeing a good deal of Annabella and Linda's *decree nisi* was not picked up by her until August.

During the *John Brown's Body* tour, in Springfield Illinois a local school graduate, Weldon Culhane, aged 18, went backstage and met Tyrone in his dressing room. The upshot was that the actor invited him to accompany the show to Chicago, where he booked Culhane into the same hotel. Later in their relationship Power suggested the boy change his first name to Ty, under which name he was to become a well-known interior decorator.

After the shooting of *The Sun Also Rises*, a friend who had met Tyrone in Rome commented on how his looks had deteriorated. He appeared tired and bloated and older than his years. Certainly he had abandoned his days of discretion to indulge in group sex parties, which became a regular occurrence. Even old friends such as Evie and Van Johnson began to avoid him. He confided in Charles Laughton that the Catholic upbringing he had tried to ignore for so long was coming back to haunt him, and the more he tried to put it aside the further he became involved in his Bacchanalian lifestyle. Laughton, who admitted he had no such com-

Above: Tyrone Power and Ava Gardner in *The Sun Also Rises* (1957).

plications in his outlook, sympathised but could not make any constructive suggestions.

They had just made *Witness for the Prosecution* (1957) together and the film was set to be a great success. But Power's theatre tour in Shaw's *Back to Methuselah* was a critical failure, although his fans flocked to see him in the provinces and the production made back its costs in New York. The flop depressed him profoundly. However, he had settled into a solid personal relationship with a girl called Debbie Minarchos and, when she became pregnant, they were married immediately in the Presbyterian Church in Debbie's hometown of Tunica Mississippi. The couple flew to California and checked into a bungalow at the Bel Air Hotel where Van and Evie threw a party for their best friend so that they could get to meet the new bride.

On their way to Spain for the location work on Tyrone's new film *Solomon and Sheba*, the Powers stopped off in London to see the Laughtons, who were appearing in the play *The Party* at the St Martin's Lane Theatre and staying in Tyrone's unoccupied flat off the Brompton Road. The two couples dined together; the impression Elsa Lanchester formed of the new Mrs Power was her strength. 'I suppose all of his women were strong,' was her comment.

By the second month of shooting in Madrid, Power had completed 60 per cent of his work on *Solomon and Sheba*. One scene involved a duel between Tyrone and George Sanders, playing brothers fighting for the right to rule Israel over the fallen body of Sheba (Gina Lollobrigida). The actors were wearing heavy robes and fighting with real swords, each weighing 15lb. Sanders kept asking for retakes to get his angles right. After 90 minutes and eight takes, Power flung his sword down and said, 'I've had it! If you can't find anything there you can use, just use the close-ups of me!' It was the only time he had been less than accommodating to a difficult actor. Power's make-up man helped him down from the platform staircase landing where the duel was being shot. His face was ashen and he was shaking violently. He was driven to the nearest hospital in Lollobrigida's car but was dead on arrival. At 44 he had suffered a massive coronary, as had his father 27 years before him. The film was re-shot with Yul Brynner in the role of Solomon.

Tyrone Power Jr was born on 22 January 1959, two months after his father's death. His godfather was Rock Hudson and he was adopted by Arthur Loew Jr, whom Debbie married a year after her husband's death.

LIBERACE (1919-1987)
(Wladziu Valentino Liberace)

'Lee', to his associates in show business, was a pianist-god to his fans. These included millions of blue-rinsed ladies who were ready to defend his masculinity to the last hatpin, despite his syrupy tones, feathered cloaks and bejewelled jump suits. He was a joke to non-admirers but genuinely liked and respected in the profession. Above all, Liberace was the supreme showman whose sense of his own omniscience expanded to infallibility with his ever-increasing success. Only he could have had the self-confidence to sue *Confidential* and the English *Daily Mirror* for implying that he was anything but heterosexual, winning thousands of pounds which sent him 'laughing all the way to the bank'. He insisted to the end of his days that he was still waiting for 'Miss Right', even after the palimony suit brought by his ex-chauffeur/companion, Scott Thorson, for $113 million. The matter was settled out of court, after which Liberace expressed amazement at the allegations and even queried Thorson's existence.

When I visited the London Dungeon for a press story, Lee was appearing at the Palladium accompanied by the amiable Mr Thorson and I had no idea that I was witnessing legal history in the making. The star was graciousness itself and Thorson was revealed as a friendly, handsome young American. The lawsuit in 1982 was a genuine surprise which did not affect Liberace's popularity in the slightest; in fact, his fans rallied just as they had during the newspaper scandals, which makes it the more surprising that he insisted the AIDS rumour was another libellous fabrication to be strenuously denied, even from beyond the grave. As he lay dying, those around him threatened libel suits if anyone dared whisper the words 'gay' or AIDS, and it was not until an autopsy that the matter was settled once and for all. It was sad that with his unassailable popularity, Liberace did not use the opportunity to come out and say just what was wrong with him and how everyone should be doing something about it to help others. The

New York Native's obituary ran, ' Yes, the beloved Liberace was a liar.'

Born in Milwaukee, his expertise as a pianist, plus his own flair for self-advertisement, soon gained him the entrée to concert hall, ballroom and nightclub celebrity with his successful wooing of the right-wing Daughters of the American Revolution, putting Mom and pepped-up classics on the map among candelabra and sequins. While males scoffed, their womenfolk applauded him to the echo. For 40 years the teasing game went on. In public he could wag his finger and flirt with chosen husbands and boyfriends of his adoring ladies and everyone thought it a huge joke.

He saw no reason why he should not extend his magic spell to the movies, as had the star after whom his beloved mother had given him his second name of Valentino. He made his debut in *South Sea Sinner* (1949) with Shelley Winters and MacDonald Carey, in which he played a pianist in a remake of Dietrich's *Seven Sinners*. Liberace's one and only starring role came in 1955 in *Sincerely Yours*. This was a remake of *The Man Who Played God/The Silent Voice*, with Liberace inheriting George Arliss' role of a blind pianist and receiving his first (and only) screen kiss from Dorothy Malone. The film was a massive flop and, though Liberace claimed he turned down many straight roles because they would not have pleased his fans, he also said he had declined the lead, eventually played by Rod Steiger, in *The Loved One* because the character was 'an effeminate mamma's boy, ten feet off the ground at all times. A great actor could pull off the role.' Director Tony Richardson said he was never offered the part. All the more strange, then, that Liberace *was* in the film, playing a flamingly gay casket salesman. Even stranger is the fact that Rock Hudson confirmed they had a fling in Rock's early days – 'Just a few weeks…' There's nowt so queer…

MONTGOMERY CLIFT [1920-1966]
[Edward Montgomery Clift]

Clift was one of the most handsome film actors to win the hearts of filmgoers in the forties and fifties. His extraordinary good looks made it easy for him to become a much sought-after model at the age of 13 and to progress to a successful stage career starting in *Summer Stock*. Alfred Lunt and Lynn Fontanne, America's leading theatrical couple, were struck by his looks, especially Lunt, whose gay proclivities on the Broadway stage were something of an open secret. But both were also deeply impressed by his combination of a sensitive acting talent with remarkable sensuality. After being in the original production of *The Skin of Our Teeth* he counted the playwright, Thornton Wilder, and the Lunts among his best friends, having played their son in *There Shall Be No Night*. Clift remained in the theatre for 11 years and was a founder member of the Actors Studio, having turned down a lucrative offer from MGM in 1941. Five years later he signed a contract to co-star with John Wayne in *Red River*, Howard Hawks' classic Western.

Of the 16 films which Clift made after his notable debut, 13 were of outstanding quality. While James Dean became an icon in only three movies, Clift's personal tragedy was more protracted – but he had longer to establish his unique value as a screen actor. *The Search* (1948), directed by Fred Zinnemann, a moving and gentle follow-up to his first performance, cast Clift as an American soldier stationed in post-war Germany who befriends a young Czech boy separated from his family and home. In 1949, after Zinnemann, he had another great director in William Wyler's *The Heiress*. The title role and the Oscar went to Olivia de Havilland, hardly as plain as the heroine of Henry James' original novel but superb in one of her greatest performances. Ralph Richardson is equally

RED RIVER

1948 United Artists/Monterey 133/125 mins b/w
Producer: Howard Hawks; Director: Howard Hawks; Screenplay: Charles Schnee, Borden Chase (from Chase's story 'The Chisholm Trail');
Cinematographer: Russell Harlan
John Wayne, Montgomery Clift, Joanne Dru, Walter Brennan, Coleen Gray, John Ireland, Noah Beery Jr, Harry Carey Jr, Paul Fix

Although this film was made in 1946, Montgomery Clift's second movie, Fred Zinnemann's *The Search*, actually reached the cinemas first and won a clutch of Academy Award nominations for Clift, director Zinnemann and writers Richard Schweizer and David Wechsler. This ensured that Clift became a box-office name during his first year in films. *Red River* was probably the best of all the 1940s westerns and one of Wayne's finest performances in the genre he had made his own. Wayne plays Tom Dunson, a powerful waggoner owning a substantial expanse of land. With his companion Groot (Walter Brennan), he is heading towards Texas and the Red River. They encounter young Matthew Garth (Clift), a survivor from an Indian attack, and take him along with them. Garth becomes Tom's right-hand man and the unspoken love between them turns to animosity when Tom decides to drive his cattle and men along Texas' Chisholm Trail, against the advice of Matthew's friend, the cowpoke Cherry Valance (John Ireland).

Sexual repression is expressed between the main characters – there is a flirtatious bond between Matthew Garth and his friend Cherry and tension between Tom's girlfriend Tess Millay (Joanne Dru) and her rival Fen (Coleen Gray). Hawks specialised in portraying gutsy women and virile male camaraderie. Guns, as phallic symbols, are pinpointed in *The Celluloid Closet*. Cherry says to Matthew, 'That's a good-looking gun you were using back there; maybe you'd like to see mine?' He blasts away with his gun and his friend says, 'That's good, too.' Then they fire away together – a Horse-Frightening few minutes.

good as her hateful father, Dr Sloper, and Miriam Hopkins is effective in one of her best later roles as the good-natured aunt. Clift gives perhaps his weakest performance as the opportunist who romances the heiress. He was clearly too sensitive to play just a gigolo in this fine film.

In George Stevens' *A Place in the Sun* (1951), adapted from Theodore Dreiser's novel *An American Tragedy*, Clift's role was again a man on the make. He plays a drifter having an affair with working girl Shelley Winters but aspiring to marry rich beauty Elizabeth Taylor. This time he is both ruthless and forceful; Clift won his second Oscar nomination and Winters her first. The studio's attempt to promote a romance between Clift and Taylor did not require much effort. He, a bisexual who revelled in conquests both male and female, fell in love on sight with the 17-year-old Taylor, in the full flower of her beauty, and was delighted to help her through her most difficult scenes with spectacular results. They remained close until his untimely death.

Alfred Hitchcock was not exactly on top form when he directed Clift in *I Confess*. Yet Clift's performance as a priest under pressure to break his vow of silence after he has heard a murderer's confession is a masterly portrait of a man wrestling with his conscience. Mental torment was something he became increasingly adept at purveying. Increasingly, his panaceas were drugs and drink, and his behaviour, even on set, became what his co-workers described as 'odd'.

Strange behaviour was rampant among the characters in Fred Zinnemann's 1953 dramatisation of James Jones' bestselling novel *From Here to Eternity*. Clift's performance as Robert E Lee Prewitt – a GI, gifted bugler and former boxer stationed in Pearl Harbor right before the bombing – has been hailed as his greatest. It won him his third Oscar nomination. The picture and director both gained Oscars. The brutal and adulterous commanding officer, played by Philip Ober, promises Prewitt the post of company bugler if he will box on the unit team. Prewiit refuses. For his obstinacy, the captain orders Sergeant Warden (Burt Lancaster) to give the soldier every dirty detail in the company. Warden starts a torrid affair with Karen Holmes (Deborah Kerr), wife of the CO. Prewitt is comforted by nightclub hostess Lorene (Donna Reed) and his frail but resilient

Above: Ernest Borgnine and Montgomery Clift in *From Here to Eternity* (1953).

best friend, Angelo Maggio (Frank Sinatra), himself the victim of sadistic Italian-hating Sergeant Fatso (Ernest Borgnine). The interactions between these volatile people make for high drama and won Oscar nominations, besides Clift's, for Lancaster, Kerr, Sinatra and Reed, plus Oscars for Best Cinematographer (Burnett Guffey) and editor (William Lyon), plus three more assorted awards.

Raintree County (1957), directed by Edward Dmytryk, formed a watershed in Clift's life, less for its entertainment value than for the almost fatal car crash which disfigured his beauty and kept him away from filming during months of recuperative surgery. The event also took a terrible mental toll on Clift's already tormented mind. His leading lady in this Civil War epic, Elizabeth Taylor, was still distraught from the so recent (1955) and so tragically similar accident which had killed her beloved James Dean. Nevertheless, she was a loving and consoling factor in Clift's recovery.

The change in his features, which even the most careful photography and subtle lighting

Above: Hope Lange and Montgomery Clift in *The Young Lions* (1958).

could not wholly conceal, nevertheless gave added gravitas and pathos to his screen presence. This was noticeable in his next movie for Dmytryk, *The Young Lions* (1958), in which Clift was cast as Noah Ackerman. A young Jewish draftee, Ackerman faces anti-Semitism even before getting to confront the Nazis, but becomes fast friends with enlisted singer Michael Whiteacre (Dean Martin). Their story is paralleled with that of Christian Diestl (Marlon Brando), an idealistic German who believes in Hitler and becomes a lieutenant in the Wehrmacht. Diestl gradually becomes disillusioned with the brutality he encounters in the Nazi regime and the characters eventually intersect outside a concentration camp. Brando is at his most charismatic and Dean Martin remains very much Dean Martin. Rumours were rife suggesting an affair between Brando

and Clift, even hinting that photographs depicting their intimacy had been taken, but the whole concept may well have been the product of an inventive subterranean gay press agent.

Lonely Hearts (1959), a light-hearted confection mainly notable for Clift's only teaming with his friend Myrna Loy, was directed by Vincent J Donohue. 1959 also saw Clift's powerful involvement with the work of Tennessee Williams in the last film the actor made with Elizabeth Taylor, *Suddenly Last Summer*.

The last five years of Clift's life were notable for worthwhile movies with sad connotations. Elia Kazan's *Wild River* (1960) is an affecting drama beautifully played by Clift. He plays a Tennessee Valley authority official and Jo Van Fleet plays his grandmother, who is fighting not to have to give up her land. His next film, John Huston's *The Misfits* (1961) is a sombre movie, with Clift as a disillusioned rodeo rider who crosses paths with Marilyn Monroe as an equally discontented divorcee. Clark Gable plays an ageing cowboy in the drama written by Arthur Miller for his then-wife, Monroe. It was the last film for both Gable, in one of his most intuitive performances, and Monroe. Both Monroe and Clift were heavy drug users at this time. Her absences from the set were very trying to everyone, while Clift's alcoholism was another cross both he and John Huston had to bear. It appears that Gable hastened his death in insisting on doing his own stunts, being dragged around and lassoing mustangs, but he treated both his near-to-breakdown co-stars with unexpected compassion and understanding, though he continued to refer to Clift as 'the Faggot'. This was an unendearing trait he had towards people whose sexuality was less well-guarded than his.

Clift undertook an agonising ten-minute cameo as a Holocaust survivor in Stanley Kramer's *Judgement at Nuremberg* (1961), which won him his fourth Oscar nomination.

Right: Montgomery Clift, Katharine Hepburn and Mercedes McCambridge in *Suddenly Last Summer* (1959).

Judy Garland was also nominated as another Nazi victim. John Huston, who directed the actor again in the title role of *Freud* (1962), remarked that 'The combination of drink, drugs and being homosexual was a soup that was too strong for Clift.' During the production, which centred round the five-year period when Freud formed his Oedipal theories, Clift had an operation for the removal of cataracts from both eyes. He was becoming difficult to insure and it was four years before his next and final film, *The Defector*, in 1966. This was a French/German co-production, directed by Raoul Lévy, in which the ravages of his traumatic life were all too plain to see. He died the same year of a heart attack at 46.

I met Montgomery Clift in 1950 when Jessie Royce Landis ('Call me Royce!', she would boom) starred at the Savoy Theatre for Stanley French in *Mrs Inspector Jones*, for which I was handling the press. When she introduced us I was impressed by his gallantry towards her and the total charm of his greeting to us both. It was for me a brief few moments of privilege.

FRANKIE HOWERD (1921-1992)
(Francis Howard)

One of the most original of British comedians, Howerd was once described as 'having more cheek than a row of bottoms.' His fluctuating voice and catchphrases like 'Ladies and gentle-*men*! and 'Titter ye not' were all part of his gloriously flustered and ingratiating manner. His accompanying facial contortions could rightly be described as eccentric or camp (in the sense of frivolous or paradoxical), without descending to the effeminacy exemplified by Kenneth Williams or Charles Hawtrey.

Thus it came as a surprise to many of the public to learn that Frankie was, in fact, gay. The nearest analogy in American movies was perhaps Edward Everett Horton with his hand-wringing 'Oh my!', or Eric Blore, the perennial butler or manservant, with his downcast look followed by a baleful double-take, more expressive than any denial or invective. Howerd's nervous patter, sucked-in cheeks and finger-wagging transferred ideally from

Above: Anton Diffring and Frankie Howerd in a publicity still from the ill-fated stage production *Mister Venus* (1958).

the variety stage to radio and TV from the fifties on, and were carried into movies, spasmodically, for some 20 years.

I myself had no particular thoughts about Howerd's sexual orientation until I went to interview him after one of his variety appearances at the Golders Green Hippodrome in the early fifties. I was doing PR for the Ronald Jeans comedy *Young Wives Tale* with Joan Greenwood at the Savoy Theatre. She came back from a *Variety Bandbox* broadcast raving about Frankie Howerd. 'You must meet him,' she husked in her inimitable tones, midway between a croak and a gargle. It was the most startling encounter with a stranger I'd ever had. As soon as the door closed behind me, Frankie motioned me to a couch, hurled himself on me and bit my nose!

I met Frankie off and on through the years. He was always charming, with no reference to the 'dressing room incident', which I assumed he had forgotten. At one time I was writing for

the firm which published his autobiography, *On the Way I Lost It* (1976). Years later, when I had to review one of Howerd's pantomimes, I mentioned in passing to the producer the story of my first meeting with the comedian. He passed on the story, explaining who I was and that I was working for the *Stage* newspaper. Howerd apparently responded with one of his famous 'Ooohs!'

Frankie's first film, in 1954, was Val Guest's *The Runaway Bus* with Petula Clark and Terence Alexander, who soon became adept at fielding Frankie's passes. As the conductor of the eponymous bus, Howerd had one of his best parts and most successful films. In 1955, for Alexander Mackendrick, he joined a cast of accomplished character actors, including Alec Guinness and Peter Sellers, in the Ealing Comedy classic *The Ladykillers* and the year after he made *A Touch of the Sun* (see box).

In 1958 Frankie again appeared for Val Guest in *Further Up the Creek* and in 1962 once more was cast with Dennis Price in Michael Winner's *The Cool Mikado*. Howerd's appeal was sexless and ageless. Every time he considered his career was about to peter out he became a cult figure for another generation of admirers. This process continued right up until his death in 1992. An example was his sensational comeback in the sixties with *That Was the Week That Was*. In fact he had never really been away. Coral Browne became friendly with him when they were together in *A Midsummer Night's Dream* at the Old Vic in 1957 and found him mostly gloomy and full of dire foreboding, despite his considerable success in the role of Bottom. She, however, could cheer him up and make him laugh, as she could most people who were not liable to be shocked by her barrack-room language.

In 1966 Launder and Gilliat cast Howerd in *The Great St. Trinian's Train Robbery* with George Cole and Dora Bryan. Howerd briefly

A TOUCH OF THE SUN

1956 Eros/Raystro 80 mins b/w
Producer: Raymond Stross; Director: Gordon Parry: Screenplay:
Alfred Shaughnessy; Cinematography: Arthur Grant
Frankie Howerd, Ruby Murray, Dennis Price, Dorothy
Bromiley, Gordon Harker, Katherine Kath, Reginald
Beckwith, Richard Wattis, Alfie Bass, Miriam Karlin, Colin
Gordon, Esma Cannon, Willoughby Goddard, Viola Lyell,
Marianne Stone

As a hotel clerk called Darling, who ends up owning the
hotel after a grateful patron leaves him a fortune, Frankie
Howerd goes to extravagant lengths to entice the public to
patronise his by-now run-down establishment. One of the
ruses is to get the hotel staff to pose as rich punters to
impress the potential backers. Howerd himself performs a
hilarious drag act as Lobelia, Duchess of Pulborough, a tall
lady who towers over the amorous backer who insists 'she'
dance with him. Dennis Price has a choice role calling for
a typically urbane upper-class performance. Gordon
Harker, the cockney comedian for whom thriller writer
Edgar Wallace wrote a number of character roles,
appears in one of his last parts as the elevator 'boy' who
poses as the Duke of Pulborough.

Gordon Parry, the workmanlike director of the 1951 film version
of *Tom Brown's Schooldays*, keeps a firm hand on the farcical
goings-on. Frankie Howerd makes a genuinely likeable character of
Darling, while fifties chart-topper Ruby Murray, in her one and only
film role as a chambermaid also called Ruby, sings two charming
songs: 'In Love' and 'O'Malley's Tango'.

became a member of the wildly successful
team of British *farceurs* produced by Peter
Rogers and directed by Gerald Thomas,
appearing in *Carry On Doctor* in 1968 and
Carry On Up the Jungle the following year.
One of the images of Frankie Howerd that
tends to linger in the mind was a vision of him
in the 1970 series *Up Pompeii!* as the leering
slave Lurcio, surrounded by a bevy of bosomy
beauties but still, in the words of his biographer, Mick Middles, 'as camp as a boy scout

Above: Frankie
Howerd in *A Touch
of the Sun* (1956).

jamboree'. In the seventies he continued with
his film career in the same mode in *Up the
Chastity Belt* (1971), *Up the Front* (1972) and
his only American movie, *Sgt Pepper's Lonely
Hearts Club Band* (1978). There had been a
slight variation in *The House in Nightmare
Park/Crazy House* (1973) with Hollywood's
Ray Milland, a comedy-horror spoof that did
not win many hearts.

Born Francis Howard – the 'e' was substituted when he went on the stage – Frankie
wept bitterly at failing to be accepted for
RADA; what could they have made of him?
But he was an instant success at the end of
World War Two at the Stage Door Canteen for
the Forces, run by Dorothy Dickson. 'He was
funny both on and off stage,' she recalled,
'and never more so than when he was trying to
be serious, probably because of his air of
melancholy.'

LIZABETH SCOTT (1922-)
(Emma Matzo)

Scott has the unenviable distinction of being the only film actress whose 'outing' by the late unlamented scandal sheet, *Confidential*, actually ruined her career. Many others have been 'named and shamed' and continued regardless after their 'transgression', having created little more than a nine days wonder. For most of her career Lizabeth Scott had dodged questions about boyfriends and romance in general, saying she was far too busy, was married to her career, and so on. She was one of three Hollywood blondes of the era marketed for their sex appeal, the others being Veronica Lake, with her 'peek-a-boo bang', and Lauren Bacall, 'the voice'. Scott became 'the threat', playing exactly the same kind of husky-voiced carabet entertainers, although the singing voices of the other two were dubbed. Hal Wallis signed Scott to a Paramount contract as a handy replacement for Lake, should she turn recalcitrant.

The 1954 *Confidential* exposé, couched in the purple prose reserved for such publications, alleged that 'Liz, according to the grapevine buzz was taking up almost exclusively with Hollywood's weird society of baritone babes … Those who did catch a glimpse of 'Scotty', as she calls herself, reported spotting her from time to time in off-colour joints that were favourite hangouts for movieland's twilight set … In an interview she gave to columnist Sidney Skilsky she confided that she always wore male colognes, slept in men's pajamas and positively hated frilly, feminine dresses … On one jaunt in Europe she headed straight for Paris's Left Bank where she took up with Frede, the city's most notorious lesbian queen and the operator of a night club devoted exclusively to deviates like herself.' And so on.

By hiring Hollywood's most famous attor-

THE STRANGE LOVE OF MARTHA IVERS

1946 Paramount 116 mins b/w
Producer: Hal B Wallis; Director: Lewis Milestone; Screenplay: Robert Rossen (based on the story 'Love Lies Bleeding' by Jack Patrick); Cinematographer: Victor Milner
Barbara Stanwyck, Van Heflin, Lizabeth Scott, Kirk Douglas, Judith Anderson, Roman Bohnen

This movie proved to be the most prestigious and best-produced film of Lizabeth Scott's entire career. Officially, *Martha Ivers* was a vehicle for Barbara Stanwyck, showcasing her skill at depicting twisted emotions. Scott is third-billed as Toni Marachek, a girl on parole who finds herself in the country town run by Martha Ivers (Stanwyck) and her alcoholic district attorney husband, Walter O'Neal (Kirk Douglas in his film debut). Toni is protected by Sam Masterson (Van Heflin), the childhood love of Martha, who murdered her aunt (Judith Anderson) while planning to elope with him. To protect the family name, an innocent man was executed for the crime.

Stanwyck, a dab hand at this kind of *film noir*, plays the title role with force and conviction, but Scott more than holds her own in the scenes where they battle over Heflin, whom Scott wins in the end. Her performance created a subtle portrayal of an emotionally bruised woman who is never bitter. Heflin, as usual, creates his effects by underplaying, while Douglas' first film appearance is remarkably impressive.

ney, Jerry Giesler, in 1955 to institute a $2.5m libel suit against *Confidential*, Scott only ensured the maximum international coverage for the case. Giesler alleged that his client had been portrayed in a 'vicious, slanderous and indecent manner', and the fact that the suit failed to materialise left only a malodorous cloud hanging over the star's name. Had she, like Dietrich, ignored the similar kind of article directed against herself in the same magazine, the matter would probably have blown over in a matter of weeks.

As it was, Scott was happy to get away from the pressure focused upon her by the media by going to England to star with Steve Cochran and Herbert Marshall in *The Weapon*, directed by Val Guest in 1955 but not released in the

Right: Lizabeth Scott and Humphrey Bogart in *Dead Reckoning* (1947).

USA until 1957, the year she terminated her Paramount contract by co-starring with Elvis Presley in his second movie, *Loving You*. The *Hollywood Reporter* said that Scott and Presley 'are responsible for a large amount of the friendliness and charm that the film generates.' As Glenda Markle, a tough publicity girl who takes Elvis and his career under her wing, she is both convincing and sympathetic.

When the movie roles dried up, Scott turned to a recording career with an LP, *Lizabeth Sings*, complete with attention-grabbing titles like 'Nice to Have a Man Around' and 'Deep Dark Secret'. In the sixties she made several TV appearances in both dramatic and musical shows but no films materialised until she flew to Malta in 1972 to appear with Michael Caine and Mickey Rooney in Mike Hodges' *Pulp*. She was cast in a nebulous role, described as an 'aristocratic nymphomaniac', a woman who travels the world with a cortege of unidentified women.

Scott was born in the industrial mining town of Scranton Pennsylvania. After high school, she took piano lessons and voice training 'because my mother wanted me to become a well-rounded human being.' When her mother ruled out Lizabeth's desire to become a nun she moved to Manhattan, determined to be an actress. She studied at the Alvienne School of Dramatic Art and eventually landed a job in the touring version of Olsen and Johnson's *Hellzapoppin'* in 1940, in which she played for a year and a half. Later she understudied Tallulah Bankhead in Thornton Wilder's *The Skin of Our Teeth* as Sabina, the Lilith-like maid who represents man's survival through the ages. Scott got to play the part just once. Jack L Warner, busily promoting Lauren Bacall's career and seeing Scott as a potential rival, turned her down. She took to modelling to earn a crust and an introduction to Hal B Wallis – who was moving to Paramount – led to him signing her in 1944 to a seven-year contract.

Named as one of the Stars of Tomorrow for 1946 by the *Motion Picture Herald*, Scott claimed she had no time for romance and told the *Boston Sunday Post* in January of that year: 'Launching a career is a serious business, a full time job … I'm tired of that smart New Set who blast Hollywood, calling it an intellectual void … They do fine things in the theatre and splendid things out here, too. Baddies crop up on both coasts. I dislike it when critics sell Hollywood short.'

Her first movie was *You Came Along* in 1945, second-billed to Robert Cummings and directed by John Farrow. As a treasury department official assigned to take three GIs, including Cummings, on a War Bond tour, she had plenty of scope for emotional acting when she falls in love with Cummings, only to lose him when he dies from leukaemia. *Life* magazine recorded its opnion that 'slim, husky-voiced Miss Scott is reminiscent of three other actresses … Dorothy MacGuire, Lauren Bacall and Katharine Hepburn.' The film was a respectable success. Her next film role was in the cracking melodrama *The Strange Love of Martha Ivers*.

Loaned to Columbia for the 1947 *Dead Reckoning* with Humphrey Bogart, the studio courted comparisons with his usual co-star and real-life wife, Lauren Bacall, by presenting on the billboards BOGART and, underneath, SCOTT. The plot has Bogart on the trail of the murderer of his service friend William Prince, to whom Scott was engaged. As Coral Chandler, a cool nightclub singer in Morris Carnovsky's club, she is too interested in Carnovsky's wealth to let a little thing like murder bother her and she shares a scene with Bogart reminiscent of the scene with Mary Astor in *The Maltese Falcon* in which, as the guilty party, she begs him to overlook her crime for the sake of love but he hands her over to the police. The film was a financial success and the *New Yorker* commented 'Miss Scott not only resembles

Miss Bacall closely but can flare her nostrils even more vigorously.'

The same year Lizabeth, in her first film in Technicolor, *Desert Fury*, 'inherited' Mary Astor as her mother, who runs a whorehouse and controls the cops and politicians. The all-star *Variety Girl* rounded off 1947. Her nemesis, Veronica Lake, was one of the 45 or so assorted stars and other personalities in director George Marshall's entertaining kaleidoscope of Paramount talent.

In the 15 further films on her contract, Scott had the pick of young male co-stars, frequently on loan-out to other studios. For United Artists there was the tightly knit drama, *Pitfall* (1948), with echoes of *Double Indemnity*, directed by Veronica Lake's then-husband, André De Toth. Dick Powell plays a claims adjuster lured away from his sweet wife, Jane Wyatt, by grasping model Lizabeth Scott. Her other 1948 release was *I Walk Alone*, playing a nightclub singer in the post-prohibition period torn between club owner, Kirk Douglas (baddie), Burt Lancaster (OK) and Wendell Corey (weak henchman to Douglas).

Scott's career may be said to have hit rock bottom in 1949 in *Too Late for Tears*, in which she played a female Bluebeard who falls to her death from a tenth-storey window. The same year, on loan to RKO, she took third billing to Victor Mature and Lucille Ball, both under contract to that studio, as the unpleasant wife of pro-football coach (Mature), with Ball as his club's secretary, who secretly loves him. The *New York Times* commented, 'Lizabeth Scott turns her lip chewing to advantage!' Questioned about her social life at this time she was ready with such pronouncements as 'I believe in sex – completely and absolutely' and 'I'm in love with a wonderful life, a life of living alone. Peace, quiet, solitude – they're all mine.'

In 1950 Scott appeared with Charlton

Heston in his feature film debut, *Dark City*, directed by William Dieterle. He played a bruised romantic turned into a cynical gambler. She is again a nightclub diva, singing 'If I Didn't Have You'. They were teamed again for Columbia's *Bad for Each Other* (1953), directed by Irving Rapper. The excellent John Cromwell directed Scott in *The Company She Keeps* (1950) as probation officer to Jane Greer, for whom she sacrifices herself to keep the parolee on the path of righteousness after another misdemeanour. Both girls fight for the love of Dennis O'Keefe, whom the ungrateful Greer tries to lure away from Scott.

1951 was the year Scott broke free from the Wallis stock company co-stars. On loan-out to RKO again, she acted with Robert Mitchum in *The Racket*, with John Cromwell as director of this sombre study of corruption in a big city. Mitchum is the honest police captain who must come to grips with the racketeers, led by Robert Ryan. Scott is the nightclub songstress Irene, in love with Robert Hutton. Ryan delivers one of the classic put-downs of filmdom: 'Why, you cheap little clip-joint canary!'

Playing opposite Alan Ladd in *Red Mountain*, her first Western, directed by William Dieterle, did Scott no favours. In her role as Chris, Yankee-loving woman of gold miner Arthur Kennedy, she trailed around in her long dresses looking abject. The *Chicago Daily Tribune* commented: 'Lizabeth Scott performs with all the animation of a chunk of cement!' Though seldom the critics' darling, this was really going too far. Hal Wallis' biggest money-makers at the time were Dean Martin and Jerry Lewis, on whose radio show Scott appeared frequently. She was happy to be cast with them in *Scared Stiff* (1953). As an heiress, Mary Carroll, she inherits a 'haunted' castle on a remote Caribbean island. Martin and Lewis help her to track down the villain, who tries to prevent her from discovering the

fortune in gold hidden under the castle. George Marshall, one of Hollywood's top directors for over 20 years, had made the original version, the Bob Hope vehicle *The Ghost Breakers*, and Lizabeth Scott quoted this as her second favourite film after *You Came Along*. She maintained that *Scared Stiff* showed a different facet of her screen personality. The role played by Brazilian bombshell Carmen Miranda, however, is, as so often, quite pointless.

Scott then starred with John Payne and Dan Duryea in the Western, *Silver Lode*, for RKO. This movie caused a stir among film buffs because it was the work of cult director Allan Dwan, the last surviving link with Hollywood's earliest days. Dwan began directing in 1911 and is credited with having invented the dolly shot. He had been in charge of the Douglas Fairbanks silents. At the time of *Silver Lode* he had been a top director for nearly 45 years and, although Lizabeth Scott's role as the richest woman in town was hardly rewarding, the film itself packed a characteristic punch, using the western genre to make a cryptic statement about Senator Joseph McCarthy's political witch hunts. By the time of his death in 1981, Dwan had some 400 films to his credit.

Prior to *Confidential*'s tabloid bombshell, Scott's career was already somewhat in the doldrums but she continued to parry press questions about her social life. In 1953 she told United Press reporter Vernon Scott: 'I'm really not a recluse, you know. Is there anything wrong with a gal just because she doesn't show up at every premiere and party in Hollywood? … It's just that the rat race isn't for me. People say that you can't lead a normal life in Hollywood, but they're wrong. I'm having a wonderful time doing just what I want! It depends on one's definition of the word 'normal'.'

Left: Alec McCowen and Maggie Smith in *Travels With My Aunt* (1972).

ALEC McCOWEN [1925-]
[Alexander Alec McCowen, CBE]

In 1953 my business partner, the late Anna Matthews, and I were starting out as a PR firm in offices at the Savoy Theatre. We walked across the road to the nearby Strand Theatre to see a play called *Escapade* by Roger McDougal, starring Phyllis Calvert. We were particularly impressed by a young actor playing a runaway schoolboy. The actor's name was Alec McCowen and we became friends after I interviewed him for a column in a showbusiness magazine.

We were both somewhat addicted to cycling and, at his suggestion, planned to cycle to Brighton one weekend, just for the hell of it. He never started that ride and I set off indignantly on my own – and never stopped. For the next 45 years or so that became my mode of transport for business and pleasure, at home and abroad. I forgave his tardiness; after all, actors have

more pressing things to do, like keeping in work. As time went by, Anna and I moved from the Savoy to a private house in Earl's Court and Alec came into our lives again. Acting roles were scarce and he was not too proud to mind our phone for a tiny fee while we were out.

McCowen was born in Tonbridge Wells in Kent. His mother was an actress and dancer and his father ran a pram shop. Alec once said, 'As soon as I knew there was such a thing as a theatre, I wanted to be part of it.' Accordingly, he won a place at the Royal Academy of Dramatic Art, after which he spent some ten years in various repertory companies and made his film debut in *The Cruel Sea* in 1952. Having joined the Old Vic Theatre Company, he made his New York stage debut with the Oliviers in *Antony and Cleopatra* in 1959. This was two years after a notable film appearance in *Time Without Pity* as the son of an alcoholic father, Michael Redgrave. The father fights to stay sober in order

Right: Danny Schiller, Julie Walters, Shirley Stelfox and Alec McCowen in *Personal Services* (1987).

to have the son reprieved from a murder charge, of which he is innocent but condemned to die within the next 24 hours. McCowen's performance was both sensitive and deeply moving under the direction of Joseph Losey.

Apart from notable success on the West End stage, including Mercutio in Franco Zefferelli's production of *Romeo and Juliet*, McCowen had roles of increasing importance in such films as *The Loneliness of the Long-Distance Runner* (1962), with Tom Courtenay. In the main, however, stage work provided his most rewarding roles, with National Theatre successes in *The Browning Version*, *Equus* and *The Misanthrope*. But Hitchcock provided a role that remains one of McCowen's most memorable to date. In *Frenzy* (1972), one of the director's most brutal thrillers, Barry Foster is the 'neck-tie murderer' and Jon Finch the man he succeeds in framing for the crimes. The lighter side of the case is provided by McCowen as the police inspector in charge of

the investigation, a beautifully underplayed performance as a man whose main problem is represented by his dotty wife – a wonderful piece of acting by Vivien Merchant, who insists on cooking him ever more eccentric gourmet meals.

Another excellent film role in 1972 was in *Travels With My Aunt*. McCowen is Henry, the stodgy nephew of Maggie Smith, Oscar-nominated for her playing of Aunt Augusta in George Cukor's sparkling version of Graham Greene's novel. They make an inspired twosome as she obliges him to leave behind his banking career and the flower garden which is his main interest in life. He begins to open up and shed, very reluctantly, his sullen exterior.

In 1968 Alec asked Anna and myself to help with the PR for his starring part in Peter Luke's witty clerical comedy-drama *Hadrian VII*, based on the novel by Frederick Rolfe, in which McCowen had played previously at Birmingham Rep. Hadrian's private life was not such as to appeal to the authorities; it was a great role and a great performance. After a prolonged run at the Mermaid Theatre, play and star transferred to New York for most of 1969, where he won his second Tony Award – the first having been for *The Philanthropist*. He was to win a third for his record-breading one-man show *St Mark's Gospel*, in which he explored fully the wisdom and warmth to be found in the New Testament.

In 1983 McCowen played the Algy the Armourer, the brains behind James Bond's remarkable life-saving devices, in the film in which Sean Connery returned one more time to reclaim the role he had made his own, *Never Say Never Again*. Four years later, Alec said he had never had more fun than playing one of the high-ranking officials who attended Madam Cynthia Payne for *Personal Services*. Julie Walters gave a memorable performance as Madame Cyn. McCowen's character is a World War Two Commander who boasts of his 207 missions over enemy territory while wearing a bra and panties. The actor claims it to be 'one of the finest memories of my working life!'

As a friend and admirer of Martin Scorsese he also enjoyed working with him and a remarkable cast in *The Age of Innocence* (1993). This was very untypical Scorsese but nonetheless enchantingly enjoyable. Most recently McCowen has appeared under the same director's banner for a return to basics in *Gangs of New York*, starring Leonardo De Caprio, Cameron Diaz and Daniel Day Lewis. McCowen plays a priest.

McCowen has always been openly and joyously gay and in 1991 was quick to show support for Ian McKellen when the gay community was divided over the actor accepting a knighthood through the mediation of an anti-gay government. After all, it is the Queen who bestows the knighthood and it should be in her domain alone to bestow or withhold. At least, that is the way it should be.

ROCK HUDSON (1925-1985)
(Roy Fitzgerald Scherer)

Above: A portrait of Rock Hudson from *Send Me No Flowers* (1964).

One of the greatest and most popular box-office stars of the fifties and sixties, Hudson was not only ruggedly handsome but an impressive actor. He was adept at both drama and comedy, successful in action films and westerns, following his first appearance in a small role in *Fighter Squadron* in 1948 to his first lead in *Peggy* (1950). He learned his craft in such movies as *Bend of the River* (1952) with James Stewart, directed by Anthony Mann, and *The Scarlet Angel* with Yvonne De Carlo the same year, directed by Sidney Salkow. In the musical *Has Anybody Seen My Gal?* Hudson was second-billed to Piper Laurie in Douglas Sirk's early success, set in small-town America in the 1920s.

Right: Rock Hudson and Elizabeth Taylor in *Giant* (1956).

Hudson received top billing for the first time in Raoul Walsh's *The Lawless Breed* (1953), playing notorious gunman John Wesley Hardin. Walsh directed him again the same year in *Sea Devils*, set in the early 1800s, as a smuggler involved with spy Yvonne De Carlo – their second teaming. He was directed again by Douglas Sirk in 1954 in *Taza, Son of Cochise*. Next came *Magnificent Obsession*, the film which raised him to major stardom. Hudson played opposite Jane Wyman, who was Oscar-nominated but lost out to Grace Kelly for *The Country Girl*. One of the best weepies of the fifties gives Hudson the role of a playboy whose irresponsibility leads to the blinding of Wyman. His 'magnificent obsession' is to become an eye surgeon, dedicated to restoring her sight. This was an enormous success, as was the original version in 1935, starring Irene Dunne and Robert Taylor.

The director-actor combination of Sirk and Hudson was to re-team several more times in the fifties, including *Captain Lightfoot* (1955), with Hudson incongruously cast as a 19th century Irish rebel, *All That Heaven Allows* (1955) with Jane Wyman as a widow falling for her gardener, and *Written on the Wind* (1956) with Lauren Bacall, Robert Stack and Dorothy Malone, who won an Oscar for her performance as Stack's nymphomaniac sister. This was such a success that Hudson, Stack and Malone were reunited in *The Tarnished Angels* (1957). This time Malone plays Stack's wife and Hudson a newspaper reporter who gets caught up in their lives while Stack is kept busy as a stunt pilot in a travelling airshow. By this time Sirk and Hudson regarded each other as mutual lucky charms.

Although Hudson did not flaunt his sexuality, he was not exactly discreet and when a scandal sheet threatened to reveal that he was gay, the studio quickly arranged a marriage to a devoted member of his fan club. The marriage lasted three years. Despite his Oscar-nominated performance as Bick Benedict in George Stevens' *Giant*, and his consummate comedy performances opposite his favourite co-star, Doris Day, the world now knows him

PILLOW TALK

1959 Universal/Arwin 105 mins Eastmancolor
Producers: Ross Hunter, Martin Melcher; Director: Michael Gordon;
Screenplay: Stanley Shapiro, Maurice Richlin (based on a story by Russell
Rouse and Clarence Greene); Cinematographer: Arthur E Arling
Rock Hudson, Doris Day, Tony Randall, Thelma Ritter, Nick Adams, Julia
Meade, Allen Jenkins, Marcel Dalio, Lee Patrick, Mary McCarty

The first of the witty, sophisticated sex comedies starring Day and Hudson. The others were *Lover Come Back* (1961) and *Send Me No Flowers* (1964). They were all, in a way, semi-biographical for those in the know about Hudson's true sexual preferences, dealing as they did with men pretending to be what they're not. In *Pillow Talk*, Rock is a songwriter who shares a party telephone line with Day. After hearing his constant sexual overtures to young women when she wants to use the phone to carry on her business as an interior designer, she takes him to task and they form a mutual detestation. However, having seen what she looks like – he had pictured her as a frigid old bag – he masquerades as a wealthy Texan to woo her. She soon realises his true identity and from then on they cross and double-cross until the inevitable ending.
Tony Randall is around as a Broadway show-backer, supposedly in love with Day, and his naturally ambivalent persona blends well with the premise. Randall repeated the role in *Lover Come Back*, in which Day is an ad executive determined to land the account of scientist Hudson's new invention – only he's really an ad man himself and there is no invention. In *Send Me No Flowers*, hypochondriac Hudson mistakenly believes he's going to die and sets out to find a suitable successor for his wife, Doris Day. Best friend Tony Randall tries to console him and they even share an innocent night in bed together. The *double entendres* proliferate; Rock gets into drag for plot purposes in *Pillow Talk*, and in *Lover Come Back* he feigns impotence: 'Now you know why I'm afraid to get married.' Doris Day and Thelma Ritter, cast as her maid, were both Oscar-nominated for *Pillow Talk*.

predominantly as the fifth famous person to die of AIDS. In so doing he gave homosexuals an identity which went far beyond the popular (or unpopular) idea the general public had of gay people. The writer, Vito Russo, says that Hudson's identity 'is a watershed in shattering the myth (prevalent before). He really is gentle and macho and soft-spoken – and gay. It shat-

ters that old limp-wristed stereotype.'
He even convinced President Ronald Reagan, who for four years had not once publicly acknowledged the existence of AIDS, that it was time to do so. Hudson himself left a quote, read in an AIDS fundraiser: 'I am not happy I have AIDS but if that is helping others I can at least know that my misfortune has had some positive worth.' *Giant*'s director, George Stevens, said of the star's pre-packaged male sex appeal: 'The image may be synthetic but the man is real. There is an inner core of warmth and decency there that can't be counterfeited – and it plays on the screen.'
It is, in hindsight, a puzzle as to why Rock Hudson allowed his scriptwriters to pepper his movies with so many teasers. Was he testing the water for a possible 'coming out' in the future? Were his scriptwriters and directors in *Pillow Talk* (1959) and *A Very Special Favor* (1965) putting in sly hints for their friends or for the more sophisticated section of the film-going public? The last-mentioned movie went further than most. Charles Boyer, once one of the screen's great lovers, asks playboy Hudson to win his daughter's affection away from her 'girlie' and less well-adjusted fiancé, Dick Shawn. Leslie Caron, the daughter, is both frigid and a psychiatrist – is such a combination probable? – and to encourage her to 'cure' him, Hudson pretends to be gay. 'Hiding in closets isn't going to cure you,' she reasons.
A study of his CV sheds no light on the complexities of Hudson's persona. Born in Winetka Illinois, after graduating from high school he worked as a mail carrier and was a navy airplane mechanic during World War II. After a spell as a truck driver, he was signed up by an agent who was certain the young Roy Scherer had potential, banking on his manly good looks and impressive stature (6'4") to get him into movies. His name was changed to the more resounding Rock Hudson, his teeth were capped and he was

coached extensively in acting, singing, dancing and riding. It took 38 takes before he could speak one line to the director's satisfaction; in his first film, it was evidently not only his agent who had faith in him.

Among the 38 films he made after *Magnificent Obsession*, there were several notable performances. *Battle Hymn* (1957), another for Douglas Sirk, features Hudson as a pilot helping to evacuate orphans in the Korean War. *Something of Value* (1957), about the Mau Mau uprising, co-starred Sidney Poitier and was directed by Richard Brooks. *A Farewell to Arms* (1957) was based on Hemingway's novel of love and war and co-starred Jennifer Jones. There were two films with Gina Lollobrigida, Robert Mulligan's comedy *Come September* (1961) and *Strange Bedfellows*, directed by Melvin Frank in 1965. 1966 saw Hudson's fine performance, comparable to the one in *Giant*, in *Seconds*. John Frankenheimer's riveting thriller concerns a distraught middle-aged man (John Houseman) who undergoes plastic surgery and emerges as Rock Hudson!

There were other unusual offerings. These include the musical *Darling Lili* in 1969 with Julie Andrews, directed by her husband, Blake Edwards – an unaccountable flop, though charmingly entertaining, with Andrews as a German spy/entertainer and Hudson as a WWI American commander with whom she gets involved. Another surprise, directed by Roger Vadim as his first American film, was *Pretty Maids All in a Row* (1971), a black comedy-thriller in which high school counsellor Hudson seduces and kills half the student body. Weird casting, indeed, especially for those fans who were lapping up his tremendously popular TV series, *McMillan and Wife* (1971-76).

Hudson's penultimate movie, directed by Guy Hamilton in England in 1980, was an entertaining Agatha Christie whodunit, *The Mirror Crack'd*, with Angela Lansbury as Miss Marple, a forerunner to her everlasting TV series *Murder, She Wrote*. Rock is married to Elizabeth Taylor, playing a film star who was once Sweetheart of the Forces! Did Dame Vera Lynn know about that? Kim Novak plays Taylor's arch rival and, naturally, a suspect.

Hudson's TV appearance in 1984, the year before his death, was a sad one in which, gaunt and haggard, he shared a kiss with Linda Evans in *Dynasty*, causing outrage among those who were unaware that AIDS cannot be transmitted by a kiss.

ANTHONY PERKINS [1932-1992]

The son of Osgood Perkins, a popular actor of the early 20th century, Anthony, born in New York, started acting as a teenager in summer stock. In 1953 he was snapped up for the movies by George Cukor, who cast him as Jean Simmons' boyfriend in *The Actress*, based on Ruth Gordon's autobiography. He next took over from John Kerr in the stage version of *Tea and Sympathy*, but failed an audition for *East of Eden* – had he been successful, the career of James Dean could have been very different.

Another sensitive young man part as Gary Cooper's son in William Wyler's *Friendly Persuasion* (1956) brought him an Academy Award nomination, and during the fifties he excelled in a variety of shy and retiring roles, notably the biographical *Fear Strikes Out* (1957) as Red Sox outfielder Jimmy Piersall. The film was directed by Robert Mulligan and was Perkins' first starring role. Delbert Mann directed him in a film version of Eugene O'Neill's *Desire Under the Elms* (1958) in which, as farmer Burl Ives' son, he has an affair with stepmother Sophia Loren. They made a curiously unconvincing pair of lovers. Fine actor though he was, Perkins' almost fey personality gave rise to early conjectures over his sexual orientation.

The 1958 film version of Thornton Wilder's *The Matchmaker* gave him a welcome opportunity to play comedy, away from the constraints of romantic passion. Perkins plays Cornelius Hackl, head clerk of a grocery store who finds love and happiness in the Big City. Shirley Booth, Shirley MacLaine and Robert Moore rounded out this inspiration for the hit musical *Hello Dolly*. The director was Joseph Anthony. Too fey by half was the 1959 *Green Mansions*. This was director Mel Ferrer's sadly unsuccessful attempt to find an ideal role for his wife Audrey Hepburn – as a bird girl in the Venezualan jungle. Perkins is ill-at-ease as the fortune-hunting refugee who becomes involved with her. The same year, Stanley Kramer's powerful film version of Nevil Shute's novel *On The Beach* provided rewarding roles for Perkins (as a young Australian naval officer), Gregory Peck, Ava Gardner and Fred Astaire (in his first dramatic role), all facing annihilation from nuclear fallout. In *Tall Story* (1960), Perkins plays a college basketball star who falls for co-ed Jane Fonda, in her first film role, directed by Joshua Logan.

There could hardly have been a more marked contrast between his comic college boy role and his watershed movie for Hichcock the same year: *Psycho*.

For years after *Psycho* Perkins turned down any role involving drag (which he had assumed for plot purposes in *The Matchmaker*) or non-heterosexuality. Eventually, the scarcity of rewarding parts caused him reluctantly to accept bisexual, asexual or homosexual roles. Before this eventuality, he gave several fine performances. These included Mike Nichols' *Catch-22* (1970), an all-star anti-war film with Jon Voight and Orson Welles; Claude Chabrol's *Ten Days' Wonder* (1971), with Welles and Marlene Jobert, and John Huston's *The Life and Times of Judge Roy Bean* (1972), with Paul Newman, Jacqueline Bisset, Tab Hunter (allegedly a romantic partner for Perkins, who described him as 'like a Greek

God') and Ava Gardner as Lily Langtry. The same year, Perkins starred with Tuesday Weld in *Play It As It Lays* as her gay griend, a suicidal producer. The couple had teamed previously in *Pretty Poison* (1968), a black comedy with Perkins as a parolee who lures Weld, as a beautiful and innocent cheerleader, into joining him in various illegal activities, directed by Noel Black.

From 1974 onwards, Perkins' roles included a fair sprinkling of sexually ambiguous characters. Among these were Sidney Lumet's *Murder on the Orient Express*, one of the superior Agatha Christie thrillers starring well-loved players, no longer top drawers on their own, but together a powerhouse of box-office attraction. Supporting Albert Finney's garlic-flavoured Hercule Poirot were Richard Widmark as the nasty murdered industrialist, Perkins as his hysterically gay secretary, Lauren Bacall, Sean Connery, Vanessa Redgrave, John Gielgud, Ingrid Bergman and Dame Wendy Hiller. In 1975 Perkins appeared in Berry Gordy's ridiculous *Mahogany* with Diana Ross as an aspiring model, Billy Dee Williams as her boyfriend and Perkins as the bisexual photographer who discovers her and turns bitchy when she rejects his advances. There is a wrestling match between Perkins and Williams in which Williams inserts a phallic-shaped gun in the mouth of his almost willing victim. Daniel Daniele plays a hanky-waving fashion agency manager.

In 1978, Inspector Javert provided a good role in the British made-for-TV version of *Les Misèrables*, directed by Glenn Jordan. *Winter Kills* (1979) starred Jeff Bridges as the half-brother of a murdered US president, trying to track down his relative's killer. Eli Wallach plays a gay underworld villain who may be the murderer, and Elizabeth Taylor appears in a cameo as a famous actress who once had an affair with the dead president. Bridges as Nick Keegan has a bisexual girlfriend (Belinda Baxter), while Perkins effectively plays the Keegan family's

Opposite: Anthony Perkins and Janet Leigh in *Psycho* (1960).

PSYCHO

1960 Paramount/Shamley
109 mins b/w
Producer/Director: Alfred Hitchcock;
Screenplay: Joseph Stefano (based on
the novel by Robert Bloch);
Cinematographer: John L Russell
Anthony Perkins, Janet Leigh, Vera Miles,
John Gavin, Martin Balsam, John
McIntire, Simon Oakland

When Anthony Perkins took on the role of the crazed Norman Bates, motel proprietor – a nervous, bird-like creature totally under the dominance of his aged invalid mother – he not only changed the perception of his own persona but that of horror movies in general. This was mainly thanks to the inspired direction of Alfred Hitchcock, who created a new twist on the subgenre of spine-tinglers dealing with eerie characters in remote, benighted lodgings, a form harking back to James Whale's *The Old Dark House* (1932) and beyond. The murder of Janet Leigh in a shower is unlikely to be forgotten by anyone who sees it, as are the final scenes revealing the truth about the relationship between Norman Bates and his 'mother'.

Among the many imitations were several belated sequels, one of which (*Psycho III*, 1985) Perkins directed himself. George Cukor, who 'discovered' the young actor for the movies, said: 'He had a fresh, nervous, somewhat boyish quality ... I was attracted by his attractiveness and his difference ... Then Norman Bates began catching up with him. Not merely professionally, which had already happened, but facially, particularly the eyes. The actor who played all these lunatics and scary characters and kooks in all these exploitation pictures is not the actor I chose. As for all the anecdotes about him making the rounds ... they indicate he's not the same boy either.' At the time Cukor referred to him as a boy, Perkins was well into his fifties. He retained a boyish quality, however – no longer a boy-next-door but rather an ageing, haunted Peter Pan.

financial adviser. The film was directed by William Richert – a wild but entertaining movie.

In 1980, Andrew V McLaglen cast Roger Moore opposite Perkins, playing the manic leader of a gang of terrorists who have taken over a supply ship, in *North Sea Hijack*. Then it was back to Norman Bates, 23 years later, released from the asylum and trying to steer clear of murders and showers in *Psycho II* (1983), directed by Richard Franklin. Between this and *Psycho III* came Ken Russell's *Crimes of Passion* (1984), with Perkins as a deranged (and highly ambiguous) street preacher trying to save the soul of Kathleen Turner, who is a fashion designer by day and a prostitute by night. This was filmed in Britain while *Twice A Woman* was made in Holland by George Sluizer in 1985. This was a have-your-cake-and-eat-it affair with Perkins and Bibi Andersson as a divorced couple who, unknowingly, start a relationship with the same woman (Sandra Lumas). In 1986 Perkins made his only attempt at direction with *Psycho III*, in which Bates becomes attracted to his latest tenant (Diana Scarwid), who bears an unfortunate resemblance to his shower victim from the original film. This time the star/director manages to infuse humour along with the thrills.

Perkins had married Berinthia Berenson, in 1973, the photographer sister of actress Marisa Berenson. He claimed to have had his first heterosexual affair with actress Joan Hackett, who voiced her opinion that Perkins was 'nuts'. Reputedly, Brigitte Bardot, during *The Ravishing Idiot* (1965), Jane Fonda (*Tall Story*, 1960) and Ingrid Bergman (*Goodbye Again*, 1961) all failed in their attempts to seduce him. When asked how he got on with Bardot, he replied 'We didn't.' All denied the allegation of attempted seduction, while Victoria Principal scorned the suggestion that she was once his heterosexual partner.

Perkins and Berinthia had two children and he claimed that his lifestyle had completely changed. He continued to take male lovers during their marriage, however, and in the late eighties the *National Enquirer* revealed that Perkins had AIDS. A doctor whom he had visited for a minor ailment tested him surreptitiously and the news was leaked to the tabloids. He considered suing but his wife suggested he have himself officially tested to confirm his HIV status. In order to keep on working he ignored the situation to the end, though some of the media chronicled his growing gauntness. Perkins declined to take part in AIDS fundraisers but issued a statement from his deathbed which was posthumously broadcast around the world: 'I have learned more about love, selflessness and human understanding from the people I have met in this great adventure in the world of AIDS than I ever did in the cut-throat, competitive world in which I have spent my life.'

DAVID BOWIE [1947-]
[David Jones]

Bowie was probably the most famous musical performer to come out as bisexual. This was in the seventies, the days of glitter and heavy make-up – and that's only the men. Bowie, with his androgynous persona, flamboyant outfits and the sexual flaunting that went with it, gave a positive queer voice to gays everywhere. At that time he talked frankly about his gay affairs, claiming that he met his first wife, Angie, when they 'were both laying the same man.' She, in her book about their marriage – they were divorced in 1980 – wrote about finding him in bed with Mick Jagger. She says she made them breakfast. A diverting story which may or may not be apocryphal. After his marriage to the model Iman in 1992, Bowie rejected early claims about being gay, saying 'I was young and just experimenting.'

Bowie is London-born with, he said, a father who was 'a drinker and a layabout'. He claims that he and his brother and sister were all illegitimate. His father reformed and became a publicist in a children's home, while his mother worked as a cinema usherette. Leaving school at 16, he worked in an advertising firm, which did not give him an opportunity to indulge his eccentricities. So he embarked on a musical career, breaking through with the topical single 'Space Oddity' in 1969, and underwent training in mime from Lindsay Kemp, who, he said, 'taught me more about what one can do on a stage than anyone.'

From this specialised theatrical education Bowie broke back into the musical mainstream in 1972 with the epoch-making tour of Ziggy Stardust and the Spiders from Mars, based on his bestselling album of the same name. Ziggy was a sexually ambivalent rock star from outer space, making Bowie a trend-setter for Glam Rock. In drag and imaginative make-up he became an androgynous icon for a generation. From Ziggy he went into the Thin White Duke character of his cocaine-using days; his frequently changing image earned him a reputation as the chameleon of rock.

In 1975, Bowie starred on screen for Nicolas Roeg as *The Man Who Fell to Earth*, ideally cast as a mysterious visitor from another planet. Buck Henry plays a gay lawyer who helps the spaceman build his earthly empire. Four years later Bowie made his second film, *Just a Gigolo*.

Merry Christmas, Mr Lawrence (1982), a British/Japanese co-production directed by Nagisa Oshima, is a fascinating drama set in a World War Two Prisoner of War camp, a study in conflicting cultures. Bowie is Celliers, a New Zealander, whose rebellious nature and stiff-upper lip bravery puzzle his guards and intrigue the new camp commandant, Yoni (Ryuichi Sakamoto), who is greatly attracted to him and plans to make him the prisoners' CO. The development of their relationship deserves further amplification, but is one of the most attractive features of this complex and provocative film. This is Bowie's best performance to date; he inhabits the role, which fits him like a glove, and Sakamoto, a Japanese pop star in his first dramatic role, is superb too.

In Tony Scott's *The Hunger* (1983), Bowie was cast in the most way-out role he has ever played. He portrays the vampiric 200-year-old toy boy of the ageless and ever-lovely Catherine Deneuve, who takes on a new lover every second century or so, bestowing on them temporary 'eternal beauty', presumably until she tires of them. John (David Bowie), after a hard life of satisfying Deneuve year in and year out, bloodsucking, disco dancing, replenishing his wardrobe with all the latest trends in *haute couture*, is shocked but surely not surprised to find himself ageing rapidly. He reaches his 251st year and expires, looking every bit his age. His loving mistress tenderly salts him away before turning to her next conquest, the sexy lesbian Susan Sarandon. A bizarre and beguiling variation on the vampire theme for lovers of the genre, but probably not for *Ziggy Stardust* fans.

Bowie's next three major films were varied and, each in its own way, brilliant. Jim Henson's *Labyrinth* (1985) has his puppets intermingling with human and fantasy characters. A latterday Alice in Wonderland weaves her way through a treacherous maze, where she encounters Bowie as the King of the Goblins, who sings her a couple of songs. Julian Temple's imaginative film version of Colin Macinnes' 1958 cult novel *Absolute Beginners* tells the story of two Notting Hill teenagers, Eddie O'Connell and Patsy Kensit, set against the background of the emerging youth culture and racism at the time the book was written. O'Connell plays a photographer, Kensit the fashion designer with whom he is in love. Bowie is Vendice Partners, the cool associate of the unscrupulous James Fox. Bowie gets to sing the title tune amid a set of characters mostly as queer as coots. Eve Ferret is Big Jill, who goes for chicks only; Jo McKenna is the sprite Fabulous Hoplite, 'our own low-rent Oscar Wilde'; and Lionel Blair plays the record producer Harry Charms ('Nobody's Wild about Harry'). The music, orchestrated by Gil Evans, is superlative, and there's a wickedly seductive number by Sade.

It's a giant leap from fifties Notting Hill to Martin Scorsese *The Last Temptation of Christ* (1988). Scorsese's adaptation of Nikos Kazantzakis' controversial book seeks to present Jesus as both fully God and fully man, picturing all the familiar stories of the disciples and the miracles, with the dramatis personae as set forth in the Bible vividly recreated by a remarkable team of actors. These are headed by Willem Dafoe's subtle depiction of the Christ as a man locked in a battle with his own destiny, making him more comprehensible than the always-perfect Redeemer presented in the Gospels. Predictably, this did not please the Elders of the Church. Bowie's Pontius Pilate makes his indecision and capitulation understandable, as are the motivations of Harvey Keitel's Judas and

Barbara Hershey's Mary Magdalene.

Three years later, Bowie played Monty, the new English barman in the latest New York theme park restaurant, in Richard Shephard's *The Linguini Incident* (1991). This is a vastly entertaining comedy about Manhattan's super-rich set, packed with examples of deception, robbery, snobbery and Monty's quest to marry in order to get a green card to continue working in the USA. The cast includes Rosanna Arquette, Buck Henry and Viveca Lindfors.

After a 20-second flash as an FBI agent in David Lynch's *Twin Peaks: Fire Walk With Me* (1992), Bowie made no films for four years. In 1996 he played Andy Warhol in a biographical study of the artist, *Basquiat*, directed by Julian Schnabel, and in 1998 he made two movies, a

Above: David Bowie in *The Linguini Incident* (1991).

crime drama called *Everybody Loves Sunshine/B.U.S.T.E.D.*, directed by Andrew Goth, and the Italian *Il mio west*, directed by Giovanni Veronesi and not released in English-speaking countries. In 2000, Bowie's last film to date was *Mr Rice's Secret*, directed by Nicholas Kendall. He remains an icon and something of an enigma.

BRAD DAVIS (1949-1991)

In his 15-year film career, Davis made 19 films. From 1985 until his death from AIDS at the age of 41, he suffered from the disease but kept it hidden in order to keep on working. He left behind a stinging indictment of Hollywood homophobia. 'I make my living in an industry which professes to care very much about AIDS, that gives umpteen benefits and charity affairs, but in actual fact, if an actor is even rumoured to be HIV-positive, he gets no support on an individual basis – he does not work.' Davis was, however, not homosexual. His friend Larry Kramer wrote that 'He was one of the first straight actors with the guts to play gay roles.' After his death his widow, Susan Buestein, continued his activist work, which he had begun during the final years of his life.

Born in Florida, Davis moved to Georgia after high school graduation and from thence to New York to begin acting off-Broadway, where he studied at the Academy of Dramatic Art. Theatre work led to his film debut in *Sybil* (1976), directed by Daniel Petrie, and two years later the most notable movie of his career, *Midnight Express*.

For all that he made other excellent films, Brad Davis never reached the top stardom he deserved. He played in three movies in 1980. First was *A Small Circle of Friends*, directed by Rob Cohen, a rare, charming comedy in which Davis, along with Karen Allen and Parker Stevenson, play college friends during the late sixties. Then there was *The Greatest Man in the World*, an *American Short Story Collection* from a

James Thurber tale, in which Davis is a pilot who becomes the first person to fly non-stop across the world. He gives an outstanding performance in the made-for-TV drama about the Vietnam war, *A Rumour of War*, as a GI whose unswerving support of the war leads to tragedy. Richard T Heffron directs a strong cast, including Keith Carradine, Michael O'Keefe and Brian Dennehy.

Davis has a telling cameo as an American athlete in Hugh Hudson's classic Oscar-winning *Chariots of Fire*, an Olympic study of Eric Liddell and Harold Abrahams, two runners competing for Britain in Paris in 1924, played respectively by Ian Charleson and Ben Cross. The devoutly Christian Scott, Liddell, runs for the glory of Jesus, the Jewish Abrahams, sensitive to anti-Semitic prejudice, runs simply to be accepted. Liddell went to China as a missionary and died in a Japanese Prisoner of War camp. Ian Charleson himself died of AIDS in 1990, aged 39. He had made his film debut in 1977 as one of the amoral twins in Derek Jarman's *Jubilee*. Following *Chariots of Fire*, he worked most notably on the stage, winning acclaim in *Cat on a Hot Tin Roof* and *Hamlet*.

Querelle (1982), the West German film which was the last directed by Rainer Warner Fassbinder, probably means more to gay audiences than *Chariots of Fire*. It is based on Jean Genet's homo-erotic story of lust and murder *Querelle of Brest*, and Davis plays the ruggedly handsome, violently sexual sailor with 'a guy in every port'. For good measure, Jeanne Moreau, the mature saloon chanteuse, sings a song based on Oscar Wilde's 'Each Man in His Time Kills the One He Loves', which proves prophetic. The sailor creates erotic fulfilment and mayhem while on shore leave in the process of facing up to his true nature. Critics have pondered what Fassbinder 'meant' by the film. Under the alienating macho posturing, is there a parable about a man whose life has been obsessed with having or getting? Alternatively, is it a send-up of hyper-

MIDNIGHT EXPRESS

1978 Columbia/Casablanca 121 mins Eastmancolor
Producers: David Puttnam, Alan Marshall; Director: Alan Parker;
Screenplay: Oliver Stone
(based on the autobiography by Billy Hayes, with William Hoffer);
Cinematography: Michael Seresin
Brad Davis, Randy Quaid, Bo Hopkins, John Hurt, Paul Smith, Norbert Weisser, Irene Miracle, Paolo Bonacelli, Michael Ensign

Based on Billy Hayes' autobiography, this movie traces his hellish years spent in a Turkish prison for drug smuggling. Brad Davis' performance is a *tour de force*, displaying a great range of human emotions. Hayes enjoys a brief liaison with a gay Scandinavian prisoner, Erich (Norbert Weisser), here confined to a kiss in the showers – although actually Billy and Erich were lovers in real life. John Hurt's character Max is, as always, spot-on – a drug-besotted but philosophical Englishman. Randy Quaid, as the slightly unhinged American Jimmy, is outstanding. Weisser's Erich is credible and touching and Paul Smith as Hamidou, the prison official who meets a fitting end when he tries to rape Billy, presents a chilling study in sheer evil. A Horse-Frightening sight. When the hero eventually catches the 'Midnight Express' (ie, escapes), it is a thrill to watch Davis caught in freeze-frame as he executes an ecstatic jump for joy *en route* to freedom. Director Alan Parker and editor Gerry Hambling both won British Academy Awards for their work, besides Oscar nominations.

masculinity, with its grunted terms of endearment, violence, attraction to dominance/submission and total anal phallocentricity? Whatever the answer, Davis presents a multi-layered performance of considerable power and Moreau is radiant in an underdeveloped role.

Of the 11 films during the remainder of his career, Davis' two most compelling performances were in the title role *Robert Kennedy and His Times* (1984), based on the book by Arthur Schlesinger and directed by Marvin J Chomsky, and the remake of *The Caine Mutiny Court Martial*, directed by Robert Altman in 1988. Davis takes the Bogart role of the infamous Captain Queeg. In contrast to Bogart's neurotic interpretation, Davis shows a smug and offi-

RUPERT EVERETT (1959 –)

Some years ago, a headline asked why there has never been an openly gay leading man. The question is now answered: Rupert Everett came out in 1992 so there was one even then, although at that time he had not reached the peak of eminence he now inhabits so handsomely. He is unique in another way, in having a personality that recalls the great days of the movies' English gentlemen, like Ronald Colman, Herbert Marshall and George Sanders. Everett is a younger version, with an experience of life to which they could never have owned up – and he has broken new ground in being able to play straight or gay with equal conviction.

His professional acting career started at the prestigious Glasgow Citizens Theatre. His life until then had hardly been uneventful. Born in Norfolk, the son of an army officer and a Scottish mother, his early days were spent in army camps around the world before attending Ampleforth, a Catholic public school, until he was 15, when he dropped out and went to Paris. At a party he heard some queer goings on: a queen singing soprano and another playing a piano with candles on it. He decided he'd finally arrived at his milieu. After a brief spell at the Central School of Speech and Drama he was expelled for subversion. He joined the heroin set in London – 'Everyone I knew was into it,' he has said – but his determination to become an actor gave him the will to ditch heroin.

His first novel *Hello Darling, Are You Working?* revealed Everett's sense of humour and high-camp awareness of style. After *Another Country* (1984), he did several jobs, including modelling for Yves St Laurent's Opium aftershave. He made a pop record, *Generation of Loneliness*, which was not a success. He has admitted that he worked for a while in London as a rent boy, about which he says he is not going to be defensive because it has nothing to do with him now. He has had dates with Bianca Jagger, Cher and Paula

cious control-freak – an interpretation just as telling, but quite different from the original.

The year before his untimely death, Davis gave a performance that shows he possessed comedy talents, virtually untapped, in Percy Adlon's *Rosalie Goes Shopping* (1990), as the charming husband of Marianne Sagebrecht in a satire on American consumerism. She's a housewife juggling 37 credit cards and he is the man who tries to keep her a few paces ahead of her creditors. His last film, *Hangfire* (1991), directed by Peter Maris, cast Davis as one of a group of escaped convicts who create chaos in a small New Mexican town. That he could carry on working so long shows the remarkable strength of character which always shone through his screen performances.

Above: Rupert Everett and Colin Firth in *Another Country* (1984).

Yates, and Madonna is one of his best friends.

Another movie which gained Everett accolades was *Dance With a Stranger* (1984), directed by Mike Newell, with a sensational film debut by Miranda Richardson as Ruth Ellis, the last woman to be hanged in England for murder. Everett played the glamorous but worthless boyfriend whom she kills. Alternating between stage and screen, Everett has since appeared in, among others, *Duet for One* (1986), *Chronicle of a Death Foretold* (1986) and *The Comfort of Strangers* (1992), directed by Paul Schrader. The latter film is a visually exquisite production of Harold Pinter's screenplay about a young English couple (Everett and Natasha Richardson) involved in the twisted games of Christopher Walken, who runs a gay bar, and his invalid wife Helen Mirren. Walken desires Everett, a passion that is not fully requited, and the ending is seemingly unmotivated.

After *The Madness of King George* (1995), a smallish but well-characterised and noticeably padded part as the Prince Regent, came the film that made him more in demand than ever, *My Best Friend's Wedding* (1997). This was a gay role that was gradually written up from a cameo into one of the biggest successes of an outstandingly popular movie.

In 1998 Everett presented a stylish Oberon opposite the beautiful Michelle Pfeiffer as Titania in Michael Hoffman's film of *A Midsummer Night's Dream*, with an all-star cast of whom several seemed unable to get to grips with the iambic pentameter, especially Pfeiffer and Sophie Marceau's Hippolyta. The role of Lord Goring in Oliver Parker's *An Ideal Husband* (1999) fitted Everett like a glove. The Oscar Wilde prototype – witty and, for all his elegance, antisocial – is perfect for him and, if there are to be more Wilde remakes, he should, if he cares to, be in all of them. He is not, however, confined to upper-class gents in his characterisations, as he showed so ably in *Inside Monkey Zetterland* (1992), when he

MY BEST FRIEND'S WEDDING

1997 Columbia TriStar/Predawn 105 mins Technicolor
Producers: Ronald Bass, Jerry Zucker; Director: P J Hogan; Screenplay: Ronald Bass; Cinematographer: Laszlo Kovacs
Julia Roberts, Dermot Mulroney, Cameron Diaz, Rupert Everett, Philip Bosco, Rachel Griffiths, M Emmet Walsh

A simple tale – Julia Roberts and Dermot Mulroney agree to marry when they reach the age of 28, if no one else gets there first. With just weeks to go, in walks Cameron Diaz, whom Mulroney intends to marry in a few days' time. Determined to sabotage the wedding and win Mulroney back, Roberts enlists as a maid of honour, undermining her love rival at every opportunity. In between her acts of subversion, Roberts seeks consolation from her gay friend Rupert Everett, giving one of the funniest performances of his career. The sparkling teamwork of Diaz, Mulroney and, particularly, Roberts, guided by P J Hogan's brilliant direction, makes this one of the most pleasant comedies of recent years, *Muriel's Wedding* (1994) – another Hogan triumph – notwithstanding.

played a working-class Australian doing his time in LA. He is also a gay activist who falls in love with a lesbian Patricia Arquette.

Everett has homes in LA, New York, Miami and presumably one in England, now that the quarantine laws have been changed. His labrador Mo is the only part of his private life about which he will talk freely. He loves Mo, who must by now have his own passport. Everett has written a script for himself about a supposedly heterosexual film star who is really gay. He also has ready a film script from his novel *Hello, Darling, Are You Working?* Despite his air of langour in interviews, he is a hard worker, an avid traveler and likes the excitement of working in other countries. He has made films in such diverse countries as Italy, Colombia and Russia, where he had a happy time making *Quiet Flows the Don* (1992) in the year of his coming out. He said then, 'It's time for people to be honest about what they do.' It was this kind of thinking that prompted him to play the small part of a man dying of AIDS in *Remembrance of Things Past* (1993). □

became deemed worthy of the royal accolade, conferred by the monarch on the advice of the Prime Minister. People whose names are published in the Queen's Birthday Honours or New Year Honours usually receive the award at an investiture at Buckingham Palace. The Queen remains standing throughout the ceremony, which takes about an hour. After the playing of the National Anthem, the Lord Chamberlain announces the name of the recipient and the achievement for which he or she is being honoured.

Those who are to receive a knighthood, and who are therefore entitled to be called Sir, kneel on the investiture stool before the Queen. She uses the sword that belonged to her father, King George VI, to dub the knight,

8 THE QUEEN'S KNIGHTS

The origins of knighthood are said to date back to Ancient Rome, when there was a knightly class of mounted nobles. Later, in Europe, a knight would have to prove himself to be worthy according to the rules of chivalrous behaviour, such as faithfulness to his saviour and his sovereign; he also had to be financially capable of providing a required number of armed followers to render military service to his sovereign for a minimum period each year or pay a tax, which proved handy for the royal coffers.

Through the centuries, as the sovereign ceased to lead the troops into battle, knighthood developed so that it could be conferred for other services to the country. The Arts

Above: A latterday portrait of Dirk Bogarde.

Opposite: Nöel Coward in *The Italian Job* (1969).

tapping him on the shoulder before congratulating him on receiving the award. The theatrical Dames of the British Empire are not tapped with the sword but the Queen pins on a medal conferring the Damehood.

In the past the accolades were exclusively awarded to actors or actresses whose achievement in the theatre had been outstanding. Nowadays the cinema and television or the musical field can render people eligible – eg, Sir Elton John, who received the Sword of Honour from Queen Elizabeth II in 1998. Until fairly recently, a blameless personal life and, where applicable, a respectable marital record were also considered necessary. Time has altered all that.

SIR NOËL COWARD
(Noël Pierce Coward) 1899-1973

The 20th century's greatest English-speaking wit, playwright, lyricist and, along with Ivor Novello, composer of light music. Coward made no bones about his homosexuality but did not exactly flaunt it, apart from lounging about in silk dressing gowns and smoking cigarettes in long holders. But, as his fame grew, the establishment learned to tolerate him, without approving. In the twenties, when the Bright Young Things, among whom he was the brightest, made their own rules of behaviour, Coward's play *The Vortex* (1924), in which he himself starred, dealt with such untapped topics as a drug-addicted son of uncertain morals and sexual orientation and a mother who avariciously pursued what would now be called toy boys. In 1932 Coward's *Design for Living* dealt wittily with a *ménage à trois* in which two men love a girl and, equally, each other – a theme that was lightly skipped over in the 1933 Hollywood version.

Born in Teddington, Middlesex of respectable middle-class parents, Coward was into acting at the age of 12 in a children's play called *The Goldfish* and from then on never stopped. In 1913 he played an angel in a play called *Hannele* at Liverpool Rep, where he met and formed a life-long friendship with Gertrude Lawrence. A year older than he, she appeared as another angel. When both were grown up, Coward wrote the classic comedy *Private Lives* for himself and Lawrence. Later speculation that they may have had an affair has been effectively ruled out – Coward was simply not interested sexually in women and she, although twice-married and bisexual, was more career-orientated than anything else. An actress friend of hers said, when she married producer Richard Aldrich: 'He thinks he's marrying Miss Gertrude Lawrence; he will soon find he has married Mr Lawrence!'

After he became an international star and made his grown-up Hollywood debut in *The Scoundrel* (1933), Coward achieved one of his greatest film successes as star and co-director of *In Which We Serve* with David Lean, a patriotic tribute to the British Navy lightyears removed from such brilliantly conceived comedies as *Blithe Spirit* (1945), which starred Rex Harrison, Kay Hammond and Constance Cummings as well as featuring Coward's humorous narration. There was a five-year gap before Coward's next appearance on screen: *The Astonished Heart*. Coward took over the leading role from Michael Redgrave in this triangular romance, which finds him torn between wife Celia Johnson and mistress Margaret Leighton. Johnson was one of his favourite actresses on both stage and screen, and with her he enjoyed some of his greatest successes, including *In Which We Serve*, *Brief Encounter* (with Trevor Howard, adapted from one of Coward's playlets) and *This Happy Breed*, in 1945, in which she had played with him in the theatre. In *The Astonished Heart*, however, the liaison was not so felicitous: his personality had become so familiar by that time that it was almost as though he were parodying himself – and he was no longer acceptable as an ardent lover. With Redgrave, the part might have worked.

Graham Payn played Coward's efficient secretary. Coward was by then sharing his life with Payn at their home in Montreux, Switzerland. Payn had appeared on stage in the revue *Sigh No More* and the musical *Ace of Clubs* with Pat Kirkwood, written for him by Coward, besides several appearances opposite Gertrude Lawrence in Coward playlets in the USA. It was through Payn, for whom my partner and I were doing PR, that I met Noël Coward. (Payn had been the dancing partner of Dorothy Dickson in the revue *Fine and Dandy* in 1942 and she had been Coward's friend since she arrived in England in the revue *London, Paris and New York* in 1919.) Coward proved as scintillating a companion as his work suggested, but with a kindness at variance with some of his more caustic remarks.

He and Graham came to one of my parties in Notting Hill Gate, which was dimly lit as Noël had asked not to be singled out from the other guests in order to avoid fuss; he just wanted to 'mingle quietly'. That was as likely as Elvis singing 'Blue Suede Shoes' in a darkened room without being recognised. Within minutes he was surrounded. In fact, he didn't mind a bit. Through the years we kept in touch: on one occasion I left him, as a going-away present, a box of plastic prehistoric monsters from Shreddies packets, which amused him. He wrote to say thank you: 'The Monsters have their own cabinet here in Les Avants, where I'm sure they'll be very, very happy.'

In 1944 Dorothy Dickson had asked Coward to help her in the organisation of a Stage Door Canteen in Piccadilly. This was to be on the lines of the one in New York for the Armed Forces on leave, where they could be entertained and dance with the stars, be wined and dined and, in general, relax away from the stresses of war. Coward refused, saying it was too late, he was too busy, and a host of other excuses. Dickson went ahead with the help of a committee and a host of her friends in showbusiness. The project, within sight of the Eros statue, was opened by the politician Anthony Eden on 31 August 1944, in front of a packed house full of the Allied Forces in London. Among the entertainers were Dorothy Dickson herself, Fred Astaire, Bing Crosby and a surprise visitor, Nöel Coward, unannounced, who had come quietly through the stage door and knelt, in true theatrical style, before hostess Dickson. 'Darling, you were right, I was wrong,' he announced. 'Tell me what you want me to do – anything to help!' The slight rift was healed and Noël joined the stars, who gave of their best.

The Canteen was an immediate triumph and remained open until after the end of WWII. The cream of British and American stars appeared, including Marlene Dietrich, Beatrice Lillie,

Above: Nöel Coward and Elizabeth Taylor in *Boom!* (1968).

Cicely Courtneidge, Jack Hulbert, Julie Andrews and Petula Clark. Two decades later, Simpsons of Piccadilly, for their part in the Festival of London Stores, invited Dorothy Dickson to organise a get-together of many of the original Stage Door Canteen performers, which garnered massive publicity. The *Evening Standard* of 21 May 1968 displayed posters headed 'The Stars Who Helped Win the War!' Coward was abroad, making a film in Hollywood, and could not be present. The event was such a success that another reunion was arranged for later in the year, this time in honour of Coward and including all three leading ladies from the original productions of his musical success *Bitter Sweet*. These were Peggy Wood from His Majesty's Theatre London (1928), Evelyn Laye from the Ziegfeld New York (1929) and Anna Neagle from Herbert Wilcox's film of 1933. This time, however, the press coverage was comparatively sparse. The event had taken place on the day of Bobby Kennedy's assassination.

In 1968 Coward appeared in one of the odd-est films of his career, and probably the oddest in that of his friends Elizabeth Taylor and Richard Burton. The film – directed by Joseph Losey, no less – was based on Tennessee Williams' play *The Milk Train Doesn't Stop Here Anymore*. The play was adapted by Williams himself into the over-ripe script of *Boom!* Williams called it the 'most perfect' of all the screen versions of his plays. Neither the public nor the critics concurred, but the film has a spe-cial appeal to gay people and recently gained an extra cachet when presented by the LA County Museum of Art as part of its celebration of the Nöel Coward centenary in 1999. Coward's role, as the bitchy Witch of Capri (originally written for a woman; Constance Collier would have been perfect or even Hermione Gingold), 'is played to the faggy hilt by Sir Nöel', according to Raymond Murray's *Images in the Dark*. Taylor plays a hugely wealthy but dying writer, Sissy Goforth, who becomes besotted with a wander-ing poet and 'Angel of Death', Richard Burton.

The same year Losey directed another film with an offbeat relationship for Elizabeth Taylor, *Secret Ceremony*, in which she, as a middle-aged nympho mourning her dead daughter, becomes involved with a mentally unbalanced girl (Mia Farrow). At first they play mother and daughter games, then their relationship becomes increas-ingly Sapphic, complicated by the unexpected return of Farrow's sexually abusive stepfather, played by Robert Mitchum. Two films in a row calculated to please one section of her admirers and to dismay the more 'normally' orientated.

Coward's final film appearance was in the Michael Caine vehicle *The Italian Job* (1969). The movie presented Coward as the type of character in which he excelled – the dominant inmate of a men's prison who becomes involved in a brilliantly organised bullion heist, masterminded by Caine. Graham Payn

amusingly plays Coward's buddy in the jail.

Coward's work on *In Which We Serve* gained Sir Nöel a special Academy Award. His achievement of successfully juggling theatre, film, cabaret, writ-ing, composing and recording careers, besides some secret service work for Britain during WWII, made him indeed special – perhaps the most ver-satile all-rounder of the 20th century in the field of entertainment. His knighthood came late in life, delayed, it is thought, until a more enlightened establishment attitude became prevalent than the one holding sway when his contemporary, Sir John Gielgud, fell foul of an *agent provocateur*.

For some years Sir Nöel had become increasingly frail. He died of a heart attack at the age of 74 at his home in Bermuda. Graham Payn and Nöel's devoted secretary and friend, Cole Lesley, were in residence at the time.

SIR JOHN GIELGUD
(Arthur John Gielgud) 1904–1998

Born in London of a theatrical family – his mother was Kate Terry-Lewis – Gielgud studied for the stage at Lady Benson's School and at RADA. He made his first professional appear-ance at the Old Vic and soon became distin-guished as a leading exponent of Shakespearean roles, playing Romeo at the age of 20 with Sir Barry Jackson's Company and his first *Hamlet* at 25 – a performance he looked back on with some scorn in an *Omnibus* interview in the nineties.

However, Gielgud's versatility was such that he made a personable Innigo Jollifant in J B Priestley's musical *The Good Companions* in 1931 and repeated the role in the film version in 1933, opposite Jessie Matthews at the start of her rise to pre-eminence in British musicals. In 1937 came Hitchcock's *Secret Agent*, from W Somerset Maugham's Ashenden spy stories, opposite Madeleine Carroll and Peter Lorre. Gielgud was hardly the ideal leading juvenile,

Right: Peter Lorre, John Gielgud and Madeleine Carroll in *Secret Agent* (1937).

despite his mellifluous speaking voice, and the theatre claimed his attention, for the most part, except for occasional character roles, of which the earliest and most outstanding was *The Prime Minister* (1940), as Disraeli.

Gielgud produced and played the title role in *Macbeth* in 1942. When the tour reached Edinburgh, where I was stationed in the Royal Artillery, I was taken backstage by my friend John Shepherd, who was in the company. I was surprised and excited to be asked to meet Gielgud for lunch at the elegant Aperitif cocktail bar/restaurant. The only problem was getting a replacement for my duties as switchboard operator at the 63rd LAA BHQ in Moray Place, where the army had requisitioned one of many grand residences in that area. The invitation came at short notice as *Macbeth* was only in town for a week and there were no takers. The old army dictum 'Never Volunteer' proved all too true that afternoon, but I was not going to miss the opportunity of being wined and dined by the

first real star I had ever met. The glimpse across a crowded tea-room of Mary Morris, which had so disturbed my equilibrium the same year, paled into insignificance beside this opportunity to mingle with the *crème de la crème*.

Calls to BHQ at this stage of the war were infrequent, especially in the afternoons, so I took a chance and, with a brief prayer to my guardian angel, unplugged the switchboard before setting out in my best battledress. This was not very impressive, as my buttons had a green tinge from the nail varnish I put on them to avoid the boring chore of having to polish them too often. I arrived before my host and just hoped that the few shillings I had on me might cover the cost of a Pimms at Aperitif prices. I need not have worried. The Scots, contrary to all rumours, are apt to be generous, especially to a scruffy artillery gunner, who quite clearly was an unusual sight in that bar. Very soon I was sipping as graciously as I knew how from a Pimms number whatever, flavoured with vodka and bequeathed by a kind lady in a large flowered hat who was over-whelmed when I was joined by John Gielgud, to whom I was proud to introduce her. My special treat in those days was lobster mayonnaise and that was what we had, with more Pimms.

The remainder of the lunch remains a blur, apart from the procession of people who came to our table to pass compliments and even to ask for autographs, all of whom Gielgud handled with his customary courtly grace. He sent me back to barracks in a pre-paid taxi, then, sur-prise surprise, I was on a charge for dereliction of duty. Sergeant Major Newbold – he who had taken me to see a Cicely Courtneidge film from the training camp – was impressed by my lunch date and insisted on polishing my buttons prop-erly, after I'd applied the nail varnish remover. The Commanding Officer was not remotely impressed by my explanation, however, and I was sentenced to ten days confined to barracks with hard labour in the form of washing up the unit's dirty dishes, plus potato peeling.

John Shepherd arranged a tea party at the home of married friends of his, to which Gielgud and I were invited, after which we did not meet again until he produced, but did not appear in, Eric Linklater's *Crisis in Heaven*, with Dorothy Dickson as Helen of Troy. In the meantime, word reached John Shepherd that the redoubtable Martita Hunt, who was to be an unforgettable Miss Havisham in David Lean's *Great Expectations*, had been trumpeting the news round the West End that 'John has been going out with a young gunner in Edinburgh!' That was as far as it went, as my unit was sta-tioned in far-flung places like Liverpool, Bognor Regis, Eastbourne, Stanton, Leeds and Sheffield, and Gielgud virtually never stopped working. We corresponded spasmodically.

There was a notable gap in Gielgud's film appearances until his outstanding performance in 1953 as Cassius in Joseph L Mankiewicz's *Julius Caesar* – for which he was awarded the

British Academy's Best Actor of the Year acco-lade. This was also the year he was knighted. In 1955 he was directed by Laurence Olivier in the superlative film of *Richard III*, dominated by Olivier in the title role, repellently grotesque and villainous. The supporting cast included Claire Bloom, Ralph Richardson and Gielgud as the gentle Duke of Clarence – spectacularly exe-cuted by being up-ended in a butt of Malmesey.

The years since Gielgud's knighthood had been as busy as ever but he was under consider-able strain since a press bombshell headlining his arrest for 'importuning' in a public toilet in Chelsea one night in October 1953. At the time, Gielgud was in the final stages of directing John Perry's *A Day by the Sea* for Binkie Beaumont, the gay but always discreet head of H M Tennent Productions. Sir John was depressed, drink had been taken, and an attractive *agent provocateur* had little difficulty in attracting his attention. As the actor had given his real name there was no way the affair could be hushed up, as had sever-al recent cases of arrest on similar charges. Gielgud was fined £10, with resultant newspa-per headlines. What he should have done, had he not been so confused, was to phone Binkie Beaumont – who was extremely well-connected and had an extra vested interest in the success of the play as it was written by his lover, John Perry, who had coincidentally been Sir John's first real love. The furore eventually settled down but it is thought to have been the reason Nöel Coward's knighthood was so long delayed.

In 1957 I cycled to the Memorial Theatre at Stratford upon Avon to see Sir John's perform-ance in his production of *King Lear* and was welcomed back to his dressing room with my friend, Jimmy Laurie, an entertainer who had been a school friend and fellow weight trainer of Sean Connery. We were surprised and delighted to find Charles Laughton and Elsa Lanchester already there, having returned to England recently after completing the film *Witness for the*

Prosecution. Sir John had made *The Barretts of Wimpole Street* in the part originated on screen by Laughton and had just played the Inquisitor, Warwick, in Preminger's *Saint Joan*, starring Jean Seberg in the title role. They were discussing the film's various performances, especially hers, in critical terms and I presumed to interject with 'I thought she definitely had some moments in the part.' Sir John said crushingly, 'You can't have *moments* as Saint Joan!'

Gielgud's stage and screen work continued apace, especially after fine roles like that of the charming King Louis VII of France in Peter Glenville's 1964 *Becket*, which won him an Academy Award nomination. The gay director, working from the screenplay crafted by Edward Anholt from Jean Anouilh's play, explored the subtle homo-erotic tension between Peter O'Toole's Henry II and Richard Burton's Chancellor, created Archbishop of Canterbury by the King — a theme which was absent from the original play. Both stars received Oscar nominations for Best Actor, while Gielgud's was for Best Supporting Actor.

Many consider Sir John's finest screen role to be in Alain Resnais' *Providence* (1977). Gielgud plays Clive Langham, a noted elderly author, who is terminally ill, foul-mouthed and alcoholic. He spends a night trying, through his hallucinations, to plot out a new novel involving his stressed-out sons, David Warner and Dirk Bogarde, the latter at odds with wife Ellen Burstyn. Fact, fantasy, his unconscious thoughts and growing senility are all woven into the fabric of the old man's tale. Elaine Stritch, also playing a character with a terminal illness, is a part of his fact and fiction.

From this masterpiece Gielgud moved on to *Caligula* (1979), with Malcolm McDowell as the crazed young Emperor whose excesses included homosexual orgies; these were eventually excised by the movie's director, Tinto Bass. This supposedly led to Gore Vidal insisting he have all his credits deleted from the film. Peter

O'Toole co-starred with McDowell and Gielgud played Tiberius' tutor, Nerva, who commits suicide by cutting his wrists in the bath. Gielgud regarded the film as 'pure pornography'.

At the age of 77, Sir John won his first Oscar for Best Supporting Actor in Steve Gordon's *Arthur* (1981), co-starring Dudley Moore and Liza Minnelli. *Arthur* is a crazy comedy with Moore as a dotty millionaire who risks his fortune to woo the charming but penniless Minnelli. Hobson, Arthur's devoted but acerbic gentleman's gentleman — delivering such uncharacteristic lines as 'Do you want me to scrub your dick, sir?' – is the comedy highlight of Gielgud's career in the movies. In *Arthur 2: On the Rocks* he reappears briefly as a ghost, having died in the first film; the sequel has the original stars but little of the original wit.

As film historian David Thomson put it, after the birth of his serious interest in film work, Gielgud '...plunged into film with magnificent, indiscriminate zest'. There had been Orson Welles' *Chimes at Midnight* (1966) as Henry IV, Tony Richardson's *The Charge of the Light Brigade* (1968) as Lord Raglan opposite Trevor Howard's Lord Cardigan, and David Lynch's *The Elephant Man* (1980), as the compassionate hospital administrator. There were also two guest appearances in Agatha Christie's all-star murder fests, *Murder on the Orient Express*, Sidney Lumet's blockbuster from 1974, and *Appointment with Death*, directed by Michael Winner in 1988, in both of which Sir John provided an elegant red herring. Gielgud's prize turkey was, perhaps, the ludicrous 1972 musical remake of James Hilton's *Lost Horizon* (1937). Financially and emotionally these manifold film challenges, averaging a couple of movies a year, provided the stability Sir John had long sought. He was able to move from his London flat in Regents Park to a palatial country establishment in Wootton Underwood with his companion Martin Hessler, who had shared his life for some

Left: John Gielgud in *Prospero's Books* (1991).

30 years and who pre-deceased him.

The finest late flowering of Gielgud's film career has to be *Prospero's Books* (1991), Peter Greenaway's kaleidoscopic vision of one of Sir John's greatest Shakespearean roles, in which he not only stars in the title role but also gives voice to every other character in the film. Greenaway spatters the screen with an endless procession of naked bodies and Bacchanalian revels, only sketchily following the development of the original narrative. This is an audacious representation of *The Tempest* and one which may outrage as many as it will delight. In any event, the film is a crowning achievement for the 87-year-old actor, whose career on the screen began in a 1924 silent, *Who is the Man?*, playing a dope fiend; in his own words, 'The most ridiculous part I've ever played on screen.'

His last stage appearance was in 1988 in *The Best of Friends*. In 1994 the Apollo Theatre in London's West End was renamed the Gielgud Theatre in his honour. The cur-tain fell on his film performances with 1996's award-winning Anglo-Australian co-produc-tion *Shine*, directed by Scott Hicks. Best Film and Direction Academy Award nomina-tions were supplemented by an Oscar for Geoffrey Rush as David Hellgott, the gifted pianist whose brilliant career was cut short by severe mental problems. Sir John's per-formance as Cecil Parkes, who becomes involved in the traumatic family tensions, was, as always, immaculate.

SIR MICHAEL REDGRAVE
(Michael Scudamore Redgrave) 1908-1985

Sir Michael was the son of actor Roy Redgrave and actress Margaret Scudamore, a dear old lady with whom I was privileged to work when she played the childrens' nanny to Joan Greenwood and Naunton Wayne's offspring in the comedy *Young Wives' Tale* by Ronald Jeans at the Savoy Theatre in 1949. I did not know until much later that, between engagements, she was given to bouts of desperate alcoholism, during which her friend Coral Browne used to nurse her.

I met her son only once, in the White Room Club with John Gielgud, and found him handsome but remote from us. 'Don't you believe it', said Sir John. I was reminded of this years later, after Redgrave had starred with Joan Greenwood and Richard Attenborough in *The Man Within* (*The Smugglers* in the US) in 1947. Dennis Price remarked, 'Wasn't that a touching scene when Michael locked Joan in a cupboard, then made love to young Dickie Attenborough?' Slight exaggeration, of course, but that was the way the scene played to those in the know.

In fact, bondage with guardsmen was more Redgrave's cup of tea… and thereby hangs a tale. It was rumoured that he had brought home a soldier one evening when Mrs Redgrave, Rachel Kempson, was out and the children safely tucked up in bed – and asked his guest to undress him and tie him to the kitchen table. Mission accomplished, the young man helped himself to the cash available in Redgrave's discarded garments and departed. When cook came in from her night out… The scene can only be imagined.

Nevertheless, Michael founded the most impressive dynasty in the world of theatre and film: father of Vanessa, Corin and Lynn, grandfather of Natasha and Joely, and husband of the fine actress Rachel Kempson, born 1910 and still acting into her eighties. A lady of infinite tolerance and charm. With her help and unfailing support, Redgrave maintained the image of a dutiful family man, which was useful when his name came up for a knighthood; such credentials helped allay the misgivings of a Palace still experiencing shock waves from the Gielgud affair. There were slight whispers of an 'unusual' family background but

Redgrave became Sir Michael in 1959. Soon after, he encountered his peer, Sir John Gielgud, one of those inevitably in the know about his friend's predilection for bondage games, who greeted him with 'Ah, Sir Michael, I'll be bound!'

Redgrave was born in Bristol when Margaret Scudamore was on tour with a play called *The Christian*, and was carried on stage in the arms of his father Roy (George Ellsworthy) Redgrave. When touring in Australia his parents separated; his mother returned to England with Michael while his father stayed Down Under. The two never met again. The family's acting lineage dated back to the mid-19th century: the precedent of 'unusual' family patterns was thus early established. Michael received university honours degrees in Modern Languages and English Literature and his MA degree from Cambridge in 1930. He served in the Royal Navy for a while and taught French and German for a few years before getting into the Liverpool Repertory Company, where he met Rachel Kempson. They married ten days later. She knew of his bisexuality from the beginning and was the one who kept the family together. In 1946 they played husband and wife in the film *Captive Heart*.

Before his film career, Redgrave had swiftly risen to eminence at the Old Vic, later performing with John Gielgud's company at the Queen's Theatre and building an impressive record of theatrical successes before making his New York stage debut as *Macbeth*. Like Sir John, Redgrave specialised in Shakespearean roles but his versatility was boundless, in more ways than one. A liaison with Dame Edith Evans in later years may have been more of a trial to the long-suffering Lady Redgrave than any barrack room peccadilloes.

With his photogenic good looks, Sir Michael's film debut could not be long

delayed. Alfred Hitchcock is often given credit for having cast him with Margaret Lockwood in the 1938 success *The Lady Vanishes* as his film debut. In fact, the great director had given him a small part in the 1936 *Secret Agent* with Gielgud, and was ready to take a chance with the newcomer opposite Britain's already established and fast-rising Margaret Lockwood. The same year he partnered two more of Britain's most prestigious film ladies, Jessie Matthews in the non-musical *Climbing High* and Elisabeth Bergner in *Stolen Life*. The highly strung Matthews did not warm to him: he had made fun of the small bridge she used to put in the gap between her two front teeth for close-ups. Worse, much worse, she heard, or thought she heard, the forbidden words 'chorus girl' being used between her co-star and director Carol Reed. The Matthews-Redgrave teaming was not a marriage made in Heaven, although the comedy, Jessie's last under her Gaumont-British contract, was amusing and quite charming. It was also very funny, especially

when Alastair Sim, with his magnificently eccentric personality, appeared on screen.

With this promising kick-start in cinema, Redgrave proceeded to a highly successful career as a romantic lead into the sixties – including acting as narrator for several documentaries to which his dulcet tones were particularly suited. From then on he turned to character roles, while combining his acting with his role as paterfamilias and with some lasting liaisons, including 20 years with a lover referred to as Alan in his son Corin's biography, *Michael Redgrave – My Father*, published in 1995. There were eight years with the handsome, half-American actor Bob Mitchell, who was succeeded in the early seventies by another American actor, Fred Sacoff. These men were referred to by the children as 'Uncle'.

Other movie highlights of Redgrave's career included *The Stars Look Down* (1939) with Margaret Lockwood, from A J Cronin's bestseller. In 1941 there was *Kipps* with

Phyllis Calvert and Diana Wynyard, in 1942 *Thunder Rock* and *The Way to the Stars* with John Mills and Rosamund John in 1945. In the same year Redgrave scored one of his most eerie successes in the portmanteau horror/thriller *Dead of Night*, as a ventriloquist whose identity is slowly but surely being taken over by his dummy. Redgrave's episode in this film is the most famous and, directed by Alberto Cavalvanti, he produces perhaps the most apt of all his characterisations, surely reflecting some of the confusion in his own mind as to his several identities. The same may be true, to a lesser degree, of his superb portrayal of Andrew Crocker-Harris in *The Browning Version*, a Classics master unable to communicate with his pupils, about to lose his teaching post and discovering that his wife Millie (Jean Kent) is being unfaithful. Terence Rattigan adapted his own play, in which Eric Portman had created the part of Crocker-Harris with Mary Ellis as Millie in 1948. The film was lovingly directed by Anthony Asquith, as was the 1952 *The Importance of Being Earnest*.

After *Time Without Pity* (1957), Sir Michael was directed again by Joseph Losey in his last great part in 1971, as an old man recalling his memories of being a go-between for high-born Julie Christie and her true love, Alan Bates, a lowly farmer. Christie's character is engaged to Edward Fox, a member of the British aristocracy. The young go-between is played by Philip Guard: he stays single for seven decades because he falls in love with Christie while acting as her intermediary. An undeniably worthy, and very fine, film – but Harold Pinter's script from L P Hartley's original novel is too subtle for some tastes. After this, Parkinson's Disease kept Sir Michael from acting: with Corin he wrote an autobiography, *In My Mind's Eye*, published in 1984. He died two years later, aged 77.

Above: A portrait of Sir Alec Guinness from 1959.

SIR ALEC GUINNESS
(A Guinness de Cuffe) 1914-2000

Cambridge's Chief Registrar in the forties was John Gentle, a man who lived up to his name in an elegant house virtually on the bank of the river Cam. He also gave interesting parties for visiting celebrities, especially those who were appearing at the Arts Theatre. It was at one of these soirées that I met Alec Guinness for the first time. He had studied for the stage privately under Martita Hunt and from 1936 to 1937 acted for the Old Vic Company, mostly in Shakespearean parts. Later in 1937, he joined John Gielgud's company at the New Theatre.

When we met at John Gentle's party in 1940 he was playing at the Arts Theatre in the leading role of Charleston in a nationwide tour of Robert Ardrey's *Thunder Rock*; the part was

Left: Filming of *HMS Defiant* was interrupted when Sir Alec Guinness is visited by 1961's Miss World contestants.

being played at the Globe Theatre London by Michael Redgrave. At the age of 26 Guinness was prematurely bald and totally un-actorish. I would never have associated him with the theatre despite his six years of varied experience, had I not already seen *Thunder Rock* at the Arts. In the company of such unmistakably thespian guests as Robert Helpmann, ballet dancer supreme and actor, and the broadcaster and recording star Arthur Marshall – whose school-mistressy monologues on Decca Records were very popular at the time – Guinness shone modestly as an honest example of a rational human being.

The following year he joined the Royal Navy as an ordinary seaman, returning full-time to the stage in 1946. In the meantime he had leave for various projects and we met again,

quite unexpectedly, at Highbury – a small film studio where the Rank Organisation made some of their B-movies featuring such Charm School starlets as Diana Dors and Maxwell Reed, the first husband of Joan Collins. As part of my duties as a minor assistant director for Rank, stationed at Denham Studios, I was deputed to look after aspiring actors being tested for major roles in films. One memorable day at Highbury, David Lean was testing people for his forthcoming *Great Expectations*; including the teenage Jean Simmons, there with her mother to be tested for the role of the young Estella. Anthony Wager was also present as the young Pip (who grows up into John Mills) and Alec Guinness, in a handsome blond wig, was testing for Pip's friend, Herbert Pocket.

They all excelled in their roles in the finished film and it was lovely to see Alec, modest as ever but considerably glamorised by the studio's make-up wizards. It happened that he had played Herbert Pocket before, on stage in 1939: he had also adapted the Dickens novel for the theatre, so who better, the astute David Lean had reasoned, to recreate the part on screen.

It was exciting in this way to be in at the birth of a genuine superstar of motion pictures. Alec told me later that Lean had paid me a compliment: 'That boy [sic] is the only assistant who actually watches and takes in what is happening during filming.' Unfortunately, I was transferred from *Great Expectations* halfway through shooting to Frank Launder and Sidney Gilliat's *I See A Dark Stranger*, filming on a nearby set – but at least I worked for and became firm friends with Deborah Kerr before her departure for Hollywood.

While on David Lean's film I made another notable friend – the formidable Martita Hunt, whom I had to escort to and from make-up to be transformed from a grouchy grey-head, moaning about her hangovers, into the tragic Miss Havisham. She could be fun when in a good mood and I was a witness during the tricky filming of the scene where Miss Havisham's smouldering wedding gown catches fire: she had to step back from the flames in the nick of time as the tricks department took over. As she narrowly escaped being incinerated she roared, 'This fucking dress is a bastard!' The atmosphere on Deborah Kerr's set was much more restful.

Alec Guinness' rise to screen pre-eminence was virtually instantaneous, from a sinister Fagin in *Oliver Twist* – more Dickens for David Lean in 1948 – to Robert Hamer's *Kind Hearts and Coronets* the next year. This *tour de force* as eight members of the D'Ascoyne family, including Lady Agatha, all of whom are polished off by the heir to their fortune (Dennis Price) made Guinness an international star. Guinness' virtual facelessness as a human

Above: Cleo Sylvestre and Sir Alec Guinness in the stage production *Wise Child* (1968).

being made him the ideal chameleon actor, able to submerge himself in any role.

What more propitious time could I have chosen than 1949 to reappear in Alec Guinness' life – this time as his PR. After the acclaim for *Kind Hearts* he took a breather to return to the stage for Stanley French at the Savoy Theatre in *The Human Touch*. This was a play about the discovery of anaesthesia by Dr James Y Simpson, with Sophie Stewart as his wife, Adrienne Corri and John Gregson – who was about to become a young leading man in the movies. A lovely cast and an inspiring subject with which to start one's career as a theatre PR. Guinness and I enjoyed an emotional reunion, each regarding the other as some kind of a lucky talisman.

After the run he was to return to the screen in a lighthearted comedy, *A Run For Your Money*.

This co-starred Donald Houston, the glamorous golden-haired Welshman who had become a star in his first film *The Blue Lagoon*, in which he and Jean Simmons had spent a major part of the movie swimming in the said lagoon as lightly clad as the mores of the time allowed. Alec had not seen the film and asked my opinion of his prospective co-star. 'Well, he's very pretty,' was all I could find to say. 'Obviously,' said Guinness in satirical mode. 'But can he act?' There were no complaints about their partnership and the movie, with Guinness' star charisma and Houston's youthful appeal, pleased the public.

Guinness' work from then onwards was mostly concentrated on the cinema: after *The Mudlark*, playing Disraeli to Irene Dunne's Queen Victoria, he went on to a run of brilliantly successful Ealing comedies, including *The Lavender Hill Mob* and *The Man in the White Suit* (1951), for which he was Academy Award-nominated, *Father Brown* (1954) and *The Ladykillers* (1956), in which he played a master crook. When I met him again on location near King's Cross Station while looking after PR for Peter Sellers, we had a pleasant reunion over tea in the canteen. Guinness co-starred with Grace Kelly in her last film, *The Swan* (1957), the year in which his two Oscars (American and British) for the Commanding Officer in *The Bridge on the River Kwai* led to his knighthood in 1959. He returned to the theatre in 1967, playing the transvestite criminal, Mrs Artminster, in Simon Gray's *Wise Child*. In the dressing room, Dorothy Dickson remarked on how 'brave' he was to play such a part. He said, 'Why shouldn't I? I've nothing to hide.'

Guinness had been happily married since 1938 to Marula Salaman, a copywriter in an advertising firm, and he became a Catholic in 1954 after a little boy mistook him for a priest and called him 'mon père' when he was in his habit as Father Brown. He took this as a sign to lead him into the faith to which he had been increasingly drawn through the years.

As one of his obituary writers said, his sexuality was complex but he did not care for people to assume anything. In the thirties he was displeased in the extreme by the Oliviers' assumption that John Gielgud was his boyfriend. 'Not that he could not have been but, in fact, he was not.' He did not suffer fools gladly. He continued to work and more AA nominations followed: in 1958 for *The Horse's Mouth* in his own adaptation of Joyce Carey's novel; then for *Star Wars* (1977) and *Little Dorritt* (1988). Guinness gained a whole new youthful following for *Star Wars*, besides his television triumphs in John le Carré's *Tinker, Tailor, Soldier, Spy* and *Smiley's People*, which added BAFTA Awards to his other accolades in the seventies. Our last meeting was a lighthearted one at the stage door of the Richmond Theatre, where his son Matthew was appearing. Sir Alec said, 'Eric, you're prettier than ever!' It was, of course, nonsense, but I lapped it up regardless.

He and his wife had a close circle of friends including Michael Redgrave and Rachel Kempson, of whom only Lady Redgrave has outlived him. Sir Alec died at 86 at the Edward VII Hospital in Midhurst. For years he had lived with his family in Petersfield, outside Portsmouth.

SIR DIRK BOGARDE
[Derek Niven van den Bogaerde] 1920-1999

One of the handsomest, potentially most charming and gifted actors ever to find stardom in films, Dirk Bogarde was a paradox. Adored by teenagers during his Rank years, increasingly courageous in his choice of film subjects, yet fiercely closeted regarding the truth about his sexuality and increasingly bitter over the recognition he felt his own country denied him. I knew him quite well at the beginning of his career in movies.

Bogarde had worked his way up to stage manager at the Q Theatre near Richmond, in Surrey, from 1939, and made his West End debut in J B Priestley's *Cornelius* in 1940. At Wyndham's Theatre, he appeared under the name Derek Bogaerde as Dorothy Dickson's walk-on partner in a dance sketch called 'Exit to Music' in Herbert Farjeon's World War II revue *Diversion*. He then joined the army and only resumed his acting career on being discharged. I saw a lot of him when working at Shepherd's Bush Studios as an assistant director on tests for film parts he didn't get, one of which was *Broken Journey*, starring Phyllis Calvert in 1947. The role for which Dirk had tested as a young pilot was eventually played by Grey Blake.

Another role which eluded him, as the film was never made, was the part of a young killer in *Power Without Glory*, which he had acted brilliantly in 1947 at the go-ahead fringe theatre, the New Lindsey, in London's Notting Hill Gate. I was impressed by him, the play and a wonderful cast of later-to-be well-knowns, including Kenneth More as the good brother in the story, Dandy Nichols as their mother and character actresses Beatrice Varley and Maureen Pook (later Pryor). Nöel Coward was impressed enough to call on Dirk and advise him to persevere with his acting career. After the play I went for drinks with Bogarde and playwright Michael Clayton Hutton: both were depressed, and Clayton Hutton's depression must have been terminal as he committed suicide not long after. Bogarde, however, signed a seven-year contract with the Rank Organisation.

After his first starring role in the somewhat dreary *Esther Waters* (in a part turned down by Stewart Granger), Bogarde shone in 'Alien Corn', one of the sections of the Somerset Maugham portmanteau film *Quartet*, for which the author filmed an introduction. Dirk was cast opposite the great French actress Françoise

Above: Dirk Bogarde in *The Singer Not the Song* (1960).

Rosay as the famous pianist who comes to assess that his playing is not good enough for him to pursue a career in music. The story also provided another Rank employee, Honor Blackman, with one of her early English Rose parts, from which it took her years to escape. This was a much happier and more cheerful Dirk Bogarde than the one on whose tests I kept working, when he had told me 'I'll never make it in films.' I won my five-pound bet that he'd soon be a star.

At 29, Bogarde was convincing as one of the *Boys in Brown* – the one who corrupts innocent Richard Attenborough, a mere 26. Another of the mature lads was Sir Nöel's friend, Graham Payn. As a watered-down version of the play, the film was effective without being half as sexually explicit: if such a thing had been possible, Lord Rank might well have expired in a

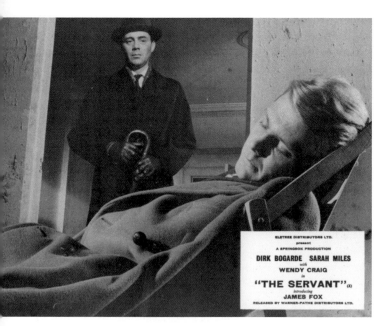

DIRK BOGARDE SARAH MILES

with
WENDY CRAIG
in
"THE SERVANT" (x)

introducing
JAMES FOX

RELEASED BY WARNER-PATHE DISTRIBUTORS LTD.

role as Inigo Jollifant he inherited in the 1957 remake of *The Good Companions* opposite Jannette Scott, and Fraser gave Bogarde a run for his money as one of the romantic leads in *The Wind Cannot Read* the following year.

A highlight of Fraser's film career was as Lord Alfred Douglas in Ken Hughes' *The Trials of Oscar Wilde* in 1960. Another gay role Fraser played in the sixties was as the secretary to the ill-fated lesbian dancer Isadora Duncan, notoriously strangled when her own scarf caught in the wheels of her moving limousine. Vanessa Redgrave memorably played the lead role in the 1968 movie *Isadora*, directed by Karel Reisz.

In a newspaper article, Fraser remarked on the singularity of Bogarde's relationship with his manager, Anthony Forwood, who had left his wife, Glynis Johns, to devote the rest of his life to Dirk. Forwood always insisted that theirs was nothing more than a business association, although they seemed as close as the happiest of married couples. There was never a hint in any of Bogarde's brilliant part-autobiographical books that he and 'Forwood' (as he always called him, making him sound like a butler) were anything but just good friends. This was surely long after the days when any disclosure of a personal relationship between them could have disillusioned any of his early fans who were still alive.

When Bogarde returned to England after Tony Forwood's death from cancer at their home in Provence, he was bitter about the country which had given him such a wonderful start to his career and was about to reward him with a knighthood in 1992. He blamed everybody but himself that his Hollywood debut in 1962 in George Cukor's *Song Without End* was not a great success. Fond as he was of his tragic co-star Capucine, the affair he claimed to have had with her was likely to have been studio-inspired. Nor was his next movie *The Angel Wore Red* with Ava Gardner a success. Yet he had been given several rewarding roles in his native country, includ-

cloud of outraged cigar smoke. Bogarde, after his real start in the Maugham film in 1948 and his resonant hit as the cop-killer in *The Blue Lamp* the following year, hit his mark as Britain's top teenage idol in 1954's *Doctor in the House*, directed by Ralph Thomas, which catapulted him to the position of Rank's biggest star, even if it was not in quite the way he would have wished. In 1955's *Doctor at Sea* his leading lady was Brigitte Bardot, on her way to becoming France's greatest sex symbol – although her singing voice had to be dubbed by a leading recording and TV star, England's Jill Day. Bogarde was always baying for the moon and later used to decry this stage of his career.

Bogarde's friend and sometime co-star John Fraser himself had his share of youthful admirers: a signed picture of him in my hall mysteriously disappeared after one of my parties. He was definitely a top fifties pin-up and it was quite a feather in my cap to persuade him to run with me through Hyde Park – his flat was barely a quarter of a mile from mine – for an early dip in the Serpentine, though he did not repeat the experience. As a recording artist he was definitely a better singer than John Gielgud, whose

Above: Dirk Bogarde and James Fox in *The Servant* (1963).

ing, in 1955, a murderer in *Cast a Dark Shadow* (Margaret Lockwood's last for Rank), *A Tale of Two Cities* as Sydney Carton (1958), *The Doctor's Dilemma* (1959), directed by Anthony Asquith, and *King and Country* for Joseph Losey in 1964.

Paradoxically, Bogarde had been sending out signals towards sexual liberality in his films, tentatively, since 1956. A strangely cast Bogarde, not too convincing as a Spanish working man in A J Cronin's *The Spanish Gardener*, is accused by his employer, diplomat Michael Hordern, of stealing. The man is jealous of the gardener's friendship with his lonely and neglected son, Jon Whitely. The original motive of his jealousy, that he was sexually attracted to his employee, is omitted from the film, directed with some subtlety by Philip Leacock.

Subtlety is hardly the word for Bogarde's 1960 *The Singer Not the Song*, which delves into the relationship between Bogarde's bandit, Anacleto (in tight black leather gear) and John Mills' priest trying to reclaim him for the Church. The critics were scathing, one of them comparing Bogarde's bandit to a 'latter-day *Queen Kelly*', referring to the uncompleted film Gloria Swanson started for Erich von Stroheim in 1928. Personally, I found both Mills and Bogarde moving and convincing. From this to 1961's barrier-breaking *Victim* was only a short step, but one Dirk Bogarde was brave to take. He admitted that 'It was the wisest decision I ever made in my cinematic life.' Bosley Crowther of the *New York Times* called film and performance 'unprecedented and intellectually bold, presented honestly and unsensationally.' Yet, apparently, all done without upsetting his real fans. So why did Bogarde feel himself unable to carry this 'intellectually bold honesty' into his private life?

In Losey's *The Servant*, Bogarde went further, in presenting with equal boldness a subtly malign character who deliberately and ruthlessly sets out to pervert his weak and easily led young master, James Fox, in order to make him his slave. In the

mid-sixties, John Schlesinger's *Darling* won accolades galore for its 'modern' slant on life at that time: this time Roland Curram plays the gay character and the film revolves round Julie Christie, who won an Oscar. Why Bogarde accepted his role of Robert Gold, a mere adjunct to the Darling of the title, is a mystery. At least, in Losey's cartoon spoof *Modesty Blaise* (1966), opposite Monica Vitti, Bogarde is blondined, dolled up to the nines and camper than Chloe.

The following year, Bogarde stayed with Losey for *Accident*, in which the director guided the star to give one of his finest performances. Harold Pinter's script presents a compelling study of an Oxford don and his infatuation with a beautiful student, Jacqueline Sassard. In films like this and Liliana Cavani's *The Night Porter* (1974), Bogarde was able to choose as rewarding a selection of roles as any actor in his mid-fifties could have wished. The highlight of this period, however, has to be Luchino Visconti's *Death in Venice*, based on Thomas Mann's story of the dying Gustav Mahler falling in love with a beautiful 17-year-old boy, Bjorn Andersson. Bogarde is magnificent as the composer and Silvana Mangano lends grace to the occasion as the mother of the boy, who is quite unaware of the emotions he has inspired in the man.

In 1976 Bogarde worked for his old 'victim' from all those years ago, Sir Richard (now Lord) Attenborough. He gave a meticulous performance as the incompetent and insensitive General Sir Frederick ('Boy') Browning, husband of Daphne du Maurier, in *A Bridge Too Far* – the general who led a disastrous raid behind German lines in World War II. Among the others in this all-star epic were James Caan, Sean Connery, Robert Redford, Gene Hackman, Anthony Hopkins and Laurence Olivier.

It is hard to fathom what Sir Dirk had to complain of in these and other rewarding offerings, especially as he chose to return in a homo-erotic made-for-TV film in 1986, directed by Bob

Left: Wesley Snipes and Nigel Hawthorne in *Demolition Man* (1993).

Mahoney from a short story by Graham Greene, called *May We Borrow Your Husband?* A gay offering indeed, in which Bogarde plays a writer befriended by a gay interior decorator (David Yelland), who helps them seduce a sexually confused young husband while Sir Dirk sees to the wife. Sounds more like Coward than Greene – I'm sure Sir Nöel tackled a similar theme some years before this.

Bogarde's valedictory film performance in the Franco-British *Daddy Nostalgie/These Foolish Things*, directed by Bertrand Tavernier in 1990, was, sadly, a fitting one, as the sick and at times insufferable father of Jane Birkin. Bogarde gives a brilliant and emotionally devastating portrayal of a bitter and grouchy old man. In 1996 Sir Dirk suffered a severe stroke which necessitated 24-hour round-the-clock nursing, until a heart attack carried him off in May 1999.

I shall always remember with affection the beautiful and friendly young man who was convinced he would never become a star. He did, despite himself.

SIR NIGEL HAWTHORNE
1929-2001

Most of the goods things in life came late for Sir Nigel Hawthorne, after more than 45 years of working as an actor on stage and in films and television. Born in Coventry and brought up in South Africa, he decided at 21 it was 'an actor's life for me'. Having started as stage manager in rep, success in the theatre came relatively quickly in classics like *The Philanthropist*, *The Alchemist*, *As You Like It* and *Oh! What a Lovely War*. Hawthorne was also in the last play to be banned by the Lord Chamberlain, Edward Bond's *Early Morning*.

Hawthorne started in films in 1978's *Sweeney II*. Although he won BAFTA Awards and an Olivier Award and was regularly in work, all the time he was feeling depressed and a complete failure. He could not seem to find his own particular niche, either in his work or in his private life. Although he had never been closeted regarding being homosexual, he was not the type

Right: Helen Mirren, Nigel Hawthorne and Amanda Donohoe in *The Madness of King George* (1994).

to flaunt or be militant about it. He once said, 'What's the point in offending people if you are trying to win their respect?' He admitted, however, having enormous respect for Ian McKellen and everything he has done for Gay Rights, but he succeeded, in his own way, through having an innate sense of the fitness of things.

When he turned 50, everything seemed to gell for Hawthorne. He had met his partner and inseparable companion, writer Trevor Bentham, as far back as 1968, when he was stage managing one of Nigel's plays, but they only began to live together some years later in a farmhouse in rural England – a 15th century manor house he bought from Chris Lowe of the Pet Shop Boys. He said: 'I think we're very privileged. We appear always as a couple ... and we don't *frighten the horses*!'

In 1981 Sir Nigel was cast in the BBC sit-com *Yes, Minister* as the scheming civil servant Sir Humphrey, for which he won four BAFTA Awards. The character became a particular favourite of Margaret Thatcher. The timing was

just right and gave Hawthorne the reputation of being one of Britain's favourite light comic actors. In 1991 he won a Tony Award on Broadway for Best Actor in *Shadowlands*, although Anthony Hopkins played the C S Lewis role when the 1993 film was made. Hawthorne enjoyed a big comedy success in the 1993 Hollywood-made *Demolition Man* as Dr Cocteau, the seemingly benign leader of a future Fascist utopian society. Renegade cop Sylvester Stallone, frozen for his part in a battle with bad guy Wesley Snipes, is defrosted along with Snipes into this unsettling future. Cue action mayhem.

The highlight of Sir Nigel's film career was his marvellous interpretation of the tragic George III in Nicholas Hytner's *The Madness of King George*, which, in its original theatrical incarnation, won him the Best Actor Award from the London Critics Circle (plus the Laurence Olivier Award for Alan Bennett's play) and, for the 1994 film version, an Academy Award nomination.

Less welcome was the press 'outing' of his private life, which followed an interview he gave in the US to *The Advocate* magazine before the awards ceremony. The British press reaction was scurrilous and insulting and hurt both Nigel and Trevor deeply. As extremely well-adjusted people, the wound healed – but the affair did expose the vestiges of a deeply rooted homophobia in certain media circles. Another serious, this time physical, problem with which Hawthorne had to cope was his sudden diagnosis in March 2000 as having blood clots in his lungs, necessitating an immediate emergency operation which left him with a 12-inch scar across his stomach.

Among the many movies with which Sir Nigel was associated, a notable production in 1998 was the Restoration comedy *The Clandestine Marriage*, which he and his good friend Joan Collins baled out when it ran into financial difficulties and in which they were credited as associate producers. The film, directed by Christopher Miles, had leading parts for Nigel Hawthorne as Lord Ogleby and Joan Collins in a highly uncharacteristic role as the monstrous sister and dominatrix, Mrs Heidelberg. The film was released in 1999, the year in which Hawthorne was knighted in the New Year Honours. His health, however, continued to deteriorate and he died, aged 72, on 26 December 2001.

SIR IAN MCKELLEN
1939-

Acclaimed as the foremost of our younger actors – Olivier had called him 'the greatest young actor in the English theatre' – McKellen's early fame came on stage. He made his London debut in *A Scent of Roses* in 1964 with the National Theatre at the Old Vic, and then enjoyed a remarkable four-year run of successes with the Royal Shakespeare Company.

On Broadway, McKellen won the Tony Award for playing Salieri in *Amadeus*, in 1979-80.

McKellen also won four Olivier Awards – the UK equivalent of the Tony – including one for the part of Max in the London production of the greatly successful homosexual drama, *Bent*. This groundbreaking 1979 play by Martin Sherman revealed the persecution of homosexual men in Dachau. At the Royal Court Theatre, McKellen and Tom Bell were the leading players; McKellen and Michael Cashman then played Max and Horst in a 1990 West End revival. On Broadway, Richard Gere played Max and, when the film was eventually made in 1997, McKellen was cast as Uncle Freddie, with Clive Owen and Lothaire Bluteau as Max and Horst. Sherman wrote his own screenplay, which was directed by McKellen's partner, Sean Mathias. The scene where the two make love without any physical contact, while aimlessly humping big boulders back and forth, retains the intensity achieved on stage. Mick Jagger scores as Greta/George, a transsexual cabaret singer, and Jude Law is briefly seen as a stormtrooper – clearly a star in the making even then.

It was not until he outed himself in 1988 that McKellen's career took off in a big way, whether by coincidence or because his personal act of liberation gave him a new zest for the movies is unclear. He had, however, given an outstanding performance in Waris Hussein's 1969 *A Touch of Love*, in which he played a bisexual newscaster who is the father of student Sandy Dennis' illegitimate child. In 1981 he gave an even more impressive characterisation as author D H Lawrence in Christopher Miles' *Priest of Love*. A remarkable cast included Janet Suzman as Lawrence's dominant wife Frieda, with whom his relationship was always tempestuous, Ava Gardner as one of Lawrence's society admirers, Sarah Miles (sister of the director) and John Gielgud in a cameo as a repressive English censor.

McKellen played John Profumo, Minister of War, in Michael Caton-Jones' impressively directed reconstruction of the Profumo affair, *Scandal* (1988). John Hurt starred as the osteopath, socialite and sexual *provocateur* Stephen Ward, the catalyst for the whole sorry affair, which was instrumental in bringing down the Conservative government in 1963. Joanne Whalley-Kilmer was remarkably convincing as call girl Christine Keeler, and the whole cast breathed life into what was once the nation's daily dose of press titillation. Leslie Phillips reincarnated Lord Astor, at whose residence the drama took place, Bridget Fonda was Mandy Rice-Davis, Keeler's companion in arms – later an actress, and Britt Ekland, Mariella Novotny, Daniel Massey, and Mervyn Griffith-Jones rounded out the cast. In 1993 McKellen received an Emmy nomination for *And the Band Played On*, an all-star made-for-TV film co-starring Matthew Modine, Richard Gere, Phil Collins, Lily Tomlin and Alan Alda, directed by Roger Spottiswoode from Randy Shilts' novel. He played a San Francisco gay activist who campaigns for AIDS education.

McKellen's own screenplay adapted from Shakespeare's *Richard III* is an updating of the classic tragedy to the thirties, in which he plays the king as a ruthless Fascist dictator who creates a Nazi-like society. This is one of his finest screen performances, directed by Richard Loncraine, with Nigel Hawthorne as Richard's supportive brother, George, Duke of Clarence, who pays for his loyalty by being executed in the Tower. Their mother is played by Maggie Smith, who denounces her scheming son in an especially powerful scene. Even more dramatic is the drowning of the aforementioned Clarence in a butt of Malmesey.

McKellen's knighthood in 1991 was the centre of much controversy; he was the first openly gay person to be so honoured. He came out in a BBC interview in response to the anti-gay Clause 28, after some of his friends had argued that there was not a single gay celebrity who would come out to protest against it. He was supported in his action by friends and fellow artists including Alec McCowen, Stephen Fry, Simon Callow (an openly out actor whose only gay role to date has been in the smash hit *Four Weddings and a Funeral*), producer Cameron Mackintosh and director John Schlesinger. The *Guardian* called it 'one of the most remarkable examples of gay solidarity since homosexuality was de-criminalised in Britain in 1967.' As a fervent gay and AIDS activist, Sir Ian, one of the Founders of the Stonewall Group British Civil Rights Organisation, through his success in both art films and mainstream productions has shown that one can be openly gay without being pigeonholed into stereotypical roles.

A landmark in his film career is the 1999 release of Bill Condon's film *Gods and Monsters*, in which he portrays with aching intensity the great and ultimately tragic film director James Whale. This is interspersed with reunions with old acquaintances, George Cukor, Elsa Lanchester, Boris Karloff and his sometime lover, producer/studio executive David Lewis. Whale's infatuation with his hunky but heterosexual gardener (Brendan Fraser) is woven into this mingling of fact and fiction, for which McKellen and Condon gained Oscar nominations along with Lynn Redgrave as Best Supporting Actress in the untypical role of Whale's devoted but deeply religious and disapproving housekeeper. A film and performances to treasure.

2001, contrastingly, saw McKellen's acclaimed performance in Peter Jackson's New Zealand-shot blockbuster *The Lord of the Rings: The Fellowship of the Ring*, for which he was also Oscar-nominated for his performance as Gandalf the Grey. With two further parts of this epic to be released, McKellen is set to remain firmly in the public eye for some time to come. □

9 OUT OF THE CLOSET

Film critic and biographer Alexander Walker wrote, in his 1966 book *The Celluloid Sacrifice*, of 'The Love That Dare Not Speak Its Name' as a love that, at the time of writing, 'could hardly be persuaded to keep its mouth shut.' This was a clear allusion to the proliferation of films dealing with gay relationships which followed the modification of the Production Code the same year and it was, in the circumstances, a bold statement. The sixties certainly heralded a new permissiveness in the treatment of homosexual themes and characters.

As we have seen, in 1960 Peter Finch played the title role in *The Trials of Oscar Wilde* and the following year deemed it advisable to decline the bisexual lead in Basil Dearden's *Victim* in favour of Dirk Bogarde. Barrister Melville Farr is happily married to Laura (Sylvia Sims), who is aware of his past affairs but accepts him nonetheless, assuming that marriage has assured his heterosexuality. However, blackmailers bring up his relationship some years before with construction worker Jack Barrett (Peter McEnery), which Farr has always denied. When caught by the police for stealing money from his employer, Barrett hangs himself in order to avoid involving Farr, who had avoided him when he tried to contact him.

The blackmailers are extracting money from several people and Farr decides to stop the rot by exposing and prosecuting them himself. This film was a landmark because of the stress it laid (back in 1961, when homosexuality was illegal in Britain) on the fact that the majority of blackmail cases involved gay men. The film's plea for

Opposite: Candice Bergen and Shirley Knight in *The Group* (1966).

tolerance was the reason *Victim* was refused the seal of the Motion Picture Association of America. Direction by Basil Dearden and production by Michael Relph are superlative and the acting, from Dirk Bogarde as Farr down to the smallest roles, is absolutely convincing. That a star of Bogarde's eminence should undertake such a controversial role lent added weight to the argument. It was a significant performance.

Sylvia Sims' subtle acting as Laura saves the character from being unsympathetic in the face of her husband's defiant 'I wanted him' – though he does not go as far as saying 'I had him.' Peter McEnery as the actual victim and Dennis Price as a blackmailed actor are excellent, while the blackmailers, revealed as a slimeball weight trainer with a penchant for male pin-ups and a tight-lipped dykey librarian, are shudderingly well presented by Derren Nesbitt and Margaret Diamond. Authenticity is lent to the film's gay milieu by scenes shot in the famous Duke of Wellington pub, where theatre people have always gathered, among them a generous proportion of homosexual actors.

The relaxation of the 1934 Production Code came in 1966. This was a very significant watershed, brought about by social change, civil liberties groups and Supreme Court decisions. The revised Code still condemned sin and paid tribute to virtue, but suggested restraint in dealing with sexual themes, rather than banning them completely. This had, in effect, been happening from the end of the fifties and the early sixties.

Sidney Lumet directed *The Group* (1966), adapted by Sidney Buchman from the novel by

Mary McCarthy. Buchman also produced. The story traced the emotional development of eight Vassar girls after their graduation and emerged as extremely gripping drama, in which Lumet's sensitive direction does full justice to every nuance of McCarthy's blockbuster book. The girls are played by Joanna Pettet, Kathleen Widdoes, Joan Hackett, Elizabeth Hartman, Jessica Walter, Shirley Knight, Mary-Robin Redd and Candice Bergen, whose film debut this was. Joan Hackett was also making her first movie appearance, after years of success on the New York stage. Her performance was perhaps the most moving of a group of mostly unknowns, but it was Bergen who garnered the maximum publicity.

This was partly due to her being the daughter of America's best-loved ventriloquist, Edgar Bergen, creator of Charlie McCarthy, his ever-cheeky dummy. Even more noteworthy, in 1966, was the fact that she, as Lakey, was the first female in an American film to be addressed as

a lesbian, when she returns from Europe with a butch Baroness as her lover, played by Lydia Prochnicka. The character played by Larry Hagman says to her: 'I never pegged you as a Sapphic – to put it crudely, a lesbo.' This was, reputedly, the first time the term lesbian had been used in a Hollywood movie.

Lesbianism was the theme of the 1968 American-Canadian production, *The Fox*, directed by Mark Rydell and adapted from a novella by D H Lawrence by Lewis John Carlino and Howard Koch. Two girls, living in contented isolation on a farm in a remote region of Canada, work their land and are happy just to be with each other. Jill (Sandy Dennis) is the feminine partner, Ellen (Anne Heywood) wears the pants, and all goes well until a drifter (Keir Dullea) comes into their lives. He seduces Ellen and taunts Jill, who is devastated by her lover's defection, suggesting that her problem is that she has never had a man.

There is heavy use of symbolism (Dullea as

the Fox who brings destruction into the hen-house; a phallically suggestive tree falls on Dennis and kills her) and a simplistic ending, suggesting that, after Jill's failure to adapt to heterosexuality (or, at least, to bisexuality) she needs to be got out of the way to leave room for the normal-ish straight ending. The last shot is of the grinning head of the dead fox, a final homophobic take on a movie far removed from Lawrence's original subtle storyline. The film has been viewed as a parable, suggesting all that is needed to cure any wayward signs of sexual affection is a good normal liaison. Anne Heywood, a very good actress who has played in some strangely chosen movies, has been married for some 40 years to *The Fox's* producer, Raymond Stross, who may have been responsible for the denouement.

The Killing of Sister George (1968) is one of the breakthrough films (and plays) of the sixties. It marked a change of attitude from the general public, a large percentage of whom, if lesbianism in the movies is discussed, will mention the film. The original play by Frank Marcus was far more understated, and won Beryl Reid a Tony Award on Broadway. (The word lesbian was never mentioned). It also marked a change of direction for the actress, for many years a popular star of variety and revue in Britain. For the try-out at the Bristol Old Vic in 1965 she took a substantial cut in salary (from several hundred pounds to ten pounds a week), against the dire warnings of her agent for taking a risk with such an 'unwholesome' subject. The play limped round its provincial tour to dreadful notices and deafening silences. Reid wrote in her autobiography *So Much Love*: 'In Bath we were deafened by the old chaps in their bath chairs being wheeled out by their nannies, their urine bottles rattling as they went, saying "disgusting, disgusting"'.

When Michael Codron bravely decided to open in the West End, at the Duke of York's in June 1965, suddenly the laughter was deafen-

Above: Beryl Reid and Susannah York in *The Killing of Sister George* (1968).

ing, the notices mostly wonderful. After a long run Beryl left the cast, along with Eileen Atkins, who played George's girlfriend, Childie, to open in New York at the Belasco in October 1966, again with enormous success. Director Val May had seen the play through from the beginning.

Robert Aldrich directed the film version, with a screenplay by Lukas Heller, in 1968. The theatrical story concerns an ageing lesbian actress in a wildly popular radio soap opera, playing the sweet-natured district nurse who bikes around a country community, spreading happiness and health in equal proportions. In the movie this becomes a television soap.

ENTERTAINING MR SLOANE

1969 Pathé/Canterbury 94 mins colour
Producer: Douglas Kentish; Director: Douglas Hickox;
Screenplay: Clive Exton (based on the play by Joe
Orton); Cinematographer Wolfgang Suschitsky
Beryl Reid, Harry Andrews, Peter McEnery, Alan Webb

Beryl Reid was happy to tackle on screen a part she would play later on stage at the Royal Court, directed by Lindsay Anderson: Kath in Joe Orton's *Entertaining Mr Sloane* in 1969. Clive Exton adapted the original play, which won the Drama Critics award in 1964 but which folded on Broadway after only 11 performances. Straightforward lesbianism was one thing, but apparently Orton's quirky mixture of murder, blackmail, implied incest and gay-battering was too much of a bad thing. Reid had been offered the part in London in 1964, but was not free to do it so Madge Ryan created Kath, with Dudley Sutton as Sloane. After *The Killing of Sister George*, Reid was free to do the movie, which went further than the play, with the ageing nympho Kath and her homosexual brother Ed bargaining over the dead body of their Dadda, kicked to death by lover-boy Sloane.

What was inferred in the play is, again, made explicit on the screen. The film Sloane, directed by Douglas Hickox, was played by Peter McEnery, overly butch and with badly dyed blond hair. Kath picks him up in a graveyard, suggestively sucking an ice lolly and wearing see-through chiffon. 'Forgive me Mr Sloane, I'm all in the rude,' she says, pulling the dress towards her ample dimensions as she drapes herself over a tombstone.

She invites him to be her lodger, against the will of her Dadda (Alan Webb), who recognises the boy as someone he's had trouble with before. Her brother Ed (Harry Andrews) also objects until his lustful eyes take in what Mr Sloane has to offer, which is on display for all takers. 'Do you keep fit, my boy? ... Healthy mind in a healthy body,' he purrs, feeling his leg. Soon Kath has a 'bun in the oven', Ed has

given Sloane a flashy car, and Sloane has kicked the Dadda to death when he threatens to reveal what he knows about his past.

Sloane, as chauffeur, is attired from head to foot in tight leather. After the murder, Ed and Kath discuss turning their lodger over to the police unless he swears eternal allegiance to them. The film ends with a remarkable three-in-one ceremony, one-part funeral rite and two-parts marriage ceremony (not for the squeamish!). The film pulls all stops out to shock and succeeds very well in this. The dialogue is mostly Orton (Kath: 'I've had the upbringing a nun might envy'), part Reid (she put in 'I've some urgent knitting to do'). All the performances are superlatively good, especially Reid and Andrews. Morbid humour and grotesque fancies are the order of the day.

The play resumed its record-breaking theatre incarnation with Malcolm McDowell as Sloane – again, custom-built for the part. Harry H Corbett played Ed and James Ottoway the Dadda, with director Lindsay Anderson snugly at home with the material. Orton, bludgeoned to death by his boyfriend Kenneth Halliwell two years previously, would have been pleased with the set-up. His sister Marilyn, visiting Beryl Reid in her dressing room, told her how much her performance as Kath had reminded her of their mother, on whom the character must have been partly based.

Above: Peter McEnery and Beryl Reid in *Entertaining Mr Sloane* (1969).

George's private life has caused disquiet at the studios and her attack on two nuns in a taxicab (filmed in the City of London) brings the matter to a head. George is going to be written out of the series and a smooth-talking, venom-dripping 'lady from the BBC', Mrs Mercy Croft (Coral Browne), is dispatched to break the news. George, foul-tempered and terrified, takes it out on girlfriend Childie (Susannah York), whom Mrs Croft is all too ready to console. A scene was set at the famous lesbian club, The Gateways, where Mrs Croft has spun her web to trap the (not too innocent) Childie. George loses her girlfriend and her job, and is demoted to impersonating a 'flawed and credible cow'. Her 'moos' bring down the curtain on a genuinely moving scene, which works as well in the cinema as on the stage, despite many critics complaining about the 'coarsening' of the play.

On stage there were no overtly sexual love scenes, but Aldrich had one written into the film, which Reid flatly refused to play, even at the risk of having to relinquish the role, coveted by Bette Davis, who had it put about as a *fait accompli* that she would do the film. Davis made the mistake of saying to Robert Aldrich, 'I won't be wearing those awful clothes Beryl Reid wears on stage.' He replied, 'No, you won't, because *she'll* be wearing them!' However, Reid held firm about the sex scene with Susannah York. An awkward impasse was averted when Coral Browne proved quite happy to film the passionate snogging with Childie – on closed sets, naturally. Reid recognised that the scene was a potential crowd-puller and publicity catalyst, but always insisted, 'I never did think all that nipple-sucking was necessary!'

Reid seldom bothered to correct the idea so many fans had that her lifestyle followed that of Sister George. But to a New York taxi driver who said, 'May I kiss you? I've never kissed a lesbian before,' she replied, 'Well, you may, if you like, but you still haven't!'

In 1968 Rod Steiger took on a role in *The Sergeant* that few Hollywood actors at that time would have dared, that of Master Sergeant Callan, a bullying, macho military man, desperately covering up his closet homosexuality by immersing himself in all facets of his army life. One facet is to prove his undoing, the blond, disturbingly handsome Private Swanson (John Philip Law), with whom he falls desperately in love. The private is obviously heterosexual and the sergeant has no one in whom he can confide his seething passion. His emotions eventually become ungovernable, to such a degree that, in a moment of desperation, the sergeant seizes the startled private and kisses him passionately. Overcome with remorse and shame, Callen takes his pistol, heads for the woods and shoots himself.

John Flynn allows no gleam of humour to lighten this distressing tale, set in the Paris of 1952. Steiger's acting makes the sergeant's tragic inability to confront his own sexuality believable and moving, while John Philip Law has little to do but look vulnerable and beautiful, which obviously comes naturally to him. Released shortly after the same subject was dealt with in *Reflections in a Golden Eye* (1967), *The Sergeant* lacks the complexity of John Huston's film, but also avoids the risibility of some of its situations.

Frank Sinatra plays a tolerant New York City detective in Gordon Douglas' absorbing cops and gay-bashers drama, *The Detective* (1968). Sinatra's cop, Joe Leland, is assigned to track down the murderer of a rich gay antiques dealer, Teddy, whose head is smashed in with a statue. He has also been castrated. Abby Mann adapted the screenplay from the novel by Roderick Thorp, while producer Aaron Rosenberg kept a close eye on the proceedings, which were so explicit for the period that it would have been easy to go over the top. The action is mostly centred around the city's homosexual haunts. The gays portrayed are terrified,

MacIver (William Windom), who killed what he feared in himself, preferring to be a murderer rather than allow himself to develop into a loathsome acknowledged queer. He leaves behind a tape recording, confessing that he thinks one homosexual can always recognise another: 'It's in the eyes.' Although this is very much a 'man's' movie, the wives, respectively, of Detective Sinatra and Murderer Windom are sympathetically played by Lee Remick and Jacqueline Bisset, who contribute welcome beauty amid the general sordidness, in this third of Sinatra's 'wild side' excursions.

Detective Sinatra's 'tolerance' towards homosexuals had been two years gestating. In 1967's *Tony Rome*, also directed by Gordon Douglas, private eye Rome is assigned to investigate the goings-on of society girl Ann Archer (Jill St John), with Lieutenant Santini (Richard Conte) also on her trail. Drugs are involved (when are they not?) and *en route* the private eye interviews a lesbian stripper called Georgina and her whining roommate, Irene. He clearly disapproves of their way of life, making a wry face and saying they're in the wrong 'ballpark'. Perhaps the uncredited actresses preferred to remain anonymous, or their studio thought it politic. He also visits Vic, a gay drug dealer (Lloyd Bochner, who figured in *The Detective*). His apartment leaves one in no doubt as to his sexual orientation: the campest extreme of sixties decor. Martin H Albert's book was adapted by Richard L Breen.

The second Tony Rome movie, *Lady in Cement* (1968), reunited the Breen/Douglas writer/director team, though Breen died during pre-production. This time the heiress involved is Raquel Welch, who may or may not have known the naked female corpse. In addition there is a homosexual Miami nightclub owner (Frank Raiter), a Mafia boss (Martin Gabel), a lovable thug (Dan Blocker) and the lady herself among the suspects, but the general effect is neither as exciting as the first Tony Rome movie nor as well

furtive creatures who hide in trucks by the East River, where they go for their pick-ups. Leland's assistant in the murder hunt is the homophobic Lt Curran (Ralph Meeker), while Robert Duvall plays a violent queer-bashing cop.

The victim's former roommate, Felix (Tony Musante), is arrested, tried and executed for a crime he manifestly did not commit, following a confession bullied out of him. The detective's conscience troubles him, as he recognises that he obtained the confession for the sake of promotion. Another case, ironically, leads him to an apparently respectably married man, Colin

Above: Frank Sinatra and Deanna Lund in *Tony Rome* (1967).

Right: Natalie Wood and Christopher Plummer in *Inside Daisy Clover* (1965).

plotted as *The Detective*. Welch's beauty was at its peak, but Sinatra seems a little uninvolved.

Gavin Lambert, novelist/biographer (Norma Shearer, Nazimova), adapted his own novel into the screenplay for *Inside Daisy Clover*, starring Natalie Wood as the precocious 15-year-old whose aspirations to become a musical film star are fulfilled after her discovery by film executive Raymond Swann (Christopher Plummer). She falls in love with and marries thirties screen idol Wade Lewis (Robert Redford), without suspecting that he is a homosexual who 'never could resist a charming boy.' He leaves her after one day. Studio executives, however, turned him into a bisexual, fearing box-office antipathy to bright new grown-up Natalie Wood, for years one of Hollywood's favourite child actresses, being wed, however briefly, to a 'faggot'. She was fine, despite her singing voice being dubbed. Christopher Plummer was professional

as always, while senior and junior stalwarts such as Ruth Gordon and Roddy McDowall lent capable support, but the film was less than a blockbuster. The gay role did no appreciable harm to Redford's career. In the new millennium he is still up there, blond and handsome as ever, with a little help from soft-focus photography that even Lucille Ball might have envied.

In a class of his own, when it came to pushing the barriers to breaking point and beyond, was Kenneth Anger. Anger's output was either not completed, withheld from release or completed but not shown. His main work *Scorpio Rising* (completed in 1963) was a ritual *hommage* to that masculine fascination with the 'thing that goes', ie, the hot-rod racer, gently polished by some rough trade while the theme song 'Dream Lover' floats gently in the background and sexually explicit images fill the screen. Unfortunately, Anger used people's music without their permission, with the result that lawsuits have kept the movie from distribution, except for a brief release in the mid-1980s. Nevertheless, Anger is as important in the development of homo-erotic film imagery as was his *avant-garde* compatriot Andy Warhol, whose films actually were released to a selected public.

In fact, the films credited to Warhol between 1963 and 1968 were mostly directed by his protégé Paul Morrissey – a prodigious output of eight movies. The Warhol films were made in an East 47th Street studio dubbed 'The Factory', where Warhol developed his own star system. He called his performers Superstars. They included drag queens Holly Woodlawn and Candy Darling, women such as Edie Sedgwick, Viva and Bridget Polk, and hustlers Paul America and Joe Dallesandro. The latter came nearest to making it to mainstream stardom and the Morrissey films most widely shown were those devoted to the exploitation of Dallesandro's personality and body. The emphasis was on the latter, caressed by the camera to a degree probably never seen before in mainstream films. At that time, the late Gaumont Cinema in Richmond, now a bank, was managed by a film buff devoted to the *avant-garde*, so I was able to catch movies which rarely escaped to the main film houses.

Warhol's most famous film, *The Chelsea Girls* (1966), the first underground movie to receive commercial distribution, was a three-and-a-half hour blockbuster made for $7500. It features New York's Chelsea Hotel and tells stories from various hotel rooms. The characters include gays, transvestites, drug addicts and, of course, hustlers. It became an art-house hit throughout America but was banned in Boston. Warhol's own summing-up was, 'The lighting is bad, the camerawork is bad, the sound is bad, but the people are beautiful.'

Paul Morrissey's *Flesh* (1968) is a notable example of the 1960s sexual revolution, as well as of the independent filmmaking that came out

of the Warhol factory. Dallesandro plays a gay hustler sent by his wife (Geraldine Smith) onto the streets to earn $500 to pay for an abortion for her live-in lesbian lover. Dallesandro's physique is more impressive than either his personality or his acting. He avoided the danger of typecasting in the seventies, having played Holly Woodlawn's impotent druggie lover in *Trash* (1970). In *Heat* (1972), Dallesandro becomes involved with fading film star Sylvia Miles, her lesbian daughter Jessie and the boyfriend of the daughter's former husband. In another change of pace, Dallesandro plays the virile handyman pitted against the mad Baron Frankenstein (Udo Kier) in *Flesh for Frankenstein* (1974), originally released in 3D. In *Blood for Dracula* (1974), he is the stud who makes sure that Dracula/Kier's intended victims are no longer virgins by the time he gets to drain their blood. The life of a superstar hustler must be an exhausting one!

Crumbling barriers and the demise of the Production Code did not, however, spell the immediate end of offensively stereotypical portrayals of gay sexuality and even deliberate mickey-taking. *The Gay Deceivers*, directed in 1969 by Bruce Kessler, is a hilarious (if you don't mind that kind of thing) farce about two straight friends, Danny (Kevin Coughlin) and Elliot (Larry Casey), who set up home together and pose as gay lovers to dodge the draft. Their neighbours are *bona fide* homosexuals, Malcolm (played by Michael Greer as the ultimate swishing, mincing, lavender-wearing, 'queer as three dollar bill' stereotype pansy) and his friend Craig (Sebastian Brook), who become suspicious when they see women being smuggled into the *soi-disant* gay bungalow complex. Amid all the lisping, hand-flapping, prancing goings-on there is one genuine satirical laugh, when the intimidating Recruiting Officer is revealed as having a male lover. Jerome Wish developed the script from an idea by Abe Polsky and Gil Lang.

The second 1969 'queer' offering is very

queer indeed. *Staircase* was developed from the play by Charles Dyer, who wrote his own screenplay. It was directed by Stanley Donen, who should have known better. There may be an in-joke in the casting of Rex Harrison as Charlie, older and more dominant of the two gay barbers. Harrison used to be regarded as a homophobe, standing out among the usually tolerant actors of his day. His posturing and Professor-Higgins type off-key rendering of some genuinely funny lines (which worked well in the theatre when spoken by Patrick McGoohan) are a blatant send-up of what he probably thought was your average 'queen'. They contrast markedly with Richard Burton's bravely touching Harry, bald and rejected by his vicious-tongued partner.

Burton played Harry for real. He once said in an interview for the *People*, 'perhaps most actors are latent homosexuals and we cover it with drink. I was once a homo, but it didn't work.' This may have been the inspiration for the claim that not only did Burton have an affair with Eddie Fisher at the time he was married to Elizabeth Taylor, but that he and Laurence Olivier had been lovers. Burton's last wife and his brother have claimed the idea to be nonsense and to date Dame Elizabeth has not uttered on the subject. After all, you cannot libel the dead. There have, perhaps, been stranger liaisons: Dame Edith Evans and Sir Michael Redgrave?

The *Staircase* movie begins with a drag act by Rodgers and Starr, lampooning the Russell/Monroe 'Two Little Girls from Little Rock' number in *Gentlemen Prefer Blondes* (1953) – a cheerful enough opening to an often embarrassing experience. Cathleen Nesbitt, who once said 'I'm the only one old enough to play Rex's mother', did just that in this film at 81, while Avril Angers, once an outstanding stage *Sister George*, played a neighbour.

In 1970, *The Boys in the Band* presentend a microcosm of a party of gay men – for the first time served up as entertainment for the masses.

Above: Kenneth Nelson and Cliff Gorman in *The Boys in the Band* (1970).

The party is to celebrate the birthday of Harold, Jewish and caustic and played by Sammy Frey. Mart Crowley wrote the screenplay from his own stage play and William Friedkin directed with brio and a great sense of comedy. The film, like the play, is funny and uncomfortable at the same time and the acting is an outstanding example of teamwork. Painful revelations abound as the evening proceeds and drink is taken. The guests include one camp queen, Emory (Cliff Gorman); one sweetly ineffectual – Frederick Coombs as Donald; one black man – Reuben Greene as Bernard; and the host, Michael, Catholic and self-hating, with a bitter tongue. There are also a couple, married Hank (Laurence Luckinbill) and promiscuous Barry (Keith Prentice). The party ends with a Truth Game in which everyone has to declare who he really loves. There are, naturally, several surprises. Both play and film were barrier-breakers in their time.

Midnight Cowboy (1969), from the bestseller by James Leo Herlihy with a script by Waldo Salt, was the first Hollywood film to look squarely at male prostitution and, as lovingly directed by John Schlesinger, portrays a moving relationship between two unlikely characters, Joe Buck (Jon Voight, in one of the most poignant performances of the sixties) and Dustin Hoffman in a brilliant depiction of the semi-vagrant Ratso Rizzo, homophobic, crippled, foul-mouthed and full of nervous tics. From mutual disgust they begin a mutual caring relationship – non-sexual but almost along the lines of a platonic 'marriage', with Ratso cooking for Joe and Joe becoming violent in his hustling to earn money so they can make a new life together. His gay clients, like Towny (Barnard Hughes), are depicted as pathetic creatures, as are his women customers, including a sharply etched study of a tough broad by Sylvia Miles, a Warhol protégée.

The film made an enduring star of the round-faced and definitely appealing Jon Voight, who presents Joe as an idealist who expects to take Manhattan by storm and finds that all people are after him for is his body (and not too many even want that). The ending is tragic and beautifully acted as Ratso, who has become Joe's 'manager', dies on a Florida-bound bus. This is perhaps Hoffman's most moving performance of his early career. He, Voight and Miles were Oscar-nominated, while Schlesinger and the film itself won Oscars.

Another John Schlesinger highlight came in 1971 with *Sunday, Bloody Sunday* (which the director co-wrote with Penelope Gilliatt), depicting a *ménage à trois* between the heterosexual Glenda Jackson, a divorcee who works at an employment agency, Peter Finch, a middle-aged bachelor doctor in London who shares her answering service, and the bisexual Murray Head, a young designer of modern sculpture who sleeps with both of them. During one weekend

the situation is resolved. The scene at the beginning, when Finch and Head share a tender kiss, provoked an outcry when shown on BBC2 in 1978. The situation comes to a head when Jackson and Head offer to look after the five children of their friends, Vivian Pickles and Frank Windsor, so the couple can have a quiet weekend at a seminar without the children. When Head excuses himself from Jackson on the Saturday morning, merely saying he's 'going out', she realises he is off to an assignation with Finch and is angry at having to share her lover with a man. The two male lovers discuss a forthcoming holiday in Italy, then Head returns to Jackson.

The acting, which includes a convincing sketch from Peggy Ashcroft as Jackson's mother and Maurice Denham as her father, is mainly excellent, although the character played by Head is underdeveloped to the extent that it is difficult to fathom why two such intelligent people as the characters played by Jackson and Finch should fall so heavily for him, undeniably pretty and blandly accommodating to all comers though he is. However, an Academy Award nomination went to Jackson and Finch as Best Actress and Actor, as well as to Schlesinger and Gilliatt as director and for Best Adapted Screenplay.

Bob Fosse's award-winning musical *Cabaret* in 1972 was based on Christopher Isherwood's novel *Goodbye to Berlin* rather than John Van Druten's play *I am a Camera*. The play tended to heterosexualise the hero, whereas the gay Isherwood based the stories on his own experiences. The character played by Michael York – name changed to Brian Roberts – meets the promiscuous singer, Salley Bowles, who falls for him only to find that they are sharing the favours of the German Baron (Helmut Griem) who is her meal ticket.

As Sally, supposedly a mediocre performer, is played by Liza Minnelli, how could she fail to become, very quickly, a glittering cabaret star? (In the London stage version, Judi Dench,

Right: Dustin
Hoffman and Jon
Voigt in *Midnight
Cowboy* (1969).

though nearer the author's conception of Sally, was also just too good a performer to be a failure.) However, with Minnelli, who won the Oscar, playing the part to the hilt, it would be churlish to complain of the depiction of Weimar Berlin, with Nazism ever more evidently on the rise, and the seedy Kit Kat club where Sally performs. Minnelli shares the limelight with the gorgeously camp MC played by Joel Gray, another Oscar-winner for Best Supporting Actor, as were Bob Fosse for direction and Geoffrey Unsworth for cinematography. Minnelli, York and Griem make an attractive *ménage à trois* in one of Hollywood's best-ever musicals.

In 1975 Sidney Lumet's *Dog Day Afternoon* provided Al Pacino with an exemplary role as Sonny, a bisexual who robs the First Savings Bank of Brooklyn to pay for a sex-change for his transvestite lover/wife Chris Sarandon, although at home Sonny has a female wife (Susan Peretz) and two children. Frank Pierson gained a richly deserved Oscar for Best Original Screenplay, but Lumet merited more than the nomination he received for his stunning control of the kaleidoscopic action. Sonny wins over the crowd outside as he holds innumerable phone conversations with his wife, his lover and various FBI and police authorities. The situation is both funny and tragic, as Sonny, tough but inexperienced, creates a situation beyond his control.

Pacino is magnificent and both Sarandon and John Casale as Sal, Sonny's inept accomplice in the bank heist, play up superbly in their far from conventional roles. The taut script and Lumet's sympathetic and insightful direction simply could not be bettered. The story is based on a true incident and has been subsequently used, with variations, on screen and television but never as brilliantly as here. Academy Award nominations went to Pacino, Sarandon, Lumet and D D Allen for best editing. There is a witty discussion on a news broadcast about the merits of Sonny's 'marriage' to Leon (Sarandon). The part was to have been played by Warhol regular Holly Woodlawn but Pacino was worried about his image and it was decided that they did not want any real homosexuality in the script – probably a wise decision. There was nevertheless one of the first glimpses in the cinema of the anger of Gay Liberation: transvestites and bearded men are shown waving banners bearing the legend 'Sonny all the way'. A real boundary-breaker.

For an actor so concerned about his image, it is surprising that Al Pacino accepted the role of the heterosexual copper in *Cruising* who kits himself out to haunt the gay bars of Greenwich Village, on the trail of a serial killer of homosexual men. The film has its values as a peep-show and eye-opener; a naïf friend of mine thought that a naked man strung between two poles with a fist in the proximity of his buttocks was being 'helped down'! The notorious S&M bars of New York become boring when toured *ad nauseam* and the only 'average' gay man is butchered out of the picture before he gets uncomfortably close to the undercover cop. William Friedkin, the director, explained that this isn't a film about gay life: 'It's a murder mystery with an aspect of the gay world as background.'

Six minutes were cut in the UK. The film united the gay community, with calls for it to be banned: this was Hollywood's most notoriously homophobic movie of the late seventies. The film postulates that Steve Burns, Pacino's character, brought into contact with muscular men in skin-tight shirts and leather ensembles, plus the prospect of excitingly violent sex, questions his own sexuality. The idea that mixing with gays in the luridly depicted leather bars and a night in the 'Coalhole' multi-storied sex emporium could turn any male queer, infuriated gays

at the time and groups boycotted cinemas showing the film. Now that the furore has died down, the movie may prove entertaining to those interested in what gay life was like in the pre-AIDS days. Pacino's career has not been noticeably harmed, but such a fine actor could get away with anything.

Caravaggio (1986) may be taken as typical of the later work of Derek Jarman. Perhaps not his finest film, but all of his movies have been, of their very essence, landmarks in the progress of extending the limits of gay themes – in fact, Frightening the Horses – as few other filmmakers have done. Jarman's fanciful account of the life of Michaelangelo Merisi Caravaggio, the last and for some the greatest of the Italian Renaissance painters, was seven years in the preparation but only five weeks in the filming, in an Isle of Dogs warehouse. It is probably the most accessible of Jarman's works. As virtually nothing is known of the painter's life, the director is on safe ground in marrying his unconventional religious beliefs to a homo-erotic interpretation of his putatively bisexual way of life. His depictions of saints were probably modelled on real-life people he knew, including street urchins – his portrait of St John is unusually musclebound – pimps and prostitutes.

Nigel Terry plays Caravaggio as the bad-boy of the Italian aristocracy who scandalises the establishment with his pictures of often nude saints. A man of intense passions with a taste for 'rough trade'. There is a three-way love affair between his rugged lover, the bisexual Ranuccio (Sean Bean), and Tilda Swinton as Lena, the beautiful mistress who comes between them. Lena is the model for the Virgin Mary and Mary Magdalene in some of the painter's best-known canvases. In the end the painter stabs Ranuccio. It was, in fact, a murder charge which sent Caravaggio into exile: virtually all that is actually known about his life.

Jarman, for lack of patronage, worked on a

Right: Steven Waddington and Andrew Tiernan in *Edward II* (1991).

minuscule budget, yet produced (often critical-ly disparaged) *avant-garde* masterpieces such as *Sebastiane* (1976), a highly homo-erotic vision of the saint who died on a cross, pierced by arrows for his Christian beliefs. In Jarman's version this is because he refuses the advances of the sadomasochistic Severus, captain of the Emperor Diocletian's guards. Co-directed by Paul Humfress, the film, despite an overload of beautiful nude male bodies, was accorded a surprisingly strong commercial showing in Britain and key cities of the US.

Like the Andy Warhol film unit, Jarman had his own repertory company of actors whom he regularly employed. These included Nigel Terry, who reappeared in Jarman's 1991 adaptation of Marlowe's *Edward II*. Terry played the evil Mortimer who, with his mistress Queen Isabella, subjected the tragic Edward (Steven Waddington) to the cruellest assassination of a monarch in history. As the Queen, Tilda Swinton, another Jarman 'regular', won the Best Actress

Award at the 1991 Venice Film Festival. The director died of AIDS in 1993 at the age of 51.

Gus Van Sant, still in his thirties and going very strong, has achieved both public and criti-cal success with his 'trilogy of the streets': down-and-outers scrounging for a living on the wet streets of the Pacific Northwest and unre-quited gay love among hustlers. Outstanding in this category is Van Sant's *My Own Private Idaho* (1991). This modern gay classic is out-standing in every department, especially the acting. Keanu Reeves stars as Scott, the rebel-lious son of the Mayor of Portland, who drifts into prostitution as a gesture of defiance against the culture in which he has been raised. The tragic River Phoenix co-stars as the narcoleptic street hustler, Mike, searching for his long-lost mother. At the start of the film, Mike awakes from a narcoleptic fit in a flophouse, where he is being fellated by a fat bald man. The youth is taken to the house of a rich matron where he meets and falls in love with the unresponsive

Left: River Phoenix and Keanu Reeves in *My Own Private Idaho* (1991).

Scott, who nevertheless looks after him to the extent of taking him to a safe haven to sleep off one of his fits. After being picked up by a rich German (Udo Kier), Mike again passes out and ends up with Scott in Portland.

Led by the Falstaffian Bob Pigeon, a rebellious loner played by William Richert, Scott, Mike and other hustler friends take over a derelict building, presumably as a kind of headquarters for nefarious activities, but they are cleared out in a police raid, after which Scott is told he must go and seek out his disapproving father. Then Scott joins Mike to help him look for his mother, setting out on their motorbikes. Mike stumblingly tries to express his love to his friend in a moving scene in front of an outdoor fire: much of the dialogue here was improvised by River Phoenix. The film's mood swings from tragic to hilarious to highly erotic. Van Sant's weaving of a subplot based on Shakespeare's *Henry IV Part II* lends a poetic touch, with Reeves as the Prince Hal prototype.

Not all critics approve of this but, for others, it adds an extra dimension to this beautifully conceived and highly original love story – one that definitely dares to speak its name.

Surprisingly, one of the most satisfying gay movies in the nineties was from Taiwan, *The Wedding Banquet* (*Xiyan*) (1993), released by Central Motion Picture Corporation Good Machine Inc, directed by Ang Lee and produced by him with James Schamus and Ted Hope. Lee and Schamus also wrote the script, along with Neil Peng. If there is such a thing as a family-orientated gay movie, this is it. There are faint echoes of *La Cage aux folles* in a same-sex couple having to resort to various subterfuges to throw potential in-laws off the scent of their actual relationship, but this is gentler and less farcical in mood, apart from the hilarious aftermath of the wedding banquet. Wai Tung (Winston Chao) and Simon (Mitchell Lichenstein) have lived together happily in Manhattan for six years: both are young, attractive and successful. The only fly in the ointment is that Wai Tung's parents in Taiwan are pressuring him to marry. When his father has a stroke, mother keeps sending tapes with her pleadings, containing details of ideal girls – measurements and all – saying that his father is only hanging on to life to be able to hold his grandchild in his arms.

Simon suggests his friend marry his lodger, Wei Wei (May Chin), an unconventional artist who cannot make enough money from her paintings to pay her rent and needs a green card to stay in the country. Reluctantly on both sides, after the parents have sent over a young opera singer as a candidate, Wei Wei and Wai Tung agree to a marriage of convenience. The unexpected arrival of his father, Mr Gao (Shung Lung), and mother (Ah-Leh Gua), who think Wei Wei is lovely and suitable, brings about a panic resolution: an immediate marriage in a registrar's office. This reduces Mrs Gao to tears, as she is cheated of a proper church wedding with guests.

Simon takes everyone out to dinner to try to assuage his mother's disappointment. When the restaurant manager (Anthony 'Iggy' Ingoglia) learns that the young couple have just married, he insists on inviting them to a proper wedding banquet, to the delight of the parents and the embarrassment of the young people. Meanwhile, at home in Simon's town house, he and Wai Tung have to sleep apart while the newlyweds pretend to share one bed: she, totally undomesticated, serves immaculately prepared Chinese meals, actually cooked by Simon, who can even speak a little Chinese and passes as Wai Tung's lodger. Mrs Gao plies Wei Wei with gifts and money and they strike up a happy relationship.

The wedding banquet is a riot and even the Gaos are impressed by the number of people present. This is followed by the traditional honeymoon aftermath, at which almost everyone gets pie-eyed, edging the young couple under an eiderdown, from which they throw out their

garments one by one: the guests creep away after the first article of clothing flies out. The sequel is not entirely unexpected. Tensions mount in the household as the parents stay on, but the twist at the end leaves virtually everyone satisfied as the parents sail away and the parents' wish is about to be satisfied.

The performances are universally delightful, the film provides some moving introspective moments, and the photography of Jong Lin is superb, especially the in-depth and richly caparisoned banqueting hall and subsequent party (sets by Rachel Weinzimer). Delicate touches complete the *mise en scène*, such as the swift substitution of Chinese scrolls in place of the male pin-ups on the lovers' walls (Wai Tung works out at a body-building gymnasium). The only drawback could be the subtitles. Apart from that, a cracker of a film that crosses all sexual and racial divides.

Hesitantly in the 1980s, and increasingly apparent from the early 1990s, was an openness in attitudes towards sexuality that was quite new in Hollywood's movies. For decades the industry had tacitly subscribed to a comment attributed to mogul Samuel Goldwyn: 'Most of our pictures have little, if any, real substance. Our fear of what the censors will do keeps us from portraying life the way it really is. We wind up with a lot of empty fairy tales that do not have much relation to anyone.' This was changing, not only on screen but also in the manner in which films were marketed. A mite cynical perhaps, but it is tempting to assume that it was through this period of time that the corporate bean counters gradually realised that they had been missing, indeed often actively antagonizing, a large potential audience. Not only were gays and lesbians a substantial audience in numbers, they were also an audience with disposable income.

Of course, the word 'Hollywood' no longer means what it once did. Generally speaking, and certainly so as far as gay-themed films are concerned, Hollywood is more a gathering place where movies are talked about and, maybe, green-lighted for adequate funds, and marketed; and it is still where everyone comes in the hope of receiving the ultimate accolade, an Oscar. But a very high proportion of productions, especially so when considering gay themes, are made independently of Hollywood's moguls and image makers. Many of them are written and directed by the same person, a one-man band who, somehow, scrapes together the funding in order that he can bring his brainchild to the screen and only then, and rarely, finds a studio that will take an interest in the finished product and market it in a manner that will allow the film to actually be seen outside a small core of art-house theatres and, perhaps, make a little money. Not surprisingly, therefore, many indies are made extremely cheaply with all the deficiencies that implies: less than perfect camera work, actors no one has heard of (actually, a plus in many instances because the genre has brought forward new and clearly competent actors), bad sound and tacky sets; the latter avoided in many cases by outdoor shooting, in which the sound is even worse.

With a little luck, following the growing acceptance of gay-themed films, all of the foregoing inadequacies will become a memory (although, for inexplicable reasons, we seem to be stuck with poor sound quality, even in some big budget productions).

Acceptance, or at least tolerance, of gay films didn't happen overnight, but eventually the qualities evident in, for example, *Latter Days* (2003), *Mysterious Skin* (2004) and *Brokeback Mountain* (2004) became relatively common-place. The trend, however, began a decade or more earlier even if few, if any, early 1990s filmmakers would have dared dream of winning an Oscar for an openly gay-themed film.

By the 1990s, Hollywood could be reasonably certain of box-office success for a remake of the French *La Cage Aux Folles* (1978), which had spawned two sequels and, as we have seen, had its general theme explored in *The Wedding Breakfast* (*Xiyan*). Hollywood's confidence was not so much because of the popularity of the original, which was superbly acted by Ugo Tognazzi and Michel Serrault, as Georges and Albin, a gay couple (Serrault playing his character, Albin, as an outrageously camp transvestite) in conflict and contrast with Georges' son's prospective in-laws, but through awareness of the Broadway success of the stage musical, which ran for 1,176 performances from 21 August 1983 (with nine months for its 1986 London production). In the event, the Hollywood remake, *The Birdcage* (1996), was adequate although it missed not only the glittering surface of the original but also largely failed to mine the suppressed tragedy, which the French film did so well. Perhaps surprisingly, the principal actors, Robin Williams and Nathan Lane, failed to match their French counterparts, while Gene Hackman, as the prospective father-in-law, seemed as bemused as his character was supposed to be.

Outside the USA, filmmakers were less hesitant, less circumspect and more open. In 1987, the team of Ismail Merchant and James Ivory had made *Maurice*, a careful and reflective adaptation of an E.M. Forster novel that explores how a young Englishman comes to terms with his latent homosexuality in the years before the Great War. Scripted by Kit Hesketh-Harvey and Ivory, and with a first-rate cast including James Wilby, Hugh Grant, Rupert Graves, Denholm Elliot, Simon Callow and Ben Kingsley, the film attracted respectful attention but while it circumnavigated the barriers, it did not crash through them. By the early 1990s it was possible to be more forceful, as was shown by Neil Jordan's *The Crying Game* (1992), in which the contemporary and seemingly unending conflict in Northern

Ireland is the backcloth for a haunting love story. A bond of sorts develops between a kidnapped British soldier, Jody (Forest Whitaker), and a member of the Irish Republican Army, Fergus (Stephen Rea). Later, and now hiding in London and regretful of Jody's death, Fergus meets the British soldier's girlfriend, Dil (Jaye Davidson). Fergus and Dil are drawn to one another and it is only when they are about to have sexual intercourse and Dil is revealed in full frontal nudity that Fergus is startled to discover the truth about Dil. It is a measure of Davidson's performance, as well as Jordan's directing and writing (he won an Oscar for Best Screenplay), that the film's audience was just as startled as is Fergus when he sees that however feminine Dil might appear to be, 'she' is unmistakably a man. Although it would be misleading to describe *The Crying Game* as a gay film, its moving account of love and loyalty, in which Dil's sexuality is, however potent the twist, an almost incidental issue, makes it a remarkable film.

From Australia came *The Adventures of Priscilla, Queen of the Desert* (1994), which is about three extrovert drag queens (is that, one wonders, a redundancy?) driving across the Outback in a pink bus ostensibly to perform their show in Alice Springs. With Anthony, known as 'Mitzi' (Hugo Weaving), are Adam, 'Felicia' (Guy Pearce), and Ralph, 'Bernadette' (Terence Stamp), as well as Anthony's young son. Awaiting them at the end of their journey is Anthony's estranged wife. The flamboyance of the trio, set against the desert landscape, and the equally arid attitudes of the townspeople they encounter along the way, invites inevitable conflicts but also, surprisingly, brings romance with Bob (Bill Hunter), who is to tightly closeted that even he is quite unaware of his latent desires. Most creditably, *Priscilla* showed that it was possible to have fun with (not make fun of) characters such as these, and be moving without being mawkish while maintaining an adult attitude

Above: Guy Pearce as 'Felicia' in *The Adventures of Priscilla, Queen of the Desert* (1994).

when dealing with formerly restricted subjects. Equally adult was the German *Bent* (1996), which is set in Berlin during Nazi-dominance and centres upon a character who is not only gay but also a Jew and who ends up in Dachau concentration camp where either trait was enough to set him on course for the gas chamber. In France there were films such as *Ma Vie En Rose* (1997, English-language title: *My Life In Pink*), about a boy named Ludo (Georges Du Fresne), who hopes to be transformed surgically into a girl. In the UK, *Like It Is* (1998) took its central gay relationship and blended it quite successfully with a view of the north-south cultural divide that had by then been a 30-year theme for successful British films. In this tale, a tough young boxer from the north of England, Craig (Steve Bell), meets Matt (Ian Rose) and begins a relationship that brings conflict with Matt's flat-mate, pop singer Paula (Dani Behr), and his boss, music producer Kelvin (Roger Daltrey). Gritty in its portrayal of the problems facing young men coming out even as late as this, the film has an admirable measure of assurance and authority. And from Cuba there came *Before Night Falls* (2000), an account of the life of poet Reinaldo Arenas, whose fight for acceptance was as much about politics as it was about his sexuality.

Meanwhile, American filmmakers were not at a standstill; they, too, were slipping into a higher gear, albeit still circumspectly. Although Sam Mendes' *American Beauty* (1999) is not a gay film, the gay thread it contains is crucial to its resolution. Throughout, middle-aged, middle-class, middle-American Lester Burnham (Kevin Spacey), endures agonizing self-reappraisal through the attraction he feels for his daughter's young friend, Angela (Mena Suvari). Concurrently, his entirely innocent befriending of the male teenager next door, Ricky Fitts (Wes Bentley), is misinterpreted by the boy's homo-phobic father, Frank Fitts (Chris Cooper). This awakens in Frank terrifying doubts about his own sexuality. He comes on to Lester, is rejected with barely-disguised horror, and reacts by shooting Lester in the head. It is the manner in which this gay facet is presented, with simple, non-exploitative candour that is commendable. In *Boys Don't Cry* (1999) Brandon Teena (Hilary Swank) is a teenager who breaks through the barriers separating her true sexuality by posing as a boy in her small Nebraska hometown. Although not exploitative, despite a grim finale, this is based upon a true story, yet there is a curious distancing between the characters and the audience, hinting that perhaps the makers were not wholly convinced of how audiences would respond. These films and others of the period were important in setting down markers that suggested how far it might be possible to go but no one yet had jumped in, feet first.

There were many other films in these years that dealt with one or another of the numerous themes open to gay-orientated filmmakers. Indeed, in the next chapter it will become apparent that very nearly every theme used in non-gay films is available for use, plus those that are largely if not exclusively bound to the subject of gayness.

For all the movement taking place among independent filmmakers, however, a hefty shove was needed. When it came, this push was from a surprising source: television.

Broadway's success had fuelled Hollywood's growing confidence in the possibilities of exploring gay themes in feature films – after all, it was fairly easy to dismiss theatrical attitudes towards homosexuality as an adjunct to the perceived gayness of the theatrical community. Much more to the point and, it must be admitted, rather startling was the manner in which American television took gay and lesbian concepts into American homes. Not just those areas equipped with cable and pay-to-view, but heartland homes accustomed to an often unsophisticated approach to primetime television. It wasn't just Ellen DeGeneres, whose coming out brought consternation among advertisers to the detriment of her popular show, *Ellen* (1994-1998); there were also shows such as *Dawson's Creek* (1998-2003) and *Will & Grace* (1998-2006). Admittedly, the latter brought an often immature approach to its depiction of homosexuality, but it was high in the ratings and successful in the awards it scooped. Then there was *Six Feet Under* (2001-2005), in which the gay relationship between undertaker David Fisher (Michael C. Hall) and black cop Keith Charles (Matthew St. Patrick) was much less off-the-wall than many other relationships in the series, and *The L-Word* (from 2004), which brought lesbianism into close-up. Overall, on television homosexuality was not only prime-time and open, it was also as often as not taken seriously even if it was usually in the never-never land of sitcoms.

Occasionally, though, it was not sitcomland but serious television drama that provided the means by which gay themes were explored. Using AIDS as the binding issue for a fascinating view of the USA's political and philosophical morass of the 1980s, *Angels In America: A Gay Fantasia On National Themes* (2003) was a six-part television mini-series directed by Mike Nichols from a screenplay that Tony Kushner based on his own play. Weaving together fact, fiction and fantasy, the storyline connected, sometimes tenuously, a group of gay men, most of them tightly closeted, as they made and broke the rules by which Reagan-era America was governed. Notable among those in the closet are Joe Pitt (Patrick Wilson) and Roy Cohn (Al Pacino), the latter a real-life closeted homosexual who persecuted other homosexuals just as vigorously as he did communists when he wreaked vicious havoc behind Washington scenes for many years, first as a scheming acolyte of Senator Joseph McCarthy. Ironically, if that's the right word, Cohn would die from AIDS. Central to the story of *Angels In America* is Prior Walter (Justin Kirk), who is dying of AIDS, and whose lover has fled in fear of the invisible death. And Pitt's wife, Harper (Mary-Louise Parker), schemes to find sexual release. Meanwhile, overhead and also in the corporeal world, Angels gather as harbingers of death (Meryl Streep, Emma Thompson, Jeffrey Wright, Ben Shenkman). Complex and demanding, *Angels In America* was yet another sign that television was prepared to take gay topics straight into the homes of middle America.

When Hollywood's producers saw the success of these shows, and the prizes they won, cash as well as kudos, they must have slavered more than a little. These shows were, of course, attacked by those elements of press and church that regarded themselves as arbiters and upholders of public morality in what was soon to become Fortress America. As right-wing authoritarianism in state and central government tightened its grip and the fundamentalists of the religious right gained in power, dangerous attitudes emerged in American society. This was a time of often vicious repression when violent impulses were encouraged, not always subliminally, by Establishment attitudes; the savage killings of gay student Matthew Shepard and lesbian lawyer Diane Alexis Whipple come to mind. Yet it was also a time when television expanded its presentation of gay and lesbian characters in shows. Remarkably, they did this with little or no condemnation and usually with empathy even if the fun was sometimes at the characters' expense. Astonishingly, viewing figures were not adversely affected; indeed, many of the aforementioned shows were very highly rated, won awards and (bottom line) were renewed, not cancelled. The difficulties surrounding *Ellen* were, it seems, exceptions, not the start of a new rule. That the popularity of these television shows should somehow survive the iron-clad mentality that gripped the USA from 2001 onwards was really quite remarkable, and it also encouraged glimmers of optimism among those who feared for the survival of America's soul.

Whether or not those responsible for greenlighting the financing of big-budget feature films were responding to ethical and sociological considerations or simply following the money, the rise in power of the far-right in American political and religious circles was matched in the 2000s by a boom in big-budget, studio-backed films that dealt openly and honestly with gay and lesbian issues. Looking back, though, we can see that in the 15 or so years before the steel curtain began to fall and civil liberties were curtailed if not completely withdrawn in some areas of American political, commercial, private, social and cultural life, some filmmakers had already begun to make their marks. ☐

10 AND INTO

From its earliest days, Hollywood has favoured the pigeonhole. Any film that could not be described by an immediately understood and preferably one-word tag were likely, it was believed, to be box-office disasters. Thus the word 'film' was often preceded by a word such as 'western' or 'gangster' or, after talkies came in, 'musical'. It would be quite a while before a 'gay' film would carry box-office clout and even through the 1990s and early 2000s, it was apparent that many films with growingly more visible gay elements were falling into one or another of the many genres and sub-genres that Hollywood so loved.

A sub-genre tied only to gay-related films is that of medical dramas dealing with AIDS. Although there were those who chose to look the other way, the calamitous effect of AIDS upon the gay community not only became common knowledge it also grew steadily more difficult for

it to be ignored. The general public's familiarity with the topic, together with the irresponsible attitude adopted by many in government and religious groups, especially those of fundamental Christian leanings, led almost inevitably to it becoming a routine topic for filmmakers; one that, in time, found it hovering on the edge of being treated as just another Disease-of-the-Month.

Although the vast majority of gays adopted a responsible attitude towards the threat of AIDS, a few did not. In *The Living End* (1992), written and directed by Greg Akari, the two principals, Luke (Mike Dytri), a hustler, and Jon (Craig Gilmore), a film critic, greet the news that they are both HIV positive with a cry of 'Fuck the world!' before cutting a sexual swathe through the city. People like this are fortunately in a marked minority and depictions such as this in films is similarly uncommon. Although not central to its purpose, AIDS inevitably plays a role in the documentary film *Rock Hudson's Home Movies* (1992), in which writer-director Mark Rappaport examines the star's career and the manner in which his homosexuality was concealed. Using hindsight to ill effect, the film presents numerous clips in which Hudson's lines are excerpted from context to imply a hidden agenda; one which, quite clearly, is at odds with the intentions of the makers of the original films as, although they were party to the concealment of Hudson's sexual activities, the last thing they were going to do was fill his films with nudge-nudge, wink-wink moments that would have given the game away.

Most often, though, filmmakers followed the

principled lawyer Joe Miller (Denzel Washington) to fight his case and they take on Charles Wheeler (Jason Robards), the smug senior partner who has fired Andrew. Although it was Hanks who won the Oscar as Best Actor, he received outstanding support from Washington, Robards and Banderas.

It was not only the physical effect of AIDS that was devastating; the psychological and emotional damage wreaked by the disease was catastrophic. Making matters even worse was the blinkered attitude of the outside world that for so long looked the other way. Whether this was through ignorance or choice mattered little in the degree of effect but was certainly harmful in the manner in which it ostracised victims and their loved

THE SPOTLIGHT

attitude of the majority of real-life gays and were understanding, sympathetic and responsible. That said, even in frontline productions such as *Philadelphia* (1993), it was corporate attitudes towards AIDS victims and homosexuality that were the central topics, rather than the intimate relationships that had led to the film's principal character, lawyer Andrew Beckett (Tom Hanks), contracting the disease. Andrew's struggle to fight a court case for wrongful dismissal against the law firm that fired him was the core of the story while his concurrent battle as he strove to combat the disease was depicted through his deteriorating physical condition rather than through a detailed exploration of the devastating emotional and psychological damage it wreaked upon him and those he loved, in particular his partner, Miguel Alvarez (Antonio Banderas). Andrew hires struggling, homophobic but

Opposite:

Rock Hudson.

ones. In the early 1980s, as public awareness of the disease began to spread, *The New York Times* decreed that mention of those loved ones, especially in the growing number of obituaries, required the euphemism 'longtime companion'. This was the title used for one of the early films to seriously examine the effect of AIDS. In *Longtime Companion* (1990), damaged lives are examined with honesty and sensitivity through Craig Lucas's screenplay, which he based on his own stage play. Directed by Norman René, the film stars Campbell Scott, Patrick Cassidy, John Dossett, Mary-Louise Parker and Bruce Davison and is a landmark in the development of gay films by responsible filmmakers.

It took far too much time for the American government to take seriously the extent of AIDS and the effect it would have upon the country. It was all too easy for people in a position to do something to do nothing, to side with, even if only through neglect, those who dismissed the disease as a plague visited upon gays by a wrathful god. Although the push for understanding and action came from the scientific community, that group as a whole was not without blame. The story of the eventual awakening within the medical profession was told in a HBO television film, *And The Band Played On* (1993). Directed by Roger Spottiswode and featuring Matthew Modine as Dr Don Francis and Alan Alda as Dr Robert Gallo, the plot displays the breakthrough that led not only to the discovery of the AIDS virus but also to changes in governmental attitudes towards AIDS, albeit one that somehow left largely unaltered attitudes towards gays. In his treatment of government and scientific responses scriptwriter Arnold Schulman is less than unbiased; labelling them as the 'bad guys' is simply too pat. It must be acknowledged, however, that Randy Shilts' book, on which the script was based, was also less than even-handed. This last point is not an easy one to make; Shilts was gay and died of AIDS and for all imbalance of his book deserves considerable credit and respect for opening up a subject that too many people ignored for too long.

Sometimes, it seems, it is when a film does not try too hard to be confrontational that it succeeds in getting across meaning and messages. Thus, *Jeffrey* (1995), directed by Christopher Ashley from a screenplay Paul Rudnick based on his own stage play, is a film about the meaning of love in which is made an almost incidental statement about gay relationships that speaks more strongly than many gay-themed films. Here, Jeffrey (Steven Weber) decides to give up sex, partly because of frustration with the kind of people with whom he daily interacts and partly because of his growing awareness of the danger of AIDS. Having decided upon celibacy and committed to it, he promptly meets the man of his dreams. As Jeffrey adjusts to the conflict between his intended life and his emotional needs as well as

accommodating the psychological trauma of witnessing the slow and painful death suffered by those he loves, the film touches more deeply than many better known and more highly praised films.

AIDS is central to *Love! Valour! Compassion!* (1997), which uses a reunion of a group of long-time friends and lovers as the vehicle for an examination of complex interrelationships that are both damaging and healing. This was directed by Joe Mantello from Terrence McNally's screenplay, which he based on his 1994 stage play. The eight-man group gather at the luxury home of one of their number, Gregory Mitchell (Stephen Bogardus), to spend their summer vacation in comfort and luxury. Omnipresent, though, is the threat of disease and death because almost all of the group are sick, some gravely so, others not yet under sentence of death. Gregory's blind lover, Bobby Brahms (Justin Kirk), becomes the sexual target of Ramon Fornos (Randy Becker) who is there with his friend John Jeckyll (John Glover). Arthur Pape and Perry Sellars (John Benjamin Hickey and Stephen Spinella) are using the occasion to celebrate the 14th anniversary of their relationship. Also at the gathering is John's dying twin brother, James (also John Glover), and Buzz Hauser (Jason Alexander), who is trying to find a way in which he can accommodate the fact that he is HIV-positive. The openness of the film is enhanced by the honesty of its approach and a strong and witty script that is fluently interpreted by the cast.

The plot of Henry Murger's tale of struggling artists, who have to deal with failure, of sickness and death, and of love, lost and found, has been used often over the decades, most notably by Giacomo Puccini for his 1896 opera, *La Bohème*. More recently, Jonathan Larson turned it into a stage musical for which he wrote the book, music and lyrics. This award-winning rock opera was then adapted by Stephen Chbosky whose screenplay was directed by Chris Columbus for *Rent* (2005). Set in New York's East

Village in 1989-90, the characters are faced with similar crises to the original but coloured with contemporary concerns, of which AIDS is paramount. For Mark Cohen (Anthony Rapp), his surroundings form the subject of a film he is trying to make; for his roommate, musician Roger Davis (Adam Pascal), these same surroundings are something he strives to block out as he sinks into despair over his sickness, he is HIV-positive, and struggles to stay clean from drugs. His struggle is not helped by his new girlfriend, dancer Mimi Marquez (Rosario Dawson); she, like Roger, is HIV-positive and, unlike him, remains drug addicted. Mark is also seeking, somewhat hopelessly, to win back the attentions of his former girlfriend, Maureen Johnson (Idina Menzel), who is now in a lesbian relationship with lawyer Joanne Jefferson (Traci Thoms). Also among this group are computer whizz Tom Collins (Jesse L. Martin), who is also HIV-positive, as is his lover, drag artist Angel Dumott Schunard (Wilson Jermain Heredia); and their former friend and soulmate Benjamin Coffin III, who married into money and now owns the seedy apartments in which the tale is set. The strength of the plot and the diversity of the characters helps maintain momentum although the seediness of the setting, allied to the emotional and physical pain in which all the characters are trapped conspire to prevent the film from creating an effect akin to that which occurs when Puccini's music soars gloriously out from a similar, if disease-free, setting.

A genre done very nearly to death by Hollywood, and even more relentlessly hammered into the ground by television filmmakers, is that of teenage growing pains. The opening up of gay themes has prompted several productions that look at the special difficulties encountered by young gays who have enough to worry about in getting through their teens without having also to field the derision of their peers in school. In *Edge Of Seventeen* (1998), directed by David Moreton from Todd Stephens' screenplay, Eric Hunter

Above: *Rent* (2005).

(Chris Stafford) finds his last day in school a hotbed of unrealised needs and unfulfilled hopes. The story is set in 1984, when admitting to anything that hinted at something other than straight sexuality was an invitation to stonethrowers to do their worst. Thanks to skilful performances by Stafford and Andersen Gabrych, as the overtly gay and painfully vulnerable Rod, and Tina Holmes, as Eric's until-now girlfriend Maggie, the film is amusing and entertaining and the underlying plea for tolerance and understanding is made with subtlety.

Coming of age and coming out are also the core of *Get Real* (1998). Directed by Simon Shore from Patrick Wilde's screenplay, the story centres on a love affair between Steven Carter (Ben Silverstone) and John Dixon (Brad Gorton). Steve, a 17-year-old who has accepted his homosexuality and has begun having casual sexual relationships, mainly with older men, chances to meet up with schoolmate John in circumstances that make clear John's latent homosexuality. This discovery startles Steve because John is known to be the school's sporting hero and is outwardly aggressively heterosexual. Their relationship starts off as solely sexual but slowly they realise that they are falling in love, something that is surprising to Steve and shocking to John who is only now confronting and starting to understand his sexuality. The script allows the characters to develop believably and Shore's direction and the acting of the two principals is both assured and sensitive.

Almost as much concerned with assimilation of immigrants as coming out is *Mambo Italiano* (2003), a Canadian film directed by Émile Gaudreault from a screenplay on which he collaborated with Steve Galluccio, writer of the original stage play, which was based upon his own real life story. The story follows the attempts by Angelo Barberini (Luke Kirby) to tell his parents, Gino and Maria (Paul Sorvino and Ginette Reno), that he is gay. Even something as relatively commonplace as finding a place of his own is shocking to his parents, whose grip on reality is a touch tenuous to start with – they planned to settle in the USA but ended up in Canada by mistake – and acceptance of their son's homosexuality is beyond their grasp. Meanwhile, Angelo's lover, policeman Nino Paventi (Peter Miller) is much less ready to reveal his sexual proclivities; what's more, his nightmarish mother, Lina (Mary Walsh), is enough to make even a policeman pause. Played largely for laughs, *Mambo Italiano* might take its subject lightly but it scores a lot of points through the barbed witticisms of the script.

Having come out does not mean that life becomes suddenly free from tensions, confrontations and damaging conflict. In many respects, *The Broken Hearts Club: A Romantic Comedy* (2000) is another familiar movie story told in a traditional manner. A group of post-adolescent friends gather to bemoan what they have done or failed to do with their lives and loves, finding support from one another and somehow surviving through personal tragedy. Written and directed by Greg Berlanti, the film is set in West Hollywood and stars Timothy Olyphant, as Dennis, a photographer, and features Zach Braff,

as the mildly lustful Benji, Matt McGrath, as bookish Howie, Dean Cain, as glamorous Cole, Ben Weber, as wisecracking Patrick, and Billy Porter, as the outrageous yet stable Taylor. All these characters circle around elderly restaurateur and dispenser of advice Jack (John Mahoney), whose steadying influence is essential to the friends' survival. It is only the fact that the friends are all gay that makes *Broken Hearts Club* different from many other movies that deal with groups under social and personal pressures. These pressures are not linked directly to their gayness; in many respects what happens to these people as friendships are tested could happen to anyone and this is one of the film's strengths.

Another device, although one that remains uncommon, is that of telling a story from different and differing viewpoints. Co-writers and co-directors Tom Hunsinger and Neil Hunter bring to *Lawless Heart* (2001) this *Rashomon*-like technique with a fluidity that sweeps along the outwardly complex tale of three people brought together following the death of a man they all knew. As has been implied, it is how they knew the man, and how different he appears to each of them, that lifts *Lawless Heart* well above the norm. In a sense, the film is not gay-themed, although gayness is ever present. The dead man is Stuart, who was gay, and now his lover, Nick (Tom Hollander), his brother-in-law, Dan (Bill Nighy) and one of his old friends, Tim (Douglas Henshall), separately recall moments in his life and it is how these same events differ in the minds of the three men that builds the complex fabric that is surely everyone's life. Quietly but intensely, the film has much to say about love and loss, about jealousy and need, about pain and passion. Although of the three only Nick is gay (to be a little more accurate he is bisexual), each has longings that transcend arbitrary sexual boundaries and all are strikingly well-rounded characters.

In *A Home At The End Of The World* (2004), the lives of two friends are chronicled by the changes made between childhood in Cleveland to their becoming young adults in New York some 15 years later. Directed by Michael Mayer from Michael Cunningham's adaptation of his own novel, the storyline examines the needs and desires of Bobby Morrow and Jonathan Glover. At different ages Bobby and Jonathan are played by different actors, with Colin Farrell and Dallas Roberts playing them as men. In addition to their coming to terms with their sexuality, Bobby and Jonathan also learn how to deal with birth and death and with jealousy and compromise, the latter characteristics being tested when they meet Clare (Robin Wright Penn) with whom they both form attachments. Nude scenes with Farrell, a contemporary gay icon, were reportedly cut from the film following reactions of audiences at test screenings of the film who found the scene distracting. Weren't they supposed to notice?

Sleeping around and its potential for a lighthearted if not entirely realistic story was not a complete casualty of the advent of AIDS. There were still pictures that chose this theme, among them *Slutty Summer* (2004), which was written and directed by Casper Andreas, who also stars as Markus. Using the ploy of a rejected lover seeking support and new relationships, the story follows Markus who takes a job waiting on tables in a Chelsea restaurant where everyone, staff and customers alike, is not only larger than life but also sexier and funnier. Among the characters Markus meets are Luke (Jesse Archer), who asserts his desire to try anything with anyone, Peter (Jeffrey Christopher Todd), just the opposite in his search for the right one with whom to share his life, Marilyn (Virginia Bryan), who has strictly-observed rules by which she lives her life, and Tyler (Jamie Hatchett), who is determined to avoid close attachments. Unsurprisingly, it is Tyler that Markus falls for, thus complicating still further his disrupted private life.

In some respects *Ethan Mao* (2004) could have been made without any gay reference whatsoever.

Teenager falls out with his family, is shown the door, struggles to survive, comes home to collect some belongings, and ends up, almost accidentally, holding his parents hostage inside their barricaded house. What gives this film distinctive qualities is that the reason why Ethan (Jun Hee Lee) was thrown out is not for merely failing to conform to his family's concepts of life but because he is gay. After a spell hustling in the city and now befriended by Remigio (Jerry Hernandez), Ethan comes back home to what he believes to be an empty house, his parents are supposed to be on holiday, and he and Remigio are catapulted into a stand-off with the police, while his parents are the only hope he has of getting out of the mess he has stumbled into. Directed by Quentin Lee, the film not only has the tension of the will they-won't they survive the police blockade scenario, it also concerns itself with family issues and interracial conflicts.

For a man who has never doubted his own heterosexuality to be suddenly questioned by friends and family offers interesting ideas to filmmakers. The concept was exploited in *In & Out* (1997), which stars Kevin Kline as schoolteacher Howard Brackett. On the brink of becoming happily married, Howard's life is shattered when a former student, Cameron Drake (Matt Dillon), mistakenly believing him to be gay, outs him. He does this not just casually to a few friends but on national television during an Oscar-acceptance speech. Directed by Frank Oz from Paul Rudnick's screenplay, the film provides Kline with many genuinely funny moments as he moves from numbed shock to the slowly emerging thought that maybe, just maybe, Cameron is right after all.

Also cheerfully poking fun at attitudes towards homosexuality, *But I'm A Cheerleader* (1999), directed by Jamie Babbit from Brian Wayne Peterson's screenplay, follows the coming-of-age struggles of a young girl, Megan Bloomfield (Natasha Lyonne). Pretty and popular, a

cheerleader with a regular boyfriend, Megan has everything a girl could want. Or has she? Her parents, Nancy and Peter Bloomfield (Mink Stole and Bud Cort), and friends gather the evidence: she doesn't much like kissing her boyfriend, in her locker she keeps pictures of girls, she listens to the most unsuitable kind of pop music (Melissa Etheridge no less), and she is a vegetarian. No doubt about it, she's gotta be a lesbian. And there's only one way to deal with that; Megan must spend six weeks at a special camp, True Directions for Gay People, where as its name implies sexual deviates are shown the error of their ways and brought back to the straight and narrow. Under the guidance of hopelessly inept counsellors such as Mary and Mike (Cathy Moriarty and RuPaul Charles), Megan, who never for a moment has believed herself to be a lesbian, is directed onto the path that leads towards what is deemed to be normality. Unfortunately for all, except Megan, her roommate at the camp is a young woman, Graham Eaton (Clea DuVall), a lesbian to whom Megan is soon attracted. Through Graham, Megan discovers that her parents and friends were right all along about her sexual leanings; but they were wrong to think that she should be changed. With her sexuality confirmed, Megan is ready to find true happiness in the world as a lesbian.

Above: Members of the rowing club in *Sommersturm* (2004).

Treating lesbianism as a central yet non-exploitative subject for a film remains quite rare and we must look back to *Desert Hearts* (1985) for one of the best of its kind. Directed by Donna Deitch from a screenplay by Jane Rule and Natalie Cooper, based on Rule's novel, the plot examines the love affair that develops between Vivian Bell (Helen Shaver) and Cay Rivers (Patricia Charbonneau). Vivian has come to Nevada to seek a divorce that will end her deeply unsatisfying marriage. It is here, in 1950s Nevada, that she finds the root of her dissatisfaction with orthodox sexual relationships and begins to acknowledge her true nature. Without exploitation and with care and thoughtfulness, the story follows Vivian's gradual acceptance that Cay, openly lesbian from the start, is the person she needs in her hitherto troubled life. Doubtless troubling to those who seek to bind together on-screen and off-screen proclivities, Charbonneau was pregnant during production.

While not central to the plot, the fact that the two central characters in *Bound* (1996) are lesbian lovers makes it a very different matter indeed. Although presented outwardly as a thriller, the story of a couple who seek to rip-off the Mafia is almost incidental to a scorching romance between the pair. They are Corky and Violet (Gina Gershon and Jennifer Tilly) and their romance, as they first delude then seek to rob minor mafioso Caesar (Joe Pantoliano) of $2 million he is holding for his ruthless and soon to be angered bosses, develops whenever they can find a moment together and to do so without setting themselves up for a hit. Although a minor film, the strength of writing and direction led to Andy and Larry Wachowski being green-lighted for *The Matrix* (1999), a movie that put them in the bigtime.

A sporting setting was chosen for the German film, *Sommersturm* (2004, English-language title: *Summer Storm*), which tackles the subject of homosexuality full-frontally. Directed by Marco

Kreuzpaintner from a screenplay he co-wrote with Thomas Bahmann, the storyline follows student friends Tobi and Achim (Robert Stadlober and Kostja Ullmann), who are both members of a rowing club. Their lives are complicated by their growing awareness of their homosexuality, something that does not jibe too well with Achim's girlfriend, Sandra (Miriam Morgenstern), who is also a rowing team member, and of whom Tobi becomes increasingly jealous. Meanwhile, a girlfriend of Sandra's, Anke (Alicja Bachleda-Curus), begins to develop a crush on Tobi. Adding to their personal tensions, the team members are building up towards a competition with an all-girls rowing team. At the last minute, the visitors back out and in their place comes an all-male team – all of whom are gay. The effect of this on Tobi and Achim is such that they are forced to face up to their hidden desires and admit to and accept their true sexuality.

An Icelandic film, *Strákarnir Okkar* (2005, English-language title: *Eleven Men Out*), which was screened at the London Lesbian and Gay Film Festival, is also set in the world of sport. When gay footballer Ottar Thar (Björn Hlynur Haraldsson) decides that is it time for him to come out, he does so without warning his club. The knee-jerk reaction of the board of directors is to promptly fire Ottar, who joins an amateur team. There, he meets some sexual soulmates and proves to be a welcoming beacon that attracts other gay footballers. Soon, the team is all-gay and, now named Pride United, they become very successful even if most of their 'victories' are walkovers because other teams refuse to play them. At home, things take odd turns as Ottar's son, Magnus (Arnaldur Ernst), the product of a failed marriage to a former beauty queen, finds life more than a little unsettling through his father's media fame. Written and directed by Róbert I. Douglas, the film lightheartedly follows the plight and then the success of a group of individuals, underdogs all, who are not given a

Above: Glen Berry and Scott Neal as Jamie Gangel and Ste Pearce in *Beautiful Thing* (1996).

chance by society in general and their chosen milieu in particular. Well written, funny and with some sharply etched characterisations, the film offers stringent comments on society's attitude towards gays. The suggestions of the professional football team's board as to how Ottar might be brought back to the straight and narrow are especially funny; one member recommends castration, another insists on wearing an oxygen mask in case he should catch anything.

A touching romantic comedy set on a South-East London council estate, *Beautiful Thing* (1996), centres upon a growing relationship between next-door neighbours Jamie Gangel and Ste Pearce (Glen Berry and Scott Neal), each of whom finds in the other an escape from the harsh reality of life. Jamie, determinedly unathletic, is unpopular with the other kids at school; Ste, the reverse, seems to have everything, but is the subject of violent attacks by his father and older brother. Directed by Hettie MacDonald from Jonathan Harvey's screenplay (which he based on his own stage play), *Beautiful Thing* finds charm and surprising tenderness in a setting that is outwardly charmless and harsh. There are also some nicely thrown away lines, such as when Jamie assures Ste that the HIV virus cannot be transmitted by frottage. 'What's frottage?' Ste asks, and is told, 'It's yogurt. It's French.'

Depiction of female impersonators has long been one that filmmakers have treated with scant regard for reality, seeking to raise a few cheap laughs rather than spotlight a branch of entertainment that has existed for more than a thousand years. As for seeking understanding of those who inhabit the world of the female impersonator, it almost goes without saying that filmmakers showed little or no interest in the possibilities. Of those that have tried, few come up to the standards set by *The Adventures Of Priscilla, Queen Of The Desert*. Among those that do is one that started out as a stage play, written by and starring Harvey Fierstein. *Torch Song Trilogy*, did all that Hollywood so often failed to do and was hugely successful on Broadway. In 1988, Fierstein brought his creation to a wider audience in a film version that was directed by Paul Bogart. The result was an eye-opening spectacle that laughs with and not at the participants, and was an often moving exploration of the nuanced relationship that exist in this demimonde within the world of showbusiness.

Drag queens were at the heart of events that took place in New York's Greenwich Village in the late 1960s. The Stonewall Inn was a popular bar frequented by gays and regularly raided by police seeking to enforce licensing laws that were largely ignored when non-gay clubs and bars were involved. The police raid that took place on Friday evening, 27 June 1969 was therefore nothing unusual. What was unusual was that this time the bar's clientele had had enough and fought back. On that June night, crowds from inside the bar were reinforced by supporters from the neighbourhood to do battle with the police who also brought in reinforcements. The political movement that sprang from these events became more than merely a hassle over licensing laws, it became the cornerstone for action that would

seek and eventually secure (begrudged) basic civil rights for an oppressed minority. The Stonewall Rebellion is remembered by the annual Gay and Lesbian Pride celebration held in New York (and matched in Los Angeles) on the last Sunday in June. The screenplay for *Stonewall* (1995), a film account of these events, was based by Rikki Beadle Blair on Martin Duberman's book. The film was directed by Nigel Finch who was to die of AIDS shortly after production ended. The story is seen through the eyes of Hector (Guillermo Díaz), known as 'La Miranda', a habitué of the Stonewall Inn. The film explores the tensions of customers such as Matty Dean and Bostonia (Fred Weller and Duane Boutte), and the owner of the Stonewall, Vinnie (Bruce MacVittie), while setting out an account of the events that led up to that extraordinary night.

Pretty much free of tension, but good-naturedly funny, *Connie and Carla* (2004), looked at a similar world through the frantic eyes of a pair of somewhat inept singers, Nia Vandalos and Toni Collette in the title roles, who inadvertently witness a drug world killing. On the run, they end up in Los Angeles where they pretend to be men pretending to be women and are hired to sing at a club where they quickly become the toast of an almost all-gay troupe and clientele. Woven into Vandalos's screenplay, directed by Michael Lembeck, is a subtle and touching portrayal of the effect a man's decision to enter this world has upon his family, in this case his brother, but overall it is all done for fun with the choreography of the club's audience a distinct plus as the singers make a not too sly dig at the sometimes limited repertoire used and enjoyed by drag artists thanks to excerpts from *Oklahoma!*, *Evita* and, endlessly, *Mame*.

Apart from female impersonators there are the sometimes intersecting worlds of transvestites and transsexuals, and they too have attracted filmmakers; often as figures of unkind fun. In *Breakfast On Pluto* (2005), written and directed by Neil Jordan from Pat McCabe's novel, the story follows the life of Patrick Braden, a young Irish lad who is eager to reach an age when he can leave behind his stifling environment and head for the bright lights of early 1970s London. There, he becomes Patricia, known as 'Kitten', a transvestite cabaret singer, and in the newly swinging capital he is able to live a life free of the sexual inhibitions imposed back home. Braden is played as a child by Conor McEvoy and as an adult by Cillian Murphy and it is the latter's bravura performance that brings out the best in Jordan's script. There is also solid acting support from Liam Neeson, as Father Bernard, Stephen Rea, as Bertie, and Brendan Gleeson, as John-Joe.

Transsexuality forms the glue that binds the main characters in *Different For Girls* (1996), although it is cleverly applied in Tony Marchant's screenplay, which was directed by Richard Spence. While still at school, Karl Foyle rescues Paul Prentice from a beating in the shower meted out because other students take exception to his pretence at being a girl. That was back in the 1970s, but when the pair meet up again in London today a surprising change has taken place. Now, Karl (Steven Mackintosh) has become Kim, a transsexual, and to the dismay of Paul (Rupert Graves), they are mutually attracted and begin to fall in love. Their path is far from easy and true love has a hard time in surviving the obstacle course to which the duo are submitted. Making all the difference to what could have been a minor film, the characters are not at all stereotyped. Female on the outside Kim might be, but deep down he is still Karl, tough and worldly, capable, as he showed long ago, of being a two-fisted rescuer of Paul who was then, and remains, a 'typical' film female, dithery and emotionally unstable albeit shrouded in an aggressively macho exterior.

The effects of a sex-change operation are not restricted solely to the individual who undertakes the psychological and surgical journey. Quite

Above: Cillian Murphy as Patrick Braden/Patricia in *Breakfast on Pluto* (2005).

clearly, the effects, from ripples to shock waves, surge through family and friends. In *The Adventures of Sebastian Cole* (1998), which is set in New York in 1983, the individual at the centre of the storm that breaks is Hank (Clark Gregg) who announces to his wife, Joan (Margaret Colin), and stepchildren, Jessica and Sebastian (Marni Lustig and Adrian Grenier), what he intends to do. The family instantly disintegrates, Jessica heading for California with her boyfriend, Sebastian being dragged off to Europe by his mother. A few months later, Sebastian comes back to New York to return to school. He finds his most secure relationship with his stepfather, who now calls himself Henrietta as he awaits final surgery. Along the way, Sebastian struggles to find comfort with his girlfriend, Mary (Aleksa Palladino), and is also reunited with his natural father, Hartley (John Shea), but his actions are mostly those of a rebellious teenager, typical in all respects save the cause of the destructive force that drives him. Written and directed by Tod Williams, the film is wry and understanding, and draws its humour from the bewilderment experienced by characters all of whom are fumbling in a darkness for which nothing could have ever prepared them.

The road movie has long been a Hollywood tradition, and one that has resulted in many fine films examples, such as *Easy Rider* and *Thelma and Louise*. Writer-director Duncan Tucker uses the form for an entertaining and insightful look at the problems facing anyone taking the huge step of having gender-changing surgery. In *Transamerica* (2005), it is a man planning to become a woman so that he can fully enter the world that has for a lifetime been an uncomfortable compromise. Unfortunately for Los Angeles-based Bree, 18 years ago, when still searching for a sexual identity, an encounter with a woman produced a child. That child now lands in jail in New York and needs help. The authorities call Bree, rightly believing that they are speaking to the boy's father, and insist that this is to whom the youth must be handed over. At first Bree wants to avoid this but the psychiatrist who has yet to sign off the pre-operative process before Bree has the final operation, only a week away, insists that the confrontation is a psychological necessity. Bree flies to New York and meets Toby (Kevin Zegers) who assumes that the woman facing him is some sort of do-gooder who wants to save his soul for Jesus. It suits Bree to leave Toby in the dark and, aware that the boy seeks to go off on his own anyway, decides to drive back to LA by way of Toby's stepfather and dump him there. As the road-movie genre demands, along the way the pair learn much about one another and even more about themselves. They encounter all manner of entertaining oddballs and simultaneously offer the audience an opportunity to understand something of the problem-strewn path facing those members of society who, like Bree, are born without a clearly defined sexual identity. Bree is played by Felicity Huffman who was Oscar-nominated as Best Actress.

Revelations of sexual abuse of minors by priests in the Roman Catholic Church has been picked up as a weapon by some who compare this to the hard line taken by the Church against homosexuality. In so doing, this has revealed just how shaky is the grasp many have on the subject. Whatever newspapers and the police might choose to express, links between practicing adult homosexuals and child abusers are decidedly tenuous. Although the reactions of many religious factions towards homosexuality are rich with dramatic potential, filmmakers have not exactly fallen over themselves to exploit them; certainly not in sufficient quantities to form an adequate sub-genre. Ela Troyano's *Latin Boys Go To Hell* (1997) goes a little way to redeeming this lack even though religion is not an issue, just an abiding state that has determined how the principal characters behave. In this tale, which Troyano directed from his own script that was based on Andre Salas's novel, Justin Vega (Irwin Ossa) is hot-bloodedly aware that his sexuality is out of step with the ideal preferred by the church. When his cousin, Angel (John Bryant Davila) comes to stay with Justin's family in their cramped home in the Los Angeles barrio, he finds himself in a state of acute lust. His desire for Angel is not reciprocated; instead, Angel pursues Andrea (Jenifer Lee Simard) whose closest friend is Braulio (Alexis Artiles), who may be gay but he is also jealous and controlling over what Andrea does and with whom. Into the mix are swirled all manner of barrio mores and pop culture trends. Religion is just one ingredient, but the influence of the Church and its attitude is by no means insignificant.

In *Conspiracy of Silence* (2003), written and directed by John Deery, a newspaper reporter, David Foley (Jason Barry) investigates the suicide of parish priest Frank Sweeney (Patrick Casey), and the expulsion from the seminary of Daniel McLaughlin (Jonathan Forbes), who has been accused of sexual impropriety. Foley seeks to connect these two incidents but comes up against the Church's ability to seal itself off from outsiders and to deny any suggestions that it might have some responsibility. The film finds a delicately balanced line to follow that neither attacks nor defends the Church, although is clearly does not accept the covert behaviour of the hierarchy. Strongly cast (Brenda Fricker plays Daniel's mother, Annie McLaughlin), the film avoids a rush to judgement but does hit home with its subtle points and succeeds in making the audience think.

Also thought-provoking is *Priest* (1994), directed by Antonia Bird from Jimmy McGovern's script. This production delves deeply into the emotional and psychological torment endured by a man who has taken the vows of the priesthood only to find that his love of God is countered by his growing realization that he is gay. The problems of Father Greg Pilkington (Linus Roache) are exacerbated when he learns through the confessional that a member of his congregation is sexually abusing his daughter. As he struggles to find a way to rescue the young girl from her very real physical torment without breaking the rules of confession, the priest's own sexual relationship is exposed. Any credibility he might have had are lost and he can no longer intervene to protect the girl from her predatory father. His hounding by press, congregation and hierarchy stand in stark conflict with his genuine love of God and humanity.

An intriguing aspect of Catholicism and homosexuality is touched upon in *Boys To Men* (2001), a portmanteau of four short films that looks at life for gays from different angles and at various ages. The first section, *Crush*, is about a very young girl who falls for a young teenage boy, not knowing that he is gay and unable to understand the concept; two other sections are *The Mountain King* and *...lost*. It is in the final section, *The Confession*, written and directed by Carl Pfirman, that a seldom dwelt upon aspect of gayness is considered. Two men, Joseph and Caesar (Bert Kramer and Tom Fitzpatrick), have lived together for three decades and now the former is dying. A Catholic, Joseph want to make his last confession to a priest, Father Marcus (Christopher Lieke) but Caesar resists. This is not an act of thoughtless cruelty, rather it is that Caesar believes that the inevitability that Joseph will include their long relationship in a confession is to admit that their loving life together has been a sin.

Even more frowned upon in Hollywood's past than were gay-themed films have been any tales that touched upon incest. Those that have, and they were never major films, have taken one of three fairly obvious routes: brother and sister, father and daughter and, although rarely, mother and son. Combining the two taboos and making a film about incest between two brothers seems on the surface to be box-office suicide, but that is what writer-director Christopher Münch did in *Harry + Max* (2004). The brothers are Harry (Bryce Johnson), a 20-something boy band artist whose career is already on the skids, and Max (Cole Williams), six or seven years younger and rising fast up the same pop idol ladder. (The protagonists roles in flashbacks are played by Mark L. Young and Max Picioneri.) Harry and Max meet up after time apart and before their careers take them in opposite directions decide to take a camping trip they had planned long ago. It wasn't only Harry's career that got in the way, it was also his drinking and their emotional instability brought about by being raised in what could be termed, with some understatement, a dysfunctional family. The boldness of making a film on this theme is creditable although its worthiness is somewhat undercut by a discernible reluctance to grasp the subject as firmly as might have been.

But then it is hard to be critical of any movie that tries to break new ground, especially so at a time when the ground is in a state of ongoing upheaval as filmmakers, in Hollywood, the UK and all around the world are engaged in projects that, until so very recently, would have been unbelievable in any consideration of popular cinema. □

It was not only the movies themselves that underwent marked intrinsic changes in the 2000s. The manner in which gay and lesbian films were promoted was also different. No longer coy, no longer shrouded in innuendo and larded with coded references, films with gay themes were promoted as being films with gay themes. What had once been potential depth charges were now flaunted as important sales aids.

Actors, too, approached their roles in gay-themed films somewhat differently than had been the case in the past. Indeed, where a gay or lesbian actor had once upon a time gone to enormous lengths to hide his or her sexual proclivities, it was no longer thought necessary to be secretive. This did not mean that the closet door was yanked off its hinges; there are still reportedly many leading Hollywood names hiding inside. Often, though, the promotion by the leading actors of gay-themed films in which they appear is treated as just another part of being a movie actor. Well, almost.

While many heterosexual actors were no longer afraid to take gay roles, most of them still seemed to find it necessary to use interviews to distance private life from screen life

without saying that the reverse side of media interviews, the questions asked by interviewers, concentrated on the actors' sexuality. While no interviewer appears to have ever asked post-Hannibal Lecter Anthony Hopkins if he ate people, actors playing gay roles are peppered with questions that seek to determine if they have ever had same-sex relationships. Most actors respond to these probes with good humour, some allowing hints of ambivalence to surface, a few have gone to considerable lengths to assert their heterosexuality. Occasionally, and refreshingly, a heterosexual actor would appear in a homosexual role and prove himself to be sufficiently secure in his sexuality to make little or no reference to the matter in interviews. The Spanish actor, Antonio Banderas, unmistakably heterosexual, comes to mind; having appeared in a number of homosexual roles in big-budget pictures, he treated them all exactly as they should be treated, as just another acting job.

As in the past, the new wave of movies brought with it additions to the list of actors as gay icons. As before, the icon might be gay or lesbian or bisexual or transgender or be straightforwardly heterosexual but have a raw

11 GAY ICONS FOR A

and assert their heterosexuality. It is an interesting aspect of attitudes towards gayness that no actor ever appears to have found it necessary to distance himself from a role in which he played the part of a murderer or rapist or anyone truly reprehensible. It almost goes

Opposite: Antonio Banderas as Pierre Dulaine in *Take the Lead* (2006).

emotional appeal to the gay and lesbian audience that defies simple or even rational explanation. In the early 2000s, the list of gay icons was still filled with names from the past – often the distant past – brushing shoulders with recent additions. Thus, many of those already

NEW AGE

named in earlier chapters of this book will be found on gay icon lists of the 2000s, among them, alphabetically, Dirk Bogarde, Cher, Joan Crawford, Bette Davis, James Dean, Judy Garland, Cary Grant, Rock Hudson, Madonna, Bette Midler, Barbra Streisand and Mae West. Others, not listed herein but who appeared in films for many years might include Joan Collins, Audrey Hepburn, Ethel Merman, Elizabeth Taylor, Lauren Bacall and Liza Minnelli. As before, individual sexual proclivities often have little to do with their acceptance by gays. Some people – almost always 'celebrities' – have an appeal that transcends the corporeal and their known or perceived sexuality. In Minelli's case there is a sense of qualification by association. Not only is she the daughter of gay icon supreme, Judy Garland, and bisexual film director, Vincente Minelli, but she is herself a frequent associate of gays, including Peter Allen, to whim she was married for a while.

Among latterday actors are some whose recent work has been especially notable for its integrity, one that they have acquired for not always obvious reasons. Will this following remain faithful for twenty or more years, as has been the case of many gay film icons of the past? While certain knowledge lies only in the future, in the meantime we have the luxury of speculation.

A small sample might include Keanu Reeves, Jude Law, Hugh Jackman, Gael Garcia Bernal, Jake Gyllenhaal and Daniel Craig.

Keanu Charles Reeves was born 2 September 1964 in Beirut, Lebanon, to an English mother and an American father, the latter being of Hawaiian-Chinese descent. Following the break up of his parents' marriage he was raised by his mother first in New York City, then in Toronto; Reeves eventually became a naturalised Canadian. At age 17 he dropped out of school,

taking various dead-end jobs while pursuing a dream of becoming an actor. He appeared on the stage in Toronto, and also appeared on television and made films from 1979. In the early 1980s he moved to Los Angeles to concentrate on screen acting and made an impact in the 1986 film *River's Edge*. Other films from the late 80s and early 90s include *Permanent Record*, *Bill & Ted's Excellent Adventure* and *Bill & Ted's Bogus Journey*. His 90s films show a roller-coaster ride through the good and the best-forgotten, the former category including 1991's *My Own Private Idaho*, from which might be dated his status as a gay icon. His breakthrough role came in 1994's *Speed*, a nail-biting all-action drama in which he and Sandra Bullock frantically drive a bus that has been booby-trapped by demented Dennis Hopper to explode if the road speed is allowed to fall below a preset limit. Reeves followed this with films in which he co-starred with two of Hollywood's biggest guns, *The Devil's Advocate* with Al Pacino, and *The Replacements*, with Gene Hackman. Reportedly, in both instances, Reeves deferred a portion of his salary so that the production companies could afford these major stars. The first of these two films was on the upswing, the second wasn't. In the mid-1990s Reeves returned briefly to his theatrical roots, appearing in a production of *Hamlet* in Canada, but by the end of the decade was back in Hollywood with a box-office smash, *The Matrix* (1999). Then came some poor films before two sequels to *The Matrix* clicked with audiences, as did *Constantine* (2005). Later films, such as *A Scanner Darkly* (2006) did only middling business, although Reeves appeared remarkably indifferent to success. Indeed, his decision to turn down the sequel to *Speed* was based upon his stated preference for going on the road with his pop trio, Dogstar. Apart from *My Own Private Idaho*, there is little in the list of films Reeves has made to

Above: Keanu Reeves in *Constantine* (2005).

illuminate his iconic status. Rather more to the point have been his ranking by *People* magazine in a list of the world's 50 most beautiful people, dubious praise indeed, and comments he has made to the press in interviews regarding his sexuality, including telling *Vanity Fair*: 'There's nothing wrong with being gay, so to deny it is to make a judgement. And why make a big deal of it?' He has also made a point of refusing to answer some direct questions, always a signal to the gutter press to launch an attack. Attracting particularly lurid headlines was a report that appeared in gossip magazines claiming that Reeves had married film producer David Geffen. In his response to this, Geffen suggested that the likely source was a woman scorned; other comments suggested that at the time Geffen and Reeves had not even met. By

the mid-2000s, Reeves had abandoned his pretensions to be a rocker, disbanding Dogstar, and was involved with film projects including *Fishing For Moonlight* and *Stompanato*, playing the title role in the latter film as the hoodlum involved with film star Lana Turner and stabbed to death by her daughter.

David Jude Law is one of few British actors to avoid Hollywood stereotyping. Born 29 December 1972 in London, he turned to acting while still a small child. At age 12 he enrolled with the National Youth Music Theatre and was soon appearing in stage and television productions. In his teens and early twenties he made a few films but concentrated on his stage career, notably in a West End production of *Les Parents Terribles*, which was followed by his Broadway

by taking to court and winning costs against the *Sun* newspaper. His new relationship was in fact with Sienna Miller, an actress he had met while working in 2003 on a remake of *Alfie* in which he took the title role. When this new relationship foundered, the press gleefully fastened upon his problems, which included difficult arising in the divorce proceedings. Other films of the period include a cameo role as Errol Flynn in *The Aviator*, the lead in *Sky Captain and the World of Tomorrow* and *i ❤ huckabees*, and leading roles in *A Series of Unfortunate Events*, *Closer* and *All the King's Men*, a 2006 remake of a classic film, this one starring Sean Penn and Anthony Hopkins. Through 2006 and into 2007 Law's films included *Breaking And Entering*, *The Holiday* and *My Blueberry Nights*. Given his clearly heterosexual private life and the rich variety of his screen roles, of which only those in *Wilde* and *Midnight in the Garden of Good and Evil* touch upon the gay world, it is clear that Law's iconic standing lies in his physical good looks rather than any personal kinship.

Another actor far removed from the gay world is Hugh Michael Jackman, who was born in Sydney, Australia, on 12 October 1968. He acted in school plays and musicals while still very young and by his teens was sufficiently interested in the stage as a career to study at Sydney's Actors' Centre. In the early 90s he was offered an ongoing role in the popular Australian soap, *Neighbours*, and was simultaneously accepted by the Western Australia Academy of Performing Arts in Perth. He showed his seriousness about his career by choosing the three-year course of study over the possibility of instant stardom on television. He chose well and immediately on graduating in 1994 landed a leading role in an Australian production of *Beauty and the Beast*. After this he turned to television with a string of

debut in the same play, retitled *Indiscretions*, in 1995. For his work on this production Law was nominated for an Olivier award in London and a Tony in New York. His film work in the late 1990s and early 2000s included appearing as Bosie opposite Stephen Fry as Oscar Wilde in *Wilde*, playing hustler Billy Carl Hanson in *Midnight in the Garden of Good and Evil*, the doomed Dickie Greenleaf in *The Talented Mr Ripley*, for which he was nominated for an Oscar and won a BAFTA; he was a Russian sniper in *Enemy at the Gates*, a cyborg in *AI: Artificial Intelligence*, a remorseless hitman in *Road to Perdition*, and a war-weary Confederate soldier in *Cold Mountain*, another Oscar-nominated role. It was while he was making the latter film that Law's personal life was severely disrupted. His marriage to Sadie Frost, with whom he has three children, was under stress and gossipmongers suggested that he was having an affair with *Cold Mountain* co-star Nicole Kidman, rumours she scotched

Above: Jude Law in *Alfie* (2004).

appearances in various dramatic productions, on one of which he met actress (later director) Deborra-Lee Furness, whom he married in 1996. Late in 1996 he took the leading male role in a production of the musical *Sunset Boulevard*; this was directed by Trevor Nunn and would pave the way for a future break-through. In the meantime, Jackman played in more Australian television productions until Nunn called him to London to play the lead in a revival of *Oklahoma!* His performance as Curly McLain won rave reviews from critics and audiences; but then it was back to Australia for films, such as *Paperback Hero* and *Erskineville Kings*, his role in the latter bringing him a Best Actor nomination by the Australian Film Institute. Then came *X-Men*, a film already in pre-production in Hollywood when the actor cast in the lead was unable to play the role when his previous film overran. Jackman's performance in *Oklahoma!* had been noticed and this won him the role. Cautiously turning down a subsequent rush of offers for roles in action-man movies, he chose instead to play in a variety of films, such as *Someone Like You*, *Swordfish* (temporarily withdrawn following the attack on the World Trade Center), and *Kate & Leopold*, the latter bringing him a nomination for a Golden Globe. After turning down the lead in the film version of *Chicago*, he made *X-Men 2* and was then offered a Broadway role that turned him into a superstar, and which was pretty much the only reason for his appearance on gay icon lists. In *The Boy From Oz* he played the role of Peter Allen who was, in real life, a bisexual Australian singer and dancer who became Judy Garland's protégé and was married briefly to Liza Minnelli. Later, Allen wrote some hit songs, then died young, a victim of cancer and AIDS. Jackman's vibrant performance brought him rave reviews and packed houses through until autumn 2004. Film roles continued to come his way and

although he made *X-Men: The Last Stand*, they were usually varied and far removed from the gay tinge of *The Boy From Oz*. These film roles include the lead in *Van Helsing*, *The Fountain*, Woody Allen's *Scoop* and *The Prestige*. One role he did not get was as the new James Bond; this went to Daniel Craig, who would also find his way into gay icon lists.

Although it is not easy to grasp the reasons for the iconic status of Jude Law and Hugh Jackman, it is not too hard to understand why Gael Garcia Bernal has made the lists. Born on 30 November 1978 in Guadalajara, Mexico, he first appeared on stage with his parents while he was still a small child. He studied acting for-mally, then appeared in more stage productions as well as on television and some movie shorts. His first feature film was *Amores Perros*, which was Oscar-nominated in 2000. He then appeared in films such as *Y Tu Mamá También*, *El Crimen Del Padre Amaro*, playing the role of a priest internally at war with ethical issues, and *La Mala Educación*, in which he portrays a junkie transvestite. In all of these films, Bernal attracted favourable attention. This was especially so in the case of the last of these films, which was first screened at the 2004 film festival at Cannes. Meanwhile, Bernal had appeared as Che Guevara in the television miniseries *Fidel*, once more catching the eye of critics and audiences. Although drawing favourable reviews, Bernal had to wait a while before he could be seen by the wider audience in the USA; the foregoing films had to depend upon art-house showings. By the mid-2000s Bernal was poised to make that breakthrough thanks to roles in *The King*, *The Science of Sleep* and *Babel*. In interviews, Bernal has made few attempts to hide his varied sexuality and this has heightened anticipation for his forthcoming appearances in big budget Hollywood movies. Co-starring with big names, as he does in *Babel* with Brad Pitt and Cate Blanchett, means that before many more films have been made he will have had a chance to broaden his appeal and capitalise on his iconic status, which has hitherto depended heavily upon Internet images and the news drifting north from Mexico.

Already firmly on those lists of gay icons is Jake Gyllenhaal, who has been in films for many more years that might be thought after a glance at his date of birth. Jacob Gyllenhaal was born 19 December 1980 in Los Angeles, California, USA. His father, Stephen Gyllenhaal, is a film director, his mother, Naomi Foner, is a screen-writer. With both parents thus immersed in the business, their children were inevitably in regular contact with film people and hence son Jake and daughter Maggie were raised in an atmosphere from which acting careers were almost foregone conclusions. (Maggie Gyllenhaal starred notably in 2004's *Strip Search*, written by Tom Fontana, directed by Sidney Lumet, a damning indictment of the frightening erosion of civil liberties in the USA in the post-WTC-attack years.) Gyllenhaal attended Harvard-Westlake, a private high school in California, then studied briefly at Columbia University but was set on an acting career. He had already made his screen-acting debut, playing Billy Crystal's son in *City Slickers* (1991), and as a young adult concentrated all his efforts into building a career as an actor. Among Gyllenhaal's early films as an adult were *Donnie Darko* (2001), in which his sister was played by real-life sister Maggie, and for which role he won an Independent Spirit Award as Best Actor, *Bubble Boy* (2001) and *Good Girl* (2002). Although he received favourable reviews, none suggested the sharp rise to stardom that lay not far ahead. He appeared on the stage in London, playing an eight-week run in *This Is Our Youth* at the Garrick Theatre and winning the 2002 London

Evening Standard Award for Outstanding Newcomer. Gyllenhaal was in *The Day After Tomorrow* (2004), but it was his role in *Jarhead* (2005) that gave him his big step upwards. This was also the film that attracted the attention of the gay audience, not because of its subject matter but because of the on-screen presence of several well-built and semi-naked men. When Gyllenhaal took the role of Jack Twist in *Brokeback Mountain*, he was aware that no one connected with the production was in for an easy ride, acknowledging that people would have problems with it. He was doubtless unaware that the movie would meet with such unprecedented success and that for his portrayal of the complex Twist he would be nominated for an Academy Award as Best Supporting Actor. Far less distinguished than an Oscar nomination, he has been named by *People* magazine as one of the world's 'hottest bachelors', which is at best a questionable honour. In *Details* magazine he commented on reports that he was bi-sexual, saying, 'I'm open to whatever people want to call me. I've never really been attracted to men sexually, but I don't think I would be afraid of it if it happened.' Tongue firmly in cheek, after *Brokeback Mountain* was released he remarked, 'I fooled around with Heath Ledger and Michelle Williams got pregnant.'

An actor whose appearance on lists of gay icons might be a measure more of shock value than anything else is the latest James Bond. He is Daniel Wroughton Craig, who was born 2 March 1968 in Chester, Cheshire, England. Raised by his older sister and mother following his parents' divorce, he lived in Liverpool where he acted in school plays from age six and went as often as was possible to productions at the city's Everyman Theatre. After leaving school, he joined the National Youth Theatre. This was in 1984 and four years later he was accepted at

Above: Daniel Craig in *Casino Royale* (2006).

the Guildhall School of Music and Drama from which he graduated in 1991. His first film role was *The Power Of One* and he also appeared on television. His breakthrough came with roles in the films *Lara Croft: Tomb Raider* and *Road to Perdition*, which attracted much attention. He appeared in *Layer Cake* and played the role of murderer Perry Smith in *Infamous*, an account of Truman Capote's life and in particular the writing of *In Cold Blood*. In this film, Smith and Capote have an encounter in Smith's prison cell, which ends with a passionate kiss. It was this kiss that attracted a great deal of publicity and even more outrage, most of it coming from fans of James Bond desperately unhappy at their hero being portrayed in the latest film, *Casino Royale*, by an actor who would do such a shocking thing. These fans were also incensed that the new film's script called for Bond to have

a sexually ambivalent relationship with Felix Leiter, a male baddie played by Jeffrey Wright, and were also somewhat put out that the new Bond had, of all things, blond hair. Quite clearly, Craig was up against it from the off, but by the mid-2000s the old guard of Bond fans was close to being outgunned by the small army of gay fans Craig had picked up along the way to international recognition.

As suggested, this handful of contemporary gay icons, Keanu Reeves, Jude Law, Hugh Jackman, Gael Garcia Bernal, Jake Gyllenhaal and Daniel Craig, might not stay the course over coming decades, although most if not all of these actors have the capacity to remain box-office favourites regardless of the sexual proclivities of them and their fans. Their careers will be interesting to follow. ☐

12 OPENING WIDER

The rush of independent gay and lesbian films through the 1990s and early 2000s was notable, but it should not be supposed that all were quality productions. The fact that many failed to find adequate distribution might have been discrimination against the subject matter, but there were always other factors. The same might be said of non-gay movies from earlier decades. Back in the 1920s, 30s and 40s, the era we tend to think of as Hollywood's golden age, not all movies were good. Of course, we tend to remember only those that were superior entertainment, but for every one that was memorable and remains watchable today there were dozens that are fit only for wet Sunday afternoon, and for every one of those borderline cases are hundreds that are not worth a moment of anyone's time. However much movie buffs might hate to admit it, Hollywood churned out incalculable numbers of films that are unbearably bad.

Just which of today's gay-themed films will still be watchable a generation from now cannot be anything other than guesswork. The following handful of films has been chosen not because any of them necessarily carries the hallmark of a latterday *Night at the Opera* or *Twentieth Century* or *Frankenstein* or *Double Indemnity* or *Out of the Past* or *It Happened One Night*, all of which are as good today as they were when first released, but because they have elements that suggest a measure of durability not immediately apparent in all the many other gay films that are around today.

In *Big Eden* (2000), the setting and the plot are reminiscent of many Hollywood movies from a bygone age. Written and directed by Thomas Bezucha, the tale is set in the small Montana town of Big Eden, a place in which people look out for their neighbours and are caring and open-minded and not at all vicious and malevolent. It is Capra-land, not Coen-land. Henry Hart (Arye Gross) was born and raised here, and has come back to care for an ailing elderly relative. It isn't just his grandfather's health that troubles Henry; here in Big Eden was where he met and fell in love with schoolmate Dean Stewart (Tim DeKay). It was because of this and his inability to cope with his emotional attachment to Dean that Henry left Big Eden to go to New York where he has become a successful artist. Back in Big Eden, Henry finds that his feelings for Dean are unchanged, but Dean's feelings are a very different matter. The town is also home to Pike Dexter (Eric Schweig), a Native American who owns and operates the general store and it is he who finds in Henry the soulmate he has unknowingly longed for. The townspeople of Big Eden band together to smooth the way for Pike and Henry to

Opposite: Philip Seymour Hoffman in *Capote* (2005).

find one another and despite intervening tragedy bring about a surprisingly happy ending.

Thus summarised, *Big Eden* might appear trite, but then, many Frank Capra films sound trite when so encapsulated. Benefiting from a good script and strong performances all shaped by firm but discreet direction, the film is notable because it is about the dreams and hopes of people in general who just happen, in this instance, to be gay. Critical response to *Big Eden* was mostly positive, words like 'charming' and 'sweet' and 'engaging' and 'feel-good' appeared often, none of them words much seen in film criticism these days. Well received at several festivals, *Big Eden* collected awards including Best American Independent Feature Film at the 2001 Cleveland International Film Festival, Best Feature awards at the Florida Film Festival, the L.A. Outfest, and at Gay and Lesbian Film Festivals in Miami, San Francisco, Seattle and Toronto.

Whether or not it was deliberate, the makers of *Latter Days* (2003) pretty much guaranteed confrontation with a religious body. Given that their principal character was a young Elder with the Church of Latterday Saints whose internal conflict finds him embattled with his religious beliefs and his sexuality, it is hard to imagine that a strong reaction was not expected. Adding fuel to the potential fire, among many locations nationwide into which the film was booked to open was a Salt Lake City theatre. The theatre pulled out of the arrangement citing the film's lack of artistic merit as justification. The opening went ahead elsewhere in the country and a little while later *Latter Days* was screened at another Salt Lake City theatre where, thanks no doubt to the publicity the contretemps had generated, it did very well at the box office.

Written and directed by C. Jay Cox, the story traces the difficult relationship that develops between Aaron Davis (Steve Sandvoss), a Mormon who is in Hollywood with two fellow missionaries proselytizing a particular belief in God. They room in a building which also houses homosexual Christian Markelli (Wes Ramsey), whose hedonistic lifestyle is measured by the quantity rather than the quality of the men with whom he sleeps. Taking a bet from his friends, Christian sets out to seduce Aaron but soon discovers that it is not only the Mormon attitude towards homosexuality that he must overcome; Christian also finds that, unbelievable though it is to him, he begins to fall in love with the young missionary. Meanwhile, uncomfortable though it makes him, Aaron's attitude towards the aggressively sexual Christian undergoes a marked shift. Not only does Aaron seek to save Christian, he also begins to respond to suppressed sexual longings he never knew were buried deep inside him.

The film found favour with the gay community, its intrinsic honesty in dealing with its sexual and religious content being especially commendable. The emotional difficulties that come with almost any deep love affair, gay or straight, were treated directly and with no grafted-on easy exit from the problems that confront the principals. At the 2003 Philadelphia International Gay & Lesbian Film Festival *Latter Days* won the Audience Award as Best Gay Male Feature; and at 2004's Toronto Inside Out Lesbian and Gay Film and Video Festival it won the Audience Award as Best Feature Film or Video.

A disturbing tale of the lifelong damage inflicted on anyone who suffers sexual abuse in childhood, *Mysterious Skin* (2004) traces the lives led by two young men who, as children, were molested by a trusted adult. The sexual damage done is clearly profound and yet, in some respects, and not to downplay the appalling physical abuse, the psychological damage caused by realization that no one can be trusted is even worse. Written and directed by Greg

Opposite: Joseph Gordon-Levitt and Brady Corbett in *Mysterious Skin* (2004).

Araki, who based his screenplay on Scott Heim's novel, *Mysterious Skin* explores the lives of Neil McCormick and Brian Lackey (Joseph Gordon-Levitt and Brady Corbet) who, when aged eight, were molested by their baseball coach (Bill Sage) in their home town of Hutchinson, Kansas. In the flashbacks, the natural innocence of Neil and Brian (played in these scenes by Chase Ellison and George Webster) is heartbreakingly wrenched from them by their coach. The boys are now in their late teenage years and it is at this age that Brian declares, in voice-over as the film begins, 'The summer I was eight years old, five hours disappeared from my life. Five hours. Lost. Gone without a trace ... Last thing I remember I was sitting on the bench at my Little League game. It started to rain. What happened after that remains a pitch black void.'

As Araki explores that pitch black void, his fitful light throwing more shadows for every aspect it reveals, the damaged young men come slowly but very truthfully to life. Wisely, Araki remembers that this is film and not words on a page; he is sparing in his use of dialogue, constantly aware that a picture can be more vividly revealing than long and elaborate speeches. The eyes of the two protagonists, shadowed pools in which occasionally gleam flashes of fear and self-loathing, reveal the nature and depth of the troubled lives they are doomed to lead. For one of the pair, Neil, the encounter with the coach marred his development through its revelation that he actually appeared to like what was done to him, even though it catastrophically reshaped his future. For the other, Brian, it marked the beginning of a succession of periods spent in that black void that have been scattered across the landscape of his life.

Neil has taken his childhood experience as the defining manner in which he should lead his life and become not only openly gay but also a gay prostitute. Brian has retreated deeper and deeper into that internal darkness, seeking to

MYSTERIOUS SKIN

2004 99 mins colour
Producers: Greg Akari, Jeffrey Levy-Hinte,
Mary Jane Skalski
Director: Greg Akari
Photographer: Steve Gainer
Screenplay: Greg Akari, from a novel by Scott Heim
Joseph Gordon-Levitt, Brady Corbet, Bill Sage, Lisa Long,
Chris Mulkey, Elisabeth Shue, David Lee Smith, Ryan
Stenzel Richard Riehle, Michelle Trachtenberg

As young children, Neil and Brian are molested by their baseball coach. Years later, now young adults, they try to come to terms with the permanent damage done to them. It is not just the brutal theft of their innocence, but the everlasting fear and self-loathing that have ruined their lives. Neil has allowed the childhood trauma to define his existence as an openly gay young prostitute; Brian has plunged ever deeper into the black void that was opened up before him by a trusted adult. With damaged psyches, Neil and Brian inhabit twilight worlds from which they are unlikely ever to emerge and which cannot be imagined by anyone with whom they might try to form relationships.

explain what happened then and the fact that he remains an afflicted young adult by coming to believe that instead of a trusted adult of his own society taking away his innocence, it was the work of alien beings from another world.

In the course of their search for emotional resolution, Neil and Brian move among others with damaged psyches who, like them, inhabit worlds in which it is never brighter than a marled twilight. Brian finds brief understanding and some measure of kinship with Avalyn (Mary Lynn Rajskub), who also believes that she was taken away by aliens. By the very nature of the life he leads, Neil has many relationships and one, with Eric (Jeff Licon), offers some hope of a lasting bond but it is not in Neil's afflicted character to be open to friendship. When Neil and Brian meet again as teenagers, they try to cast light into their separate and life-defining black holes. Ironically, it is with Eric that Brian forges a stable, and perhaps lasting, relationship. For Neil, it is necessary that he go back home to where it all began and try to rediscover the life that might have been.

It is one of the film's many plusses that there are no pat explanations; even Mrs McCormick (Elizabeth Shue), who is Neil's promiscuous mother, is not held up as scapegoat for her son's problems, although quite clearly she had other things on her mind rather than peering into every dark corner along his path – after all, if a mother cannot trust her son's baseball coach who can she trust.

Well received when shown worldwide, *Mysterious Skin* picked up several awards including the Jury Award at the Bergen International Film Festival for Araki, who also won the MovieZone Award at the Rotterdam International Film Festival and was Best Director at the Seattle International Film Festival. It was nominated for Best Feature at the Gijón International Film Festival, and Araki was nominated at the Independent Spirit Awards.

Gordon-Levitt's performance also attracted attention with several nominations and at the Seattle International Film Festival he won the Golden Space Needle Award as Best Actor.

The internecine squabbles that blight relationships in Hollywood form the basis for *The Dying Gaul* (2005), written and directed by Craig Lucas. A powerful producer, Jeffrey Tishop (Campbell Scott), buys a screenplay from Robert Sandrich (Peter Sarsgaard), who is trying to pick up the pieces of his life following the death from AIDS of his partner. Robert's screenplay is largely autobiographical and Jeffrey wants to make changes, notably changing the sex of his lover to avoid making a gay movie, declaring 'Most Americans hate gay people. If they hear it's about gay people, they won't go.' Nevertheless, Robert goes along, his passiveness largely a result of the emotional devastation he has suffered and his inability to overcome his grief. But Jeffrey has more in mind than merely turning Robert's story into something other than what was intended. He begins wooing Robert to have a sexual relationship with him. Meanwhile, the producer has introduced Robert to his wife, Elaine (Patricia Clarkson), who appears to be genuinely interested in the writer and his lifestyle. Soon, though, the relationship between Robert and Elaine goes beyond friendship. An unorthodox triangle develops and as the inherent cruelty of the Tishops makes itself apparent, so too is it clear that ahead lies disaster.

Although it doesn't look like it, Lucas's work started out as a stage play. It flows easily on the screen and the acting of the three principals is excellent. Both Sarsgaard and Clarkson have good followings and this film offers them their best roles to date; Scott is the son of George C. Scott and Colleen Dewhurst. The film does not concern itself solely with the central triangle; the nature of the plot is such that there are many opportunities to take stabs at the crass commercialism that lies at the heart of much of what Hollywood does. Critics were divided, some thought *The Dying Gaul* stagey and pretentious, many thought it sparkling and witty. Almost all showered high praise on the barbed dialogue and the three stars. Uncommonly for independent gay-themed films, the score is notable and minimalist composer Steve Reich also received critical praise.

The title comes from a Roman marble statue that copies a long-lost Greek bronze that depicts a defeated but respected ancient enemy, one of the Gauls who went into battle naked save for their weapons.

The life and career of openly-gay writer Truman Capote were already familiar to the American literati when, in 1959 he began work on a project that would make his name and image known around the world. That project, which resulted in his book, *In Cold Blood*, which was filmed in 1967, centred upon a brutal killing of a Kansas family by two men, Perry Smith and Dick Hickock.

In *Capote* (2005), directed by Bennett Miller from Dan Futterman's screenplay that was based on Gerald Clarke's book, the writer is followed from when he hears of the horrific events in Kansas and decides to go there and explore the possibilities of a magazine article for *The New Yorker*. Accompanying Capote (Philip Seymour Hoffman) on the trip is friend and fellow writer Harper Lee (Catherine Keener), author of *To Kill A Mockingbird* (which was filmed in 1962). In Kansas, Capote is given full access not only to the investigation but also to the culprits, Smith and Hickock (Clifton Collins Jnr. and Mark Pellegrino). Of these two, Smith is sexually ambivalent and soon Capote is able to fashion with him close rapport. As a result, Capote has at his disposal far more than would be available to just any reporter; more than that, as he soon realises, this is not merely a magazine article –

this is a book, and a big one at that. As time passes, and Smith and Hickock are tried, found guilty and sentenced to die, the rapport between Capote and Smith becomes greater with Capote irresistibly drawn to the cold-blooded killer. Disturbingly, Capote finds himself torn between any ability he might have to help the murderer in his final days and his awareness that the execution of Smith and Hickock will form nothing less than the perfect ending for his book. The ambivalence of Capote and the extent to which his gayness is relevant to his behaviour is caught to perfection by writer, director and actor and so too is the fact that this book marked the beginning of Capote's decline into alcoholism. Not surprisingly, *Capote* and Hoffman were Academy Award nominated. It was Hoffman, in competition with Heath Ledger for *Brokeback Mountain*, who walked away with the trophy on Oscar night.

Early screenings of *Brokeback Mountain* (2004) at film festivals prepared audiences for something special and for once the hype was delivered. This is a remarkable film, not only for its genre-breaking setting – a gay western? – but also for the honesty and integrity with which it was brought to the screen by writers Larry McMurtry and Diana Ossana, who adapted Annie Proulx's short story, and director Ang Lee. Their concept was aided immeasurably by outstanding performances, not only from the four principals but also from all the players in minor roles.

Ennis Del Mar and Jack Twist (Heath Ledger and Jake Gyllenhaal) are two cowboys working in the bleak high country of Wyoming. Herding sheep for their boss, Joe Aguirre (Randy Quaid), they are obliged during one bitter night to share a tent; the alternative being risk of frostbite or worse. This precipitates a homosexual encounter that shocks them both, especially Ennis who had never imagined that his pent-up sexual frustration had homoerotic roots. Indeed, he had always

BROKEBACK MOUNTAIN

2004 134 mins colour
Producers: James Schamus,
Diana Ossana
Director: Ang Lee
Photographer: Rodrigo Prieto
Screenplay: Larry McMurty and
Diana Ossana, from a short story by
Annie Proulx
Jake Gyllenhaal, Heath Ledger,
Michelle Williams, Anne Hathaway

Caught without a campfire during a bitterly cold night, cowboys Ennis Del Mar and Jack Twist share a tent and the outcome, a homosexual encounter, shocks them both. The shock develops into a mutual revelation and re-evaluation when both men realise that this is no passing fancy but something that will remain a part of their lives. But the times and the place being what they are, it is 1963 in Wyoming, each goes his own way. They marry and lead 'normal' lives for a few years before they again meet up. Then, both know that this is something that will be with them forever but they can handle it only with occasional weekends over the years. Their marriages are doomed: Jack's just drifting into disillusion; Ennis's shattering when his wife sees him in a passionate embrace with Jack. Ultimately, as the years become decades, Ennis and Jack have to accept that the love they have for one another is something that cannot be fulfilled in the society to which they belong.

harboured hints of homophobia. This chance encounter develops into a strong bond that goes far deeper than simply satisfying sexual urges. Both men begin to re-evaluate their lives. Ennis, orphaned in childhood when his parents died in an automobile accident, has never been able to open up emotionally to himself, let alone to another person. Jake, raised by a crude and malevolent father, has long teetered on the brink of acknowledging that his sexual proclivities are not straight. When both men realise that this new relationship they have formed is no passing fancy but will be the defining event of their lives, they are forced to decide what they will do.

The decision made by Ennis and Jack is not prompted by the emotional bond they have forged but by the crucible of the time and place in which it has happened. This is 1963, and they are not in one of the few rarified parts of the USA where changes are afoot but in Wyoming, which is very much country where men are men and woe betide anyone who might challenge the status quo. Ennis and Jack go their separate ways and both enter traditional relationships; Ennis marries Alma (Michelle Williams), Jack marries Lureen (Anne Hathaway) and both men set aside thoughts of that mountainside encounter. For four

Opposite:

Heath Ledger and
Jake Gyllenhaal in
Brokeback Mountain
(2004).

years, they lead lives determined by rules set by others, but when they meet again the embers of their relationship flare up and both men now begin to realise, however unspoken it might be, that what they feel for one another is real love.

Their marriages are already doomed: Jack's has drifted into disillusion while Ennis's shatters when his wife witnesses his passionate embrace of Jack after their four-year separation. Neither man, however, is able to make the break with the society that they know and which stifles them and they settle instead for occasional weekends together as the years drift by. In a very real sense this is an old-fashioned love story: two people are thrown together, feel the spark of love, are separated, meet again, know that the spark can become an everlasting fire, but are doomed by outside pressures to lose the love that should be theirs. Had this been made as a man-woman love story, it would have resembled the many bland, by-the-numbers films churned out by Hollywood over the decades. Made as a same-sex love story, the old model is cast aside to allow the emergence of a moving and ultimately tragic story.

Over all hangs a shroud of melancholy, although there are fitful glimmers that the two men might find a way to escape the stifling ties that bind them to their other commitments and undertakings and especially the crippling cultural burden that anchors them to lives lived to a pattern determined by others and guarded by rules that both ache to smash. Uplifting in a way defined by its implicit belief that there should be a place for all in a truly democratic and honestly open society, poignant in its heartbreaking underlining of the reality that is forced upon anyone who dares to be different, *Brokeback Mountain* proved to be that rarity, a film that is exceptional in every way: writing, directing, acting and scoring. Not only this, it is also thought-provoking and life-changing while never for a moment being polemical. That it could be all this and at the same time prove to

be a box-office smash brought with it hope that Hollywood might have finally grown up in its attitude towards homosexuality.

While *Brokeback Mountain* won numerous awards and ran up substantial box-office receipts, the anticipated controversy was really quite slight. In *Rolling Stone*, film critic Peter Travers called it, 'Unmissable and unforgettable! Hits you like a shot in the heart!' Kyle Smith, in the *New York Post*, said that the film 'will be rightly praised for honestly assessing the emotional wreckage done to men and women by the closeting of homosexuality.' Of course there were adverse comments. Tom Snyder, a film critic from the Christian right, thought it was 'at times twisted, laughable, frustrating, sadomasochistic, plotless and boring.' He also suggested that it was representative of Hollywood's intention to project 'a leftist homosexual agenda, which goes along with radical feminism, and a misunderstanding of what Christianity teaches.'

Much more balanced was the comment of Sean Smith in *Newsweek* who considered the likely effect on the nation as a whole and on Hollywood in particular: 'No American film before has portrayed love between two men as something this pure and sacred. As such, it has the potential to change the national conversation and to challenge people's ideas about the value and validity of same-sex relationships. In the meantime, it's already upended decades of Hollywood conventional wisdom.'

Hopefully, the upending will have taught Hollywood something that sticks long after the fuss and furore of the past few years has died down and gay-themed films have become as accepted and unexceptional as are westerns and musicals and all the other hyphenated genres. Even more important, perhaps Sam Goldwyn's remark, about the manner in which Hollywood was and to some extent still is held in thrall to the censors, political, corporate and religious, can be set aside forever. □

BIBLIOGRAPHY

The Bard in the Bush
by John Fraser,
Granada Publishing, 1978

Broadcasting It
by Keith Howes,
Cassell, 1993

*The Cambridge Biographical
Encyclopedia*,
Edited by David Crystal
(Second Edition), Cambridge
University Press, 1998

*The Celluloid Closet:
Homosexuality in the Movies*
by Vito Russo,
Harper Row, 1995

*Charles Laughton: An
Intimate Biography*
by Charles Higham,
Intro Elsa Lanchester,
W H Allen & Co, 1976

Charles Laughton and I
by Elsa Lanchester,
Faber & Faber, 1938

Deborah Kerr by Eric Braun,
W H Allen & Co, 1977;
St Martin's Press, 1978

The Elvis Film Encyclopedia
by Eric Braun,
B T Batsford, 1997

Hollywood Gays
by Boze Hadleigh,
Barricade Books Inc, 1996

*Images in the Dark: An
Encyclopedia of Gay and
Lesbian Cinema*
by Raymond Murray,
Titan Books, 1996

*The International Film
Encyclopedia*
by Ephraim Katz,
Macmillan Press, 1980;
Papermac, 1982

*The Lonely Heart: A
Biography of Cary Grant*
by Charles Higham and
Roy Mosley,
Harcourt Brace Jonavich,
1989

*The Lonely Life: An
Autobiography*
by Bette Davis,
MacDonald & Co, 1963

*Marlene Dietrich by her
daughter Maria Riva*,
Bloomsbury, 1992

*Montgomery Clift:
A Biography*
by Robert La Guardia,
W H Allen/A Howard &
Wyndham Co, 1977

Nazimova: A Biography
by Gavin Lambert,
Alfred A Knopf Inc, 1997

*Open Secret: Gay Hollywood
1928-1998*
by David Ehrenstein,
William Morrow & Co, 1998

*A Portrait of Joan:
An Autobiography of
Joan Crawford*
with Jane Kesner, Aromore,
1978

*Prick Up Your Ears:
A Biography of Joe Orton*
by John Lahr, Allen Lane,
Penguin Books, 1978

*Quinlan's Film Stars:
A Directory of Film Stars*
(Fourth Edition)
by David Quinlan,
B T Batsford, 1996

Rock Hudson: A Biography
by Brenda Scott Royce,
Greenwood Publishing
Group, 1996

*The Secret Life of Tyrone
Power: A Drama of a
Bisexual in the Spotlight*
by Hector Arce, William
Morrow and Co Inc, 1976

*The Sewing Circle:
Hollywood's Greatest Secret*
by Axel Madsen,
Robson Books, 1995

*So Much Love: An
Autobiography*
by Beryl Reid with the
assistance of Eric Braun,
Hutchinson & Co, 1984

*Starring Miss Barbara
Stanwyck*
by Ella Smith,
Crown Publishers, 1974

Tallulah: An Autobiography
by Tallulah Bankhead,
Purnell & Sons, 1952

*Those Dancing Years:
An Autobiography*
by Mary Ellis,
John Murray (Publishers),
1982

*The Time of My Life:
An Autobiography*
by Pat Kirkwood,
Robert Hale, 1999

*Vincent Price:
A Daughter's Biography*
by Victoria Price,
St Martin's Press, 1999;
Sidgwick & Jackson, 2000

Virgin Film Guide
(Sixth Edition),
Virgin Books, 1997

Who's Who in the Theatre:
compiled and edited by John
Parker (Eleventh Edition),
Sir Isaac Pitman & Sons, 1952